Key Studies in Diplomacy

Series Editors: J. Simon Rofe, Giles Scott-Smith

Emeritus Editor: Lorna Lloyd

The volumes in this series seek to advance the study and understanding of diplomacy in its many forms. Diplomacy remains a vital component of global affairs, and it influences and is influenced by its environment and the context in which it is conducted. It is an activity of great relevance for International Studies, International History, and of course Diplomatic Studies. The series covers historical, conceptual, and practical studies of diplomacy.

Previously published by Bloomsbury:

21st Century Diplomacy: A Practitioner's Guide by Kishan S. Rana
A Cornerstone of Modern Diplomacy: Britain and the Negotiation of the 1961 Vienna Convention on Diplomatic Relations by Kai Bruns
David Bruce and Diplomatic Practice: An American Ambassador in London, 1961–9 by John W. Young
Embassies in Armed Conflict by G.R. Berridge

Published by Manchester University Press:

Reasserting America in the 1970s edited by Hallvard Notaker, Giles Scott-Smith, and David J. Snyder
The diplomacy of decolonisation: America, Britain and the United Nations during the Congo crisis 1960–64 by Alanna O'Malley

Sport and diplomacy
Games within games

Edited by
J. Simon Rofe

Manchester University Press

Published by Manchester University Press
Altrincham Street, Manchester M1 7JA
www.manchesteruniversitypress.co.uk

British Library Cataloguing-in-Publication Data
A catalogue record for this book is available from the British Library

ISBN 978 1 5261 3105 8 hardback

First published 2018

Typeset in 9.5/12 pt Minion Pro by
Servis Filmsetting Ltd, Stockport, Cheshire
Printed in Great Britain by
TJ International Ltd, Padstow

David John Keir, 19 October 1947–25 March 2017:
a fine sportsman and godfather

Contents

Contents

List of figures

List of tables

Contributors

Aaron Beacom is Reader in Sport and International Relations at the University of St Mark and St John. He has a particular interest in multi-stakeholder diplomacy with actors such as the International Paralympic Committee and a range of social action groups, engaging in the diplomatic process as they pursue their objectives and advocate for wider social change. Recent publications include *International Diplomacy and the Olympic Movement* (Palgrave), as well as papers in *International Journal of Sport Policy and Politics, International Journal of Sport Communication, Journal of Sport for Development* and *Diplomacy and Statecraft*. Current research focuses on governance and development challenges relating to disability sport and has included field work for the Invictus Games Foundation (2016). Beacom is co-editor, with Ian Brittain, of the *Palgrave Handbook of Paralympic Studies* (publication forthcoming).

A native of Bogotá, Colombia, **Alexander Cárdenas** received a PhD in Peace, Conflict and Development Studies at University Jaume I focusing upon sport and peace building in Colombia and Northern Ireland. He has been affiliated with INCORE, the International Conflict Research Institute, in Derry as a Marie Curie Research Fellow in Sustainable Peace. Cárdenas has conducted extensive research on sport for development and peace in Colombia, Northern Ireland and the Philippines, and has been involved in the implementation of projects aimed at community development via sport and Olympism in Latin America, Europe and South East Asia. He is an evaluator for the Advanced Olympic Research Grant Program of the Olympic Studies Center and has an extensive collection of sports memorabilia.

Laurence Cooley is a Research Fellow in the International Development Department at the University of Birmingham and a Visiting Research Fellow in the School of Natural and Built Environment at Queen's University Belfast. He is a political scientist with research interests that include ethnic conflict resolution, the politics of the census and the governance of sport in deeply divided societies. From February 2017 to January 2019, he is an ESRC Future Research Leader, working on a project about the relationship between power-sharing institutions and census politics in post-conflict societies. Together with Jasmin Mujanović, he has written about FIFA, UEFA and football governance reform in Bosnia and Herzegovina in the journal *Global Society* and for the online magazine *Balkanist*. Outside of academia, it's all about the bike.

Suzanne Dowse is the Faculty Director of Quality at Canterbury Christ Church University and Research Associate with the Centre for Sport, Physical Education and Activity Research (SPEAR). Prior to holding these positions she was the Programme Director for theSport and Health Management and Events Management Degrees. Her teaching specialism and subject expertise include Politics, International Relations and Sport Policy, and the political and social impacts of hosting sport mega-events. Her recent research in this area has explored the intersection between children's rights and various social justice issues.

Maximilian Drephal specialises in the history of empire, colonial and post-colonial South Asia, and the methodology of new diplomatic history. Before writing his PhD thesis at Loughborough University on 'The British Legation in Kabul: the coloniality of diplomacy in independent Afghanistan, 1922–1948', he studied History and English at the Freie Universität Berlin and the University of Manchester. He joined the Department of History at the University of Sheffield as a Lecturer in International History in September 2016. His recent publications include an article entitled: 'Corps diplomatique: the body, British diplomacy and independent Afghanistan, 1922–1947' in *Modern Asian Studies*.

Joseph Eaton is Associate Professor of History at National Chengchi University. Eaton is a PhD graduate of Columbia University in New York City and former Fulbright Scholar at the Tamkang University Graduate Institute of American Studies in Danshui. His research focuses on the United States' connections with the world. Eaton's book, *The Anglo-American Paper War: Debates about the New Republic, 1800–1825* (Palgrave, 2010), examines the polemics over images of the early American republic that consumed the attention of writers on both sides of the Atlantic. Eaton's articles have appeared in *Diplomatic History*, *The Pennsylvania Magazine of History and Biography*, *The Journal of the Republic of China Military Academy*, *Nineteenth-Century American History*, *Tamkang Journal of International Affairs* and the *Taiwan Review*.

Carole Gomez has been a Research Fellow at IRIS (Institut de Relations Internationales et Strategiques) since 2013. She works on international sports issues and focuses on sports diplomacy and integrity, specialising in the study of sport boycott. Gomez holds a Master's degree in International Public Law–International Relations from Pantheon Assas University after studying European law at Queen's University, Belfast.

Lindsay Sarah Krasnoff is a historian, consultant and author of *The Making of Les Blues: Sport in France 1958–2010* (2012). Her work on sport, race, identity, immigration and youth has appeared on and in *CNN International*, *Huffington Post*, *Roads & Kingdoms*, *Sports Illustrated*, *The New Yorker* and *The New York Times*. Krasnoff previously served in the Office of the Historian, US Department of State, where she worked on the history of US–Europe relations. She serves on the Executive Committee of the sports think-tank Sport and Démocratie, where she co-leads sport diplomacy initiatives, and is a member of the Overseas Press Club of America.

Sibylle Lang holds a PhD in International Politics from the Helmut Schmidt University in Hamburg and a master's degree in Political Science, North American Studies and

Intercultural Communication from Ludwig Maximilians University in Munich. She is an adjunct teacher at the University of the Federal Armed Forces in Munich and lectures regularly on defence-related topics, among others at the Bundeswehr Command and Staff College. She has worked for several UN organisations and think-tanks/consultancies in the fields of development and peace building and for the Military Policy and Arms Control branch of the German Ministry of Defence. Her research focuses on the strengthening of the security/development nexus, a holistic approach to crisis and conflict management, mission analysis and capability development, as well as international military cooperation.

J. Simon Rofe is Reader in Diplomatic and International Studies in the Centre for International Studies and Diplomacy, and is the Programme Director for MA Global Diplomacy, at SOAS University of London. His research focuses upon diplomacy, international and global history – with a particular focus upon on the US Embassy in London – and the diplomacy of sport. He is the author of a number of books and academic articles including those in *Diplomacy and Statecraft, Journal of the Gilded Age and Progressive Era, Sport and Society* and *The Journal of Transatlantic Studies*. Selected books include: *The London Embassy – 70 Years in Grosvenor Square 1939–2009*, with Alison Holmes (Palgrave, 2012); *International History and International Relations*, with Andrew Williams and Amelia Hadfield (Routledge, 2012); and 'Nearly man: Thomas E. Dewey from crime buster to presidential contender in 1944', Andrew Johnstone and Andrew Priest (eds), *US Foreign Policy and American Presidential Elections* (University of Kentucky Press, 2017)

David Rowe is Emeritus Professor of Cultural Research, Institute for Culture and Society, Western Sydney University; Honorary Professor, Faculty of Humanities and Social Sciences, University of Bath; and an elected Fellow of the Australian Academy of the Humanities and of the Academy of the Social Sciences. He has published over ninety research articles in peer-reviewed journals (including *The International Journal of the History of Sport*) and over 110 chapters in edited collections (including *Moral Panics, the Press and the Law in Early Modern England*) and reference works (including *The Oxford Companion to Australian Sport*). Rowe's books include *Sport, Culture and the Media: The Unruly Trinity* (McGraw-Hill, 2nd edition, 2004), *Global Media Sport: Flows, Forms and Futures* (Bloomsbury, 2011) and *Sport, Public Broadcasting, and Cultural Citizenship: Signal Lost?* (edited with Jay Scherer, Routledge, 2014). His work has been translated into several languages, including Chinese, French, Turkish, Spanish, Italian and Arabic.

Amanda Shuman is a post-doctoral researcher and technical manager for the ERC-funded project 'The Maoist Legacy' at the University of Freiburg. Her research interests include PRC history, the Global South during the Cold War, soft power and transnational networks of sport. She is currently preparing a book manuscript based on her 2014 University of California dissertation, 'The politics of socialist athletics in the People's Republic of China, 1949–1966'. She has previously published articles on

China's involvement in the Games of the New Emerging Forces, a sports mega-event held in 1963 in Indonesia, as well as on sports delegation visits between China and Africa in the 1960s. A forthcoming publication discusses the relationship between sport and the national humiliation narrative in China by analysing visual images of athletic bodies in 1950s Chinese films.

Alan Tomlinson is Professor of Leisure Studies, in the School of Humanities, at the University of Brighton. He is an internationally renowned scholar and researcher on the social history and sociology of sport, leisure and popular culture with a long-standing interest in the history and politics of FIFA, alongside the Olympics and the IOC. He is the author/editor of around three dozen volumes and books on sport, leisure and consumption, including *Consumption, Identity and Style* (Abe Books, 1990), *FIFA: The Men, the Myths and the Money* (Routledge, 2014) and *Sport and Peace-Building in Divided Societies: Playing with Enemies* (Routledge, 2017/18, with John Sugden). Tomlinson has a notable media dimension to research, is a full member of the Sports Journalists' Association of Great Britain and a long-term contributor to the football periodical, *When Saturday Comes*.

Umberto Tulli received his PhD in History and International Relations from the Istituto Italiano di Scienze Umane (now Scuola Normale Superiore) in 2011. The same year, he was awarded a one-year fellowship from the Olympic Studies Center of the International Olympic Committee. He held postdoctoral positions at the University of Bologna (2012–13) and at the University of Trento (2014–17), where he is currently Adjunct Professor of American Diplomatic History. He is the author of two books – *Tra diritti umani e distensione* (Franco Angeli Milano, 2013) and *Breve storia delle Olimpiadi* (Carocci, 2012) – and a number of essays and articles in Italian and English. He is currently writing a history of the European Parliament before the introduction of direct elections in 1979 and a history of the Olympic Games during the 1980s.

Rachel Vaughan's research interests focus on sporting and cultural diplomacy during the Cold War. She has worked in a variety of research, teaching and administrative roles at Aberystwyth University and is currently editorial assistant for the journal *International Relations* and Research Impact Officer in the Department of Business, Research and Innovation.

Acknowledgements

A work of this kind is not a single endeavour and there are a number of parties to thank for what is on its pages. First of all, my thanks to the original participants of the CISD colloquium 'Sport and Diplomacy: Message, Mode and Metaphor'.[1] The conference and the discourse it captured spawned many academic relationships and three published outputs: the first was a special edition of the academic journal *Diplomacy and Statecraft* (27, 2016), and then, alongside this volume, a book, edited by Dr Heather L. Dichter, looking particularly at *Soccer and Diplomacy* (Cornell University Press, forthcoming). Heather L. Dichter deserves particular thanks for the production of this volume. Her dynamism of thought and action proved a suitable foil to this endeavour. Her contribution is manifest in the work presented here as it is in her stellar contribution to the field of Sport History.

I would also like to thank Dr Dan Plesch for his unswerving support in developing the Sport and Diplomacy project; and for the rest of my CISD colleagues who have provided institutional support for the endeavours. Inspiration has been drawn from students on the CISD MA module 'Sport and Diplomacy: More than a Game' since its inception in 2011. The rich discussion, particularly from the female majority of the student body, has been richly rewarding in furthering my own thinking. Particular mention must go to the two outstanding Associate Tutors of the class: Verity Postlethwaite and Omar Sahla. Their contribution to the field of Sport and Diplomacy is still to come. Finally, it would be remiss of me not to mention my original and ongoing collaborators with whom I began the Sport and Diplomacy project in 2011: Dr Geoff Pigman and Dr Stuart Murray.

Finally, rather than repeat the trope that 'any errors that remain are my sole responsibility', I would gently suggest that deciding whether the manuscript is error-free is an exercise left for the reader.

J. Simon Rofe
July 2017

Note

1 The conference was held under the auspices of the MA Global Diplomacy Programme, 3–4 July 2015.

Introduction: establishing the field of play

J. Simon Rofe

As an enduring and ubiquitous part of modern life, sport has a powerful capacity to touch individuals and societies around the world in ways that traditional forms of diplomacy and those traditionally thought of as diplomats rarely can. As writer and former England cricketer Ed Smith sagely notes, in the twenty-first century 'sport is bigger, grander and more diverse than ever'.[1] However, the role that sport plays in global affairs as a whole – and in diplomacy specifically – is poorly understood and often ignored. Indeed, a commonly held view is that sport and anything in the political domain are wholly distinct, but, as Lincoln Allison posited, this 'myth of autonomy' does not stand up to scrutiny.[2] Sport, therefore, demands understanding in the realm of diplomacy.

Nowhere has the diffusion and redistribution of political and economic power in our globalising world had more visibility than in international sport and its coverage by globalised media. Put simply, sport today is a multi-billion dollar global business. New media companies encompassing television networks, and their radio predecessors, have paid immense sums of money to broadcast major sporting events from the Olympic Games and FIFA World Cup. The International Olympic Committee (IOC) estimated its revenue for the Olympiad – the four-year cycle encompassing the Summer Olympic Games in its first year, culminating with the Rio de Janeiro Games – would exceed $4 billion, comprising nearly three-quarters of its entire revenue.[3] The Olympics are able to generate such vast monies because they have a global audience; their only competitor for attracting as many viewers – and thus potential consumers – is the FIFA Football World Cup.[4] It is precisely the global reach of mega sports events (MSE), such as the Olympic Games and World Cup, that attracts a range of actors to seek to utilise them to achieve their diplomatic goals. A raft of literature exists on sporting 'mega-events' to which this volume contributes directly in the shape of Suzanne Dowse's analysis of the South African FIFA World Cup; and indirectly as it embraces the transactions of the quadrennial diplomatic game.[5]

The most recognisable member in the cast of actors found at MSE is national governments, not least because they share in large part the visual imagery of the competitors at these events. States can reach millions if not billions of people across the world as audiences through these MSE. Given their transnational character they allow for the dissemination of 'public diplomacy' – to win the 'hearts and minds' in the lexicon of conflict resolution – on a grand scale and in more pervasive means than individually or nationally focused programmes. As a prime recent example: the German tourism industry published a colourful and positive factsheet extolling the many benefits that the country received from organising the 2006 FIFA World Cup, noting that 'Germany rolled out the red carpet for its guests' and that the country's image abroad had improved, at least in part due to a more positive self-image that Germany was able to portray.[6] Academic research supports the enhanced perception of Germany's increased image abroad, which helps reinforce to potential host cities or countries the potential benefits of organising a mega-event.[7] (Debates over whether the financial costs outweigh the potential benefits of hosting MSE are a challenge to address. They are addressed where relevant in this volume but are not central to its analysis.[8]) R. S. Zaharna notes that public diplomacy and tourism are two key components of 'nation-branding',[9] and hosting sporting events allows the two elements to help national governments and other diplomatic players achieve their political goals. Not every state hosts MSE; indeed, in the twenty-first century very few states have the infrastructure and/or finances to do so. From a high point in the early 2000s of up to ten cities vying for the right to stage the Olympic Games, the IOC faces a challenge in the second decade of the century to find enough cities to bid meaningfully for the games.[10] Other sporting federations face a more acute and more immediate predicament, with sport reflecting global societies facing financial challenges.

Even without the focus of hosting major international sporting events, countries, organisations and individuals can and do use sport to achieve diplomatic ends. Sport provides a lens upon the international system that gives insight into the underpinning facets of diplomacy as means of communication, representation and negotiation. The 2016 Olympic Games in Rio de Janeiro highlighted many dimensions to diplomacy. For example, for the first time the Olympics welcomed a Refugee Olympic team, highlighting the plight of millions of refugees (although the celebration of the Refugee Olympic team stands in stark contrast to the political response to the issue of refugees globally). Yulia Efimova, the Russian swimmer who had previously served a doping suspension and almost did not compete in the Olympics because of a second positive doping test, touted the line presented in the Russian media that the West is returning to a state of Cold War anti-Russian sentiment, reflecting the heightened tensions between Russia and the rest of the world.[11] The Lebanese team refused to travel on a bus with the Israeli team; a Saudi Arabian judoka withdrew from her match citing injury, which the Israeli press claimed was to avoid a potential second-round match against an Israeli athlete; and an Egyptian judoka was sent home from the Games after refusing to shake hands after losing to his Israeli competitor.[12] These episodes can also be considered 'diplomatic incidents' of the type that diplomats regularly address and as such are routine.

Equally, because of the popularity of sport, individuals have also chosen to use sporting events as a place to stage a protest or worse. When traditional diplomacy (be it international or domestic) does not appear to provide an avenue for change, athletes and others have used the tremendous audiences at sporting events as a platform for their message. Political protests have included John Carlos and Tommie Smith's actions on the podium in 1968 at Mexico City supporting the American civil rights movement; teams from the National Basketball Association and Women's National Basketball Association supporting Black Lives Matter and protesting the killings of unarmed African American citizens by law enforcement agenciesin recent years; and the 2016 Olympic silver medallist Feyisa Lilesa making an X with his arms above his head as he crossed the marathon finish line to show his solidarity with his persecuted Oromo people in Ethiopia. The en masse African boycott of the 1976 Olympic Games in Montreal contributed to the Gleneagles Agreement which ensured the sporting exclusion of apartheid states in Africa – and also that African states would participate in and not boycott the 1978 Commonwealth Games in Edmonton, Canada.[13] The Black September group used the 1972 Olympic Games at Munich to raise awareness of the Palestinean cause, their terrorist actions causing the death of eleven Israeli athletes and coaches and one German policeman. More recently, in November 2015 the Paris terrorist attacks organised by the so-called Islamic State included the friendly football match between France and Germany at the Stade de France as one of the sites of their coordinated bombings. Sport has therefore not surprisingly been used by a variety of actors as a vehicle to achieve specific political goals. This in turn reinforces the diplomatic qualities of sport as a medium for communication, representation and negotiation, but also the necessity of a nuanced understanding of how such incidents – and those away from the headlines – shape the sport and diplomacy nexus.

At another point of the spectrum of the relationship between sport and diplomacy there is the use of athletes to promote a particular, often national, image abroad. As athletes engaging in elite competition have a profile that makes them marketable commodities and potentially hugely wealthy, endemic to this quality is their ability to communicate and represent. Whether they are articulate orators or not, they can communicate through their sporting prowess; and whether they are playing an individual sport, in a team in a national league, or in international competition alongside multiple sponsors, they are representing a series of identities. The United States Olympic Committee (USOC) has its Team USA Ambassador Program for Olympians, Paralympians and hopeful athletes to prepare them for 'the expectations, roles and representing the United States', including extensive education on 'being ambassadors for their sport and country'.[14] The USOC, along with the national governing bodies and professional leagues, also works with the State Department for the Sport Envoy programme which sends athletes and coaches abroad to work with community and youth programmes organised by the US embassies and consulates.[15] The United States is not alone in this. Indeed, the visibility of athletes is why many of them, along with musicians and actors, have served as 'Goodwill Ambassadors' for the UN agency UNICEF in order to help improve the lives of children across the world.[16] 'Goodwill Ambassadors' as a title, used both officially and unofficially, is a reflection of the appropriation of diplomatic language to other realms of global society: including sport.

The guiding theme throughout this book is the practice of diplomacy in relation to sport. It focuses upon the concept of soft power in its many forms and its relation to public diplomacy and nation branding; terms that have received considerable scholarly discussion, but rarely combined with the world of sport. The Harvard scholar Joseph S. Nye Jr has argued that '[T]he soft power of a country rests heavily on three basic resources: its culture (in places where it is attractive to others), its political values (when it lives up to them at home and abroad), and its foreign policies (when others see them as legitimate and having moral authority).'[17] Governments and other actors across the globe have utilised sport to attempt to achieve their aims, particularly as they can easily promote the three aspects Nye emphasises as being central to soft power. In many cases governments directly and indirectly use sport, such as programmes for development and peace or by hosting MSE. Sport exchanges at the most basic level – organised by individuals or governments – have contributed to the 'winning of hearts and minds', to quote Nye again.[18] On the other hand, withholding the opportunity to compete in sport – the oft used and misused term 'boycott' – or even just the threat of such action has been utilised by a variety of actors in their efforts to achieve a desired political outcome.

Not all examples of sport as a form of soft power are directed by states. People-to-people exchanges, frequently organised by private individuals or organisations and often characterised as track-two diplomacy, can also contribute to the changing of perceptions. Exchange programmes perform one aspect of this regardless of whether the programme is supported by a government – such as the State Department funding of the Fulbright Program or the British Council's Premier Skills campaign – or organised by a private individual such as Martin Feinberg, who wanted to show his French basketball club his home country. Previous work has addressed agents of cultural diplomacy and what they are attempting to achieve via these programmes, and the variety of actors utilising sport within diplomacy is just as important.[19] As Giles Scott-Smith has noted, 'the informal networks established from these relations themselves have major political import'.[20] Perhaps one of the strongest pieces of evidence of the value of these exchanges is the impact of the Erasmus Programme, an educational exchange programme for students within European Union (EU) countries, begun in 1987 and enhanced in 2014 with Erasmus +, which brought together all the EU's education, training, sport and youth programmes. In the UK referendum on its EU membership (23 June 2016), the preference to remain as part of the EU was overwhelmingly supported by younger voters.[21] Time spent abroad, living in and learning about a country, can have long-lasting impacts on both populations; sporting tours have provided a ready medium for exchanges since at least the end of the Second World War.

After many years of relative neglect by their separate disciplines, the realm of sport and diplomacy together is attracting renewed scholarly attention across a range of academic fields. This book is deliberately aimed at broadening and deepening the debate about sport and diplomacy, and expanding this specific but nascent field. Scholars began to critically examine sport and international politics in the late twentieth century, but only more recently has sport and diplomacy become a site of greater interest.[22] The few books on sport and diplomacy literature tend to focus solely on the

Olympic movement[23] or remain more narrowly focused on specific periodisations of time, such as the interwar decades or the Cold War.[24] When a chapter on sport is included in a more substantial book on diplomacy, it is often relegated towards the end or mentioned within a chapter on international organisations.[25] Special issues of a variety of academic journals are increasingly addressing this intersection of sport and diplomacy,[26] and the editors of this volume look forward to the publication of more full-length monographs addressing these topics.[27]

The volume here is not restricted to MSE or the Cold War, although both of these elements appear on the following pages. Furthermore, sport, development and peace (SPD) literature has largely remained a separate, isolated component of broader sport studies literature, frequently addressed by sport sociologists and not often by those who engage with diplomacy.[28] The contributions contained herein bring that subfield into larger conversations around diplomacy with those who consider global affairs. Indeed, the inclusion of Cárdenas and Lang's chapter on the practice of SPD within this volume on sport and diplomacy helps move this field past the narrow confines of the Cold War and into the twenty-first century. With a combination of theoretical chapters grounded in historical examples and chapters which address particular episodes, the book will help guide future research on sport and diplomacy by illustrating the value of studying the two together. This has the added benefit of showing that scholars of sport and diplomacy do not view themselves as distinct but instead come together to continue to expand the nascent field while making valuable contributions to each subfield.

To address the themes of soft power and public diplomacy, and the narratives that flow from them, the book is divided into three parts followed by a separate concluding chapter. The first section brings together various conceptual dimensions of sport and diplomacy and begins by tackling issues familiar to students of diplomacy: namely peace and conflict. Laurence Cooley's chapter on the 'deeply divided' societies of Bosnia and Herzegovina, Cyprus and Northern Ireland illustrates the competing jurisdictions of different actors such as a troika of UEFA, FIFA and the IOC demanding time-sensitive reforms to Bosnia's post-Yugoslav football architecture. These pragmatic concerns are also evident in Alexander Cárdenas and Sibylle Lang's practitioner account of the use of sport in Colombia and the Philippines in programmes for development and peace. The authors' field work, vested in diplomacy at the grassroots, is integral to their thinking on the positive and progressive opportunities that sport provides. Alan Tomlinson draws on his expertise in the study of FIFA to ask questions of the sport and diplomacy relationship in three realms: the individual, the institutional and the ideological. Suzanne Dowse implicitly takes up these themes in the example of the 2010 South Africa FIFA World Cup to illustrate how a state can utilise a global mega sports event as a political tool to influence domestic and international audiences, and reveals the disjuncture between expectations and realities that cut across elites and publics. Addressing these spaces between expectations and reality is something the study of sport and diplomacy can facilitate.

The second section looks at ways governments and individuals have sought to use international sport competitions as a form of public diplomacy to achieve specific aims. Maximilian Drephal shows two dimensions of public diplomacy in Afghan–British relations: first, how a newly independent Afghanistan used sport to display its burgeoning nationhood, and secondly, how British diplomats used sporting contests, both with and as events for the local population, to continue a colonial legacy in a post-independent Afghanistan. While 'ping-pong diplomacy' famously describes the opening of US–Chinese relations in the 1970s, Amanda Shuman demonstrates how China used this sport in its relations with newly decolonised states a decade earlier in its efforts to position itself as the stronger communist state in the deepening Sino-Soviet split. Shuman's account reveals the importance of representation of the state in people-to-people diplomacy. Lindsay Sarah Krasnoff's chapter looks at informal people-to-people diplomacy. The two tours to the United States by French basketball team PUC in the 1950s and early 1960s brought enduring positive legacies for both the sport and the individuals involved against a backdrop of indifference in Franco-US relations. David Rowe's contribution is to question the position of Australia in relation to an Asian context and the role the region's leading sport – football – had to play in Australia hosting the 2015 Asian Confederations tournament.

The final section addresses the withholding of sport competitions, including the threat of boycott, as a diplomatic tool. Carole Gomez takes a broader and more theoretical approach to boycotts in the realm of sport and diplomacy; and grapples with the difficulties of pinning this concept down. Rachel Vaughan's chapter is about the melding of sport with issues of recognition and the implications of recognition in one realm upon another as she explores American diplomacy towards 'two Chinas' surrounding the 1960 Winter Olympics in Squaw Valley, California. Joe Eaton tackles perhaps the most famous sport boycott – the 1980 Moscow Olympics – by investigating Asian and African responses to American diplomatic efforts on this issue. His account starkly reveals the need for nuance and appreciation of diversity within the diplomatic sphere in considering the 1980 boycott. Umberto Tulli's contribution is to return to the debate on public diplomacy, and particularly propaganda, as he sheds light on the extensive but arm's length role the Reagan White House played in the organisation of the 1984 Los Angeles Olympics in the midst of the 'new' Cold War. The concluding chapter, by Aaron Beacom and J. Simon Rofe, provides an overview of the developing field of sport and diplomacy, picking up the issues outlined while contextualising the arguments put forward in the volume by looking to the implications for further research.

Taken together, these chapters increase our understanding of the field of sport and diplomacy. They do so by reflecting a diversity of approach and method from a range of scholars from previously distinct academic fields brought together by a desire to enhance the overall appreciation of the duality of sport and diplomacy. In discussing cultural diplomacy, Jessica C. E. Gienow-Hecht and Mark C. Donfried state that 'between 1945 and 1989–91, cultural productions became the most powerful tools for the promotion of ideological goals and strategies'.[29] Our hope with this volume is to demonstrate the primacy of sport with diplomatic endeavours, transcending the Cold War, both geographically and temporally. Much public diplomacy literature, along with broader sport and diplomacy scholarship, has focused on these ideas being part of the American diplomatic toolbox. While this idea is addressed in some of the chapters contained herein, many of the contributions in this volume expand public diplomacy discourse beyond the scope of the United States, and indeed beyond the nation state. States and organisations across the globe will continue to utilise sport within their soft power efforts. Whether those endeavours involve mega-events such as the Olympic Games or FIFA World Cup, or more localised programmes which involve either elite athletes or average citizens, sport uses diplomacy in many different ways to achieve political goals. The Cold War was a driving factor for many of the actions taken on either side of the ideological divide, as well as within the Sino-Soviet communist split, but the Cold War marked neither the introduction nor the end of the use of sport within soft power. Sport has been and remains an integral part of diplomacy. The multi-billion dollar business of sport, the drama of competition and the narratives it produces bring the world's population together like no other facet of modern society. This volume provides an enhanced critical analysis of the past as well as contributing to the debates across academic and sporting fields.

Notes

1 Ed Smith, 'Has sport ever had it so good?', 29 December 2015, espncricinfo.com, available at www.espncricinfo.com/magazine/content/story/956239.html (accessed 2 March 2016).
2 Lincoln Allison, *The Politics of Sport* (Manchester: Manchester University Press, 1986), 17–21.
3 IOC, 'IOC marketing: media guide Olympic Games Rio 2016', available at https://stillmed.olympic.org/media/Document Library/OlympicOrg/Games/Summer-Games/Games-Rio-2016-Olympic-Games/Media-Guide-for-Rio-2016/IOC-Marketing-Media-Guide-Rio-2016.pdf (accessed 8 August 2016).
4 FIFA runs a number of global championships for various age groups, with two World Cups run on a quadrennial cycle the most prominent; a tournament for senior men's teams begun in 1930 and a tournament for senior women's teams begun (as the Women's World Championships) in 1991. The differentiation born out of gender is testament to the increased focus upon sport as a reflection of global society and further justifies the attention this volume provides.
5 Two examples include Stephen Frawley (ed.), *Managing Sporting Mega-Events* (Abingdon: Routledge, 2016); and 'Going global: the promises and pitfalls of hosting global games', *Third World Quarterly*, 25:7 (2004).
6 Germany National Tourist Board, '"A time to make friends™": the 2006 FIFA World Cup™ and its effect on the image and economy of Germany', available at www.germany.travel/media/en/pdf/dzt_marktforschung/Fazit_der_FIFA_WM_2006_PDF.pdf (accessed 9 August 2016).
7 Magdalena Florek, Tim Breitbarth and Francisco Conejo, 'Mega event = mega impact? Travelling fans' experience and perceptions of the 2006 FIFA World Cup host nation', *Journal of Sport and Tourism*, 13:3 (2008).
8 Bent Flyvbjerg and Allison Stewart, 'Olympic proportions: cost and cost overrun at the Olympics 1960–1972', *Saïd Business School Working Papers* 2002, available at

http://eureka.sbs.ox.ac.uk/4943/1/SSRN-id2382612_%282%29.pdf (accessed 5 March 2016); Martin Müller, 'After Sochi 2014: costs and impacts of Russia's Olympic Games', *Eurasian Geography and Economics*, 55:6 (2014); Tracey J. Dickson, Angela M. Benson and Deborah A. Blackman, 'Developing a framework for evaluating Olympic and Paralympic legacies', *Journal of Sport and Tourism*, 16:4 (2011); Jo Jakobsen, Harry Arne Solberg, Thomas Halvorsen and Tor Georg Jakobsen, 'Fool's gold: major sport events and foreign direct investment', *International Journal of Sport Policy and Politics*, 5:3 (2013).

 9 R. S. Zaharna, 'Mapping out a spectrum of public diplomacy initiatives: information and relational communication frameworks', in Nancy Snow and Philip M. Taylor (eds), *Routledge Handbook of Public Diplomacy* (New York: Routledge, 2009), 90.

10 The withdrawal by the Italian Olympic Committee of Rome as a host city for the 2024 Games in September 2016 left only three cities vying for the right: Los Angeles, Paris and Budapest, after Boston and Hamburg also withdraw due to concerns over staging the event. At the same stage in the preparations for the 2012 Olympic Games there were nine cities still in contention, with five being shortlisted for the final competition. London was selected to host the 2012 Summer Olympic Games on 6 July 2005.

11 Shaun Walker, 'Yulia Efimova hits back at critics: "I thought cold war was long in the past"', *The Guardian*, 9 August 2016, available at www.theguardian.com/sport/2016/aug/09/yuilia-efimova-olympics-critics-cold-war-swimming-lilly-king-rio (accessed 9 August 2016).

12 'Saudi judoka forfeits Rio match, apparently to avoid Israeli', *Times of Israel*, 7 August 2016, available at www.timesofisrael.com/saudi-judoka-forfeits-rio-match-apparently-to-avoid-israeli/ (accessed 9 August 2016); Karolos Grohmann, 'Egyptian judoka sent home over handshake refusal with Israeli', Reuters, available at www.reuters.com/article/us-olympics-rio-judo-egypt-israel-idUSKCN10Q1WC (accessed 22 August 2016).

13 Aviston D. Downes, 'Forging Africa-Caribbean solidarity within the Commonwealth? Sport and diplomacy during the anti-apartheid campaign', in Heather L. Dichter and Andrew Johns (eds), *Diplomatic Games: Sport, Statecraft and International Relations since 1945* (Lexington, KY: University Press of Kentucky, 2014), 117–49.

14 'Team USA Ambassador Program', TeamUSA.org, available at www.teamusa.org/About-the-USOC/In-the-Community/US-Olympic-Academy/team-usa-ambassador-program (accessed 22 August 2016).

15 'Sports envoys and sports visitors', Department of State Bureau of Educational and Cultural Affairs, available at https://eca.state.gov/programs-initiatives/sports-diplomacy/sports-envoys-and-sports-visitors (accessed 22 August 2016).

16 'Goodwill ambassadors & advocates', UNICEF, available at www.unicef.org/people/people_ambassadors.html (accessed 22 August 2016).

17 Joseph S. Nye, Jr, 'Hard, soft, and smart power', in Andrew F. Cooper, Jorge Heine and Ramesh Thakur (eds), *The Oxford Handbook of Modern Diplomacy* (Oxford: Oxford University Press, 2013), 566.

18 Joseph S. Nye, Jr, 'Public diplomacy and soft power', *Annals of the American Academy of Political and Social Science*, 'Public Diplomacy in a Changing World', 616:94 (2008), 108.

19 Jessica C. E. Gienow-Hecht, 'What are we searching for? Culture, diplomacy, agents

and the state', in Jessica C. E. Gienow-Hecht and Mark C. Donfried (eds), *Searching for a Cultural Diplomacy* (New York: Berghahn Books, 2010), 4.

20 Giles Scott-Smith, 'Exchange programs and public diplomacy', in Nancy Snow and Philip M. Taylor (eds), *Routledge Handbook of Public Diplomacy* (New York: Routledge, 2009), 51.

21 Jessica Elgot, 'Young remain voters came out in force, but were outgunned', *The Guardian*, 24 June 2016, available at www.theguardian.com/politics/2016/jun/24/young-remain-voters-came-out-in-force-but-were-outgunned (accessed 9 August 2016).

22 Jim Riordan and Arnd Krüger, *The International Politics of Sport in the 20th Century* (London: Spon, 1999); Pierre Arnaud and James Riordan, *Sport and International Politics: The Impact of Fascism and Communism on Sport* (London: Spon, 1998); Peter Beck, *Scoring for Britain: International Football and International Politics, 1900–1939* (London: Frank Cass, 1999).

23 Roger Levermore and Adrian Budd (eds), *Sport and International Relations: An Emerging Relationship* (London: Routledge, 2004); Aaron Beacom, *International Diplomacy and the Olympic Movement: The New Mediators* (Basingstoke: Palgrave Macmillan, 2012).

24 Barbara J. Keys, *Globalizing Sport: National Rivalry and International Community in the 1930s* (Cambridge, MA: Harvard University Press, 2006); Heather L. Dichter and Andrew L. Johns (eds), *Diplomatic Games: Sport, Statecraft, and International Relations Since 1945* (Lexington, KY: University Press of Kentucky, 2014).

25 David Black and Byron Peacock, 'Sport and diplomacy', in Andrew F. Cooper, Jorge Heine and Ramesh Thakur (eds), *The Oxford Handbook of Modern Diplomacy* (Oxford: Oxford University Press, 2013), 708–14; Jeremi Suri, 'Non-governmental organizations and non-state actors', in *Palgrave Advances in International History* (Basingstoke: Palgrave Macmillan, 2005), 223–46.

26 The special issues include: 'Sport and foreign policy in a globalizing world' in *Sport in Society*, 11:4 (2008); 'Sport and diplomacy' in *Sport in Society*, 17:9 (2014); 'Sports diplomacy' in *The Hague Journal of Diplomacy*, 8:3–4 (2013); 'Sports diplomacy, politics, and peace-building' in *International Area Studies Review*, 16:3 (2013); 'Diplomacy and sport' in *Diplomacy and Statecraft*, 27:2 (2016); 'Sport diplomacy forum' in *Diplomatic History*, 450:5 (2016).

27 Two excellent sport-specific monographs are Beck, *Scoring for Britain*, and Sayuri Guthrie-Shimizu, *Transpacific Field of Dreams: How Baseball Linked the United States and Japan in Peace and War* (Chapel Hill, NC: University of North Carolina Press, 2012).

28 Ingrid Beutler, 'Sport serving development and peace: achieving the goals of the United Nations through sport', *Sport in Society*, 11:4 (2008); Bruce Kidd, 'A new social movement: sport for development and peace', *Sport in Society*, 11:4 (2008); Solveig Straume, 'Norwegian naivety meets Tanzanian reality: the case of the Norwegian sports development aid programme, Sport for All, in Dar es Salaam in the 1980s', *International Journal of the History of Sport*, 29:11 (2012); Fred Coalter, 'The politics of sport-for-development: limited focus programmes and broad gauge problems?', *International Review for the Sociology of Sport*, 45:3 (2010); Grant Jarvie, 'Sport, development and aid: can sport make a difference?', *Sport in Society*, 14:2 (2011); Richard Giulianotti, 'Sport, peacemaking and conflict resolution: a contextual

analysis and modelling of the sport, development and peace sector', *Ethnic and Racial Studies*, 34:2 (2011) and 'The sport, development and peace sector: four social policy domains', *Journal of Social Policy*, 40:4 (2011), doi:10.1017/S0047279410000930; and G. Armstrong, 'Sport, the military and peacemaking', *Third World Quarterly*, 32:3 (2011).

29   Jessica C. E. Gienow-Hecht and Mark C. Donfried, 'The model of cultural diplomacy: power, distance, and the promise of civil society', in Gienow-Hecht and Donfried (eds), *Searching for a Cultural Diplomacy*.

Part I

Concepts and history

1

The governance of sport in deeply divided societies: actors and institutions in Bosnia and Herzegovina, Cyprus and Northern Ireland

Laurence Cooley

Few issues are as central to international politics and diplomacy as conflict and its resolution. Sport, on the other hand, may on first consideration appear to be marginal both to international politics in general and to conflict more specifically. On closer examination, however, the relationship between sport and matters of conflict and peace reveals itself to be a complex and important one – whether in everyday manifestations of violence between sports fans, such as that which marred the early stages of the 2016 European football championship in France, or symbolised by the lofty goals of the Olympic movement, which profess to contribute to the building of a more peaceful world. Sport has been implicated in both inter-state and intra-state conflicts, as demonstrated by the examples of the 'soccer war' between El Salvador and Honduras in 1969, famously documented by Ryszard Kapuściński; and the riot between Dynamo Zagreb and Red Star Belgrade fans at Zagreb's Maksimir stadium in May 1990, which has sometimes been seen as the symbolic start of the violent dissolution of Yugoslavia.[1] In the case of intra-state conflicts, violence often leaves sport fractured along national, ethnic, religious or linguistic lines. At the same time, sport is often seen as a means of bringing people together and healing rifts in post-conflict societies, either in a symbolic fashion or in the form of more institutionalised Sport for Development and Peace (SDP) projects run by non-governmental organisations with the support of donors and international organisations.

While, as the contributions to this book serve to demonstrate, there is a vibrant literature on sport vested in historical studies and particularly diplomatic history, students of political science and international relations have until recently seemed content to leave the study of sport as a social phenomenon to their colleagues in history and sociology departments. Indeed, it has become something of a cliché to note that sport has been neglected (or indeed actively dismissed) by political scientists.[2] This claim is increasingly difficult to sustain, though, thanks to a now rapidly growing body of work on the politics of sport.[3] Much of this literature should be of interest to diplomatic historians, and particularly that which examines the role and power of international sports organisations and their interactions with states and other international organisations.[4] Another topic that has received significant attention in the past decade or so has been the SDP sector mentioned above – studies of the use of sport to attempt to further development outcomes and promote peace building in developing and post-conflict states have flourished.[5]

While this focus on SDP initiatives is welcome, particularly given that the declaration of the Sustainable Development Goals adopted in September 2015 proclaims to recognise 'the growing contribution of sport to the realisation of development and peace in its promotion of tolerance and respect',[6] the focus of this chapter is on a distinct issue: that of the *governance* of sport in deeply divided societies.[7] Unlike the SDP literature, the focus here is not on assessing whether and how sport can serve the purpose of lessening divisions between groups in such societies, but on how, given that such divisions exist, sport is organised and governed – and how a variety of actors have contributed to the shaping of the institutions of governance of sport.

The chapter identifies broad patterns among the types of institutions used to govern sport in three deeply divided societies, namely Bosnia and Herzegovina (hereafter, Bosnia), Cyprus and Northern Ireland.[8] The chapter draws on some of the existing research on the governance of sport in each of these cases, but it also seeks to move beyond the analysis of single cases and start to establish more general observations about how sports federations, often under the influence of diplomatic actors such as regional and international governing bodies, have been designed in the context of deep societal divisions that are reflected in sport.

The first section of the chapter provides a framework for understanding the types of institutional arrangements for governance in deeply divided societies, drawing on the political science literature on conflict management. This framework suggests that two broad approaches, termed 'integration' and 'accommodation', can be observed in the design of political institutions devised to manage inter-group conflict. The integration–accommodation framework is then used as a lens through which to assess the governance of sport in the three case studies. Each case study starts with a sketch of the political institutions employed to manage conflict in the country concerned, followed by analysis of the governance arrangements that exist in the sports sector. The rationale for this approach is to help understand not just the approach taken to the design of institutions of sports governance, but to do so in the context of considering the broader approach to managing conflict in each particular case. This analysis suggests that there has been a preference among a broad range of actors for integrative institutional designs for the governance of sport in each of the cases, and that this approach is at odds with the design of the same societies' political institutions, which are oriented more towards accommodation. In order to understand this preference, it is necessary to appreciate the power of rhetoric emphasising the social value of sport – as exemplified by its incorporation into the Sustainable Development Goals – but also more practical considerations about the demands of international competition and the desire of local sports actors to secure access to this international realm. The chapter concludes by reflecting on opportunities for further research into the institutions of governance of sport in deeply divided societies and the role of different actors in establishing and reforming those institutions.

Institutional design in deeply divided societies: integration versus accommodation

Before considering the specific issue of the governance of sport, it is necessary to briefly survey the broader literature on institutional design in deeply divided societies. A number of different attempts have been made to develop classifications, typologies or taxonomies of the types of institutions that are employed with the aim of managing conflict between groups.[9] The designs that are identified are wide ranging, incorporating strategies that attempt to eliminate divisions between groups by partitioning states along ethnic lines, for instance; through to those that attempt to make possible peaceful sharing of states through granting territorial autonomy to groups or establishing political power sharing between them.

McGarry *et al.*'s summary of a range of approaches to institutional design helpfully places them on a scale between integration and accommodation.[10] Integration, they suggest, 'turn[s] a blind eye to difference for public purposes', and its advocates 'believe political instability and conflict result from group-based partisanship in political institutions'[11] and thus 'reject the idea that ethnic difference should necessarily translate into political differences'.[12] In this sense, integration is a liberal prescription for the depoliticisation of identities through the privatisation of cultural difference.[13] As Kuperman explains, integration 'aims to erode the political salience of groups that are distinguished by identity or location and instead promote a single, unifying nationality through more centralised institutions'.[14] In such institutions, integrationists argue, representation should be of individuals, rather than groups, and should be based on principles of meritocracy, difference blindness and impartiality, rather than descriptive representation. Integrationists are generally hostile to group-based political parties and supportive of civil society organisations that transcend the relevant divisions in deeply divided societies. Moreover, while they may support the concept of a federal state, they do not favour federation based on territorial units based on national, ethnic or linguistic criteria. Indeed, where relevant they support unitary state designs over federal alternatives.[15]

According to McGarry *et al.*, accommodation, by contrast, as a minimum 'requires the recognition of more than one ethnic, linguistic, national, or religious community in the state. It aims to secure the coexistence of different communities within the same state.'[16] Accommodationists 'insist that in certain contexts, national, ethnic, religious, and linguistic divisions and identities are resilient, durable, and hard', and that '[p]olitical prudence and morality requires adaptation, adjustment, and consideration of the special interests, needs, and fears of groups so they may regard the state in question as fit for them'.[17] Accommodationist strategies of institutional design aim to provide guarantees to these groups 'based on their distinct identity or geographic location, via mechanisms such as proportional representation, federalism, autonomy, quotas, economic redistribution, and veto power'.[18] The accommodationist institutional design that is most prominent in the conflict management literature is a form of power sharing known as consociationalism.

Explained briefly, consociationalism describes a form of democracy in which divisions between groups in a plural society are managed through institutions that enable cooperation between the elite representatives of these social groups. In his influential work on consociational democracy, Arend Lijphart identified four key features characteristic of this cooperation. These are elite-level power sharing by means of a grand coalition, segmental cultural autonomy, proportionality between groups in public positions, and group veto rights over vital interests.[19] More recent scholarship simplifies the definition to two key features: executive power sharing by representatives of the most significant segments of society, and territorial forms of self-governance.[20]

Most contemporary empirical research on consociationalism focuses, understandably, on its adoption via constitutions or peace agreements, either at the state or sub-state level. Some authors, however, have started to examine the impacts of the adoption of consociationalism in particular policy domains. Fontana, for instance, explores the interplay of Bosnia's consociational political institutions and cultural policy in the country, focusing particularly on the museums sector.[21] She argues that the emphasis placed on ethnic difference by Bosnia's constitutional arrangements has played out through a tendency for cultural institutions to emphasise and preserve parallel, as opposed to intersecting, group histories. Studying the governance of sport provides an opportunity to contribute to this expansion of the study of approaches to conflict management such as consociationalism.

Where might diplomacy fit into this research agenda, though? Early research on consociationalism tended to neglect the role of external actors in establishing power-sharing institutions, but as these have become a more prominent feature of post-conflict settlements, so the appreciation of the role of these actors in establishing and maintaining power sharing has grown.[22] While McGarry *et al.* argue that integration is the dominant method of managing inter-group relations in established democracies – noting, for instance, that it is advocated by politicians as the best way to 'manage' Europe's immigrant populations[23] – in post-conflict and other deeply divided societies, external actors frequently prescribe strategies of accommodation. In particular, consociationalism has been promoted by a range of actors including the European Union and the United States,[24] and can now arguably be considered to be external actors' favoured method of managing group relations in post-conflict states.

The governance of sport in three deeply divided societies

Having identified the types of institutions that are employed to facilitate the governance of deeply divided societies, it is now possible to turn to the more specific issue of the governance of sport in such contexts. As a 'constitutive element of everyday life and popular culture', sport is not insulated from the effects of conflict in societies that are deeply divided along national, ethnic, religious or linguistic lines.[25] Indeed, contrary to the assumptions upon which SDP interventions are built, sport in deeply divided societies often serves to accentuate existing divisions.[26] As Sugden and Tomlinson argue, '[s]port in general, and football in particular, have proven to be significant theatres for the working up and expression of national unity, and its mobilized form, nationalism'.[27] Indeed, some authors claim that sport is *the* most powerful form that national performance can take.[28] Claims that sport contributed directly to the outbreak of violence in cases such as the El Salvador–Honduras 'soccer war' described by Kapuściński, or the clashes between Dynamo Zagreb and Red Star Belgrade fans at the Maksimir stadium, may be debatable, but regardless of whether the working up of nationalism through sport played a role in the initiation of violence, in the aftermath of violent conflict the very organisation of sport is often left divided along the lines of conflicts.

While sport in deeply divided societies has been the subject of some research, very little attention has been paid to how sport is governed in such contexts.[29] Notable exceptions include Reiche's study of the relationship between sport and confessionalism in Lebanon; Coppieters's investigation of the organisation of marathons in Brussels, Belfast, Beirut and Jerusalem; a number of articles and working papers on the organisation of Northern Irish sport, including football and cycling; Vanreusel *et al.*'s study of the organisation of sport in Belgium; and some works that consider the arrangements for the governance of football in Bosnia and Herzegovina.[30] It is with the case of Bosnia that our analysis starts.

Bosnia and Herzegovina

The case of the re-establishment of the institutions of governance of football in Bosnia following the end of the Bosnian War of 1992–95, and their subsequent reform under international pressure, illustrates two important themes that are central to this chapter. First, the initial approach taken in order to facilitate the reunification of the sport was characterised by accommodation – allowing three different governing bodies that emerged from the conflict to remain in control of the game in their respective territories – but, over time, both external actors and some local voices were successful in calling for a more integrative approach, which has seen the establishment of a single governing body for football in Bosnia. Secondly, the case illustrates the range of actors – both international and local – that are involved in sports diplomacy, broadly defined, and how the interests of these actors interact.

In order to be able to more fully understand the organisation of sport in Bosnia, it is first necessary to understand the broader political context of the country. War in Bosnia was precipitated by the country's independence from Yugoslavia in March 1992, although its roots can be traced back to Yugoslavia's first democratic regional elections in 1990, in which nationalists were swept to power in most of the constituent republics. According to the 1991 Yugoslav census, 43.7 per cent of the republic's population identified as Muslim (now more commonly termed Bosniak), 31.4 per cent as Serb, 17.3 per cent as Croat, 5.5 per cent as Yugoslav and 2.1 per cent as 'others and unknown'.[31] The war was initially fought between Bosnian government forces and Bosnian Serb paramilitaries, who opposed the country's independence and were actively supported by Belgrade. They sought to establish their own independent

Bosnian Serb state, which they hoped later to be able to unite with Serbia. Later in the war, conflict also erupted between Bosniak and Bosnian Croat forces as the latter attempted to gain control of territory in Croat-populated parts of Bosnia. In this they were supported by the nationalist political leadership in Zagreb, after the latter ousted the more moderate Bosnian Croat leadership.

The Bosnian conflict was ended by the internationally brokered Dayton Agreement in 1995; that Agreement established a new constitution for Bosnia. This constitution defined the country as a state composed of two entities, the Federation of Bosnia and Herzegovina and the Republika Srpska (RS), reflecting the division of the country at the end of the war. Extensive powers were reserved for the entities at the expense of the central Bosnian state. Each entity has its own president, government and parliament, and within the Federation power is further devolved to ten cantons, each with its own parliament. The Dayton constitution guarantees ethnic representation by way of quotas at all levels of government and in the civil service. It also established veto rules whereby decisions of the House of Representatives (the lower house of the Parliamentary Assembly) require the votes of at least one-third of the representatives of each entity, and decisions of the House of People (the upper house) can be vetoed by a majority of any of the Bosniak, Croat or Serb delegates. These three ethnic groups are identified by the constitution as Bosnia's 'constituent peoples'. The Agreement has been described as establishing a 'classic example of consociational settlement',[32] in which 'institutions correspond to an ideal-typical consociational democracy'.[33]

Since the mid-2000s, a number of attempts have been made to reform the Dayton constitution, in response to criticisms that Bosnian political institutions are not only incredibly inefficient, but also discriminate against citizens who do not belong to one of the recognised 'constituent peoples'.[34] Critics argue that the consociational institutions introduced by Dayton have reinforced the salience of ethnic divisions in the country and have turned elections into ethnic censuses, since the constitution provides ethno-nationalist parties with little incentive to appeal beyond the boundaries of their own groups.[35] Attempts at externally incentivised constitutional reform have failed, however, precisely because of the intransigence of local actors who have a vested interest in the maintenance of the system that ensures their continued grip on power. Even if constitutional reform were to be successful, it would be unlikely to involve a significant move away from the consociational approach, since the reform proposals that have been advanced all 'endorse some variation of Dayton's basic compromise'.[36]

At the end of the war in 1995, Bosnian sport was also left fractured along ethnic lines. In football, three distinct governing bodies emerged from the conflict, each running its own leagues.[37] It was not until 2002 that a single football federation, the Nogometni/Fudbalski Savez Bosne i Hercegovine (N/FSBiH), was formed, under pressure from FIFA, UEFA and the International Olympic Committee. As Sterchele notes, the united federation resembled the Dayton model.[38] The individual 'ethnic' federations continued to exist as sub-federations of the N/FSBiH, and a tripartite presidency and an Executive Committee composed of five members of each sub-committee were established.[39]

This arrangement for the governance of sport, with its echoes of the consociationalism employed in the Bosnian constitution, was intended to be an interim measure. As UEFA's head of sports legal services, Marcel Benz, told the football journalist Jonathan Wilson in 2011, UEFA was given assurances that, with time, the federation would adopt a single presidency in line with common international practice. Despite these assurances, progress proved to be very slow, and the 'interim' governance arrangement started to pose problems for FIFA and UEFA, with statutes easily blocked due to the voting rules of the N/FSBiH Executive Committee and the federation being represented by three presidents at international congresses.[40] The N/FSBiH seemed unwilling or unable to tackle significant problems in the domestic game, or to respond to pressure from fans to tackle corruption. Fans had been protesting against the federation since the formation of the 'BH Fanaticos' group in 2000 – most notably in an incident in Oslo in March 2007, when they caused a delay of more than an hour to a match against Norway by throwing flares on to the pitch, in order to highlight the issue of corruption within the N/FSBiH.

In response to the problems facing the governance of football in Bosnia, in October 2010 FIFA and UEFA demanded reform of the N/FSBiH within six months, including a requirement that the tripartite presidency be replaced. This demand met with significant resistance. Bosnian Serb representatives within the N/FSBiH opposed reform for fear that it would put at risk their political autonomy, but there was also some resistance from Bosnian Croats, who claimed that FIFA's actions were an insensitive foreign imposition.[41] When the deadline passed in April 2011 and reforms had not been agreed, the federation was suspended by FIFA and UEFA, meaning that the Bosnian national team and Bosnian clubs could not compete in international or European competition.

Even with the suspension, political opposition to reform remained. The RS president, Milorad Dodik, maintained that he was 'against one president being elected for the whole of Bosnia-Herzegovina in any state structure – you name it, even a bee-keeping association'.[42] FIFA's Emergency Committee immediately imposed a 'normalisation committee' on the N/FSBiH and tasked it with making the required reforms. Headed by former Bosnian player Ivica Osim, within two months the committee adopted a new statute, allowing the suspension to be lifted in late May 2011 and paving the way for the first single president in the federation's history to be elected in December 2012.[43]

In a very short space of time, then, a combination of pressure from below, in the form of fan protests, and from FIFA and UEFA above, resulted in significant changes to the governance of football in Bosnia. This achievement was perhaps also dependent on a significant degree of luck, as FK Borac Banja Luka, from the capital of the RS, had just won their first Bosnian Premier League title, and would have been denied the chance to play in the qualifying rounds for the UEFA Champions League had the suspension not been lifted. Borac fans and officials lobbied for acceptance of the reforms, resulting in the overcoming of political resistance in the RS.[44] While the reasons for this apparent success may be complex, it is notable that whereas the international community has struggled for more than a decade to reform the

Dayton constitution, reform of the governance of football in Bosnia has been achieved more quickly. Moreover, it has taken a significant step away from the consociational power-sharing approach of Dayton in a more integrative direction.[45] Understanding this outcome, as the analysis above suggests, requires that we understand the complex interaction of a range of actors – including national and sub-national federations, international governing bodies, fans' groups and politicians.

Cyprus

The division of sport on the island of Cyprus has a history that dates back much longer than the conflict that Bosnia experienced in the 1990s. Meaningful sporting competition involving both Greek Cypriots and Turkish Cypriots effectively ceased in the 1950s – long before the formal partition of the island in 1974 – and it is only recently that progress has been made towards the possible reunification of sport across the inter-communal divide. As in the Bosnian case, it is football in particular that has been in the international spotlight, thanks to FIFA-facilitated negotiations involving the island's two football federations. As the analysis in this section demonstrates, however, the process underway in Cyprus is a more domestically driven one than that witnessed in Bosnia, with the main impetus for reunification coming from within the federations themselves. Before examining these recent developments in sport, however, it is again necessary to first understand the broader political context.

Cyprus became independent from the United Kingdom in 1960, following a period of conflict between the British authorities and Greek Cypriot guerrillas, who favoured unification with Greece. During the 1960s, there were a number of periods of inter-communal violence between Greek and Turkish Cypriots. In 1963, there was a constitutional breakdown, and the following year a United Nations peacekeeping force was established and tasked with preventing further violence. While tensions between the two communities diffused in the late 1960s, in 1974 the Greek military junta and the Cypriot National Guard ousted the Cypriot president in a coup. Turkey responded by launching an invasion, which captured the north of the island. Cyprus has remained divided ever since. The internationally recognised Republic of Cyprus government has effective control only of the south of the island, and the Turkish Republic of Northern Cyprus (TRNC) is only recognised as a state by Turkey.

The most significant attempt to reunify the island came in the early 2000s, when United Nations-led negotiations resulted in a proposed plan for reunification, known as the Annan Plan, after the then UN Secretary-General, Kofi Annan. The plan underwent a number of revisions before being put to a referendum in April 2004. In the public vote, the majority (65 per cent) of Turkish Cypriots backed the plan, but it was rejected on the Greek Cypriot side, by a wide majority of 76 per cent of voters.[46] Had it been adopted, the Annan Plan would have established a constitutional structure based on principles of federalism and consociationalism. The plan itself cited Switzerland as a model for its proposed Cypriot constitution but, as Bose notes, it also resembled Bosnia's Dayton Agreement and Northern Ireland's Good Friday Agreement.[47] The proposed constitution would have established a bicameral parliament with an upper house (the senate) whose seats would have been divided evenly between Greek and Turkish Cypriots, and a lower house (the chamber of deputies) made up of representatives of each constituent state in proportion to their populations, with each being guaranteed a minimum 25 per cent of the seats. While the Annan Plan foresaw decisions being made on the basis of a simple majority, in the senate this would have needed to include a quarter of the voting representatives of each state, and for certain areas of critical interest a special majority of at least 40 per cent of the senators from each state would have been required. A presidential council was to have been established, made up of nine members with the approval of at least 40 per cent of the senators of each state, including at least two members from each state. The president of this council would have acted as head of state and government, and the office of both president and vice-president would have alternated between representatives from the Greek and Turkish Cypriot states every twenty months, such that at any one time one of these offices was to be held by a Greek Cypriot and the other by a Turkish Cypriot.[48]

The division of Cyprus since 1974 has had an inevitable impact on the organisation of sport on the island, not least because of the impossibility of most Cypriots crossing the so-called 'Green Line' that has divided the two communities geographically, at least until the easing of border restrictions in 2003.[49] In fact, as mentioned above, communal sporting division pre-dates the political and physical division of the island. Kartakoullis and Loizou note, for example, that the last season that Turkish Cypriot football teams competed in competitions organised by the Cyprus Football Association (CFA) was 1954–55, after which they were prevented from using sports facilities in the name of maintaining good community relations in the context of the Greek Cypriot anti-colonialist struggle.[50] While this was supposed to be a temporary measure, until the potential for inter-communal violence was over, it resulted in the Turkish Cypriot teams forming their own federation, the Kıbrıs Türk Futbol Federasyonu (CTFA). Because FIFA and UEFA recognise only the CFA as the legitimate Cypriot football federation, and have turned down the CTFA's requests to be recognised as a member federation, Turkish Cypriot football has remained internationally isolated.[51]

Since the 2004 referendum, however, there have been attempts to reunify the organisation of Cypriot football. Following the Greek Cypriot vote against the Annan Plan, the CTFA made a further attempt to join FIFA, and in meetings with FIFA officials its representatives accepted a plan to recognise the authority of and join the CFA. The plan was opposed by Turkish Cypriot politicians, however, and this prevented any progress towards its implementation.[52] More recently, further FIFA-facilitated talks have taken place. In November 2013, following negotiations in Zurich, the CFA and the CTFA signed a provisional agreement which, if implemented, will result in the CTFA becoming a member of the CFA, thus unifying football governance on the island.[53] A year and a half later, in March 2015, CTFA officials announced that they were going ahead with plans to join the CFA.[54] This decision attracted criticism from the then TRNC deputy prime minister and Minister of Economy, Tourism, Culture and Sports, Serdar Denktaş, who threatened to cut off funding to clubs in the event of the implementation of the agreement. There is also opposition on the Greek side, with some clubs voting against the proposed merger in a secret ballot held by the CFA.[55] However, the election of Mustafa Akıncı as the new TRNC president in April 2015 has signalled a political environment more conducive to unification.[56] At the time of writing, the football agreement had yet to be implemented, in part due to complications regarding the legal status of the CTFA.[57] However, the intent to merge the two federations on the island now seems to be well established.

The type of institutional arrangement that is envisaged for unified Cypriot football differs significantly from those of Bosnia's interim arrangements discussed above. While the text of the provisional agreement does not specify the exact arrangements to be adopted, one of its provisions is that the CFA will recognise the competence of the CTFA to organise its own competitions among its member clubs. As such, no joint league is envisaged.[58] In this sense, the arrangement is more limited than that of Bosnia, where a unified league structure was created. This difference is more a reflection of the significant financial gulf between the relatively well financed Greek Cypriot clubs and their Turkish Cypriot counterparts, which are semi-professional at most and largely dependent on state funding, than it is of a desire to accommodate the identities of the two parties. No new association would be formed either; rather, the CTFA would become a member of the existing CFA. Unlike in Bosnia, the CTFA would not be guaranteed representation through a power-sharing presidency. In their provisional agreement, the two bodies agreed to the establishment of a steering committee to consider how Turkish Cypriot representation in CFA committees and assembly would be ensured. As of September 2015, it was envisaged that this representation will be on the same basis as that of each of the existing divisions of the Greek Cypriot leagues.[59]

Another significant difference between the Cyprus case and that of Bosnia concerns the motivations of the domestic actors. Whereas in the case of the eventual reform of the interim governance arrangements in Bosnia, local actors (with the notable exception of fans) were resistant to reform and a solution was imposed from outside through FIFA's intervention, in Cyprus the initiative to unify the two federations is a largely domestic initiative. While FIFA has facilitated talks between the parties, the main driver of progress has been the CTFA's concern to end the international isolation of Turkish Cypriot football. The association's president has written that the agreement reached in Zurich in November 2013 promises to end 'more than three decades of isolation' and 'to give hope to our clubs, to our players and above all to our youth who all strive to gain access to this global village of the sport called football'.[60]

Northern Ireland

Our final case study is Northern Ireland. As the analysis will show, this case has also been characterised by an approach to the governance of sport that can be categorised as integrative, and which notably also stands in contrast to the power-sharing approach that has formed the basis for the political settlement of the wider conflict. However, whereas the two cases discussed so far have illustrated varying degrees of involvement of international governing bodies, the Northern Ireland case is one where the governance of sport has been a largely domestic affair – albeit with cross-border Irish dimensions.

In order to understand the context of the governance of sport in Northern Ireland, it is necessary to first consider the history of the state. While the partition of Ireland in 1921 created a Northern Irish state that had a comfortable Protestant majority who supported continued union with the United Kingdom, it did not resolve the conflict between those Protestant unionists and nationalists, overwhelmingly from the Catholic minority, who instead preferred a united Ireland. It was not until the late 1960s, however, that this conflict escalated into what became known as 'the Troubles' – a thirty-year violent conflict fought between republican paramilitaries (most notably the Provisional Irish Republican Army (IRA)) on one side and the British state and loyalist paramilitaries on the other. During this period, around 3,600 people were killed, making the Troubles Western Europe's most deadly conflict since the end of the Second World War.

Significant progress was made towards peace during the 1990s, with an IRA cease-fire declared in 1994. Since the 1998 Good Friday Agreement, Northern Ireland has been governed under an arrangement in which significant powers are devolved from the United Kingdom government to a power-sharing administration in Belfast. The text of the agreement acknowledges 'the substantial differences between our continuing, and equally legitimate, political aspirations', but states that 'we will endeavour to strive in every practical way towards reconciliation and rapprochement within the framework of democratic and agreed arrangements'. It established the Northern Ireland Assembly and a number of transnational bodies such as the North/South Ministerial Council and the British–Irish Council, in order to commit the parties to 'partnership, equality and mutual respect as the basis of relationships within Northern Ireland, between North and South, and between these islands'.[61] Northern Ireland's political institutions, established in 1998 and revised by the October 2006 St Andrews Agreement, 'are widely agreed to be consociational in nature, albeit with external federal and confederal aspects'.[62]

Executive power in the Northern Ireland Assembly is shared according to electoral strength. The electoral system is proportional, and ministerial portfolios are automatically allocated by a mathematical formula. All members of the assembly have to designate themselves as 'unionist', 'nationalist' or 'other'. The executive is headed by a first minister and a deputy first minister, and these roles are allocated to the leaders of the first and second largest parties in the assembly, providing that these two parties do not belong to the same community bloc. There are also voting rules within the assembly designed to ensure cross-community support for legislative decisions, with key decisions – such as those changing standing orders, on budgetary matters and for any issue where a 'petition of concern' has been submitted to the speaker – requiring the support of a majority of both unionist and nationalist members as well as an overall majority, or the support of at least 40 per cent of the members of each bloc and a 60 per cent overall majority.[63]

Whereas the design of Northern Ireland's political institutions is very clearly premised on the accommodation of unionist and nationalist identities and interests, the organisation of sport in Northern Ireland is arguably more integrative (even if individual sports have been associated more with one particular community than the other). Many sports are in fact organised on an all-Ireland basis, with international representation based on teams that span Northern Ireland and the Republic.[64] Rugby, for example, has been organised on this basis since before Irish independence in 1922, and this model survived the partition that accompanied independence. Whyte observes that 'middle-class' sports including rugby, tennis and golf are more likely to be all-Ireland in their organisation than 'proletarian' sports such as cycling and (association) football (Gaelic sports, he argues, 'have always kept as a matter of principle to an all-Ireland basis').[65]

Cycling provides an interesting example here, because there used to be three governing bodies for the sport on the island of Ireland. As Howard explains, two of these, the Northern Ireland Cycling Federation (NICF) and the Irish Cycling Federation (ICF), were recognised as national governing bodies by the Union Cycliste International (UCI), whereas the third, the all-island National Cycling Association (NCA), was not.[66] In the late 1980s, it was proposed that the three bodies be merged to form the Federation of Irish Cyclists (FIC), although a vote of the membership of the NICF did not achieve the required two-thirds majority to approve this. Individual cycling clubs responded by leaving the NICF and forming the FIC-affiliated Ulster Cycling Federation, which was recognised by the Sports Council for Northern Ireland as the official governing body. The FIC became the only governing body recognised by the UCI. While the NICF continued to resist integration of the sport across the border for many years, in December 2006 its membership voted in favour of joining the Ulster Cycling Federation.[67]

The organisational split in football, meanwhile, remains, with Northern Ireland and the Republic maintaining separate leagues and national teams. However, within Northern Ireland attempts have been made to make football more inclusive, in order to address the perception that Northern Irish football is dominated by unionist interests. In April 2000, the British government set up an Advisory Panel to the Minister of Culture, Arts and Leisure to create a strategy for football in Northern Ireland. The report of the Advisory Panel noted that many Catholics felt uncomfortable and unsafe at international matches (it is notable that many Catholic players opt to represent the Republic of Ireland instead of Northern Ireland), and that sectarian conflict among fans was a barrier to improving community relations through football. Nonetheless, the report noted that football enjoys significant support across the community divide, and offers possibilities for cross-community reconciliation. It recommended the adoption of an anti-sectarianism strategy to enable this potential to be realised.[68] As Bairner explains, '[a]s football could not be allowed to appear to operate under the hegemonic control of unionists, political encouragement was voiced for integrationist strategies aimed at making support for the Northern Ireland "national" team more inclusive'.[69]

However, Bairner suggests that this approach contrasts with, and is potentially undermined by, the broader political and institutional context in Northern Ireland.

He argues that attempts to make sport more inclusive 'are expected to bear fruit in a political context in which sectarian differences have been legitimised and even given formal recognition through those very mechanisms that are intended to help create a more peaceful and less polarised Northern Ireland', referring to the consociational nature of the Good Friday Agreement.[70] He concludes that 'in the world of sport, citizens are being asked to set aside the trappings of cultural difference in the interests of social inclusion and cross-community integration', but that 'the resultant policies are fundamentally at odds with those that have been promoted in other areas of society, not least in the political process itself', where societal divisions have instead been institutionalised.[71] As in both Bosnia and Cyprus, then, prescriptions for the governance of sport are significantly more integrationist than those for the broader political management of conflict.

In search of explanations: conclusions and directions for further research

In all three of the cases outlined above, the empirical evidence presented suggests that the governance of sport is more integrative, or at least has been moving in a more integrative direction, than the wider political institutions of the country concerned. How can we explain this pattern? What explanations might we pursue when attempting to explain why national and international sports governing bodies have pressed for more integrative governance arrangements than we find employed in constitutions and peace agreements?

One explanation is that this approach might partly reflect the rhetorical impact of the claims that sports administrators frequently make about the supposed unifying impact of sport. Eick has argued that, '[i]n marketing football publicly including its political role, FIFA emphasizes football's social use-value and constantly highlights the capacity of football to boost "social cohesion" as stated in the FIFA objectives: "to improve the game of football constantly and promote it globally in the light of its unifying, educational, cultural and humanitarian values"'.[72] Indeed, this rhetoric now extends beyond the world of FIFA and other sports governing bodies, as reflected in its incorporation into the declaration of the Sustainable Development Goals. Applied to the Bosnian case, it could be argued that when presented with evidence of division, politicisation and corruption in Bosnian football, FIFA and UEFA could hardly not act, given their rhetoric that sport has the power to unify.[73] One avenue of further investigation might therefore be to examine whether a form of 'rhetorical entrapment'[74] is associated with the importance that international organisations have attached to Sport for Development and Peace, regardless of the extent to which they actually believe in this discourse.

We should not overlook more pragmatic explanations of the actions of both international and national governing bodies. The organisation of international sport, which is premised on the representation of states by national teams, does not sit easily with local arrangements that seek to accommodate societal divisions through the existence of multiple governing bodies. There is a clear mismatch between the various forms of autonomy associated with accommodationist strategies of conflict management and the demands of international governing bodies, which, due to the nature of international sport, are likely to prefer unitary national governing bodies. In the Bosnian example, a clear motivation behind FIFA and UEFA's attempts to reform the N/FSBiH was not the desire to contribute to more harmonious inter-ethnic relations (though that might be part of the explanation), but to address concerns about Bosnia's undue influence on the international stage that stemmed from its federation's tripartite presidency, and to tackle the considerable problems that existed within the domestic game. Pragmatic concerns also help to explain the CTFA's commitment to joining the Cyprus Football Association and unifying football governance on the island. As noted above, while the CTFA has faced significant opposition to this plan from some Turkish Cypriot politicians, it continues to pursue the goal of merging with the CFA as a way of ending the almost complete isolation of Turkish Cypriot football.[75]

These concerns suggest that the integrative direction of sports governance, in the three case studies presented here, might not be a deliberate alternative to more accommodative approaches to conflict management such as consociationalism, so much as a pragmatic response to the demands of international competition. Further research should investigate not only the ways in which sport is governed in deeply divided societies, but also the driving forces behind the establishment of different institutional designs in the governance of sport. Here, there is also a need to more fully appreciate the relative importance of different actors, at both the national and international level. While FIFA and UEFA's suspension of the Bosnian football federation in order to tackle governance concerns stemming from ethnic division might be unique (Meier and García suggest that by far the most common trigger of such interventions is instead government interference), there are perhaps subtler forms of international influence over national governing bodies that are worth investigating.[76] The Bosnian case also highlights the potential importance of pressure from below – that is to say, from sports fans.

Rofe has noted the large number of actors (or players, to use his sporting analogy) involved in sports diplomacy.[77] The cases considered here demonstrate the need to take into account the motivations and interests of these different actors, and how they interact to produce the types of institutional outcomes that we witness. As a comparison of the Bosnian and Cypriot football experiences demonstrates, the motivations of local actors can differ significantly from case to case, even where the outcomes might be superficially similar. Whereas in Bosnia, FIFA and UEFA (along with fans) faced resistance to reform from within the country's football federation, in Cyprus the initiative to unify the governance of the game on the island has been driven by the local federations – and the CTFA in particular. In both the Bosnian and Cypriot cases, however, nationalist political elites have voiced their opposition to closer integration.

A further question that might inform further research into the governance of sport in deeply divided societies concerns the effects of these governance arrangements on broader issues of conflict and identity, and would thus serve to link this research back to the concerns of the SDP literature. If, as discussed earlier in this chapter, the aim of integrationist approaches to institutional design is to promote a shared sense of identity through the adoption of centralised institutions, then what impact do these types of institutions have when employed in the governance of sport? Will a unified Cypriot football federation promote a stronger sense of Cypriot identity, transcending Greek and Turkish Cypriot ethnic identities, among players and fans of the sport? Alternatively, might unified institutions in sport simply be the exception to the rule, and co-exist alongside continued societal division? The latter possibility is exemplified by the case of football in Northern Ireland, where there are 'signs of a Northern Irish football consciousness, perhaps, but not of an emergent Northern Irish political consciousness, far less a "national" identity'.[78] In the Bosnian case, while headlines in international media coverage of the national football team's appearance at the 2014 World Cup may have suggested a country uniting behind the multi-ethnic team,[79] the reality is somewhat more complex, with many Bosnian Serbs and Bosnian Croats indeed supporting the Bosnian national team, but often as a secondary team to that of Serbia or Croatia.[80]

While 'Sport for Development and Peace' initiatives appear to have captured the attention of a significant number of scholars from across the social sciences, those political scientists with an interest in sport have so far largely neglected the question of how sport is governed in deeply divided societies. This is perhaps surprising, given the attention that has been paid in general to questions of institutional design in such societies. This chapter set out to address this gap in the literature and, in doing so, has demonstrated the integrative direction of sports governance in Bosnia, Cyprus and Northern Ireland. It has provided some tentative explanations for why integrative institutions have emerged in sport, in the context of environments where political institutions are characterised more by accommodation than integration. Some of the issues highlighted here, such as the relationship between local and international actors and between institutions and identities, speak to important debates within political science, international relations and the study of diplomacy, and will hopefully provoke further comparative research into the governance of sport in deeply divided societies.

Notes

1 See R. Kapuściński, *The Soccer War* (Cambridge: Granta, 1990); A. L. Sack and Z. Suster, 'Soccer and Croatian nationalism: a prelude to war', *Journal of Sport & Social Issues*, 24:3 (2000); D. Brentin, '"A lofty battle for the nation": the social roles of sport in Tudjman's Croatia', *Sport in Society*, 16:8 (2013), 996.

2 See R. Levermore and A. Budd, 'Sport and international relations: continued neglect?', in R. Levermore and A. Budd (eds), *Sport and International Relations: An Emerging Relationship* (London: Routledge, 2004); G. Holden, 'World cricket as a postcolonial international society: IR meets the history of sport', *Global Society*, 22:3 (2008); J. Grix, 'From hobbyhorse to mainstream: using sport to understand British politics', *British Politics*, 5:1 (2010).

3 For a useful overview, see J. Grix, *Sport Politics: An Introduction* (London: Palgrave Macmillan, 2016).

4 See, for example, A. Geeraert and E. Drieskens, 'The EU controls FIFA and UEFA: a principal–agent perspective', *Journal of European Public Policy*, 22:10 (2015); H. E. Meier and B. García, 'Protecting private transnational authority against public intervention: FIFA's power over national governments', *Public Administration*, 93:4 (2015); D. Brentin and L. Tregoures, 'Entering through the sport's door? Kosovo's sport diplomatic endeavours towards international recognition', *Diplomacy and Statecraft*, 27:2 (2016).

5 See, *inter alia*, R. Giulianotti, 'Human rights, globalization and sentimental education: the case of sport', *Sport in Society*, 7:3 (2004); B. Kidd, 'A new social movement: sport for development and peace', *Sport in Society*, 11:4 (2008); R. Levermore, 'Sport: a new engine of development?', *Progress in Development Studies*, 8:2 (2008); F. Coalter, 'The politics of sport-for-development: limited focus programmes and broad gauge problems?', *International Review for the Sociology of Sport*, 45:3 (2010); S. C. Darnell, 'Power, politics and "Sport for Development and Peace": investigating the utility of sport for international development', *Sociology of Sport Journal*, 27:1 (2010); R. Giulianotti, 'The sport, development and peace sector: a model of four social policy domains', *Journal of Social Policy*, 40:4 (2011) and 'Sport, peacemaking and conflict resolution: a contextual analysis and modelling of the sport, development and peace sector', *Ethnic and Racial Studies*, 34:2 (2011); R. Levermore, 'Evaluating sport-for-development: approaches and critical issues', *Progress in Development Studies*, 11:4 (2011); S. C. Darnell, *Sport for Development and Peace: A Critical Sociology* (London: Bloomsbury Academic, 2012).

6 United Nations Security Council, 'Transforming our world: the 2030 Agenda for Sustainable Development', resolution adopted by the General Assembly on 25 September 2015, UN Document A/RES/70/1 (21 October 2015), 10, available at www. un.org/ga/search/view_doc.asp?symbol=A/RES/70/1&Lang=E (accessed 5 August 2016).

7 All societies are divided to some extent, so following Nordlinger I use the term 'deeply divided' to refer to those societies where there is significant antagonism between segments that are based on highly politically salient identities. E. A. Nordlinger, *Conflict Regulation in Divided Societies* (Cambridge, MA: Center for International Affairs, Harvard University Press, 1972); see also A. Guelke, *Politics in Deeply Divided Societies* (Cambridge: Polity, 2012), 13–32.

8 I am indebted to Jasmin Mujanović for his previous work with me on the Bosnian case, and to Constantinos Adamides, Nicos Kartakoullis, Christina Loizou and Sertaç Sonan for discussions on the Cyprus case. Dario Brentin provided helpful feedback and suggestions on an earlier draft of this chapter.

9 See, in particular, J. Coakley, 'The resolution of ethnic conflict: towards a typology', *International Political Science Review*, 13:4 (1992); S. Smooha and T. Hanf, 'The diverse modes of conflict-regulation in deeply divided societies', *International Journal of Comparative Sociology*, 33:1/2 (1992); J. McGarry and B. O'Leary, 'Introduction: the macro-political regulation of ethnic conflict', in J. McGarry and B. O'Leary (eds), *The Politics of Ethnic Conflict Regulation: Case Studies of Protracted Ethnic Conflicts* (London: Routledge, 1993); J. Snyder, 'Managing ethnopolitics in eastern Europe: an assessment of institutional approaches', in J. P. Stein (ed.), *The Politics of National*

Minority Participation in Post-Communist Europe: State-Building, Democracy, and Ethnic Mobilization (Armonk, NY: M. E. Sharpe, 2000); S. Smooha, 'Types of democracy and modes of conflict management in ethnically divided societies', *Nations and Nationalism*, 8:4 (2002); J. McGarry, B. O'Leary and R. Simeon, 'Integration or accommodation? The enduring debate in conflict regulation', in S. Choudhry (ed.), *Constitutional Design for Divided Societies: Integration or Accommodation?* (Oxford: Oxford University Press, 2008); S. Wolff, 'Managing ethno-national conflict: towards an analytical framework', *Commonwealth and Comparative Politics*, 49:2 (2011).

10 To be strictly accurate, the end points of this scale are assimilation at the integration end and secession/partition at the accommodation end, though McGarry *et al.* consider these beyond the scope of their analysis, and in contemporary situations they are rarely employed (with some notable exceptions, such as Kosovo).

11 McGarry *et al.*, 'Integration or accommodation?', 45.

12 S. Choudhry, 'Bridging comparative politics and comparative constitutional law: constitutional design in divided societies', in Choudhry (ed.), *Constitutional Design for Divided Societies*, 27.

13 B. M. Barry, *Culture and Equality: An Egalitarian Critique of Multiculturalism* (Cambridge: Polity, 2001), 19–62.

14 A. J. Kuperman, 'Designing constitutions to reduce domestic conflict', in A. J. Kuperman (ed.), *Constitutions and Conflict Management in Africa: Preventing Civil War Through Institutional Design* (Philadelphia, PA: University of Pennsylvania Press, 2015), 2.

15 McGarry *et al.*, 'Integration or accommodation?', 70–1.

16 McGarry *et al.*, 'Integration or accommodation?', 52.

17 McGarry *et al.*, 'Integration or accommodation?', 52–3.

18 Kuperman, 'Designing constitutions to reduce domestic conflict', 2.

19 A. Lijphart, *Democracy in Plural Societies: A Comparative Exploration* (New Haven, CT: Yale University Press, 1977).

20 See, for example, S. Wolff, 'Consociationalism: power sharing and self-governance', in S. Wolff and C. Yakinthou (eds), *Conflict Management in Divided Societies: Theories and Practice* (London: Routledge, 2012).

21 G. Fontana, 'War by other means: cultural policy and the politics of corporate consociation in Bosnia and Herzegovina', *Nationalism and Ethnic Politics*, 19:4 (2013).

22 M. Kerr, *Imposing Power-Sharing: Conflict and Coexistence in Northern Ireland and Lebanon* (Dublin: Irish Academic Press, 2006); J. McEvoy, 'The role of external actors in incentivizing post-conflict power-sharing', *Government and Opposition*, 49:1 (2014).

23 McGarry *et al.*, 'Integration or accommodation?', 50–1.

24 B. O'Leary, 'Debating consociational politics: normative and explanatory arguments', in S. J. R. Noel (ed.), *From Power Sharing to Democracy: Post-conflict Institutions in Ethnically Divided Societies* (Montreal: McGill-Queen's University Press, 2005), 3; R. Taylor, 'Introduction: the promise of consociational theory', in R. Taylor (ed.), *Consociational Theory: McGarry and O'Leary and the Northern Ireland Conflict* (London: Routledge, 2009), 9–10; C. McCrudden and B. O'Leary, 'Courts and consociations, or how human rights courts may de-stabilize power-sharing settlements', *European Journal of International Law*, 24:2 (2013), 480.

25 A. Tomlinson, *Sport and Leisure Cultures* (Minneapolis, MN: University of Minnesota Press, 2005), xiv.

26 J. Hoberman, 'The myth of sport as a peace-promoting political force', *SAIS Review of International Affairs*, 31:1 (2011); J. Coakley, *Nationalism, Ethnicity and the State: Making and Breaking Nations* (London: Sage, 2012), 131.

27 J. Sugden and A. Tomlinson, *FIFA and the Contest for World Football: Who Rules the People's Game?* (Cambridge: Polity, 1998), 8.

28 T. Edensor, *National Identity, Popular Culture and Everyday Life* (Oxford: Berg, 2002), cited in A. Bairner, 'Assessing the sociology of sport: on national identity and nationalism', *International Review for the Sociology of Sport*, 50:4–5 (2015), 376.

29 See, for example, J. Sugden and A. Bairner (eds), *Sport in Divided Societies* (Aachen: Meyer & Meyer Sport, 1999); J. Sugden, 'Critical left-realism and sport interventions in divided societies', *International Review for the Sociology of Sport*, 45:3 (2010); D. Hassan and P. O'Kane, 'Terrorism and the abnormality of sport in Northern Ireland', *International Review for the Sociology of Sport*, 47:3 (2012).

30 D. Reiche, 'War minus the shooting? The politics of sport in Lebanon as a unique case in comparative politics', *Third World Quarterly*, 32:2 (2011); B. Coppieters, 'The organisation of marathons in divided cities: Brussels, Belfast, Beirut and Jerusalem', *International Journal of the History of Sport*, 29:11 (2012); A. Bairner, 'Inclusive soccer-exclusive politics? Sports policy in Northern Ireland and the Good Friday Agreement', *Sociology of Sport Journal*, 21:3 (2004); A. Bairner, 'Sport, the Northern Ireland peace process, and the politics of identity', *Journal of Aggression, Conflict and Peace Research*, 5:4 (2013); K. Howard, 'Territorial politics and Irish cycling', *Mapping Frontiers, Plotting Pathways Working Paper 21* (Belfast: Queen's University Belfast, 2006), available at www.qub.ac.uk/research-centres/CentreforInternationalBordersResearch/Publications/WorkingPapers/MappingFrontiersworkingpapers/Filetoupload,175422,en.pdf (accessed 5 August 2016); B. Vanreusel, R. Renson and J. Tolleneer, 'Divided sports in a divided Belgium', in Sugden and Bairner (eds), *Sport in Divided Societies*; D. Sterchele, 'Fertile land or mined field? Peace-building and ethnic tensions in post-war Bosnian football', *Sport in Society*, 16:8 (2013); L. Cooley and J. Mujanović, 'Changing the rules of the game: comparing FIFA/UEFA and EU attempts to promote reform of power-sharing institutions in Bosnia-Herzegovina', *Global Society*, 29:1 (2015).

31 R. Petrović, 'The national composition of Yugoslavia's population, 1991', *Yugoslav Survey*, 33:1 (1992), cited in R. M. Hayden, 'Imagined communities and real victims: self-determination and ethnic cleansing in Yugoslavia', *American Ethnologist*, 23:4 (1996), 787.

32 S. Bose, *Bosnia after Dayton: Nationalist Partition and International Intervention* (London: Hurst, 2002), 216.

33 R. Belloni, 'Peacebuilding and consociational electoral engineering in Bosnia and Herzegovina', *International Peacekeeping*, 11:2 (2004), 336.

34 S. Sebastián, *Post-war Statebuilding and Constitutional Reform: Beyond Dayton in Bosnia* (Basingstoke: Palgrave Macmillan, 2014); V. Perry, 'Constitutional reform in Bosnia and Herzegovina: does the road to confederation go through the EU?', *International Peacekeeping*, 22:5 (2015); D. Tolksdorf, 'The European Union as a mediator in constitutional reform negotiations in Bosnia and Herzegovina: the failure

of conditionality in the context of intransigent local politics', *Nationalism and Ethnic Politics*, 21:4 (2015).

35 Belloni, 'Peacebuilding and consociational electoral engineering in Bosnia and Herzegovina', 337. See also S. G. Simonsen, 'Addressing ethnic divisions in post-conflict institution-building: lessons from recent cases', *Security Dialogue*, 36:3 (2005); R. Aitken, 'Cementing divisions? An assessment of the impact of international interventions and peace-building policies on ethnic identities and divisions', *Policy Studies*, 28:3 (2007).

36 R. Belloni, 'Bosnia: Dayton is dead! Long live Dayton!', *Nationalism and Ethnic Politics*, 15:3 (2009), 368.

37 P. K. Gasser and A. Levinsen, 'Breaking post-war ice: Open Fun Football Schools in Bosnia and Herzegovina', *Sport in Society*, 7:3 (2004), 460; Sterchele, 'Fertile land or mined field?', 975.

38 Sterchele, 'Fertile land or mined field?', 975–6.

39 J. Wilson, 'Three into one won't go for Bosnia as Fifa and Uefa ban hits home', *The Guardian*, 21 April 2011, available at www.theguardian.com/football/blog/2011/apr/21/bosnia-fifa-uefa-ban (accessed 26 May 2015).

40 Wilson, 'Three into one won't go'.

41 K. Morrison, 'Three's a crowd', *When Saturday Comes*, June 2011, available at www.wsc.co.uk/the-archive/917-International-football/8825-three-s-a-crowd (accessed 8 January 2016).

42 Quoted in 'Soccer bosses show Bosnia red card over ethnic rule', *Sydney Morning Herald*, 5 April 2011, available awww.smh.com.au/sport/soccer/soccer-bosses-show-bosnia-red-card-over-ethnic-rule-20110404–1cyyg.html (accessed 8 January 2016).

43 For a full account, see Cooley and Mujanović, 'Changing the rules of the game'.

44 E. Dedovic, 'The Bosnian national football team: a case study in post-conflict institution building', *openDemocracy*, 14 October 2013, available at www.opendemocracy.net/can-europe-make-it/edin-dedovic/bosnian-national-football-team-case-study-in-post-conflict-instituti (accessed 8 January 2016); Sterchele, 'Fertile land or mined field?', 989 n.43.

45 Cooley and Mujanović, 'Changing the rules of the game'.

46 C. Christophorou, 'South European briefing: the vote for a united Cyprus deepens divisions: the 24 April 2004 referenda in Cyprus', *South European Society and Politics*, 10:1 (2005).

47 S. Bose, *Contested Lands: Israe--Palestine, Kashmir, Bosnia, Cyprus, and Sri Lanka* (Cambridge, MA: Harvard University Press, 2007), 99–100.

48 C. Yakinthou, *Political Settlements in Divided Societies: Consociationalism and Cyprus* (Basingstoke: Palgrave Macmillan, 2009), 75–6.

49 This impact is not particularly well documented in academic research, however. Indeed, a recent overview of Cypriot sports governance makes no mention of the division of the island and covers only sporting organisations that are operational in the territory under the control of the Republic of Cyprus. M. Charalambous-Papamiltiades, 'Cyprus', in I. O'Boyle and T. Bradbury (eds), *Sport Governance: International Case Studies* (Abingdon: Routledge, 2013).

50 N. L. Kartakoullis and C. Loizou, 'Is sport (football) a unifying force or a vehicle to further separation? The case of Cyprus', *International Journal of the History of Sport*, 26:11 (2009), 1656–7.

51 Kartakoullis and Loizou, 'Is sport (football) a unifying force?', 1657.

52 Kartakoullis and Loizou, 'Is sport (football) a unifying force?', 1657–8.

53 FIFA, 'Cyprus Football Association and Cyprus Turkish Football Association sign landmark arrangement' (Zurich: Fédération Internationale de Football Association, 5 November 2013), available at www.fifa.com/governance/news/y=2013/m=11/news=cyprus-football-association-and-cyprus-turkish-football-association-sign-2218369.html (accessed 27 May 2015).

54 M. Kambas, 'Cyprus football officials determined to unify despite protest', Reuters, 30 March 2015, available at http://uk.reuters.com/article/2015/03/30/uk-soccer-cyprus-reunification-idUKKBN0MQ12X20150330 (accessed 27 May 2015).

55 A. Warshaw, 'CFA votes in favour of next steps to Cypriot football's reunification', *Inside World Football*, 25 November 2013, available at www.insideworldfootball.com/world-football/europe/13673-cfa-votes-in-favour-of-next-steps-to-cypriot-football-s-reunification (accessed 7 December 2015).

56 H. Smith, 'Divided Cyprus begins to build bridges', *The Guardian*, 1 June 2015, available at www.theguardian.com/world/2015/may/31/mustafa-ankinci-advocates-focus-future-for-splintered-cyprus (accessed 7 December 2015).

57 E. Andreou, 'Missing document delays TCFA-CFA union', *Cyprus Mail*, 13 November 2015, available at http://cyprus-mail.com/2015/11/13/missing-document-delays-tcfa-cfa-union/ (accessed 8 January 2016).

58 N. Lekakis, 'Can football loosen the "Gordian Knot" in Cyprus?', *International Journal of Sport Policy and Politics*, 7:2 (2015), 269.

59 This view was expressed by a number of sports officials interviewed by the author in Cyprus during September 2015.

60 H. Sertoğlu, 'Open letter to all Cypriots and the members of the Cypriot football community', Nicosia, Cyprus Turkish Football Association, 16 December 2014, available atwww.ktff.org/NewsDetail/Index/47 (accessed 29 May 2015).

61 Northern Ireland Office, 'The Agreement', agreement reached in the multi-party negotiations (10 April 1998), available at www.gov.uk/government/uploads/system/uploads/attachment_data/file/136652/agreement.pdf (accessed 5 August 2016).

62 J. Garry, 'Consociationalism and its critics: evidence from the historic Northern Ireland Assembly election 2007', *Electoral Studies*, 28:3 (2009), 459; see also J. McGarry and B. O'Leary, 'Consociational theory, Northern Ireland's conflict, and its Agreement. Part 1: what consociationalists can learn from Northern Ireland', *Government and Opposition*, 41:1 (2006).

63 Garry, 'Consociationalism and its critics', 459.

64 For a survey, see E. Saunders and J. Sugden, 'Sport and community relations in Northern Ireland', *Managing Leisure*, 2:1 (1997).

65 J. Whyte, 'The permeability of the United Kingdom–Irish border: a preliminary reconnaissance', *Administration*, 31:3 (1983), 304–6.

66 Howard, 'Territorial politics and Irish cycling', 5–6.

67 Howard, 'Territorial politics and Irish cycling'; T. Lamb, 'NICF joins forces with Cycling Ulster', *Irish Times*, 18 December 2006, 48.

68 Bairner, 'Inclusive soccer-exclusive politics?', 278–9.

69 Bairner, 'Sport, the Northern Ireland peace process, and the politics of identity', 224.

70 Bairner, 'Inclusive soccer-exclusive politics?', 282.

71 Bairner, 'Inclusive soccer-exclusive politics?', 283.

72 V. Eick, 'A neoliberal sports event? FIFA from the *Estadio Nacional* to the fan mile', *City*, 14:3 (2010), 288.

73 Cooley and Mujanović, 'Changing the rules of the game', 55.

74 T. Risse and K. Sikkink, 'The socialization of international human rights norms into domestic practices: introduction', in T. Risse, S. C. Ropp and K. Sikkink (eds), *The Power of Human Rights: International Norms and Domestic Change* (Cambridge: Cambridge University Press, 1999); F. Schimmelfennig, 'The community trap: liberal norms, rhetorical action, and the eastern enlargement of the European Union', *International Organization*, 55:1 (2001).

75 See Sertoğlu, 'Open letter to all Cypriots and the members of the Cypriot football community'.

76 Meier and García, 'Protecting private transnational authority against public intervention', 895–7.

77 J. S. Rofe, 'Sport and diplomacy: a global diplomacy framework', *Diplomacy and Statecraft*, 27:2 (2016).

78 Bairner, 'Sport, the Northern Ireland peace process, and the politics of identity', 225.

79 See, for example, D. Sito-Sucic, 'Bosnia's divided people unite behind World Cup bid', Reuters, 14 October 2014, available at http://uk.reuters.com/article/uk-soccer-world-bosnia-idUKBRE99D08Y20131014 (accessed 10 January 2016); E. Vulliamy, 'How Edin Džeko united Bosnia', *The Observer*, 8 June 2014, available at www.theguardian.com/world/2014/jun/08/edin-dzeko-united-bosnia-world-cup (accessed 10 January 2016).

80 E. K. Vest, 'The War of Positions: Football in Post-Conflict Bosnia-Herzegovina', PhD thesis, Brunel University, 2014, 256–7. See also Reiche, 'War minus the shooting?', for a discussion of the complex relationship between sport, sectarianism and national identity in Lebanon.

2

Can sport contribute to the mission success of military peace support operations?

Alexander Cárdenas and Sibylle Lang

Today's peace support operations (PSO) conducted by multinational coalitions are nearly always part of a larger, complex diplomatic and civilian endeavour by the international community to support peace and development in a certain country or region.[1] Examples from Afghanistan to the Democratic Republic of Congo show that PSOs face a number of communication, coordination and cooperation challenges, based upon diverging perceptions and situational awareness, misunderstanding, mistrust, prejudice and fear. These challenges can be observed in four main areas: among multinational coalition members, between a military operation and civilian crisis management actors, with host governments and their armed forces, and within local populations in the area of operation.

In diplomatic and peace-building terms, sport has in various cases proven its positive effects as a venue for personal encounters, communication and trust-building; a learning tool for mutual respect, fair play and cooperation, and a platform for shared positive experience. In Colombia and the Philippines, the military has started to use sport as a supportive element in internal peace processes and peace building. The UN has implemented pilot Sport, Development and Peace (SDP) projects in the framework of peacekeeping operations.[2] Yet, as stated by Giulianotti and Armstrong, direct and concerted involvement of peacekeeping forces in sporting practices during operation continues to be virtually absent.[3] Equally, academic research into this topic has been limited to date.

Based upon existing SDP and PSO literature, examination of relevant activities from the field, and interviews with military officers from Germany who have served in multinational peace support operations, and from Colombia with regard to the local peace process, the core argument put forward in this chapter is that, due to its particular qualities, sport may be fruitfully employed to mitigate peace support operations' communication, coordination and cooperation challenges and thus contribute to mission success.

Sport as a peace-building instrument

Operating under an intervention strategy known as Sport for Development and Peace, a multiplicity of social actors (notably the United Nations) have acknowledged the potential of sport to address social challenges as well as to advance peace building and conflict resolution in volatile contexts.[4] Advocates of sport as a social cohesion tool claim that this activity possesses unique characteristics that allow its use to advance peace building and promote reconciliation in divided societies. The popularity of sport, for instance, is considered to transcend political, ideological and geographical borders, thus becoming a common denominator between cultures and peoples.[5] The use of sport as an intervention strategy is supported by the belief that the global appeal of sport provides a hook to bring multiple stakeholders, at-risk populations and clashing parties into programmes and interventions, some of which are purposely designed to promote peace and reconciliation.[6]

As an instrument for peace, sport can engage fruitfully with the holistic process of peace building, which, as theorised by Galtung, includes three strategic factors: reconstruction of peoples and places after violence, reconciliation of the parties in conflict and resolution of animosities.[7] Reconstruction can be interpreted as the re-establishment of social relations through sport tournaments and sport-related activity, as well as the refurbishment of sport facilities that have been destroyed in conflict. Sport venues may allow games and tournaments to be conducted – hence providing a sense of normalcy after conflict, as well as allowing social interaction and possibly the forming of meaningful social relations which can extend beyond sport venues. Rehabilitation, as one of the sub-components of the first factor, can benefit from the employment of sport-related activities. During violent conflict, physical and psychological wounds have an effect on victims, the latter being in some cases particularly hard to heal. Sport in this framework may help individuals build a new sense of identity and gradually overcome severe trauma through psychosocial programmes that incorporate games and physical activity.[8] The process of reconciliation aims at (re)building positive relations between enemies who have formerly been both victims and perpetrators. Among the peace-building initiatives carried out in post-conflict situations, Borsani stresses sport as being a 'very powerful, neutral, simple, universal and useful means that can contribute, under certain conditions, to speed up each stage of the long process of especially reconciliation'.[9]

In spite of the positive effects of sport, this activity cannot be considered as a standalone peace-building strategy, and presents several limitations when employed as a peace-building tool.[10] In regions experiencing serious internal conflict, sport may not be a suitable strategy to foster reconciliation unless it is preceded by political and military accommodations.[11] Sport can also promote an exaggerated sense of nationalism and even physical violence.[12]

Sport, the military and peacemaking

In 2006 the UN Office on Sport for Development and Peace, the Department of Peacekeeping Operations and the International Olympic Committee (IOC) created a partnership to employ sport within the framework of UN peacekeeping operations. Three operations were identified as sites for pilot projects: the Republic of Congo, Cote d'Ivoire (UNOCI) and Liberia.[13] In the Republic of Congo, sport programmes were implemented to promote an atmosphere of peace and reconciliation prior to the announcement of the presidential and legislative election results, while in Liberia fifteen counties participated in 2007 in sport-for-peace programmes during seven weeks with the goal of contributing to 'peace-building, national reconciliation and harmony'. In Cote d'Ivoire, the most active of the three locations, the UNOCI, has been promoting sport-for-peace-building activities since 2006, when public viewings of football matches were organised on the occasion of the World Cup and built upon the team's own call for reconciliation led by then captain and star-player, Didier Drogba.[14] During the games, messages of peace and information regarding the operation's mandate were delivered, encouraging people to become involved in crisis solving and sensitising the population on the purpose of sport for peace in communities in crisis. Furthermore, the United Nations Integrated Mission in Timor-Leste provided logistical support to sport events conducted in 2009, which were used to promote the country as a 'place of peace and national unity'.[15] Under the title of 'Uniting UNDOF in passion and excellence', sport tournaments were organised within the United Nations Disengagement Observer Force (Golan Heights) (UNDOF), with the explicit aim to contribute to uniting the diverse contributing contingents to improve their cohesion and sense of a shared operation.[16]

Organisations in the sport, peace and development world have been integral to this trend, encouraging dialogue and discussion, and disseminating information on the topic via seminars and forums. For example, an international conference held in Brussels in 2010, and organised by a locally based think-tank in cooperation with NATO and the British Council, incorporated sport with defence, security and conflict prevention as a focal point of discussion.[17] The first International Forum on Sport for Development and Peace organised by the IOC in 2009 had Brigadier General Gianni Gola as a speaker, who stressed the diverse ways and channels in which the International Military Sports Council (CISM) has activated sport as a tool for peace building among the armed forces. The CISM, one of the largest multidisciplinary organisations in the world with 134 member countries, has fulfilled a pivotal role in the promotion of peace through sport and the military forces.[18] Founded in 1948, it carries out a series of activities, including the annual organisation of Military Sport Games, international symposia addressing diverse aspects of sport, and seminars and forums looking into the relationship between sport and peace. These events have drawn participation from military authorities and commanders of peacekeeping forces, NATO, the IOC, the UN and other relevant international community actors.[19]

In conflict areas such as the Philippines, the military is using sport to engage with community members through the Programme Olympeace. This initiative has brought together the armed forces of the Philippines, civil society organisations and students from Christian and Muslim backgrounds from the region of Mindanao – which has been the epicentre of decades of armed hostilities – to promote a culture of peace and intercultural understanding via sport and physical activity as related to the region itself.[20] In Colombia – a country currently undergoing a peace process that could bring the longest-running conflict in the Western hemisphere to an end – sport has been employed as a strategy to strengthen the links of the military with isolated rural communities affected by war, specifically by building sport grounds and conducting sport-related activities. As stated by a high official, sport 'enhances social relations in communities. People are more willing to cooperate with others and work collectively. Building sport grounds in mountainous areas, as we have done, awakens the initiative and desire to work for the benefit of the people. Sport is a good start to foster collective work in small communities.'[21]

Academic work into the role of sport in peacekeeping – though it remains scarce to date – has opened up a space for analysis and deliberation as to the worth of this activity as a valid strategy to assist the military in achieving specific peace-building and peacekeeping goals. In their research on Bosnia, Liberia and the Balkans, Giulianotti and Armstrong conclude that sport-for-peace interventions present the military with a new and fresh means to engage more actively with civilians, non-governmental organisations, ex-combatants, and other individuals and institutions promoting peace and reconciliation.[22] In his examination of the nexus between culture and conflict resolution, Woodhouse acknowledges sport as a viable, but still under-explored, channel to support the overall process of peace building with special attention to peacekeeping operations.[23] He concludes that when sport is located as a specific component of wider conflict resolution endeavours, it can make a legitimate and credible contribution to the positive evolution and transformation of contemporary peacekeeping operations.

Challenges of modern PSO – which roles for sport?

Today's complex emergencies require multidimensional answers from the international community. Besides involving a large number of different nationalities and mission cultures as well as cooperation between military and civilian actors, today's PSO are also characterised by their need for engagement of the local population – epitomised by the well-worn phrase of winning 'hearts and minds' – as well as for cooperation with host governments and the host country's armed forces, including the essential build-up and training of, and joint operations with, the latter. Starting from a mission achievement viewpoint, it is along those lines that challenges arise: 1) among military partners in a multinational coalition; 2) among military and civilian actors within an 'extended' peace support coalition or 'integrated mission', for example in aUN framework); 3) between the international military coalition and the local population and civilian stakeholders in the host country; and 4) between an international military coalition and the national authorities and armed forces of the host country. If those communication, coordination and cooperation challenges are not only conceived as mere technical issues, but also as a result of major cultural differences and divergence between the said actors, they can be deemed to lend themselves to the positive social effects of sport.[24]

It is interesting to note that as a function of evolving tasks, the military forces are themselves in a process of change, or, as Schnabel and Ehrhart put it, building upon US Marine General Krulak's notion of 'three-block war': 'We are witnessing the emergence of a postmodern military' and the 'postmodern soldier is not only a fighter, but also a peacekeeper, policeman, diplomat, social worker, and Peace Corps worker.'[25] According to Schnabel and Ehrhart, the militaries of the world are getting prepared for improved and more effective operations that 'both support the negative peace (i.e. the absence of direct violence) and positive peace (i.e. the creation of political, economic, and social conditions) to support sustainable justice and security'.[26] This change could lead to an adaptation or complementation of military values and required skills, where sport as a tool for peace may find its place.

Inter-military relations in a multinational military operation can profit from jointly practised sport

Although multinational military cooperation has a long history, the degree and quality of multinationality have clearly evolved. According to Soeters and Manigart, multinationality has become a 'predominant feature of military activities', and military task forces deal with a 'structural internationalisation' of their own workforce in the field, either within the framework of standing regional military organisations, for example for collective defence and beyond, such as NATO, or in multinational coalitions under a UN mandate.[27] At the same time, it is a widely acknowledged truth among practitioners and academic researchers that multinational cooperation in the context of PSO is a challenge in its own right for mission success, and that this challenge needs to be properly mitigated in order to achieve military efficacy and overall mission success.[28] While regional organisations such as NATO or also the EU with its Common Security and Defence Policy have developed common planning and operational procedures, engage in joint training and exercises and work together in standing multinational or at least multinationalised headquarters, the UN for its peace support operations recruits multinational forces on an ad hoc basis with a lesser degree of standardisation in all respects and an even wider range of culturally specific practices.[29]

According to Woodhouse, there is 'a multiplicity of inevitable inefficiencies in the strategic and operational conduct of any multinational peacekeeping operation. Many of these can be viewed from a cultural perspective. That is, they arise from occasional variances in the objectives of troop-contributing states (which affect, inter alia, the chain of command, the diverse mix of military capability, national differences in staff procedures, standards and equipment, language difficulties and cultural custom and ethos).'[30] Soeters and Manigart also emphasise national differences, pertaining for instance to the way armed forces address conflicts, operational styles, and the use of violence and force protection. Equally, they point to elements of strategic culture that point to distinct work-related differences such as in leadership styles, rule orientation, work and living conditions and workload, that may lead to less than optimal cooperation in a multinational military setting. The net effect, they argue, is that these factors may undermine the kind of force cohesion that is crucial for military effectiveness.[31]

Tresch, in his 2007 study, addressed the concept of trust among participants in a multinational coalition and what it means for multinational military interventions. Based upon a number of interviews with military officers, he concluded that: 'For a successful mission the relationships should be good. This is based on mutual understanding. If people know each other, then misunderstandings and a lack of trust can be minimized.'[32] This thinking is seen in broader writing on trust in diplomacy: Rofe states, '[i]n practicing diplomacy, and particularly personal diplomacy, trust matters because, at some level, communication relies on being able to trust the interlocutor'.[33] Tresch also looked into the value of both formal and informal 'integration' mechanisms within multinational military forces in theatre and found that 'informal integration mechanisms played an exceedingly important role', mentioning that 'sports competitions' would 'facilitate ... multinational military cooperation'.[34]

In the light of what has been said about the challenges of multinational military cooperation in line with the functions generally attributed to sport, and also according to recent practices of using sport to improve operation coherence (UNDOF) and individual voices of military officers having served in multinational PSOs, it can be asserted that sport can play a role in improving multinational cooperation in international PSOs. Sport can contribute to supporting the generation of meaningful social relations and serve as a platform for learning about each other. At the same time, sport can act as an integrative force, thus allowing for cross-cultural unifying situations, which have spillover possibilities to the professional military cooperation arena. Although sport cannot substitute a long common socialisation, under carefully planned circumstances it may create a sense of comradeship and belonging, thus reinforcing mutual confidence, trust and reliability, which are essential for the cohesion and success of any peace support operation.

Sport may contribute to improve civil–military relations in the context of a complex peace support effort

As pointed out earlier, contemporary peace operations in complex emergencies combine military, diplomatic, humanitarian and development, and peace-building efforts, and involve a wide range of actors. In a set-up like this, functioning coordination and cooperation between military and civilian actors is critical for mission success, however defined. However, as a rule such coordination is not a default position for the participating actors.[35]

Disparate approaches, roles and tasks, and resulting different organisational cultures of military and civilian crisis management actors have been widely identified as an obstacle to those actors' efficient and sustainable coordination and cooperation.[36]

Pugh stresses that '[t]here are historical disconnections between the military and civilian components, not simply because they have different roles … but because of divergent philosophical allegiances. These two disjunctions might be regarded as a ceiling on CIMIC (Civil–Military Cooperation) that in the short term at least seems to be significant.'[37] To overcome these obstacles, Manwaring found that '[e]ven with an adequate planning and organisational structure, ambiguity, confusion, and tensions are likely to emerge'.[38] Olson and Gregorian emphasise that fruitful civilian–military interaction requires more than a mere 'technical exercise that the right combination of meetings, information flow, and coordination focal points can solve'.[39]

Measures to improve meaningful coordination and cooperation between military and civilian actors in peace support efforts obviously must go beyond mere institutional and procedural management instruments. Sport can have a deeper transformational power than institutional or procedural coordination measures alone while at the same time serving as a platform for learning about one other. Sport may contribute to eliminate hostility between civilian and military crisis management actors on the playing field and allow for the creation of personal channels for information sharing, and cooperation and coordination based on mutual trust.

International military presence can improve the relations with local populations and stakeholders via sport

International PSO are often confronted by a lack of acceptance by local populations and stakeholders, ranging from mere disinterest to outright hostility and obstruction or resistance. However, local support is crucial for success in terms of achieving the long-term objectives of peace, security, and reconstruction and development. This was seen in early studies on the UN Interim Forces in Lebanon and confirmed by more recent assessments and analyses of the NATO International Security Assistance Force mission in Afghanistan and other operations.[40] However, multinational military interventions have again and again failed to win the 'hearts and minds' of local populations and stakeholders.

Rubinstein, Keller and Scherger assert that for international PSOs: '[o]ne of the challenges … is getting local people and members of a mission to share understanding of the meanings and rationales or the actions undertaken by the mission and by local people'.[41] First of all, this requires factual knowledge of the nature and activities of an international peace support operation. In March 2015, the New York Peacebuilding Group – a gathering of organisations including, among others, World Vision and the International Peace Institute, engaged in various peace-related issues at the UN and in the field – issued 'Civil Society Recommendations for the Reviews of UN Peace Operations and the UN Peacebuilding Architecture'.[42] The report argued that in many areas local populations do not have a clear understanding of the role of UN peace operations in their communities because there is no direct interaction, and called for the trust deficit between the UN and local populations to be addressed. One reason it gave for the trust deficit was that communities often perceive that the international peace support operation is there to help the government or the armed groups, and not the people.

Beyond a merely factual information policy, the attitude conveyed by communicating in a certain way, and even more obviously the action taken by an international presence, make the difference in dealing with local populations and stakeholders in a host country. Rubinstein, Keller and Scherger argue that this 'hinges on peacekeepers' ability to interact with local peoples that communicate genuine partnership and respect for the key symbols of their worldview', an exercise which peacekeeping operations generally fail to accomplish.[43] Their recommended focus is 'to look for ways to engage the local community so that its members feel respected and treated as equal partners in the rebuilding of their home communities'.[44]

Being asked how sport could be employed in military operations vis-à-vis local populations, a German officer stated:

> Sport can help to find access to young people, to communicate with them. Via sport you could transmit values, ideas, bring different subgroups of the population into contact with each other and so on. It could be part of CIMIC, with very little effort. Construction of playgrounds, sport facilities is comparably cheap and easy, provision of balls, etc., as well. In most military units you'll easily find people with the necessary knowledge and abilities.[45]

International PSOs may get inspiration in this respect from the 'Open the gates and bring the children in' project series implemented under CISM auspices in Tanzania, Burkina Faso, Guinea, Suriname and Mali. The initiative features the organisation of football training and competitions for children in barracks of the armed forces in the respective country, with the aim to give children the possibility to improve their physical and mental health, increase socialisation, integration, tolerance and self-esteem, and improve their quality of life while also extending what Iver B. Neumann identifies as a site of diplomacy.[46] Equally, the use of military infrastructure, as well as communicating with military personnel on sport and education, may serve to contribute to a positive image of the military vis-à-vis the population.

Referring to the New York Peacebuilding Group's report and experience from the field, sports can be used in a PSO context to disseminate information among local populations. For instance, due to their capacity to reach a wider audience, sports events can be used as an effective vehicle to inform the local population about an ongoing operation. When properly articulated, sports events can also be used to support reconciliation and positive engagement among local populations and stakeholders, providing a playing field for peaceful encounters, with the military for instance offering their organisational and logistic know-how and practical help. At the same time the support of sports events and activities may serve as a conduit to display the international PSO's acknowledgement of and support for local needs, enhancing its credibility among the local population.

The exercise of rebuilding local armed forces, training and joint operations can be supported through sport

The exercise of rebuilding local armed forces, training those so that they can operate independently after the multinational military coalition has left, and – for a transitional phase – joint operations between international military forces and the local armed forces have emerged as major challenges for modern PSOs. Yasutomi and Carmans emphasise that 'operational coherence' between external and internal actors is key to success in these critical fields.[47]

Setting up and training integrated armed forces is no easy task in a post-conflict environment. Former opposing, irregular forces have to be integrated into society and potentially into the regular army, and ethnic and other divisions need to be overcome.[48] The challenge is to integrate and transform these individuals into a functioning entity, which is able to serve all of a country's population in terms of peace, security and defence professionally and under democratic oversight. The effort of building integrated armed forces is usually accompanied by training and education in all aspects, ranging from practical training in defence tactics, intervention techniques, driving skills, firing, riot control, and so on, to training in soft skills and values (accountability, democratic oversight, respect for human rights, gender issues, etc.).[49] This training and education is first delivered by the multinational coalition, and then increasingly by local staff and institutions. During training and education, and later on during mentoring, contact between international and local armed forces is particularly intense and hence will not be lacking in challenges. Intercultural misunderstandings and 'misfits', on top of a problematic 'teacher–pupil' relationship along an international versus local division, are prone to cause mutually negative perceptions which also hamper efficacy.

A German officer, having served in Afghanistan, indicated that training and mentoring situations may lend themselves in a particular way to the use of sport to advance mission success.[50] This could be tackled by reverting to the playing field where both sides can meet as equals and establish positive relations and develop mutual respect, or for exampleby games of mixed teams which may serve as platforms for cross-national and cross-cultural cooperation. Especially with a view to international–local joint operations, sport may to a certain extent lend its socialising and trust-building effects. Moreover, sport can make a modest contribution to support integration, coherence and solidarity within domestic armed forces by fostering reconciliation among rehabilitated protagonists. Together with the host nation authorities and military command structures, PSOs could initiate and support such activities. Sport could also be used to assist with improving the domestic armed forces' relationship with local populations via platforms for positive interaction involving sports events in which both local populations and local armed forces participate, or by having domestic armed forces extend their assistance for sport events for the local population.

Conclusion

The four clusters of PSO challenges outlined at the start of this chapter can impede synergistic and fruitful interaction between the main stakeholders involved in a peace support operation. They rest on intercultural, inter-organisational and interpersonal relations in terms of communication, coordination and cooperation. As such, they offer many docking points for the overarching relationship between sport and diplomacy.

The trust- and team-building quality of sport can be applied both to multinational military–military and international civilian–military relations as well as relations with local counterparts, one practical example being the UNDOF practice of bringing together contingents from different nations in sports games to enhance the coherence of an operation. Addressing the challenge of good relations with and the 'buy-in' of local populations and stakeholders, sport can be used as a vehicle for communication, for instance via sporting events where the respective PSO gets time slots to inform the audience about the operation, or increase public awareness of peace benefits and/or inform on the positive role of sport in a post-conflict zone. The reconciliation and rehabilitation potentiality of sport could be used for sports-based measures within a PSO, aimed at the promotion of an atmosphere of peace and reconciliation and lending an actual contribution to peace and unity among the civilian population and stakeholders. Peaceful participation in sports events by local populations could be initiated and/or supported organisationally and logistically by PSO resources and capabilities. Support for the construction or rehabilitation of sports venues affected by conflict can ensure that local populations continue to enjoy the positive effects of sport, and beyond this to prove the PSO's positive ambition and will to support the well-being and serve the needs of the local population. The reconciliatory power of sport can also be used to improve relations between the host nation's armed forces and local populations, in support of the local armed forces, or to support the peaceful and effective integration of freshly assembled local armed forces during a time when an international force assists with the build-up and education and training of the latter. Beyond reconciliation, sport can also be used as part of the rehabilitation of victims of war and wounded and traumatised soldiers, which is a field to which PSOs could contribute in the respective country of operation.

Further research on the topic is clearly necessary, with a recommended focus on integrating evidence and testimony from the field, and bringing together empirical and theoretical knowledge of the challenges of peace support operations on the one hand and knowledge about SDP mechanisms on the other, to verify and refine hypotheses on the possibilities and ways to use sport in the context of military operations.

Notes

1 Peace support operations have garnered a great deal of attention in academic and practitioner literature. Perennially, both scholars and practitioners return to the multiple editions of Alex Bellamy, Paul Williams and Stuart Griffin, *Understanding Peacekeeping* (Cambridge: Polity, 2nd edn, 2010).

2 T. Woodhouse, 'Peacekeeping, peace culture and conflict resolution', *International Peacekeeping*, 17:4 (2010).

3 R. Giulianotti and G. Armstrong, 'Sport, the military and peacemaking: history and possibilities', *Third World Quarterly*, 32:3 (2011).

4 See A. Cárdenas, 'The Use of Football and other Sports for Peace Building in Colombia and Northern Ireland', unpublished doctoral dissertation, University Jaume I, 2015; C. B. Dyck, 'Football and post-war reintegration: exploring the role of sport in DDR processes in Sierra Leone', *Third World Quarterly*, 32:3 (2011); P. K. Gasser and A. Levinsen, 'Breaking post-war ice: open fun football schools in Bosnia and Herzegovina', *Sport in Society*, 7:3 (2004); N. Schulenkorf, 'Sport events and ethnic reconciliation: attempting to create social change between Sinhalese, Tamil and Muslim sportspeople in war-torn Sri Lanka', *International Review for the Sociology of Sport*, 45:3 (2010); J. P. Sugden, 'Belfast united: encouraging cross-community relations through sport in Northern Ireland', *Journal of Sport and Social Issues*, 15:1 (1991); and A. G. van der Niet, 'Football in post-conflict Sierra Leone', *African Historical Review*, 42:2 (2010).

5 Sport for Development and Peace International Working Group – SDP IWG, 'Harnessing the power of sport for development and peace: recommendations to governments', SDP IWG Report (2008), available at www.sportanddev.org/en/article/publication/harnessing-power-sport-development-and-peace-recommendations-governments (accessed 5 May 2015).

6 A. Cárdenas, 'Peace building through sport? An introduction to sport for development and peace', *Journal of Conflictology*, 4:1 (2013).

7 See J. Galtung, *Peace by Peaceful Means: Peace and Conflict, Development and Civilization* (London: SAGE, 1996), 8.

8 A. Fukushima, 'Peace and culture: fostering peace through cultural contributions', in Joint Research Institute for International Peace and Culture, Aoyama Gakuin University and The Japan Foundation New York (eds), *Conflict and Culture: Fostering Peace through Cultural Initiatives Report* (Tokyo: Aoyama Gakuin University – Joint Research Institute for International Peace and Culture JRIPEC, 2011), 5–14.

9 S. Borsani, 'The Contribution of Sport with the Process of Peace and Reconciliation: From Trauma Healing towards Social Integration', MA dissertation, Sant'Anna School of Advanced Studies, 2009, 61.

10 J. Lea-Howarth, 'Sport and Conflict: Is Football an Appropriate Tool to Utilise in Conflict Resolution, Reconciliation or Reconstruction?', MA dissertation, University of Sussex, 2006.

11 See J. P. Sugden, 'Anyone for football for peace? The challenges of using sport in the service of co-existence in Israel', *Soccer and Society*, 9:3 (2008), 414.

12 Woodhouse, 'Peacekeeping, peace culture and conflict resolution', 496.

13 Woodhouse, 'Peacekeeping, peace culture and conflict resolution', 495.

14 See Didier Drogba's 2005 post-match appeal to his countrymen to come together and resolve the Sierra Leone civil war, available at www.youtube.com/watch?v=KAW7DF1Ufek (accessed 26 April 2017).

15 UN Office on Sport for Development and Peace – UNOSDP, 'United Nations peace keeping', available at www.un.org/sport/node/183509. (accessed 15 July 2015).

16 United Nations Disengagement Observer Force – UNDOF, 'Peacekeeping forces sports event 2011', Article (2011), available at http://undof.unmissions.org/Default.aspx?ctl=Details&tabid=9227&mid=12271&ItemID=10440 (accessed 11 May 2015).

17 Security and Defence Agenda – SDA, 'Conflict prevention and resolution: the role of cultural relations', SDA International Conference Report (2010), available at http://capacity4dev.ec.europa.eu/culture-and-development-international-cooperation/document/conflict-prevention-and-resolution-role-cultural-relations-british-councilsda-2010 (accessed 19 June 2015).

18 Giulianotti and Armstrong, 'Sport, the military and peacemaking', 390.

19 International Military Sports Council – CISM, *About CISM*, available at www.cism-milsport.org/eng/002_ABOUT_CISM/intro.asp (accessed 11 May 2015).

20 Personal interview at Asia America Initiative in the Philippines, 18 July 2011.

21 Personal communication, 7 January 2015.

22 Giulianotti and Armstrong, 'Sport, the military and peacemaking', 380.

23 Woodhouse, 'Peacekeeping, peace culture and conflict resolution', 494.

24 R. A. Rubinstein *et al.*, 'Culture and interoperability in integrated operations', *International Peacekeeping*, 15:4 (2008).

25 Charles Krulak, 'The strategic corporal: leadership in the Three Block War', *Marine Corps Gazette*, 83:1 (1999); A. Schnabel and H. G. Ehrhart (eds), *Security Sector Reform and Post-conflict Peace Building* (Tokyo: United Nations University Press, 2006), 1–16.

26 Schnabel and Ehrhart (eds), *Security Sector Reform*, 3. For more on positive and negative peace, see Andrew Williams, Amelia Hadfild and J. Simon Rofe, *International History and International Relations* (London: Routledge, 2012).

27 J. Soeters and P. Manigart (eds), *Military Cooperation in Multinational Peace Operations: Managing Cultural Diversity and Crisis Response* (London: Routledge, 2008), 2–10.

28 See, for instance, K. Homan, 'Multinational peace support operations: problems and prospects', in O. Ribbelink (ed.), *Beyond the UN Charter: Peace, Security and the Role of Justice* (The Hague: Hague Academic Press, 2008), 114.

29 Homan, 'Multinational peace support', 115; and T. S. Tresch, 'Cultural and political challenges in military missions: how officers view multiculturalism in armed forces', in G. Caforio (ed.), *Contributions to Conflict Management, Peace Economics and Development* [Advances in Military Sociology: Essays in Honor of Charles C. Moskos, vol. 12:1] (Bingley: Emerald Group, 2007), 5.

30 Woodhouse, 'Peacekeeping, peace culture and conflict resolution', 488.

31 Soeters and Manigart (eds), *Military Cooperation*, 6.

32 Tresch, 'Cultural and political challenges', 10.

33 J. Simon Rofe, in Alison Holmes with J. Simon Rofe, *Global Diplomacy: Theories, Types and Models* (Boulder, CO: Westview Press, 2016), 39.

34 Tresch, 'Cultural and political challenges', 11.

35 See, for instance, G. Lloyd and G. van Dyk, 'The challenges, roles and functions

of civil-military coordination officers in peace support operations: a theoretical discussion', *Scientia Militaria – South African Journal of Military Studies*, 35:2 (2007), 68.

36 See, for instance, V. Franke, 'The peacebuilding dilemma: civil–military cooperation in stability operations', *International Journal of Peace Studies*, 11:2 (2006), 13; Lloyd and Van Dyk, 'Challenges, roles and functions', 86; and Woodhouse, 'Peacekeeping, peace culture and conflict resolution', 488.

37 M. Pugh, 'Civil–military relations in Peace Support Operations: hegemony or emancipation?', Overseas Development Institute – ODI, Seminar on Aid and Politics, 1 February 2001, 3, available at www.hitpages.com/ doc/4775505853153280/1#pageTop (accessed 8 June 2015).

38 M. G. Manwaring, 'Peace and stability lessons from Bosnia', *Parameters* (1998), 28.

39 L. Olson and H. Gregorian, 'Civil–military coordination: challenges and opportunities in Afghanistan and beyond', *Journal of Military and Strategic Studies*, 10:1 (2007), 1.

40 Rubinstein *et al.*, 'Culture and interoperability in integrated operations', 542.

41 Rubinstein *et al.*, 'Culture and interoperability in integrated operations', 544.

42 New York Peacebuilding Group – NYPG, 'Civil Society Recommendations for the Review of UN Peace Operations and the UN Peacebuilding Architecture', briefing note (2015), available at http://quno.org/resource/2015/3/civil-society-recommendations-reviews-un-peace-operations-and-un-peacebuilding (accessed 7 July 2015).

43 Rubinstein *et al.*, 'Culture and interoperability in integrated operations', 545.

44 Rubinstein *et al.*, 'Culture and interoperability in integrated operations', 552.

45 Personal communication, 7 January 2015.

46 Iver B. Neumann, *Diplomatic Sites: A Critical Enquiry* (London: Hurst, 2013), 121–46.

47 A. Yasutomi and J. Carmans, 'Security Sector Reform (SSR) in post-conflict states: challenges of local ownership', *Central European Journal of International and Security Studies*, 1:2 (2010), 117.

48 See Schnabel and Ehrhart (eds), *Security Sector Reform*, 7.

49 See, for instance, R. Domisiewicz, 'Consolidating the security sector in post-conflict states: Polish lessons from Iraq', in A. H. Ebnöther and P. H. Fluri (eds), *After Intervention: Public Security Management in Post-conflict Societies – From Intervention to Sustainable Local Ownership* (Vienna: Bureau for Security Policy at the Austrian Ministry of Defence; National Defence Academy; Geneva Centre for the Democratic Control of Armed Forces and PfP-Consortium of Defence Academies and Security Studies Institutes, 2005), 179.

50 Personal communication, 3 July 2015.

3

Diplomatic actors in the world of football: individuals, institutions, ideologies*

Alan Tomlinson

This chapter raises questions concerning the meanings, myths and messages that characterise selected aspects of the varied spheres of what can generally be labelled the sport diplomatic; those social settings and dynamics in which sport has contributed to aspects of international relations and diplomatic practice. The three spheres are the individual, the institutional and the ideological: selected individuals whose roles have been to some greater or lesser extent diplomatic in rationale and/or consequence; influential institutions that have functioned as operators in expansive networks of organisations beyond the formally or conventionally political; and the ways in which forms of sport diplomacy have intermeshed with, and in some cases heavily influenced and even determined, particular ideological stances concerning, for instance, national cultures, states and markets. Examples here are drawn primarily from the history, sociology and politics of football, in particular the organising body of world football, FIFA, and selected comparisons with the International Olympic Committee (IOC) and the history of the Olympics.

First, though, the appropriate background context: work on the earlier twentieth-century history of English football demonstrates the centrality of diplomatic practices and interventions to the organisation and administration of the English game, though without drawing out fully or prioritising the importance of the diplomatic in the overall picture; and the relevance of such practices and interventions to the study of Olympic politics in the second half of the twentieth century. Peter Beck's work *Scoring for Britain* is a thorough and revealing consideration of an important phase and case in the development of international football.[1] In particular, his close reading of the correspondence between the Football Association (FA) (of which Sir Stanley Rous was secretary for most of the 1930s) and related institutional actors challenges established interpretations of British football's isolationist period after it withdrew from FIFA in 1928. There was no doubt that the intransigence of the British Associations – the football associations of England, Scotland, Wales and Northern Ireland – in their collective attitude towards FIFA membership and international cooperation was a problem for the development of the game, not least in Britain itself. Rous recalled the 'insular attitude' of the British Associations that he inherited on becoming secretary of the FA: 'I certainly had no thought that this was splendid isolation. To me it was a matter of regret and a constant cause of difficulty that we were not more closely associated with FIFA.'[2] Rous – international referee, rule maker, stalwart of the rule-making International Football Association Board – also noted, though, that the 'very cordial relations'[3] that existed and were sustained between the British Associations and FIFA had offered a platform for collaborations and international cooperation, for the vital continuity of dialogue concerning the development of international football. One Hungarian member of FIFA, for instance, called the British Associations 'our leaders and advisers'; future FIFA president Rodolphe Seeldrayers noted the esteem and 'exceptional position' accorded British football on the international scene, despite being formally apart from FIFA.[4]

Beck confirms a distinctive sort of British exceptionalism in Britain's 'seeming independence' in contrast with the interpretation of 'sport diplomacy' formally fostered in continental Europe. Beck is correct to emphasise this British sense of going it alone, while simultaneously claiming to be the leading influence in the world game; and this is certainly evidenced in the views of the likes of the Hungarian FIFA member quoted above. The critical point here is, as Beck shows, that the British wanted to be perceived as different, on the whole superior; yet through the likes of Rous could involve themselves in the everyday business of the federation. This is an important discussion by Beck, a significant signpost to understanding the importance of less visible, non-state international and effectively networked, relations characterising British sport. In turn Beck's work serves to aid the recognition of previously neglected forms of public diplomacy in the development of the sport and diplomacy nexus. Careful and rigorous work such as Beck's confirms the importance of treating the 'sport diplomatic' seriously, adopting a revisionist re-focus on the orthodox historical record. This kind of historical analysis shows the value of making the sport-diplomatic dimension of sport history more explicit, and shows the potential of a fuller application of perspectives from diplomatic studies in fields such as the history of sport organisations. Beck has consistently provided insightful analysis of sport's place in international relations. For instance, he observed in a 2003 article on football and German–British relations that 'sport's role in reflecting, articulating, influencing and reinforcing current and future British images of Germany, at least at the popular and media level, should not be underestimated'.[5] Overall, though, Beck did not explicitly use the language of diplomacy, or 'public diplomacy', studies, and it is in this light that it is useful to consider the specific claims of the 'public diplomacy' subfield.

The 'new public diplomacy', as Jan Melissen argues, makes the 'ordinary individual … increasingly visible' in the practice of diplomacy.[6] It serves to recognise citizens as 'assertive participants in international politics' and embraces an 'explosive growth of non-state actors'.[7] He adds that non-official players in the diplomacy game have proven to be swifter at mobilisation of support than the typically unwieldy foreign policy bureaucracy. In international sport, certainly, this was true, and the increased profile of non-state actors has owed much to the networks that have created and sustained international sporting encounters. Across the cultural sector, Melisssen has also argued, sub-state actors such as cities increasingly combine with the state sector in joint lobbying for 'milestone events' such as an Olympic Games or a World Expo.[8] Shaun Riordan reminds us that non-governmental diplomacy has grown dramatically, with 90 per cent of the 20,000 NGO networks active on the world stage having been founded in the last quarter of the twentieth century.[9] He adds that public diplomacy offers a new model of collaborative policy development and that 'the use of public diplomacy to promote civil society should become a central (if not the central) element of Western diplomacy'.[10] The new public diplomacy, then, moves diplomacy towards expanded collaborative interests, 'in a network environment rather than the hierarchical state-centric model of international relations'.[11] This environment includes 'international companies operating in a global marketplace'; and the public relations concerns of companies are also said to chime with the interests of states/nations, as 'branding and public diplomacy are in fact largely complementary'.[12] There is a plethora of actors and interests populating – or seeking to enter – the corridors of power and influence of this new public diplomacy. It is a valuable conceptual emphasis for understanding such cross-sector trends and phenomena, though certainly vulnerable to the charge of conceptual elasticity. It could also be argued that 'Public Diplomacy' is a term for forms of international networking and lobbying that have been recognised for a very long time. Nevertheless, the term has some real relevance to the history, sociology and politics of international, sport-based institutions.

In politics and international relations as applied to the sporting context, a focus upon diplomacy is hardly new. Christopher Hill, for instance, in his *Olympic Politics* dedicates much of his chapter on 'the primacy of politics' to what are incontrovertibly issues of international diplomacy: the apartheid system and South Africa's suspension from the Olympic movement in 1960; and the political dynamics of the two Germanies, the two Chinas (the Taiwan question) and the two Koreas.[13] Hill calls the suspension of South Africa a 'failure of Olympic diplomacy', in that it undermined the core Olympic principle of universality; more successful were the maintenance of membership and participation of mainland China and Taiwan, and of the two Germanies, 'because both parts of the country, once admitted, were kept in the movement through thick and thin'.[14] The question of recognition of national Olympic committees representing partitioned or newly independent states is of course a fundamentally diplomatic issue, and though Hill's careful wording talks of 'the Olympic movement's involvement in international politics since the Second World War', his cases and examples of the Olympics as a political sphere are concerned consistently with the role of the SINGO, the sport-related international NGO, as an increasingly prominent institutional actor in the realm of international diplomacy.[15] Hill certainly hints at this, when observing that one of the earliest acts of incoming IOC president Juan Antonio Samaranch was to deflect the threat of legal action by Taiwan against the IOC, an outcome that was achieved 'thanks to the ... diplomacy of the' new president;[16] and Samaranch, of course, was a career diplomat.[17]

International sport organisations, then, have implicitly diplomatic missions: to find commonalities so that the sporting encounter can take place; to seek consensus, however idealistic and transient, between deeply entrenched political entities; and to find a shared language of communication and interaction in the reciprocally recognised rituals of sport. Hill concluded his chapter on the primacy of politics in sport with the observation that 'trivial-seeming questions are often symbols of deeper disputes' and his wry assertion that as 'time-wasting is often elevated by diplomats to an art of meticulous pettifogging', then 'in this respect Olympic officials do not differ from their governmental equivalents'.[18] This may sound somewhat unsubtle and reductionist as a summation of the diplomatic sphere, and the general point that Hill is making is considered historically and comparatively in an overview in the following section on the profiles of IOC and FIFA presidents. This precedes a section on the institutional actor FIFA, and the ways in which the growth of FIFA can be understood as the achievement of a wide range of individual actors engaging essentially in diplomatic encounters with representatives of states and non-state bodies across the world.

Individuals

The most prominent individuals in the world of sport are of course the record breakers and the champions. They break the barriers, establish the horizons of future aspiration, represent the nation or the region, or, in a form of global ambassadorship, their specialist sport. David Beckham kick-started the London 2012 Olympics from the top of a red London bus at the closing ceremony of the 2008 Beijing Olympics, kicking footballs into the arena; and then appeared at the steering-wheel of a speedboat delivering the Olympic torch to the Olympic Stadium for the opening ceremony of London 2012. If public diplomacy were simply the name for international branding, then the work done by Usain Bolt for German footwear specialist Puma, and before him Michael Jordan for Nike, could qualify them as public diplomats; whereas a perhaps more rounded analysis of such figures would surely portray them as individual, superstar celebrities, the personal embodiment of the global commodification of their sport, idols of consumption – to use Leo Lowenthal's label – on a worldwide celebrity stage, rather than solely spokespersons for any new 'public diplomacy'.[19]

In the 1930s though it was, as Peter Beck showed, Stanley Rous, not some idolised championship-winning footballer, who was at the helm of diplomatic initiatives and strategies that would counter the self-inflicted exile of the FA (England) and the other British Associations. Key positions of leadership of national and supranational bodies have been central to such diplomatic work through sport, and the means through which diplomatic ends have or have not been achieved. It is illuminating therefore to review the profiles of the most prominent such leaders in the two perhaps highest-profile sport-related international NGOs: FIFA and the IOC. Tables 3.1 and 3.2 summarise these profiles for the eighteen people who have held these positions, all of whom have been male and white.

The general trend identifiable in the tenures of the presidential figures is of a switch, in both the IOC and FIFA, from an amateurist, public-minded commitment to a more commercialised model of organisational expansion and financial growth. Biographical and/or autobiographical accounts – barring hagiographic excesses – can be revealing sources on such changes. When Lord Killanin described his dealings

Table 3.1 Past presidents of the Fédération Internationale de Football Association (FIFA)

President	Country of origin	Duration of presidency	Professional background
Robert Guérin	France	1904–6, 2 years	Engineer, newspaper editor
Daniel Woolfall	England	1906–18, 12 years	Civil servant
Jules Rimet	France	1921–54, 33 years	Lawyer
Rodolphe Seeldrayers	Belgium	1954–55, 1 year	Lawyer, administrator, sport journalist
Arthur Drury	England	1956–61, 5 years	Fishmonger/merchant
Stanley Rous	England	1961–74, 13 years	Physical Education teacher, football administrator, referee
João Havelange	Brazil	1974–98, 24 years	Businessman and lawyer
Joseph Blatter	Switzerland	1998–2015, 17 years	Marketing consultant and sport administrator
Gianni Infantino	Switzerland	2016–	Lawyer and sport administrator

Table 3.2 Past presidents of the International Olympic Committee (IOC)

President	Country of origin	Duration of presidency	Professional background
Demetrius Vikelas	Greece	1894–96, 2 years	Businessman/writer
Pierre de Coubertin	France	1896–1925, 29 years	Aristocrat/educationalist
Henri de Baillet-Latour	Belgium	1925–42, 17 years	Aristocrat
Sigfrid Edström	Sweden	1942–52, 10 years	Industrialist/businessman
Avery Brundage	USA	1952–72, 20 years	Businessman
Michael Morris (Lord Killanin)	Ireland	1972–80, 8 years	Journalist/author
Juan Antonio Samaranch	Spain	1980–2001, 21 years	Career politician/diplomat
Jacques Rogge	Belgium	2001–13, 12 years	Physician/surgeon
Thomas Bach	Germany	2013–	Lawyer

with the bidding team for the Los Angeles 1984 Olympic Games he noted that it was 'explicit that' it was 'going to run the Games as a commercial company', a form of arrogance that infuriated Killanin. The commercial dimension forced Killanin to use his diplomatic skills in his presidential role as he sustained essentially diplomatic channels of communication with the LA team, creating a climate of exchange and potential compromise: 'It took much negotiating to achieve a position in which each party found the outcome satisfactory.'[20]

Given the model of organisations such as the IOC and FIFA, as not-for-profit associations within the embrace of the Swiss Civil Code, forms of patronage could be dispensed by the leadership with little challenge to their decision-making process. So FIFA could claim to be a model of global democracy on the basis of its Congress at which all national associations (numbering 211 as this is written in 2017) have one vote on critical decisions; thus rendering Vanuatu as powerful within the decision-making process as Brazil or Germany. On the basis of universal suffrage for nation states, it could be argued that the FIFA Congress is a more representative body than the General Assembly of the United Nations. Numerous insider accounts revealing corruption at the highest levels of FIFA, though, undermine arguments lauding the representative credibility of the organisation.

A veteran of the expansionist years of FIFA and the emergence of the continental federations, New Zealand's Charlie Dempsey could write in the middle of Havelange's presidential tenure of close to a quarter of a century that, 'FIFA is a very autocratic organisation, with very little bend. But I think there is a sympathetic feeling towards Oceania and I know I get a sympathy vote.'[21] As general secretary and then president of the Oceania confederation, Dempsey could trade his support for the sympathy of the leadership, and pivotal to this was the claim that he could also continue to loyally support the president by delivering or seeking to deliver the ten or so votes in FIFA's Congress that the national associations making up the confederation's membership could bring to the Congress. If we take a general definition of international sport's diplomatic dimensions, this kind of horse trading between national football associations and the overarching international governing body can be seen as routine international diplomatic practice. Stuart Murray and Geoff Pigman write that 'international-sport-as-diplomacy concerns the diplomatic representation, communication and negotiation between non-state actors that take place as a result of ongoing international sporting competition'.[22] So as the stakes were raised in an expanding cultural economy of international sport, the profiles and statuses of non-state actors in national and international sporting federations became dramatically enhanced; when media technology progressed and international broadcasts of a World Cup finals, an Olympics or Cold War encounters between national sides grew increasingly significant within that cultural economy, big-money private interests emerged as increasingly important actors, sponsoring events that would attract the largest viewing figures/audiences on record. 'Representation, communication and negotiation' (Murray and Pigman's words above) between an international sporting governing body such as the IOC and an expanding range of partners (broadcasters such as NBC or ABC in the USA, and established or emergent sponsors such as Coca-Cola and

McDonald's) would become serious business indeed; and would underpin cycles of scheduled sporting spectacles and associated bids for marketing and broadcasting rights. This created the BINGO, business-based version of the SINGO, and before very long generated the excesses and abuses that came to characterise the bidding processes themselves.[23]

So the growth of international sport, its cultural pull and economic boom, and the political reverberations that international sport can generate and/or echo, have placed the biggest, most sought after and most popular sports at the centre of a new sphere of multi-stakeholder diplomacy.[24] And when this has brought together private interests and political goals, manifest in, as noted above, the corruptible bidding processes for the FIFA World Cup, a traditional model of diplomacy that might characterise Murray and Pigman's international-sport-as-diplomacy has given way to misrepresentation, cynically manipulated communication, and unprecedentedly hypocritical negotiating practices and mechanisms. The nadir of such trends and processes was the 2010 decision in Zurich, Switzerland, to award the 2018 World Cup to the Russian Federation, and the 2022 event to Qatar. The FIFA files, as the *Sunday Times* journalists Blake and Calvert referred to the sources that allowed them to tell the story of 'the Qatari plot to buy the World Cup', had contributed to the collapse of FIFA's credibility as the world governing body became 'a toxic brand, synonymous with corruption, greed and duplicity the world over'.[25] Yet until members of his own organisation furnished FIFA's Ethics Committee with evidence on his long-term crooked deals with UEFA president Michel Platini, leading to their suspension in October 2015 followed by heavy bans from any football-related activity, FIFA's president Blatter could continue to play a diplomatic hand.

In November 2014, in Marrakech, Morocco, Blatter was still announcing that the crisis of the moment – the revelations on the corruption underlying Qatar's successful bid for the 2022 World Cup – was resolved: 'we have again the unity in our government ... I will bring back the FIFA. But not alone. I need my executive committee and then I need also the football family ... I trust in myself and I trust in my colleagues. And together, we will do it.'[26] What such desperate pleading – along with the bogus idealism of the metaphor of the family of world football with FIFA at its head – showed was that a discourse of diplomacy could be adopted even in the most dire of circumstances. Equally, it showed that appeals of a diplomatic hue sound hollow, as FIFA's institutional apparatus of international sport governance was crumbling. In contrast, in a more idealistic time and place, the diplomatic dimensions of international sport governance were vital to the global growth of international sport, and it is to examples of that which we now turn in consideration of the early years of development of the two smallest continental confederations, CONCACAF (representing the North and Central Americas and the Caribbean, formed/founded in 1961) and Oceania (representing Australia, New Zealand and the Pacific Islands, formed/founded 1965/66).[27]

Sir Stanley Rous as diplomat: the FIFA message in the Americas and the South Pacific

CONCACAF

CONCACAF, ten years on from its formation, remained a focus of the FIFA president Stanley Rous's concerns. It was formed in the same year as Rous's victory for the FIFA presidency, though a decade of negotiation looked to have had little effect on the strained relationship between the FIFA hierarchy and the regional body. In July 1971 Rous found himself addressing a Congress celebrating the fiftieth anniversary of the Netherlands Antilles's national football association. The invitation to the FIFA president was from CONCACAF as well as from the Netherlands Antilles, though on arrival Rous found that neither CONCACAF president Joaquin Soria Terrazas, nor his general secretary Carlos Carrera, were there. It was the president of the Costa Rica Football Association, Francisco Morelli Cozza, who presided over the Congress as Rous rose to give the inaugural address. This is perhaps a difficult scene to imagine in 2017, when air travel is so much more secure and commonplace, and FIFA presidents now have unlimited budgets and huge levels of remuneration; Rous's FIFA was financially modest and constrained, and he operated as president in an unremunerated role. Yet he was something of an internationalist, and his mission was to take and develop football in as many parts of the world as possible.

Football, education and war service had given Rous the opportunities to leave the stifling atmosphere of a parochial and modest upbringing and village life in Mutford, Suffolk, and his experience as a quartermaster in Cairo and Palestine in the later years of the Great War showed him that football had a hold on peoples and populations in all parts of the world.[28] He might have mired himself in diplomatic nightmares on the South African front, however naively and unintentionally supporting the apartheid regime; his mission, nevertheless, remained to take football and the things that football could do and mean to as many people in as many parts of the world as possible, working via the continental confederations.[29] He was not going to let the discourteousness and absence of Terrazas, Confederation president since 1969 and fresh from his organisational triumphs at the 1970 Mexico World Cup in his home country, curb or dilute the FIFA message.

Rous moved slowly in his address, beginning with a polite statement of gratitude at having received the invitation, saying that he was pleased to 'have the opportunity to join the members of CONCACAF in their work'. His immediate theme was work, then, and he added that this work was 'a duty', vital to the discharge of his responsibilities and his office. 'Good communications between FIFA and the confederations' was vital, he emphasised, and his visits to Congresses of the Confederation and member countries served a dual purpose: to meet delegates to establish personal relationships; and to learn about and recognise the 'hard work and progress made … in the development of the game' in the region and members' countries. Rous, warming to the task, then expanded on his vision of the FIFA president's role. His wording was a mix of engineering and psychology geared to expanding connections and horizons, the 'bridge builder'. Such a figure, Rous went on, can 'bring information of what was going on in the centre, and at the same time learn of the particular problems affecting considerations of countries, and this was a key job in an organisation with 140 members'. Rous was proposing a reciprocal flow of benefits between the centre and the emerging peripheries in this: he could, as the representative of the centre, bring the knowledge and potential resources to those relatively marginalised countries, and he could also gain from direct experience of and communication with football people in those places. 'Tell me what your needs are and FIFA will do all it can to help you' was another way of expressing Rous's message, and problems such as the huge distances between some of the islands, particularly in the Caribbean, might be addressed. Thirty years later the candidate for the presidency, Blatter, was offering 'tailor-made solutions' to small footballing nations for their vote – with undoubted success.[30] Rous had also pledged to do everything in his power 'to further their development', though had little to offer in the way of monies, television contracts and *largesse,* adding only that he had been a key figure in establishing the Confederations and 'had devised the system of committees which linked them to FIFA'.

How, then, could the FIFA president begin and sustain effective bridge-building initiatives? He pointed to two ways of doing this, through, first, committees, and secondly, tournaments, stressing in particular the importance of the Amateur Committee and the Youth and Schoolboys Committee – less prominent to the eyes of the world's press he noted, though 'the most important of all because they were working at the grassroots of football and their success ensured the future of the game'. He was appealing to the participants, what we might now call the citizen diplomats – the football activists, the recreational players and the youth leagues; not the top administrators or the aspirant media moguls, not the manipulative rising politician.[31] Rous was building to his core message here, looking to get the Confederations to learn from each other. FIFA could take a 'broad, overall view', able to 'reinforce one Confederation because of its knowledge of the experience of other Confederations', as well as 'from its own long experience of the game and its problems'. It was a form of globally expansive knowledge exchange that was being offered to the delegates in this remote corner of the Dutch post-colonial Caribbean. Rous was saying trust me/us, work together, as the FIFA–Confederation relationship is 'of key importance. FIFA should be looked upon as a service organisation, not just as a governing body … able to provide information, expert knowledge, financial help and technical guidance in the development of the game'. Rous was not saying that FIFA could do this alone; it would need allies, and these included not just the Confederations and the national associations but also the political and educational institutions of the separate nations, and the grassroots organisations that established and sustained the game in the first place.

Rous of course owed his lofty position not just to his FA profile and his status as an international referee; his educational and military experiences took him on his long journey from Mutford to Zurich, and for over a decade he had taught physical education at Watford Grammar School, after studying at St Luke's Teacher Training College, Exeter, England. He knew a thing or two about national fitness debates and the team-building characteristics of team-games, and so told his listeners that he 'hoped every government, especially every Education Authority, would be willing to play its part in the development of the game'.

Remaining sensitive to the CONCACAF situation, Rous also raised questions concerning the importance of dialogue: the service FIFA could offer could not happen without 'a free exchange of ideas in both directions'. It is clear from his measured tone and his sensitively pitched critique of the Central Americas/Caribbean Confederation that much was to be done, that many were not to be trusted. This would not be used as a rationale for outright condemnation, though; slowly but surely was the order of the day for Rous, adopting a classically diplomatic dialogic stance, though with the aura of the imperialist. Karl Marx had not been on Rous's reading list at St Luke's College or at the Quartermaster's store in Palestine in the First World War, and Rous would not have recognised the warning that the 'tradition of all the dead generations weighs like a nightmare on the brain of the living'.[32] However well intentioned his diplomatic interventions, for some these would be seen as the empty promises of a haughty post-colonialist.

Oceania

The youngest of the Confederations, Oceania was initially floated as the 'South West Pacific Football Confederation', later dropping the 'West'. W. G. Walkley, the secretary of the Australian Soccer Federation (ASF), based in Sydney, wrote to Rous on 7 April 1965 (stamped as received in Zurich on 13 April). Walkley asked that his letter be regarded as a 'progress report', and confirmed that a few weeks earlier, on 14 March, 'we had a meeting in Melbourne … to discuss the formation of a South Pacific Football Confederation'. At the Southern Cross Hotel in Melbourne representatives of Australia, New Zealand, Papua and New Guinea, and Fiji met, and New Caledonia had indicated intent to join such an initiative. 'Unanimous approval' was given to the proposal. Walkey, who also pledged some general financial assistance from Australia to get things off the ground, recognised that the enterprise was 'exploratory'. He wrote, 'we have set our foot on the bottom rung of the ladder and I believe that in due course we will produce a strong confederation in the South Pacific'. 'My dear Sir Stanley', Walkley wrote in intimate cum deferential style, while strong lobbying was underway, and a headed letter from the incipient Confederation had also gone to Rous's London address from the 'South Pacific Football Confederation – Provisional Member of F.I.F.A. – (FOUNDED 14 MARCH 1965)'. This claimed affiliation/membership was circled in red pen by Rous – ever the schoolmaster – and the writer (a G. Bayutti, writing from the same Sydney address as that of the Australian Soccer Federation) invited himself to a forthcoming FIFA Committee of Study meeting in London. Rous's immaculate longhand asked 'Why? Agenda? Discuss new Confederation?' Clearly there were sensibilities at play here and Rous, displaying the diplomat's craft for clarity of communication, was not one for coded exchanges and presumption.

The detailed minute of the March meeting included the choice of 'South Pacific' rather than 'Oceania' as the new Confederation's name, as 'Oceania' included some territories or countries that would not be members. And so, from a pub room in Melbourne – a not unfamiliar pattern in choice of venues for sporting organisations – the world's latest football confederation was launched. In fact, FIFA had expressed an earlier preference for 'Oceania', proposed by General Secretary Käser as early as 1961, as previously noted the year Rous became FIFA president. And when Rous had advised the formation of an Oceania confederation at the FIFA Congress at the Tokyo Olympics in 1964, this was met with a lukewarm response: 'it was felt this name had no real meaning', wrote Käser. Nevertheless, the Australian Soccer Federation sent Rous (30 September 1964) a summary of the *Encyclopaedia Britannica*'s entry on Oceania, for the enlightenment of the FIFA Executive Committee in 'discussions regarding the formation of the new Confederation'. In the formative period, too, there was work to be done with bodies such as the French Football Federation, to which French territories such as New Caledonia were affiliated. Rous advised that the French Federation follow the FA model, allowing former 'English' [*sic*] colonies to join a Confederation and/or FIFA, while retaining an associate membership with the FA. This latter compromise, little more than symbolic, nevertheless achieved a kind of status equilibrium and lent itself to Rous's commitment (16 December 1965 to Pierre Delauney) to developmental goals: 'enabling them [the former colonies] to develop football withing [*sic*] their territory by arranging international matches and benefiting in other ways from closer co-operation with other associations'.

In these negotiations Rous was seen as a worldly and influential figure. As noted above, the ASF's Walkley, referring to the New Caledonia issue, had called upon Rous as FIFA president to bring his presence to bear on the issue: 'However, knowing the French people, I am writing to you to ask whether you would be kind enough to use your influence in having the French people expedite their decision in favour of New Caledonia joining the Oceania Confederation' (19 October 1965). Problems would persist in relation to representation on FIFA committees and the like, and the issue of the position of the French Confederation on New Caledonia's status, but from its base in central Sydney the approved Oceania Football Confederation could write on its headed paper 'Founded 1st January 1966', its proposal accepted formally at the FIFA Congress in London in 1966.

To negotiate the competing interests within the emerging Confederation, Rous needed the patience of the schoolmaster, the language of the diplomat and the decisiveness of the politician. He could read between the lines when Oceania's secretary Ian McAndrew wrote to General Secretary Käser (14 February 1967) on the increasingly sensitive issue of representation for the Confederation on FIFA's Executive Committee; Bayutti was scheduled to visit Zurich to talk about technical assistance, Rous's annotations noting that the Confederation 'don't want him – obvious', and here the FIFA president would be weighing up the internal politics of the rookie Confederation. He also noted to himself that action wasn't really needed until 'we hear of all countries having met, at least to accept proposed constitution'. At Oceania's first Congress, held in the Metropolitan Motel Brisbane 27 January 1968, Australia, New Zealand, Papua New Guinea and New Caledonia (by invitation) met, Fiji sending apologies. It was up and running, with just four national association members. Not all of these were represented on the Confederation's Executive Committee, which was dominated by the two big players, New Zealand and Australia. And new players were entering the arena, seeing the potential of a single Confederation. Representing New Zealand on the Executive Committee was expatriate Scot Charles Dempsey, who within two years was writing to Dr Käser (copied to Rous) bemoaning the inactivity of the Confederation in the administrative hands of McAndrew and its Australian origins.

Oceania as a project was ossifying, with Australia barely functioning in its founder/ leadership role. Dempsey wrote, from his position as Chairman of Tours for the Oceania Confederation, that its vice-president 'has asked me to express New Zealand's attitude that we wish Oceania to develop for the benefit of all our countries. New Zealand is most anxious to take part in Oceania and will fit in with any reasonable requests which Australia may bring forward to hold the meeting. Meanwhile we are eagerly awaiting some communication from Australia, as no doubt all other Oceania countries are' (14 April 1970, received in Zurich 21 April). Rous, himself ignored by McAndrew and Sir William Walkley, had written to Dempsey (26 February 1970) expressing serious concern: 'FIFA are most anxious for Oceania to become well formed and administered. An application from them has been received for Congress to authorise a representative in the FIFA Executive Committee. But I don't think the resolution will be successful until the progress has been made towards a sound organisation.'

Soundness of organisation was some way off and Australia could not bring its six states together in harmony. It was also looking to join the bigger fish in the Asian Confederation, which it sought to do in 1972. However, Dempsey saw the opportunities for football development that would be wasted should Oceania collapse. He told his biographer:

> We came out of that meeting with the Australians and went across to the Chevron Hilton Hotel. What were we going to do? Was it the finish of Oceania? I said it was not. I reminded the others of Sir Stanley's words that we must not give away the Confederation no matter what happened because if we did we would never get it back. I knew we had the confederation ... it had been approved and sanctioned by FIFA ... So we made Cowie president, Sashi became treasurer, Ahmed was put in charge of operations and I became secretary. I then informed Stanley of what had taken place. He approved and told us to get Oceania on the move.[33]

So from the potential wreckage of a fledgling Confederation, that is what Dempsey did, with one other New Zealand representative and two Fijians, supported by Rous in making the case for an Oceania position on the FIFA Executive Committee. He brought Australia – unwanted, as it turned out by the Asian Confederation – back into the fold in 1977, and in 1982 became president himself, championing 'the development of Oceania'.[34] Dempsey would become a long-serving ally of João Havelange, and was lambasted in 2000 over his abstention from a second round of FIFA Executive Committee voting which gave the 2006 World Cup hosting prize to Germany rather than South Africa.

Dempsey was adept at weaving and ducking in the power politics of the global governing body. He accomplished much through his highly effective politicking, lobbying and networking in a diplomatic-style role in his long Oceania/FIFA career, holding to an apolitical neutral line, as he claimed, throughout. His report to Oceania from FIFA's Paris Congress of August 1972 makes interesting reading (received by Rous, 23 September 1972):

> As regards the Congress itself, it was not an entirely satisfactory one. It is quite apparent that there are pressure groups emerging, and that FIFA is having many pressures brought upon it – especially by African nations, who I feel are introducing politics into football. In this respect I harbour a fear for the future, as I consider a split could come about … unless there is a change in attitudes.

A power shift occurred less than two years later when Havelange won the FIFA presidency from Rous, and much of Havelange's appeal had been to Africa. Dempsey's predicted split was averted by the change of leadership at the top of FIFA, and the New Zealand representative would have no problem surviving in Havelange's regime over the following twenty-six years, consigning his mentor Rous to history: the king is dead, long live the king. Havelange would do nothing to discourage perceptions of Rous as an out-of-touch colonialist with little to offer the expanding football business in Africa and Asia.

Rous performed the role of diplomatic midwife to Oceania in FIFA. As negotiator and encourager he stimulated the emergence of Oceania, stepped in pragmatically to save it from extinction, and monitored its recovery in the administrative hands of Charles Dempsey. His skills combined bureaucratic precision with diplomatic finesse, dealing with national football associations from numerous nations and territories. Charles Dempsey's memoirs were less public spirited in relation to Rous, however passionate his commitment to regional development. His FIFA Executive Committee lifestyle involved negotiations of sorts, though often on the golf course or in the hotel lobby rather than the committee room:

> You gradually grow into the system and gain confidence. There is no doubt that I have been able to overcome many problems for New Zealand or Oceania through my FIFA connections. It has been through making friends and contacts over the years at this level. Some of those contacts have been cemented even further with those games of golf on the other side of the world.[35]

Effusive and effective in informal settings and hospitality suites, what Iver Neumann has called diplomatic sites,[36] and omnipresent at big events as a travelling FIFA VIP, committee official or match commissar, Dempsey became used to the perks of office. He reportedly took the opportunity at Tinjian duty-free shop in China 'to buy the biggest suitcase I had ever seen to allow us to send the many gifts Annie and I had received back home as unaccompanied baggage'.[37] Annie his wife was no mean golfer too, and enjoyed her husband's FIFA schedule and lifestyle without complaint.[38]

Diplomacy is fraught with unanticipated outcomes as power-shifts and even the global *zeitgeist* change. Rous the international diplomat helped the entry into FIFA's corridors of power of the Glaswegian businessman and construction entrepreneur. Once granted entry to the FIFA inner elite, Dempsey settled in as a follower and favourite of the autocratic and charismatic Havelange, never once protesting at the pampered and luxurious privileges and experiences that an enriched FIFA would offer its committee members and allies from the Confederations. In return for continuing support for his five unopposed re-elections as president, Havelange would let the Confederations off the leash, helping their incomes grow as the World Cup boomed, and – in an approach adopted too by his successor Sepp Blatter – FIFA and the Confederations roared towards the scandals of excess, corruption and self-aggrandisement that would bring the US Department of Justice and the FBI to the shores of Lake Zurich in May 2015. Here, as the RICO (Racketeer Influenced Corrupt Organization) Act set in motion a series of roundups of Confederation officials (numerous of whom were from the CONCACAF Confederation), the diplomatic goals of Stanley Rous were a distant memory.[39]

It is arguable that Stanley Rous's presidency was the end of a *longue dureé* in the history of international sport diplomacy. He had been raised in the Edwardian period, born within months of the formation of the IOC. Just two years before he switched from schoolteacher to football administrator to take up his post as a modernising secretary of the FA (England), FIFA was celebrating the twenty-fifth anniversary of its formation in 1929. In a 1930 publication comprising twenty-five contributions from founders/members of national associations, football administrators from Chile, the USA, Ecuador and Palestine, as well as football nations across Europe, commented on FIFA, its goals and its achievements.[40] FIFA president Jules Rimet, from France, also offered a written sermon on the positive dimensions of football. He wrote that it would be the

> honour of the renaissance of sport of our time to have derived its passions from peaceful contests/jousts in stadia where the original violence is subordinated to the discipline of the rules of the game, loyal and honest, and where the spoils of the victor are limited to the intoxications of having won, and to seeing the colours of one's country acclaimed by the crowd.[41]

He welcomed the contributors' efforts, observing that the founders of the national federations (this was a quarter of a century before FIFA approved the establishment of the continental Confederations) were characterised by the same moral qualities as those of football: reciprocal confidence between national bodies/associations; sacrifice of particular/individual interests; abnegation of self-interest; and the development of common causes. These moral qualities, he added, underpinned the developing expansion of the game at the international level. The moral authority that the federations could bring to bear meant that 'each can work, in total calmness, at its particular task and participate to make the beautiful sport that we have charge of, the Chivalry of modern times'.[42] Messianic, certainly; idealistic, without a doubt; diplomatic, indisputably and discursively so.

A discourse of diplomacy is always contingent upon the fluctuating circumstances of time and place, and the motivations of individuals and the values of institutions. C. A. W. Hirschman, compiler of the anniversary book and FIFA's secretary/treasurer since 1906, contributed his own essay, exploring what he called the 'pacificist mission of sport in international relations'. The premise to this piece is the assertion that life is a struggle 'from the cradle to the grave', and that the scale of the struggle between groups of men has become increasingly large: families, tribes, regions, nations, groups of nations.[43] 'Will we finish by seeing the continents fight between themselves?' asked Hirschman, '?' And he wondered whether it was reckless to think that the human race, recognising that it is like a giant family locked in cycles of routine quarrels, would accept the need to search 'for a peaceful solution' as in the example of arbitration.[44] If things develop at all along these lines, 'sport can exercise a considerable influence' in a 'good way':

> Won't it be possible for all these civilisations, imitating the spirit of sport, to struggle peacefully between themselves and to accomplish stages of human progress by well-ordered 'team work'? [the term 'team work' is rendered in its English form] What progress might we have accomplished already if diplomacy were stimulated by the sporting spirit![45]

The spirit of FIFA here was echoing the spirit of Baron Pierre de Coubertin and his Olympic vision.[46] These were difficult times, politically in some embryonically fascist central European states and economically across the international arena following the 1929 Great Crash, and the idealism of the Olympic/IOC model continued to provide an inspiration and a template for FIFA. Hirschman's grand vision was rendered risible, though, when in 1931/32 he left FIFA in disgrace after it was discovered that he had embezzled FIFA funds and lost them in fruitless and desperate investment schemes.[47] So much, then, for his plea a couple of years earlier that 'in such times one is justified in showing full confidence in the pacifist role, which can exercise a true sporting spirit in social life, so valuing, in all aspects of human activity, justice and respect for the rights and interests of others'.[48]

Conclusion: ideological constraints on the sport-diplomatic

It is of course arbitrary to separate individuals from institutions – and in the discussions and analyses above individual actors are always rooted in an institutional context. Equally, institutions can be in large part understood as the constructions of individual actors. It is the blend of the two through which histories are made, collective narratives generated.[49] So in conclusion several overarching themes are worth recounting, with an emphasis upon what often holds the individual and the institution together, which is the sets of values and interests that constitute influence. If we have identified recurrent strands of a sport-diplomatic in the material presented in this chapter, any such cases must also be understood in the context of shaping, determining and often constraining ideologies. Here, the term 'ideology' is not used in the pseudo-neutral sense of sets of distinct ideas or belief-systems; [50] rather, in a more Marxist sense, 'ideologies' refer to sets of competing interests implicated if not fully enmeshed in power relations.[51]

First, then, it is clear that a broadening pitch and reach of public diplomacy, and more sophisticated deconstructions of the sport-diplomatic, are to be welcomed. This allows, indeed invites, a reconsideration of the key individuals and the nature of their networks in the history, politics and sociology of sport cultures and institutions. This can involve reinterpretations of classic works, bringing out more explicitly the sport-diplomatic dimension. And it offers boundless possibilities for archival work on individuals and their *modus operandi* in sport-based networks of power, politics and diplomacy.

Secondly, it is paramount to look at the actual practices of individuals and institutions – what do they really do, how, why, when and where? This leads the analysis directly to the field of ideology. In whose interests do apparent sport-diplomatic actors work? Take the example of the fraudulent FIFA frontman of 1930, or the active young idealist Charles Dempsey in New Zealand in his relationship with Stanley Rous. It has been demonstrated that the most idealistic of statements in FIFA's earlier years could mask exploitation and corruption at the top of the organisation; however sincere the principles of a Jules Rimet might have been, the organisation could nevertheless be threatened by the maverick activities of a single individual. In the early days of the newest Confederation, Oceania, we have seen how the rising sport administrator Dempsey could flatter and charm whoever was in the presidential driving seat. This is a reminder that organisations are not abstract entities, as they might appear according to abstract models and unanchored typologies so beloved of some models of social science; rather, they are peopled, and institutions can be vulnerable to exploitation by individuals of any kind. Take the infamous Chuck Blazer, the general secretary of the CONCACAF Confederation, who moved the Confederation into extensive and luxurious offices in the Trump Tower in Fifth Avenue, New York. Interviewed in February 1997 in these lavish surroundings, he talked of the potential of the expanding media markets for football, not as a means of promoting the game in the poorest parts of the Caribbean or the Central Americas, but more as a way of boosting the profile and prestige of his organisation. CONCACAF was 'pretty sick, it was haemorrhaging and it took us a period of time to get the haemorrhaging to stop'.[52] Once the money rolled in as deregulated markets continued to boom, Blazer set about enriching himself and selected colleagues, until turning FBI informer and contributing, pivotally, to the evidence base that led to the US indictments of FIFA-connected personnel in CONCACAF and CONMEBOL (the South American Confederation) in particular. Blazer could charm a media room full of world-weary journalists and was a popular figure in mid-town social circles, taken seriously too in the networks of decision making in FIFA's world. He inherited a crooked operation as chair of FIFA's Media and Marketing Committee, and escalated its excesses on an unprecedented scale. It was clear to some, if not many, that his communications skills, social charm and diplomatic *bonhomie* were a front; in reality, with his equally crooked confederation president, Trinidadian Jack Warner, he could run the CONCACAF institution like a fiefdom.[53]

Thirdly, an emphasis on the diplomacy topic in sport scholarship offers innumerable possibilities for the study of the gap between the rhetoric of the individual and/or institution and the identifiable practices of the organisation or the realities of the wider world. Examples include many of the slogans of the dominant SINGOs, such as the IOC's adoption of the term 'celebrate humanity', used in the 1990s to encapsulate the organisation's principles and ideals. The combination of celebration and universalism evoked in the term is a form of reductionism that misrepresents the nature of the social and the political world, the stress on an all-embracing notion of 'humanity' and inclusivity diverting attention from the social and cultural realities of a complex and often conflict-ridden world.[54]

Fourthly, and finally, the sport-diplomatic should be understood in the context of shifting and competing ideologies. The FIFA of the mid-twentieth century could grow in the name of inclusivity and post-colonial third-world development, whatever the tensions in the move to independence of so many newly independent states. FIFA in the more contemporary setting of the twenty-first century represents a deeper set of contradictions and its public/sport diplomacy role has become increasingly vulnerable to exploitation and abuse in a more deregulated and globalised, one might say neoliberal, world order. Toby Miller has convincingly argued that cultural citizenship has been threatened and re-framed in a neoliberal age in which a crisis of belonging has escalated for increasing numbers of people and peoples across the world. For them, and Miller quotes George Soros here, 'the spread of market values into all areas of life', alongside 'an untrammeled intensification of laissez-faire capitalism', erodes the basis for citizenship-based participation in any open and democratic society.[55] In such a context, as people become disconnected from the sources of their identity and from institutions of an increasingly unaccountable kind, ideological formations can consolidate; a neoliberal moment can become the dominant orthodoxy of an age. As Miller notes, for a neoliberal political Right, cultural citizenship becomes no more than 'a new set of market and ecclesiastical niches and sites of self-governance'.[56] When a corrupt and crooked network at the head of FIFA has preached its heady mix of universalism and idealism to the world 'football family', while running off with the family savings, we see how an overarching ideology has changed the individual and institutional experiences, realities and perceptions of the sport's culture and institutions. It is not possible to understand the ways in which non-state actors such as SINGOs work without recognising the wider ideological climate of the world in which they work.

Stanley Rous may, as noted in the body of this chapter, have believed in the good of the game, one of FIFA's later mottos, for people with little else in poorer parts of the world. In the eyes of those whom he sought to help, though, he still carried the weight of his own privileged past as he traversed a post-colonialising world, or was eyed as a means to an end in a changing game of diplomatic back-stabbing and accelerating ambitions. The study of diplomatic actors and practices in the world of international sport offers myriad opportunities to see how individuals, institutions and ideologies have interconnected in the making of the contemporary sporting spectacle and landscape. Responses to such opportunities will be enhanced by an engagement with the ideas and perspectives emanating from the field of sport-diplomatic studies; and this field itself will benefit from the recognition of empirically anchored historical and sociological work on the individuals and institutions for whom and which diplomatic practices – however labelled at the time – have been critical in negotiating the ideological currents of the day.

Notes

* I am grateful for invitations to present plenary addresses at the following conferences, and to participants at those events who made valuable contributions to the evolution of the chapter. In July 2015, a presentation bearing the title of this chapter was given to the conference *Sport and Diplomacy: Message, Mode and Metaphor* at SOAS, University of London, 3–4 July 2015, the event from which much of this book has stemmed. And on 6 July 2016, a plenary address on 'From Flawed Idealism to Racketeering: FIFA's Betrayal of the Simple Game' was presented at *Locating Leisure: Blurring Boundaries*, the Annual Conference of the Leisure Studies Association, Liverpool John Moores University, Liverpool, UK. I am particularly grateful to J. Simon Rofe for his perceptive editorial response to a rough draft of this chapter, and his invaluable suggestions.

1 Peter J. Beck, *Scoring for Britain: International Football and International Politics, 1900–1939* (London: Frank Cass, 1999).

2 Stanley Rous, *Football Worlds: A Lifetime in Sport* (London: Faber and Faber, 1978), 91, 92. Of course Rous was playing here with the term 'splendid isolation', which as diplomatic and international relations scholars well know, originated in relation to the isolationist position adopted by Great Britain in the second half of the nineteenth century. Isolationism has also been seen to characterise particular approaches to US foreign policy, persisting as an ideal and a goal for many US politicians in the twentieth century who supported the non-involvement of the US in the World Wars or post-war treaty making. See Iain McLean and Alistair Macmillan (eds), *The Concise Oxford Dictionary of Politics* (Oxford: Oxford University Press, 2003), 280. See too J. Simon Rofe, 'Isolationism and internationalism in transatlantic affairs', *Journal of Transatlantic Studies*, 9:1 (2011). That Rous could play with words in this critical fashion showed an unusual adeptness with language, and some skill in the use of the veiled critique delivered in considered and courteous style.

3 Beck, *Scoring for Britain*, 112.

4 Beck, *Scoring for Britain*, 112.

5 Peter J. Beck, 'The relevance of the '"irrelevant": football as a missing dimension in the study of British relations with Germany', *International Affairs*, 79:2 (2003), 408.

6 Jan Melissen, *Wielding Soft Power: The New Public Diplomacy*, Clingendael Diplomacy Papers 2, May 2005, 29–30.

7 Melissen, *Wielding Soft Power*, 29–30.

8 Jan Melissen, *Beyond the New Public Diplomacy*, Clingendael Diplomacy Papers 3, October 2011, 17.

9 Shaun Riordan, *The New Diplomacy* (Cambridge: Polity, 2003), 86.

10 Riordan, *The New Diplomacy*, 125.

11 Jan Melissen, 'The new public diplomacy: between theory and practice', in Jan Melissen (ed.), *The New Public Diplomacy* (Basingstoke: Palgrave Macmillan, 2005), 3–27, 20.

12 Melissen, *The New Public Diplomacy*, 12, 20.

13 These political examples number among what Rofe calls the clichés of sport diplomacy, operating as a kind of shorthand and even caricature in mainstream accounts. See J. Simon Rofe, 'Sport and diplomacy: a global diplomacy framework', *Diplomacy and Statecraft*, 27:2 (2016).

14 Christopher R. Hill, *Olympic Politics* (Manchester: Manchester University Press, 1992), 33.

15 On SINGOs, see Lincoln Allison and Alan Tomlinson, *Understanding International Sports Organizations: Principles, Power and Possibilities* (London: Routledge, 2017).

16 Hill, *Olympic Politics*, 52.

17 Aaron Beacom, *International Diplomacy and the Olympic Movement: The New Mediators* (Basingstoke: Palgrave Macmillan, 2012), has developed most fully an answer to the question of 'the way in which international affairs and diplomatic activity' are evolving in relation to the Olympics, calling his book 'an attempt to address this scholarly vacancy', and to give due attention to 'the characteristics of diplomatic discourse relating to the Olympic Movement', 2.

18 Hill, *Olympic Politics*, 53.

19 Leo Lowenthal, 'The triumph of mass idols' (written 1943/44), in *Literature, Popular Culture and Society* (Palo Alto, CA: Pacific Books, 1961). On Beckham, see Garry Whannel, 'The case of David Beckham', in David L. Andrews and Steven J. Jackson (eds), *Sport Stars: The Cultural Politics of Sporting Celebrity* (London: Routledge, 2001). On Michael Jordan, one source among many, see Walter LaFeber, *Michael Jordan and the New Global Capitalism* (New York: W. W. Norton, 2002), where Jordan is said to have become 'an immensely profitable commodity in a society that, especially with the end of the Cold War, seemed to value profit, celebrity and marketability above all else', including 'a sometime corruption of this Americanization', 128.

20 Lord Killanin, *My Olympic Years* (New York: William Morrow, 1983), 98.

21 Peter Devlin, *The Dempsey Years: The Rise of New Zealand Soccer* (Auckland: SeTo Publishing, 1988), 105.

22 Stuart Murray and Geoffrey Allen Pigman, 'Mapping the relationship between international sport and diplomacy', *Sport in Society: Cultures, Commerce, Media, Politics*, 17:9 (2014), 1099.

23 See John Sugden and Alan Tomlinson, 'Not for the good of the game: crisis and credibility in the governance of world football', in Lincoln Allison (ed.), *The Global Politics of Sport: The Role of Global Institutions in Sport* (London: Routledge, 2005), 26–45, where it is argued that FIFA in the last quarter of the twentieth century 'transformed itself from an INGO … into a BINGO (Business International Non-Government Organisation)', 26.

24 See Brian Hocking, 'Multistakeholder diplomacy: forms, functions, and frustrations', in Jovan Kurbalija and Valentin Katrandjiev (eds), *Multistakeholder Diplomacy: Challenges and Opportunities* (Malta and Geneva: DiploFoundation, 2006), 13–29.

25 Heidi Blake and Jonathan Calvert, *The Ugly Game: The Qatari Plot to Buy the World Cup* (London: Simon & Schuster, 2015), 452.

26 Blake and Calvert, *The Ugly Game*, 453.

27 The copies of documents relating to Rous's activities in these two settings are in the personal collection of the author, after being accessed in their original forms in a private collection of Sir Stanley Rous's FIFA papers.

28 On Rous's background, see Alan Tomlinson, *FIFA: The Men, the Myths and the Money* (London: Routledge, 2014); and Alan Tomlinson, 'Welcome to FIFA land: FIFA and the men who made it', *Soccer and Society*, 1:1 (2000).

29 Paul Darby, 'Stanley Rous's "own goal": football politics, South Africa and the contest for the FIFA presidency in 1974', *Soccer and Society*, 9:2 (2008).

30 See John Sugden and Alan Tomlinson, *Badfellas: FIFA Family at War* (Edinburgh: Mainstream, 2003), 150 for a reproduction of this letter.

31 See Giles Scott-Smith, 'Private diplomacy, making the citizen visible', *New Global Studies*, 8:1 (2014).

32 Karl Marx, 'The Eighteenth Brumaire of Louis Bonaparte', in *Karl Marx/Frederick Engels, Collected Works Volume 11, Marx and Engels: 1851–53* (London: Lawrence & Wishart, 1976), 103.

33 Devlin, *The Dempsey Years*, 110.

34 When in 2006 Australia left Oceania to again join the much larger Asian Football Confederation, the Lowy Institute's Anthony Bubalo provided a rationale for the move in a policy brief entitled *Football Diplomacy*. He emphasised the contribution of sport to 'conversation between societies', to a shared appreciation of the game that could cross cultural and national boundaries, and to a more developed grassroots engagement that could prosper between people from Australia and Asia. Transformation of 'local perceptions – and preconceptions – of what individual Asian societies are really like' was even projected. These grandiose goals would not have featured in the exchanges between Rous and Dempsey. The *realpolitik* of Australia's 2008 move was also bound up with more pragmatic and, some might say, mercenary motives linked to playing Asia's larger nations, and securing one of the several places at the World Cup finals that the Asian Confederation was guaranteed. For the detail on 'football diplomacy', see David Rowe, *Global Media Sport: Flows, Forms and Futures* (London: Bloomsbury Academic, 2011), 115, from where the direct quotations are taken. For a full account of the Australian federation's continuing volatility of Confederation membership, see David Rowe's analysis in this book.

35 Devlin, *The Dempsey Years*, 99.

36 Iver B. Neumann, *Diplomatic Sites: A Critical Enquiry* (London: Hurst Publishers, 2014), indicates just how important such locations as eating places and 'neutral' leisure locations are in the day-to-day world of diplomatic exchanges and encounters. It seems that the field would benefit from more close-up scrutiny and study of what the sociologist Erving Goffman called, in his dramaturgical model of sociology, the backstage settings of everyday life; see Erving Goffman, *The Presentation of Self in Everyday Life* (London: Allen Lane The Penguin Press, 1969 [1959]).

37 Devlin, *The Dempsey Years*, 103.

38 On the broader context of the world of diplomacy and personal and family life, see Anne Coles, 'Making multiple migrations: the life of British diplomatic families

overseas', in Anne Coles and Anne-Meike Fechter (eds), *Gender and Family among Transnational Professionals* (London: Routledge, 2008).

39 On the longer-term story of the emerging scales of scandal in the FIFA saga, see John Sugden and Alan Tomlinson, *Football, Corruption and Lies: Revisiting 'Badfellas', the Book FIFA Tried to Ban* (London: Routledge, 2017).

40 FIFA, *Fédération Internationale de Football Association 1904–1929* (undated, printed by J. H. De Bussy, Amsterdam). The Rimet and Hirschman contributions/quotations are translated from the French by the author (Alan Tomlinson).

41 FIFA, *Fédération*, 3.

42 FIFA, *Fédération*, 3.

43 FIFA, *Fédération*, 11.

44 FIFA, *Fédération*, 12.

45 FIFA, *Fédération*, 13.

46 In a speech in London in 1908 de Coubertin defined the 'Olympic idea' as a concept of 'strong physical culture based in part on the spirit of chivalry – what you here so pleasantly call "fair play" – and in part on the esthetic idea of the cult of what is beautiful and graceful'; see Pierre de Coubertin, *Pierre de Coubertin 1863–1937, Olympism: Selected Writings*, ed. Norbert Müller (Lausanne: International Olympic Committee, 2000), 588.

47 Pierre Lanfranchi, Christiane Eisenberg, Tony Mason and Alfred Wahl, *100 Years of Football: The FIFA Centennial Book* (London: Weidenfeld & Nicolson, 2004), 74.

48 Hirschman, in FIFA, *Fédération*, 13.

49 As C. Wright Mills argued so lucidly and clearly, and so long ago when he first published the book in 1959, the sociological imagination needs to recognise the interconnection of biography and history, and this requires an understanding of 'the institutions within which' an individual's 'biography is enacted'; see C. Wright Mills, *The Sociological Imagination* (Harmondsworth: Penguin, 1970), 178.

50 For an authoritative overview of the concept, see Jorge Larrain, *The Concept of Ideology* (London: Hutchinson, 1979).

51 Marx's concept of ideology has proved somewhat flexible, even elusive. In *The German Ideology*, written in the mid-1840s, he used the simile of the shifting, distorted image in a famous comment within a philosophical discussion of the process of what he called 'mental production', the 'production of ideas, of conceptions, of consciousness'. This mental production is expressed in 'the language of the politics, laws, morality, religion, metaphysics, etc., of a people', that is, the ideological formations and expressions of the society, which for Marx are the product of the 'being of men … their actual life process'. And it is this historical life process, rooted in 'material activity and the material intercourse of men' that shapes the ideological elements of a society, the 'phenomenon' that 'in all ideology men and their relations appear upside-down as in a *camera obscura*'. See Karl Marx and Frederick Engels, 'The German ideology: critique of modern German philosophy according to its representatives Feuerbach, B. Bauer and Stirner, and of German socialism according to its various prophets', in *Karl Marx/Frederick Engels, Collected Works Volume 5, Marx and Engels: 1845–47* (London: Lawrence & Wishart, 1976), 36. New technological developments in the first half of the nineteenth century were adapting the *camera obscura* (from the Latin, 'darkened room') principle to experimental forms of photography. In the Renaissance, artists suspected of using the principle to enhance

their work were seen as a mix of sorcerer or cheat. For Marx, the term was perfect for his sense of ideology as illusion, distortion or delusion, and, in a further rendering with Engels, false consciousness. It is the process of seeing through a small space – the pin-hole image – focusing upon a detail that in fact is a visual misrepresentation and distortion of the image that clearly attracted Marx to the simile. It would be interesting to think through the potential of this sense of ideology for detailed deconstruction of dominant discourses of diplomacy that present, articulate and disseminate views of the world that are wilfully misrepresented and distorted. For the purposes of the chapter in this book, ideology is a means of conceptualising the clusters of beliefs and values adhered to by social groups, and often used to legitimate the position of that group in the power structures and dynamics of the wider society. To achieve this legitimation, particular interests will be purveyed as universal interests (wilful distortion and manipulation), and it is in this sense that the concept is employed in the spirit of the Marxist pedigree.

52 Alan Tomlinson, 'Blazing a trial', *When Saturday Comes*, 341 (July 2015), 16–17.

53 On Blazer's excesses and downfall, see Mary Papenfuss and Teri Thompson, *American Huckster: How Chuck Blazer Got Rich From – and Sold Out – the Most Powerful Cabal in World Sports* (New York: Harper, 2016). Blazer died in July 2017 in New Jersey, USA, having turned state informant and so avoiding prosecution and imprisonment. On Warner's background, see Alan Tomlinson, 'Lord, don't stop the carnival: Trinidad and Tobago at the 2006 FIFA World Cup', *Journal of Sport and Social Issues*, 31:3 (2006). On 29 September 2015 FIFA's independent Ethics Committee banned Warner from football-related activity for life, citing his illegal money-making schemes and scams, including 'offer, acceptance and receipt of undisclosed and illegal payments'. Warner was found to be guilty of multiple violations of the ethics code, relating to general rules of conduct; loyalty; duty of disclosure; conflicts of interest; accepting and offering gifts/benefits; and obligation of parties to collaborate; see *Independent Ethics Committee Adjudicatory Chamber Media Release*, 29 September 2015, available at www.fifa.com/governance/news/y=2015/m=9/news=independent-ethics-committee-bans-jack-warner-from-football-related-ac-2701902.html (accessed 1 January 2018).. That Blazer and Warner could embezzle, deceive and exploit the football world, manipulating decisions and financial deals, for so long confirms the vulnerability of a global sport governance model in which pseudo-diplomacy has masked personal interests and criminal aggrandisement, and minimal transparency and accountability across the organisation and its networks have encouraged the racketeering that attracted the attention of the US authorities.

54 Alan Tomlinson, *A Dictionary of Sports Studies* (Oxford: Oxford University Press, 2010), 74. See too, for an application to the question of race to the Olympic rhetoric, Ben Carrington, 'Cosmopolitan Olympism, humanism and the spectacle', in John Bale and Mette Krogh Christensen (eds), *Post-Olympism? Questioning Sport in the Twenty-first Century* (Oxford: Berg Publishers, 2004).

55 Toby Miller, *Cultural Citizenship: Cosmopolitanism, Consumerism and Television in a Neoliberal Age* (Philadelphia, PA: Temple University Press, 2007), 179.

56 Miller, *Cultural Citizenship*, 179.

4

Mega sports events as political tools: a case study of South Africa's hosting of the 2010 FIFA Football World Cup

Suzanne Dowse

Although predominantly justified in economic terms,[1] mega sport events (MSEs) are widely perceived as political opportunities in relation to urban regeneration,[2] public diplomacy and soft power accrual.[3] However, while these ambitions are well recognised, the frequent recurrence of a disconnect or 'disjoint' between projected costs and benefits has resulted in a growing number of cities, including Oslo, Stockholm, Krakow, Boston and Hamburg, withdrawing their candidature from hosting opportunities.[4] This development concerns sporting organisations and to the outsider is interesting because the disjoint essentially emerges from efforts to secure the civic support required for the significant public subsidisation hosting entails. The need for this public endorsement is also recognised in encouraging an emphasis on benefits with high social value. Such things as job creation and infrastructure development contest with more abstract policy priorities like soft power and international status that may underpin political support for hosting opportunities and thereby also contribute to the disjoint between promoted and actual outcomes. Closing the gap is complicated because the opportunities presented by MSEs' hosting processes, whether they be tangible such as infrastructure development or intangible such as soft power potential, are frequently accepted as 'social facts' established via a process of repeated articulation rather than a robust and contextually informed evidence base capable of informing an effective strategic policy approach.[5] The popular rejection of hosting opportunities highlights the fragility of the situation, but achieving the required strategic evidence-based policy approach requires much more knowledge of what works in which contexts and how. This is particularly important given the current relocation of MSEs to developing country contexts where the political priorities and policy implications of hosting are likely to be somewhat different from those in developed countries and may offer political sciences another lens through which to explore and understand contemporary international relations and politics.[6]

As a developing country that sits on the semi-periphery of international relations, South Africa's hosting of the 2010 FIFA Football World Cup (FWC) provided an ideal opportunity to explore the potential for MSE studies to offer insight into contemporary international relations and the policy tools available to states at different stages of development. The findings presented in this chapter provide discussion points concerning the position of 'Middle Powers' within the international community and suggest that South Africa's political elite prioritised the foreign policy potential of the event to the detriment of the heavily promoted domestic goals which were used to justify the significant public subsidy involved.[7] Policy documents and interviews with key policy stakeholders confirmed that the political elite viewed the FWC as a means of improving the country's regional and international standing. The expectation among that elite was that this would develop meaningful foreign policy capacity essentially through the accrual of soft power generated by the presentation of South Africa as an attractive and capable regional power. Observers of South Africa's political history will be unsurprised at this expectation given that international sport has been used throughout the country's history as a tool (internally and externally) to sanction or support the country's political status and policy behaviour.[8] However, this history did not necessarily place politicians and policy stakeholders in a better position to maximise the event potential and minimise the risks involved. Analysis of the disjoint that emerged between anticipated and realised outcomes indicated that weaknesses in policy stakeholders' understandings of the dynamics of event delivery processes certainly inhibited efforts to manage the hosting initiative across the range of domestic and foreign policy areas, leading to unforeseen and in some cases unhelpful outcomes. These findings therefore reinforce the calls made for greater engagement by political scientists in the study of MSEs in order to improve the policy approach to hosting opportunities.[9]

South Africa's journey to FIFA 2010

The expectations held for the 2010 FWC in South Africa by the political elite, policy practitioners and public alike cannot be divorced from the country's history and socio-political environment which inform its contemporary domestic and foreign policy priorities and capacity to achieve them. Therefore it is important to recognise that, despite being one of the most powerful actors in the African continent, South Africa is a relatively new democracy and one that is continually challenged by apartheid legacies of social polarisation. These legacies include a domestic environment characterised by civil instability, extensive inequality and extreme poverty, all of which are reflected in policy preferences at national and sub-national levels.[10] Problematically, the capacity to improve these important policy goals, which include public service delivery improvement and the development of an inclusive national identity, is heavily compromised by weaknesses in decision making and policy implementation capacity. Similarly, as a significant regional actor South Africa exhibits the core characteristics of an emerging Middle Power, including ambitions for regional leadership and international influence which manifest in a regional policy preoccupation, the prioritisation of multilateral activity and pursuit of reform in global institutions.[11] Yet here, too, progress is challenged by apartheid legacies that undermine the country's regional relations and reputation, with the result that leadership ambitions are frequently internationally recognised and regionally resisted. In short, South Africa does not possess the soft power resources of appealing and legitimately perceived power, values and moral authority required for consensual hegemony.[12] To complicate matters further, the country's foreign policy ambitions are also frustrated by tensions between regional and international priorities which reduce progress at both levels.[13] Such tensions include, for example, the difficulties inherent in balancing Western normative expectations concerning free market liberal capitalism and democracy with pan-African interests and implementation capabilities.[14] These tensions were demonstrated, for example, in early 2000, when the South African government endorsed a developmental state policy orientation, but then pursued neoliberal policies of economic development which favour the market. This contradictory policy approach made the government appear uncommitted to African development and damaged its regional credibility.[15]

Alongside South Africa's domestic and foreign policy landscape, the country's historical engagement with international sport and the related social significance of sport provide important context for understanding the political motivations and expectations for the 2010 FWC. Colonial sports policies, international sports boycotts and, more latterly, event hosting all feature prominently in this history, which is replete with examples of how sport has been used to support, promote and defend political and civic interests.[16] Chief among these examples is the internationally recognised milestone in the country's post-apartheid history, the 1995 Rugby World Cup (RWC) which following, almost immediately, South Africa's democratisation, took place during a time where perceptions of the country were becoming more positively inclined and a process of re-engagement with international political and sport communities was underway.[17] The impact of the event was, therefore, highly contextual but nevertheless served to establish the RWC as a reference point for the political utility of sport-event hosting.[18] At the time the utility perceived was grounded in the symbolic and communication value of the event, observed in a foreign policy capacity as the ability to signal South Africa's readmission into the world community following the extensive period of anti-apartheid isolation. It was also recognised in a domestic policy capacity as support given to the post-apartheid process of nation building by facilitating and demonstrating racial reconciliation at the community level.

In both spheres of policy the importance of symbolism and the capacity of the event to facilitate a message of reconciliation and acceptance were and continue to be demonstrated by recourse to images of the internationally acclaimed moment when Nelson Mandela, the symbolic leader of the anti-apartheid movement, awarded the winner's trophy to Francois Pienaar, the captain of the national team in a sport associated with apartheid, while wearing a team shirt.[19] Yet while the symbolic value of this moment should not be dismissed, the depth and sustainability of the outcomes associated with it should not be taken for granted. For example, it has been suggested that the media hype and the euphoria surrounding the national team's victory misrepresented a temporary event-led display of domestic unity.[20] Such debates do not reject the positioning of the RWC as a positive social experience that gave the country domestic and international kudos and accordingly endorse the symbolic value attached to event hosting. However, they are important because they draw attention to the challenges inherent in achieving meaningful and sustained outcomes from hosting opportunities in relation to complex domestic and foreign policy issues.

As established in literature that reviews policy interventions, effective remedies are grounded in multi-faceted and sustained approaches that address the diversity of underlying problems and need a supportive socio-political environment if they are to endure.[21] These requisites were not in place for the 1995 RWC because the opportunities were unanticipated in the planning stage and the subsequent policy environment has been continually compromised by the failure to meet popular expectations for an improved quality of life under democracy.[22]

The salient point is that MSEs used as policy tools should be treated like any other policy intervention in terms of approach and expectations. Core to this proposition is that it is unreasonable to expect any event to deliver meaningful and sustained practical policy outcomes if it is not incorporated within a multidimensional and strategic policy approach that emphasises the achievement of the policy priority over event delivery priorities or those of the event owner.[23] Indeed, it may be reasonable to suggest that the impact of the RWC was to detract attention from this important caveat because its impact was atypically amplified by the unique socio-political landscape of the time, but this important contextual feature has not been accommodated routinely in expectations for events as policy tools. There is therefore some distance to travel to the more appropriate position whereby widely perceived opportunities associated with events, like symbolic messaging and re-imaging capacities, are not considered positive outcomes by default, and nor is the ability to obtain such outcomes uncritically applied to broader policy goals. The point is particularly important in relation to events held in developing country contexts, as they are promoted as an effective response to multiple and broad-reaching policy goals but paradoxically may emerge as barriers to realisation of these goals. This is because the resource implications and political value invested in events tend to absorb the human and financial capital that would otherwise be invested in the pursuit and delivery of social and foreign policy priorities. Evidence of this problem is, unfortunately, widely available, as has been demonstrated by media reports concerning the Commonwealth Games in Dehli 2010 and the FWC in Brazil 2014.[24]

With the benchmark established by the RWC, South Africa's subsequent pursuit of a range of hosting opportunities, including the Olympic Games and FWC, can be considered understandable, despite the fact that continuing instability raised important questions about the wisdom and/or capacity to host successfully.[25] Narratives surrounding the pursuit of these ambitions establish a continuation of the political value and utility of hosting opportunities which were used to send a variety of political messages that were nuanced according to the prevalent interests of the ANC leadership.[26] For example, the bid for the 2006 FWC was used to support regional leadership ambitions and efforts to change the terms of African and South African engagement with the international community. This was done through the framing of event-bid narratives in neo-colonial terms that reflected the region's history and positioned the structures and relations of the international community as unjust and responsible for the continued marginalisation and depression of the developing world.[27] Within this discourse, the award process was positioned as a symbolic test of the international community's commitment to a moral obligation to support progress in Africa.[28] Consequently, when the event was subsequently awarded to Germany, a highly developed European country, the decision could be derided as evidence of the continued intent to 'marginalise' the continent as an 'irrelevant appendage' in international affairs.[29]

The allegations of bribery and corruption that surrounded the bid award suggest that it was the personal interests of FIFA stakeholders rather than the prevailing asymmetry of power relations in the international community that drove the award decision.[30] However, the strength with which South Africa's (then) president Thabo Mbeki positioned the event as a proxy for ostensibly unrelated political objectives established a particularly strong political status for the FWC in a way that supports Scarlett Cornelissen's observation that hosting opportunities may be particularly valuable alternative policy tools for countries disadvantaged by resource limitations in comparison to their developed and industrialised peers.[31] Certainly, if apposite, this observation helps to explain the increased competition for such events among developing countries, given the risks they carry in terms of resource implications and prescriptive hosting requirements that are weighted towards the event owners' commercial and business interests.[32] The political status invested in the symbolic messaging status of the FWC bid award process made a South African bid for the 2010 event highly likely. However, while it has been suggested that the application for the 2010 event was essentially a reflexive response to the failure of the earlier bid, in similarity to MSE narratives generally, public support was encouraged by positioning the initiative as a strategic response to social priorities in economic development terms supported by impressive, albeit unrealistic, figures for tourism and job creation.[33] This twin domestic and foreign policy dynamic makes the South African 2010 FWC an interesting diplomatic study, particularly in terms of the ability to understand the expectations held for the event by political and policy stakeholders and the reality of the hosting experience.

The 2010 FIFA Football World Cup

South Africa's projection of the economic potential of the 2010 hosting opportunity firmly aligned with the recurrent findings of mega-event evaluations that pre-event predictions are invariably unjustifiably optimistic.[34] Yet, despite the established scepticism concerning the economic business case for MSEs, the figures released duly evolved into 'social facts' that underpinned popular *and* political expectations.[35] Likewise, significant infrastructure development across the country was presented as integral to this economic potential and a substantial dimension of the tangible legacy that hosting would deliver. Such an expectation was prevalent across South Africa at national and local government level. Officers involved in the project explained this in terms of the ability to use the event to bring forward planned or important projects as a result of the access provided to national funding and an immovable delivery deadline:[36]

> If [a city] needs money and it is linked to the Football World Cup then it is unlocked. Usually the Treasury gives it to the Province who gives it to the District who delegates it to the Municipality. Under the Football World Cup the money is passed straight from the National Treasury to the Municipality.[37]

However, while this expectation is not unique to South Africa, it should be recognised that to be truly developmental the activity catalysed by hosting processes must align with national and local priorities. Problematically, while invariably presented in these terms, the evidence from previous events is inconclusive and this certainly emerged as a feature of the South African experience:[38]

> To maximise the return, we wanted Athlone right up until after the bid was awarded. When it was made Green Point then the decision was taken to maximise the other objectives. Athlone would have presented an opportunity to develop a new growth nodule for the city, linked to Athlone Towers and the upgraded train station. Upgrades that were made for the 2004 Olympic Games ... The City was shocked at the decision, but it was either agree or not be part of the event. The decision was then made to make the best of it.[39]

Essentially this developmental issue is a result of tensions between the needs and interests of the event and those of the host state. Managing these tensions is invariably challenging given the power of event owners and reputational risks attached to delivering a prestigious sports contest under a judgemental global media spotlight. However, it appeared in South Africa that these inherent challenges were exacerbated by the government's prioritisation of the symbolic and re-imaging capacity of the FWC over the development opportunities promoted as a driver for the hosting project. A number of issues pointed towards this ordering of priorities, including a preoccupation with meeting the terms of hosting agreements which was embedded into event-planning processes and established event interests as the priority concern.[40] The consequent vulnerability of local needs became evident when conflicting interests or resource constraints forced a choice between pro-event and pro-local decisions. This situation was exemplified by one local government officer who explained that, although national funding had protected service delivery to an extent, roads to stadiums came before roads to villages.[41] It also became evident in the displacement of local communities to make way for event infrastructure that would have limited, if any, long–term value to them which was reported in both domestic and international press. This included the displacement of school facilities in Mombela to make way for the development of a new stadium that generated social unrest and compromised the education and well-being of affected students.[42] As a result, the 'legacy' of event-led development described by those interviewed appeared not only to be piecemeal, but also in a number of cases regressive – a situation that one city official suggested was largely attributable to the absence of a nationally driven strategic plan for development that would have supported the country moving forward collectively in line with a common focus.[43] Consequently, it became clear that although the potential for event-led development exists, conflicting delivery interests ensure that it is an extremely challenging goal to achieve and one that is dependent on political prioritisation and support. The information available suggests that this was not the case in South Africa and instead the economic development rationale provided a domestically palatable cover for political ambitions that were driven by the symbolic capacity of MSE hosting to demonstrate international political recognition.

The evidence also suggests that in addition to the value attached to securing hosting rights as a means of demonstrating international recognition, South Africa's political elite believed that the FWC presented an opportunity to modify the country's national image and improve its international position. This belief was articulated by (then) Deputy President Jacob Zuma, who described hosting as an opportunity to dispel 'preconceived notions and prejudices' about Africa and restore the continent's 'rightful place on the global stage'.[44] As such the hosting project was clearly perceived as a channel for diplomacy and, by association, a rational response to the foreign policy goal of communicating and redefining the terms of the country and continent's engagement with the international community.[45] Zuma's statement presents the issue of hosting rights as an issue of justice for the African continent, and this framing allowed South Africa's achievement of the 2010 event to be presented as a gain made on behalf of the continent in support of regional leadership ambitions.[46] In defining the event award decision in this way, Zuma continued to utilise the post-colonial narratives employed in the bid processes for the 2006 and 2010 event and, in so doing, provided an example of how Middle Powers may seek the revision of disadvantageous global norms and structures using processes and forums beyond those of traditional governance.[47] However, the 'justice' perceived in the award was arguably chimeric because it seemed that FIFA exploited the contractual process and South Africa's fear of failure under the global spotlight to maximise its return in apparent disregard of the domestic impact created:

> The Host City agreement which the City signed with FIFA for the 2010 World Cup had onerous provisions which had the potential to expose the City in fulfilling its contractual requirements. The City in many instances would be contractually required to meet FIFA requirements irrespective of whether these requirements were reasonable or not. These absolute obligations imposed on the City, to in effect meet whatever FIFA required to ensure a successful event, made the task of protecting the City's interests very difficult.[48]

Information concerning FIFA's resistance to amending restrictive contractual terms vis-à-vis the joint Belgium–Holland bid for the 2018/22 tournaments confirms that this approach was not unique to South Africa.[49] However, a number of those interviewed suggested that the value placed on the hosting opportunity by the political elite, together with the country's subordinate position within the international community, meant that it was particularly vulnerable to this exploitation. This under-standing was explained through reference to an inability to set boundaries around what could be reasonably expected from the host and a lack of political confidence necessary to resist 'requirements' that could compromise domestic interests:

> The framework is not the same, the context, as the level of development is differ-ent which meant there were additional requirements. But, more than this, South Africa really wanted the event, wanted to stage and host the World Cup so any institutional guarantee would have been done to the extent that it would not expose the country to problems.[50]

> Germany was in a different place in the approach to the event, it was self-confident as a mature state with the required infrastructure in place. FIFA has extracted more from South Africa. For example, the South African Government feels inclined to support FIFA's rules and requirements regarding ticketing which prohibit third party transfers. In Germany this is allowed and FIFA was not allowed to infringe on this right. German civil laws prevail over FIFA's.[51]

If apposite, these observations lend support to the potential for the study of global sports processes to provide International Relations scholars with an empirical channel for exploring theories concerning inter-state relations and norm development with international relations.[52] For example, FIFA's behaviour towards South Africa argua-bly reflects relations between entities occupying the core and the periphery.[53] Likewise, the way in which political communities, within South Africa and beyond, perceive hosting MSEs as 'normal' activity for states of a certain international standing suggests that it is or has evolved from a marker of distinction into benchmark of development.[54] In terms of the policy potential perceived in MSEs this is an important consideration, as if the exceptionalism of hosting is declining it may mean that expectations for increased influence or position within the international community become harder to achieve as a result of a reduced symbolic impact. These issues were illustrated by comments made by a member of the international diplomatic community who was sceptical of the depth and sustainability of the symbolic impact of hosting because it was normal practice for states of a certain level of development. By association this means that countries that do not host may be considered under-developed:

> I don't believe that South Africa will get all the congratulations that it thinks it will. Especially not from the developed countries where this kind of achievement, hosting a mega-event, is the norm. There will be a few pats on the back, but nothing long term.[55]

Problematically, identifying how far the status and image potential of an event actually meet expectations and may, as a result, increase the host's capacity to act within the international political community is difficult to determine. Essentially, this is because the soft power resources of positive appeal and reputation that hosting may enhance are intangible and affect the environment for foreign policy decision making rather than specific policy decisions.[56] It is also because research concerning national image change, while supportive of the potential for an event-led modification, does not appear to support the potential for an event to independently catalyse sustained and meaningful change. Primarily, this is because national images tend to be stable and although entrenched stereotypes may respond to counter-messages, the modification achieved is likely to be temporary if they are received in isolation from a broader and sustained pattern of evidence-based messaging that is consistent with the image change sought.[57] Finally, whether an image change actually results in behavioural changes within international tourism, business and political communities is unclear.[58]

When the information concerning the requirements for sustained image change is reviewed in the context of the knowledge base concerning events, it also appears that hosting may generate unhelpful outcomes even when the event is successfully delivered. For example, mega-events certainly offer the basis for the long-term strategic approach deemed essential for image change because they elevate media interest from the point of award to an undefined legacy period and thereby provide a means of increasing public, business and political audiences and projecting potentially influential public diplomacy messages. However, the longer award-to-games time period is frequently characterised by negative reporting that raises questions about hosting capabilities.[59] Sport-associated marketing also tends to be general rather than targeted in response to the diverse characteristics of global audiences.[60] Finally, as reporting of Brazil's hosting of the 2014 FWC and 2016 Olympic Games illustrates, the increased attention catalysed by the event can raise the profile of the host's more negative attributes, serving to reinforce existing stereotypes, present the event as a temporary anomaly and undermine positive public diplomacy messages.[61] This means that countries that do not have stable domestic environments, like those in the developing world, are less likely to benefit from the image opportunities presented.[62] They may also have fewer resources with which to develop a strategic approach that encompasses the full event life-cycle and is capable of managing the risks that accompany intense global media attention.[63]

In South Africa the range of problematic issues raised above was unfortunately evident, although this is not to suggest that positive impacts were absent. For example, it appeared strongly that efforts to rehabilitate international perceptions of the country and continent underway outside of the FWC project were not integrated effectively with event planning processes.[64] This possibility emerged during interviews with host city stakeholders which suggested that local approaches tended to be games-time focused. It was also supported by the findings of an FWC delivery needs analysis workshop held in 2007 which identified that media issues had not been meaningfully considered. Likewise, feedback from members of the diplomatic core based in South Africa confirmed a perceived 'double edge' to the media attention South Africa was receiving because it was drawing attention to the country's continuing social problems experienced in ways that could compromise the image of progress projected through the hosting project. Therefore, while the country undoubtedly received overwhelmingly positive games-time reporting, it is possible that the impact was moderated by the negative coverage received in the longer pre-event period and the increased profile of the country's broader social problems which aligned with pre-existing stereotypes. It is also possible that these issues were compounded by the extended public sector strike that followed the event which had the potential to position delivery capabilities as anomalous.[65] These possibilities are not clarified by the available information reviewed. For example, a BBC World Poll taken after the event suggests that they were not influential, as a pre-existing trend of continental image improvement was sustained.[66] However, this trend was not reflected in the Anholt Nation Brands Index, which reported a fall in South Africa's position between 2009 and 2010 that was not recovered in 2011.[67] In the absence of confirmation either way, it is perhaps prudent to recognise that hosting processes may generate unexpected and unhelpful outcomes and promote the need to accommodate this in planning approaches.

The difficulties inherent in evaluating the impact of MSE processes on a country's national image are equally salient in explorations of the soft power potential of hosting in terms of the host's supportive relational networks. These challenges arise because such relations are also intangible and influence the foreign policy decision-making environment rather than specific policy decisions that could be causally related to a World Cup effect. In line with this understanding, policy officers in South Africa generally agreed that hosting had contributed positively to the country's foreign policy environment, but only as part of a broader set of activities designed towards this end: 'From the point we won the bid we were right in the centre of the discussion. We got in a position where we could galvanise and organise support in the African Continent … It was an opportunity to be seen to be pulling together.'[68] This outcome was generally anticipated; therefore of greater interest was the way in which the hosting experience was viewed as developing a previously absent confidence in and within South Africa in ways that would help the pursuit of national interests going forward. The confidence generated *in* South Africa was arguably a core aim in relation to addressing the perceived underpinnings of international power imbalances and the limited ability to influence international decision making. The confidence generated *within* South Africa did not have a similar profile in expectations and was therefore especially interesting. There were two inter-related dimensions to this internal confidence. One aspect was the popular confidence generated in the ability of public sector organisations to operate effectively. The other was the way in which hosting processes had catalysed self-belief in those working within public sector organisations that they could be effective within their roles. This latter development was perceived as particularly important in the context of the significant political and public sector restructure that had taken place following democratisation which involved a significant expansion of responsibilities. While a restructure of this size alone would have overwhelmed the delivery capabilities of South Africa's public sector organisations at least temporarily, the challenges involved were compounded by austerity measures and policies designed to achieve a demographically reflective workforce which increased the number of black civil servants by displacing those that under other circumstances would have mentored them through the organisational change underway.[69] The net effect was to undermine the capacity for effective public service delivery and this was viewed as personally affecting delivery stakeholders. The hosting experience was therefore viewed as important because the demonstrated capacity to deliver a national project on time and in line with international standards provided a source of pride and confidence. These benefits, together with the skills and experience gained, were expected to enhance individual capacities for decisive and proactive behaviour going forward. It appeared that aspects of this behaviour were in evidence following the World Cup. For example, one diplomat highlighted that South Africa was displaying a new and 'surprising' level of autonomy in the conduct of foreign policy.[70] Although not causally linked to the FWC, it is possible that the combination of internal and external confidence inspired by the successful delivery supported a more determined pursuit of policy interests. Consequently, it may be reasonable to suggest that hosting processes may have particularly valuable state building or at least public sector development benefits that have yet to be fully recognised in discussions of the domestic and foreign policy potential of events.

Alongside the positive developments, potential compressions of soft power resources in terms of political relations and reputation were also identified and similarly difficult to evaluate.[71] In part this was because the full details were not made available, but mainly it was due to the difficulties inherent in assessing the substantive impact of problems that emerged in relation to the FWC, like the unhelpful inter-state exchanges on the country's broader and more intangible domestic and foreign policy environments that took place during the preparation process. For example, the event-associated safety and security concerns of one state had introduced a level of friction into relations with South Africa although representatives for both countries believed that broader bilateral engagement was unlikely to be affected.[72] However, these views are highly debatable because if it is to be accepted that positive impacts transcend the event and influence broader diplomatic relations, then the same has to be accepted as applicable to impacts of a negative nature. Certainly, this broader potential was supported by interviewee feedback (ibid.), which indicated that hosting processes could provide specific circles of political networks with helpful and unhelpful reference points. However, explanations of the incident described above indicated that the FWC issue essentially placed already strained relations under additional stress, which then suggests that MSEs essentially work to amplify the core features of inter-state relations which may be unhelpful in some cases. Consequently, governments seeking to use events as a policy tool for the development of diplomatic capabilities need to be alert to this potential in order to manage the risks involved.

The final consideration raised in this analysis is the very specific regional diplomacy dimension to South Africa's foreign policy aims for the 2010 FWC, which was emphasised in the promotion of the event as the 'African World Cup'. This was an unusual framing because the FWC is predominantly, if not exclusively, presented in national terms. For example, the 2006 World Cup in Germany was never promoted as the 'European' World Cup nor was the 2002 World Cup in Japan and South Korea promoted as the 'Asian' World Cup. However, although atypical, this framing firmly aligned with the regional orientation of South Africa's post-apartheid government and generated issues that reflected the country's broader difficulties in balancing conflicting regional and international foreign policy interests.[73] These included the tensions inherent in projecting the country as regionally integrated in line with its 'African' interests and the need to promote a regional exceptionalism in order to allay international stereotypes that conflate all African states as similarly insecure, brought into stark relief by the Cup of Nations terrorist attack in Angola.[74] This challenge aside, it was also unclear whether stakeholders had sufficiently considered the potential to project a meaningful collective identity through an event which, owing to sponsorship branding and a media focus on match venues, individualises attention to the host country.[75] These points notwithstanding, both policy officers and regional representatives based in South Africa perceived the African emphasis as supportive of regional relations because it was a highly visible demonstration of commitment to regional policy pledges, offered relation-building opportunities and broadened the range of competencies associated with the country's political elite. However, these observations were once again positioned as part of a wider process of regional relation-building activity from which the event could not be isolated. This reinforces the broader point made throughout this chapter that events used as policy tools should be similarly approached in terms of expectations, management and evaluation.

Conclusion

South Africa's political elite presented the 2010 FWC as an opportunity to support a range of policy priorities. However, although justified in domestic and largely economic policy terms, the way in which the government systematically prioritised event interests over these social concerns suggests that it was diplomatic potential of securing foreign policy interests and developing soft power resources through symbolic messaging and image rehabilitation opportunities that underpinned the political value associated with the hosting opportunity. Whether this external focus is particular to South Africa or applies more generally to the broader array of countries that now seek to host sport mega-events is unclear. The additional challenges experienced by developing country hosts would suggest that, for these countries at least, this is likely to be the case. However, the increased salience of soft power resources in international relations equally supports the potential for it to be a more general trend affecting developing and developed countries alike. It is also possible that South Africa's distinct, and atypical, regional emphasis for the World Cup and framing of the award decision as 'justice' achieved for a continent routinely marginalised by the international community could be considered an expression of 'Middle Powership' in international relations.[76]

The research presented also suggests that there are other event-led outcomes worthy of further exploration, like the ability of hosting processes to support state-building activities by developing the confidence, skills and experience required for the effective pursuit of policy priorities. It seems likely in view of South Africa's weaknesses in this area that, had such potential been recognised in the planning stages, the country may have gained an incredibly valuable legacy. Certainly it would be worth exploring the depth of this potential with future hosts, as it is possible that mega-event hosting may offer the international community a politically palatable avenue for supporting state building in developing countries. This is because it provides a means of developing capacity in government departments involved in the delivery of important and complex national projects in a way that could ameliorate sensitivities concerning external interventions in domestic policy arenas.[77]

The final point to draw from the South African hosting experience is that an event pursued as an instrument of policy should be considered in similar ways to any other policy intervention. In short, MSEs are not transformational tools that are independently capable of altering the deep structures of a country's domestic or foreign policy landscape. To have meaningful and sustainable results they need to be embedded within broader strategic policy processes, and even this may be insufficient if negative issues emerge in broader socio-political environments. To support the better use of MSEs as policy interventions, more work needs to be done to help policy developers understand the challenges inherent in delivery processes and the requirements for successful policy interventions. Left unresolved, the likelihood is that the disjoint between expectations and outcomes will remain, particularly if an event is sold on the basis of one set of policy preferences, yet used to pursue others.

Notes

1 V. Matheson, 'Mega-events: the effect of the world's biggest sporting events on local, regional, and national economies', College of The Holy Cross, *Department of Economics Faculty Research Series*, Paper No.06–10, 2006, available at http://college. holycross.edu/RePEc/hcx/Matheson_MegaEvents.pdf (accessed 2 March 2011).

2 C. Gratton and I. Henry (eds), *Sport in the City: The Role of Sport in Economic and Social Regeneration* (London: Routledge, 2001); C. Matheson, 'Legacy planning, regeneration and events: the Glasgow 2014 Commonwealth Games', *Local Economy*, 25:1 (2010); A. Smith, '"De-risking" East London: Olympic regeneration planning 2000–2012', *European Planning Studies*, 22:9 (2014).

3 R. Levermore and A. Budd (eds), *Sport and International Relations: An Emerging Relationship?* (London: Routledge and Taylor and Francis Group, 2004); S. Murray and G. Allen Pigman, 'Mapping the relationship between international sport and diplomacy', *Sport in Society: Cultures, Commerce, Media, Politics*, 17:9 (2014); W. Manzenreiter, 'The Beijing Games in the Western imagination of China: the weak power of soft power', *Journal of Sport and Social Issues*, 34:1 (2010); J. Grix and B. Houlihan, 'Sports mega-events as part of a nation's soft power strategy: the cases of Germany (2006) and the UK (2012)', *British Journal of Politics and International Relations*, 16 (2014).

4 R. Baade and V. Matheson, 'Bidding for the Olympics: fool's gold?', in C. Barros, M. Ibrahimo and S. Szymanski (eds), *Transatlantic Sport* (London: Edward Elgar, 2002), 127–51; L. Abend, 'Why nobody wants to host the 2022 Winter Olympics', *Time Magazine*, 3 October 2014, available at http://time.com/3462070/olympics-winter-2022/ (accessed 8 July 2016); K. Grohman, 'Hamburg withdrawal no major

concern at IOC', *Reuters*, 9 December 2015, available at http://uk.reuters.com/article/uk-olympics-hamburg-idUKKBN0TS14X20151209?feedType=RSS&feedName=sportsNews (accessed 12 January 2016); K. Seelye, 'Boston's bid for Summer Olympics is terminated', *New York Times*, 27 July 2015, available at www.nytimes.com/2015/07/28/sports/olympics/boston-2024-summer-olympics-bid-terminated.html (accessed 7 July 2016).

5 S. Cornelissen, 'Scripting the nation: sport, mega-events, foreign policy and state building in post-apartheid South Africa', *Sport in Society*, 11:4 (2008)3; M. Weed and S. Dowse, 'A missed opportunity waiting to happen? The social legacy potential of the London 2012 Paralympic Games', *Journal of Policy Research in Tourism, Leisure and Events*, 1:2 (2009).

6 D. Black and J. van der Westhuizen, 'The allure of global games for "semi-peripheral" polities and spaces: a research agenda', *Third World Quarterly*, 25:7 (2004); J. Grix and D. Lee, 'Soft power, sports mega-events and emerging states: the lure of the politics of attraction', *Global Society*, 27:4 (2013).

7 E. Jordaan, 'The concept of middle power in international relations: distinguishing between emerging and traditional middle powers', *Politikon*, 30:2 (2003).

8 P. Hain, *Don't Play with Apartheid: The Background to the Stop The Seventy Tour Campaign* (London: George Allen & Unwin, 1971); R. Archer and A. Bouillon, *The South African Game: Sport and Racism* (London: Zed Press, 1982); J. van der Merwe, 'Political analysis of South Africa's hosting of the Rugby and Cricket World Cups: lessons for the 2010 Football World Cup and beyond', *Politikon*, 34:1 (2007).

9 D. Black, 'Dreaming big: the pursuit of "second order" games as a strategic response to globalisation', *Sport in Society*, 11:4 (2008).

10 South Africa: The Presidency, State of the Nation Address of the President of South Africa, Thabo Mbeki, Houses of Parliament, Cape Town, 14 February 2003, available at www.info.gov.za/speeches/2003/03021412521001.htm (accessed 5 May 2010).

11 M. Schoeman, 'South Africa as an emerging middle power: 1994–2003', in J. Daniel, A. Habib and R. Southall (eds), *State of the Nation: South Africa 2003–2004* (Cape Town: Human Sciences Research Council Press, 2003), 349–67, available at www.hsrcpress.ac.za (accessed 12 March 2012).

12 C. Alden and G. le Pere, 'South Africa in Africa: bound to lead?', *Politikon*, 36:1 (2009).

13 M. Lipton, 'Understanding South Africa's foreign policy: the perplexing case of Zimbabwe', *South African Journal of International Affairs*, 16:3 (2009).

14 L. Nathan, 'Consistency and inconsistency in South African foreign policy', *International Affairs*, 81:2 (2005).

15 P. Kagwanja, 'Introduction: uncertain democracy – elite fragmentation and the disintegration of the "nationalist consensus" in South Africa', in P. Kagwanje and K. Kondlo (eds), *State of the Nation: South Africa 2008* (Cape Town: Human Sciences Research Council Press, 2009): xv–1, available at http://www.hsrcpress.co.za (accessed 21 November 2010).

16 G. Jarvie, *Class, Race and Sport in South Africa's Political Economy* (London: Routledge & Kegan Paul, 1985); M. Bose, *Sporting Colours: Sport and Politics in South Africa* (London: Robson Books, 1994).

17 D. Black and J. Nauright, *Rugby and the South African Nation: Sport, Cultures, Politics, and Power in the Old and New South Africas* (Manchester: Manchester University Press, 1998).

18 J. Carlin, *Playing the Enemy: Nelson Mandela and the Game that Made a Nation* (London: Atlantic Books, 2008).
19 Carlin, *Playing the Enemy*.
20 A. Grundlingh, 'From redemption to recidivism? Rugby and change in South Africa during the 1995 Rugby World Cup and its aftermath', *Sporting Traditions*, 14:2 (1998); Van der Merwe, 'Political analysis of South Africa's hosting of the Rugby and Cricket World Cups'.
21 Mike Collins, 'Sport, physical activity and social exclusion', *Journal of Sports Sciences*, 22 (2004).
22 Interview, RWC Delivery Manager, 2010; S. Terreblanche, 'the developmental state in South Africa: the difficult road ahead', inKagwanja and Kondlo (eds), *State of the Nation*, 107–30, available at www.hsrcpress.ac.za (accessed 21 January 2010).
23 A. Smith, 'Leveraging sport mega-events: new model or convenient justification?', *Journal of Policy Research in Tourism, Leisure and Events*, 6:1 (2014).
24 Reuters, 'Brazil 2014: less than half of country favour hosting World Cup', *The Telegraph*, available at www.telegraph.co.uk/sport/football/world-cup/10752888/Brazil-2014-less-than-half-of-country-favour-hosting-World-Cup.html (accessed 12 January 2016); J. Burke, 'Delhi battling human and financial cost of hosting Commonwealth Games', *The Guardian*, available at www.theguardian.com/sport/2010/aug/04/commonwealth-games-delhi-preparations (accessed 12 January 2016).
25 H. Hiller, 'Mega-events, urban boosterism and growth strategies: an analysis of the objectives and legitimations of the Cape Town 2004 Olympic bid', *International Journal of Urban and Regional Research*, 24:2 (2000); K. Swart and U. Bob, 'The seductive discourse of development: the Cape Town 2004 Olympic bid', *Third World Quarterly*, 25:7 (2004).
26 Van Der Merwe, 'Political analysis of South Africa's hosting of the Rugby and Cricket World Cups.
27 P. Alegi, '"Feel the pull of your soul": local agency trends in South Africa's 2006 World Cup bid', *Soccer and Society*, 2:3 (2001).
28 S. Cornelissen, '"It's Africa's turn!" The narratives and legitimations surrounding the Moroccan and South African bids for the 2006 and 2010 FIFA finals', *Third World Quarterly*, 25:7 (2004).
29 BBC Online, 'Mbeki lashes Fifa', 12 July 2000, available at http://news.bbc.co.uk/1/hi/world/africa/830703.stm (accessed 1 September 2012).
30 S. Cornelissen, 'Sport mega events in South Africa: processes, impacts and prospects', *Tourism and Hospitality Planning and Development*, 1:1 (2004).
31 S. Cornelissen, 'Scripting the nation: sport, mega-events, foreign policy and state building in post-apartheid South Africa', *Sport in Society*, 11:4 (2008).
32 Van der Merwe, 'Political analysis of South Africa's hosting of the Rugby and Cricket World Cups.
33 South Africa: Portfolio Committee: Sport and Recreation, 'Soccer bid 2010 briefing, 15 April 2003', Parliamentary Monitoring Group, available at www.pmg.org.za/node/2701 (accessed 31 March 2009); Cornelissen, 'Scripting the nation', 486.
34 S. Dowse, *Power Play: International Politics, Germany, South Africa and the FIFA World Cup*™, SAIIA Occasional Paper No. 82, May 2011 (South Africa: South African Institute of International Affairs, 2011).

35 Cornelissen, 'Scripting the nation', 486.
36 R. Tomlinson, 'Anticipating 2011', in U. Pillay, R. Tomlinson and O. Bass (eds), *Development and Dreams: The Urban Legacy of the 2010 Football World Cup* (Cape Town: Human Sciences Research Council Press, 2009), 96–113.
37 Interview, Host Province Government Officer (1), 2010.
38 C. Schulz Herzenberg (ed.), *Player and Referee: Conflicting Interests and the 2010 FIFA World Cup* (Pretoria: Institute for Security Studies, 2010).
39 Interview, Host City Government Officer (1), 2010.
40 South Africa: Limpopo Provincial Government, *Draft Limpopo 2010 World Cup Masterplan/(Work in Progress) July 2007* (unpublished); South Africa: City of Johannesburg, *2010 Case Study – Report 1: Progress towards Delivering the 'Best World Cup Ever'* (Johannesburg: Office of the Executive Mayor, 2008).
41 Interview, Provincial Government Officer (3), 2011.
42 *Farenheit 2010*, directed by Craig Tanner [DVD] (Leviathan Films / Rogue Productions, South Africa, 2009).
43 Interview, City Government Officer (2), 2011.
44 South Africa: The Presidency, 'J. Zuma: handover of SA 2010 Bid Book, 29 September 2003', available at www.polity.org.za/article/j-zuma-handover-of-sa-2010-bid-book-26092003-2003-09-26 (accessed 5 May 2010).
45 Nathan, 'Consistency and inconsistency in South African foreign policy'.
46 South Africa: The Presidency, J. Zuma: handover of SA 2010 Bid Book'.
47 Cornelissen, 'Scripting the nation', 488.
48 Interview, Host City Officer (3), 2011.
49 Letter from Jörg Vollmüller, FIFA's Commercial Legal Team to Mr Henny Smorenburg for the foundation, 2018/2022 Belgium–Holland bid regarding changes made to the contractual guarantee template provided for the bid application, available at www.transparencyinsport.org/The_documents_that_FIFA_does_not_want_fans_to_read/PDF-documents/(10)FIFA-aan-NL.pdf (accessed 14 July 2016).
50 Interview, National Government Department Officer (1), 2010.
51 Interview, Foreign Policy Practitioner (1), 2010.
52 A. Beacom, 'Sport in international relations: a case for cross-disciplinary investigation', *Sport Historian*, 20:2 (2000).
53 P. Darby, 'Africa's place in FIFA's global order: a theoretical frame', *Soccer and Society*, 1:2 (2000).
54 A. Smith, 'Sporting a new image? Sport-based regeneration strategies as a means of enhancing the image of the city tourist destination', in Gratton and Henry (eds), *Sport in the City*, 144–45.
55 Interview, Diplomat (2), 2010.
56 J. Nye, *Soft Power: The Means to Success in World Politics* (USA: PublicAffairs, 2004).
57 M. Kunczik, *Images of Nations and International Public Relations* (Mahwah, NJ: Lawrence Erlbaum Associates, 1997); S. Anholt, 'Beyond the nation brand: the role of image and identity in international relations', *Exchange*, 2 (2011).
58 Smith, 'Sporting a new image?', 143.
59 MediaTenor, *WC 2010: Correct Misconceptions? Pre-World Cup Coverage of the Host of WC 2010* (South Africa: Media Tenor, 2010).
60 Smith, 'Sporting a new image?', 144.
61 BBC News, 'Brazil tracks World Cup lessons for Rio Olympics', available at www.

bbc.co.uk/news/world-latin-america-28357124 (accessed 14 July 2016); W. Worley, 'Rio de Janeriro bike path collapses, killing two ahead of2016 Olympic Games', *The Independent*, available at www.independent.co.uk/news/world/americas/rio-de-janeiro-brazil-bike-path-collapses-2016-olympic-games-a6996196.html (accessed 14 July 2016).

62 P. Dimeo and J. Kay, 'Major Sports Events, image projection and the problems of "semi-periphery": a case study of the 1996 South Asia Cricket World Cup', *Third World Quarterly*, 25:7 (2004).

63 Dimeo and Kay, 'Major Sports Events'.

64 International Marketing Council, *Brand South Africa National Communications Partnership (NCP) 2009 Conference Report*, 17 August 2009, available at www.imc.org. za/content/ncpc2010/ncp_2009 report.pdf (accessed 5 September 2012).

65 D. Smith, 'South African public sector strike "endangering lives"', *The Guardian*, available at www.theguardian.com/world/2010/aug/23/south-africa-public-sector-strike (accessed 14 July 2016).

66 BBC World Service, BBC World Service County Rating Poll 2011, available at www. bbc.co.uk/pressoffice/press releases/stories/2011/03_march/07/brazil.shtml (accessed 4 April 2011).

67 GfK Roper Public Affairs & Corporate Communications, *The Anholt-GfK Roper Nation Brands Index 2010 Report, October 2010, Prepared for: Sweden* (New York: GfK Roper Public Affairs & Corporate Communications, 2010); SouthAfrica.info, *Brand South Africa Up in the Rankings*, SouthAfrica.info, 13 October 2010, available at www.southafrica.info/business/success/brandsa-anholt11.htm#.UnZnqMsgGSM (accessed 15 September 2012).

68 Interview, National Government Department Officer (1), 2011.

69 A. Habib, Public Lecture: 'Understanding contemporary South African politics', Johannesburg, 13 May 2010.

70 Interview, Diplomat (3), 2011.

71 South Africa, *2010 FIFA World Cup South Africa: Draft Report on Government Guarantees and Obligations*, November 2010 (supplied by interviewee).

72 Interviews, National Government Department Officer (3), 2010; Diplomat (2), 2010.

73 Nathan, 'Consistency and inconsistency in South African foreign policy'.

74 Interview with National Government Department Officer (4), 2010.

75 A. Desai and G. Vahed, 'World Cup 2010: Africa's turn or the turn on Africa?', *Soccer and Society*, 11:1 (2010).

76 Cornelissen, 'Scripting the nation', 488.

77 S. Van de Walle and Z. Scott, 'The political role of service delivery in state-building: exploring the relevance of European history for developing countries', *Development Policy Review*, 29:1 (2011).

Part II

Public diplomacy

5

Contesting independence: colonial cultures of sport and diplomacy in Afghanistan, 1919–49

Maximilian Drephal

Introduction: Afghanistan's independence celebrations

Afghanistan became independent in 1919, and the Afghan state commemorated the moment of statal independence and the making of an Afghan nation during week-long celebrations in each following year, staging military parades, organising cultural programmes and hosting sports competitions. Amir Amanullah Khan established the festivities shortly after the declaration of Afghan independence. They initially took place in Paghman, the summer retreat of the Afghan court on the outskirts of Kabul, but were later moved to Kabul, forming an important event in the Afghan state's and diplomatic calendars. The week began with a speech by the Afghan king. According to Afghanistan's ceremonial code for the *corps diplomatique*, foreign representatives were asked to 'proceed in full official uniform with decorations to the place appointed for the Military parade where they will offer their congratulations to His Majesty'.[1] The celebrations were also known for their social life, featuring extravagant electrical illuminations of architectural structures, cinema shows, and arts and crafts exhibitions. The programme included Afghan dance and theatrical performances. Afghans 'shut up shop for a whole week'.[2] In the privacy of the Afghan court, there were garden parties and masked balls.[3] Clay pigeon shooting took place daily, and Queen Soraya, Amanullah Khan's wife, 'proved herself to be no mean performer'.[4] Horse, elephant and donkey races, ram and bull fighting, re-enactments of Afghan military history, wrestling, gymnastic displays and tent pegging, among many other events, rounded off the diverse programme.[5] The celebrations displayed Afghanistan's statal independence, its military power, its customs as well as its athletic prowess. The independence celebrations included several instances of sport, as the Afghan state sought to forge and display an Afghan nation to domestic and international audiences. Afghan athletes came to embody Afghanistan's independence in sporting contests and, according to one report, played 'to win, or at any rate not to lose, their matches in public'.[6]

The celebrations were public spectacles. They represented a special space, which allowed for contact between Kabul's cultural, political, social and diplomatic lives.[7]

For instance, the intelligence summaries of the British Legation's Military Attaché, which were usually reserved for the collection and circulation of matters of state security, commented on the opening of a café in Kabul.[8] During the independence week in 1928, Amanullah Khan articulated his social reform project, which contributed to his downfall only a few months later.[9] Attendance that year was also extraordinarily high for the 'lure of seeing an unveiled Eastern Queen', a reference to Queen Soraya's evening attire during the grand tour of 1927/28.[10] A good turnout of visitors at the independence celebrations was an important objective for the Afghan state, and attendance was, on occasion, enforced. For instance, Amanullah Khan summoned villagers in the vicinity of Paghman in order to make up for the alleged 'scantiness and apathy of the crowd'.[11] However, in the following years, Paghman and Kabul seem to have attracted large numbers of visitors and travellers.[12] The number of spectators at the sports events varied according to the spatial conditions of the venues. Contests taking place in open spaces, such as cricket, football, hockey and buzkashi, as well as the parade of the athletes, attracted larger numbers than those entertainments taking place in more confined spaces, such as tennis and billiards. While descriptions of audiences are rare, there are references to a group of 'extremely prosperous noblemen' during a rifle-shooting event in a 'small hot tent' in 1922.[13] High ticket prices of up to fifteen Kabuli rupees made some events unaffordable for the general populus.[14] Yet, with reference to the independence games of 1944:

> There is no doubt that they are extremely popular with the people and serve their main purpose which is to foster a spirit of patriotism and national unity. Throughout the week Kabul is thronged with cheerful crowds gathered from all parts of the country. The main sporting events attract thousands of interested spectators including large numbers of school boys.[15]

The sports contests during the Afghan independence celebrations provided opportunities for a competitive British–Afghan encounter on various playing fields. This chapter studies these encounters in the context of British–Afghan relations after 1919. Several moments of independence in South Asia between 1919 and 1947 set its overall timeframe. British–Afghan interactions from the early nineteenth century onwards have been marked by several violent instances, including no less than three Anglo-Afghan wars. Following two British-Indian invasions of Afghanistan during the nineteenth century, in 1839 and 1878, the Third Anglo-Afghan War in 1919 ushered in Afghanistan's independence.

Before 1919, Afghanistan's foreign affairs were conducted in consultation with British colonial officials in India, limiting Afghanistan's sovereignty to its colonially defined borders. During the negotiations following the conclusion of the Third Anglo-Afghan War in 1919, Amir Amanullah Khan insisted – like his grandfather Abdur Rahman Khan had before him – that Afghanistan's foreign relations should be conducted with the British Foreign Office in London, rather than with the colonial government of India as before 1919.[16] This demand was only partially fulfilled. While the diplomatic mission came to be labelled the 'British' Legation in Kabul, it was staffed with colonial officers, administrators and labourers from India, who arrived in Kabul in early 1922. This pattern would remain: between 1922 and 1947, the majority of the Legation's diplomats were recruited from the colonial services in India, first and foremost from the Indian Political Service, which in turn drew its members from the Indian Army and the Indian Civil Service.[17] As the 'diplomatic corps of the government of India', the Indian Political Service administered colonial India's relations with the Indian princes, as well as with neighbouring polities in South Asia and in the Gulf.[18] Throughout the nineteenth cenutry, the colonial state in India contributed, materially, financially and epistemologically, to the shaping of the Afghan polity, variously conceived of as Elphinstone's kingdom of Kabul, the land of the Afghans and Afghanistan.[19] The transfer of colonial personnel from India into independent Afghanistan as internationally accredited diplomats of the British Legation in Kabul after 1919 laid the foundations for the continued circulation of colonial knowledge of Afghanistan beyond the temporal threshold of independence.

British diplomats in Kabul embodied colonial knowledge, expressing it in their participation in and observation of the Afghan independence celebrations and its sports contests. This series of contests attempted to support – from an Afghan perspective – and challenge – from a British-Indian point of view – the narrative of the political relations between Afghanistan, India and Britain. In this sense, the British–Afghan encounter in sport during the independence celebrations contested Afghan independence. As much as successive Afghan rulers sought to imprint the nation on to the bodies of its athletes, British diplomats in Kabul sought to challenge Afghanistan's independence. For instance, the parade of the athletes at the beginning of the independence week was perceived by the British to be '[r]ather childish but it appeals to the Afghan love of display and fosters the idea of sport'.[20] British diplomats recognised the public diplomacy dimension of the independence games *and* sought to undermine it, unsettling Afghanistan's nationalist narrative of athleticism. Others, like Francis Verner Wylie, British head of mission in Kabul from 1941 to 1943, dismissed the celebrations altogether: 'The whole thing is so ridiculously pretentious and the available resources so pathetically meagre and yet so bravely tricked out that sometimes I hardly knew whether to laugh or cry.'[21] The British–Afghan encounter in sport during the Afghan independence celebrations brings to light the continued presence of colonial registers of knowledge regarding Afghanistan. Even after the moment of statal independence in 1919, Afghanistan's history continued to exist in a colonial twilight that extended to and beyond the end of the Raj in 1947.

The Afghan independence festivities and the British–Afghan encounter in sport capture two trends that are of particular importance for the discussion in this chapter. First, imperial control was increasingly directed into diplomatic channels during the end of empire in South Asia. The creation of a British-Indian diplomatic mission in Afghanistan in the shape of the British Legation in Kabul in 1922 is testament to this development. During the transformation of imperial power, colonial practices and knowledge were exported from India into the wider remit of the Indian Empire, including Afghanistan. As a consequence, colonial notions regarding sport and its concomitant moral and ethical codes informed the diplomatic recording of

5.1 The photograph shows the dress code in action. Three Legation diplomats can be recognised by the *topi* in the front row

and reporting on independent nations. British diplomacy in Kabul between 1922 and 1947 was, thus, characteristically colonial in origin, practice and expression. In terms of clothing, for instance, '[t]he official dress on these occasions was a morning coat and white topee' (figure 5.1).[22]

Secondly, as a result of this transfer of colonial ideas, sport occupied a sizeable part in the culture of British diplomacy in Afghanistan. Therefore, this chapter conceptualises the Afghan independence celebrations as instances of public diplomacy, which merged the complexes of diplomacy and sport, and adds to them a colonial dimension. In other words, the colonial officers from India who practised diplomacy in Kabul emerge as colonial diplomat-athletes. The Legation's colonial physical regimes also distinguished its diplomats' self-perception: 'This friendly rivalry [during the British–Afghan encounter in sport], on the right lines, is a monopoly of our Legation, and of very great value', wrote P. C. R. Dodd, the military attaché.[23] Colonial administrators engaged in sport as leisure but also as representatives of the colonial state in public. British diplomatic culture in Afghanistan was intensely physical.[24] With their varied instances of public displays and competitions, the Afghan independence celebrations provided a stage for British diplomats to engage Afghans, quite literally, in a public sphere. The independence festivities were symbolically charged occasions, which prompted the projection of colonial notions of sport on to Afghanistan.[25]

Indian colonial administrators as diplomat-athletes in Afghanistan

The Legation staff enabled the transfer of colonial ideas from India to independent Afghanistan. They came with recommendations from the British Foreign Office and letters of accreditation from the British monarch, but returned to colonial – not diplomatic – service after their posting in Kabul. The elite members of the British Legation in Kabul were socialised in several systems of physical education and training reflecting their respective education and background. Physical education was a central aspect of the British public school curricula to which these individuals had been exposed, especially since the middle of the nineteenth century.[26] Sport was much more than a pastime. Games in particular provided and encapsulated key concepts of imperialism. Sport was 'an instrument of imperial moral persuasion'.[27] According to James Mangan's concept of the 'games ethic',

> the public schoolboy supposedly learnt inter alia the basic tools of imperial command: courage, endurance, control and self-control. However, there was a further and important dimension to the later concept of 'manliness': its relevance to both dominance and deference. It was widely believed, of course, that its inculcation promoted not simply initiative and self-reliance but also loyalty and obedience. It was, therefore, a useful instrument of colonial purpose. At one and the same time it helped create the confidence to lead and the compulsion to follow.[28]

Public schooling sought to convey an imperial culture of sport and ensure the diffusion of its ideals across the empire.[29] Universities sported their own physical cultures and led an individual to the colonial entrance exams and potentially into the colonial services. Finally, each individual colonial service had its own requirements. The *esprit de corp* of the Raj comprised all administrative layers from soldiers to governors-general and viceroys.[30] In essence, then, sport was a key element of colonial culture, which sought to prolong the physical fitness of the colonial state's personnel and display key concepts associated with imperial power.[31] As such, sport ranked among the 'colonial technologies of conquest and rule'.[32] In addition, bodies displayed powerful moral images: 'Late nineteenth-century anthropology conceived of the body as the physical outer map of the moral inner man':

> Indulging in an evening game of polo, squash, or tennis before a bath and dinner, the athletic civilian displayed his possession of an appropriate physique while simultaneously demonstrating his possession of the essential qualities of the ruling race: the ability to observe rules, loyalty and comradeship towards his team members, fair play to the other side – in other words, honesty, uprightness, courage and endurance.[33]

By the time a candidate joined the Indian Political Service, he – this was an exclusively male domain – had already been equipped with and trained in a variety of sports and games. Applications to the Indian Political Service also asked for a candidate's history of field sports and the quality of his horsemanship, making athletic exploits part of the selection process of potential colonial officers. The focus on athletic candidates contributed to the Indian Political Service's reputation of 'intellectual mediocrity'.[34] Referees were asked if a respective applicant was 'of active habits and proficient in field sports'.[35] In response, Francis Henry Humphrys, British Minister in Kabul from 1922 to 1929, was described as 'a good all-round athlete' and as a '[v]ery good' horseman.[36] He had captained the cricket team at Shrewsbury School.[37] Biographical dictionaries corroborate the centrality of physical recreation in colonial servants' lives. Humphrys's *Who Was Who* entry lists cricket, shooting and fishing, as well as aviation.[38] British Minister in Kabul from 1930 to 1935, Richard Roy Maconachie's decision to apply for the Indian Civil Service in the first place was partly due to the fact that 'life in India was preferable to life in London for anyone who loved the open air and all field sports'.[39] William Kerr Fraser-Tytler's hobbies – he was British Minister after Maconachie between 1935 and 1941 – are described as fishing, gardening and weaving.[40] Finally, Giles Frederick Squire, British Minister in Kabul from 1943 to 1948 and British ambassador from 1948 to 1949, 'played for the Occasionals at hockey when he was at Oxford, and had a talent for other ball games, especially lawn tennis'.[41] Henry Hawes Elliot, a Legation surgeon, was 'fond of tennis & hockey'. Asked if he was 'a good, bad, or indifferent horseman', the referee replied: '[g]ood'.[42] Another Legation surgeon, Edmund Stanley Sayers Lucas, 'rides, shoots, swims & plays squash'.[43] Several of the Legation members were also sportsmen of international stature. For instance, Arthur William Fagan, secretary at the Legation in the early 1920s, represented Britain in fencing at the Olympic Games in Stockholm in 1912.[44] George Cunningham, secretary at the Legation from 1925 to 1926, and governor of the North-West Frontier Province from 1937 to 1946 and 1947 to 1948, played international rugby for Scotand prior to his colonial career.[45]

Thus the diplomats who came to Kabul after 1922 to set up Britain's first permanent diplomatic representation emerged from a colonial system whose various physical cultures were immensely pronounced and finely tuned through decades of attention to the colonial officer's bodily qualities. Due to their cultural and political proximity to the colonial services in India, they exercised plenty in a variety of games, including tennis, squash, cricket and hockey.[46] Fraser-Tytler 'engaged in every form of sport available' throughout his time in Afghanistan, including riding, shooting and fishing.[47] Some of these activities were incorporated into the larger institutional life of the British Legation, which kept a fishing record and hunting diary until the 1960s.[48]

Contesting history in the British–Afghan sporting encounter

Sport generated occasions for social interaction between the Legation diplomats and elite members of Afghan society, which were monopolised by the British–Indian diplomatic mission as 'the only foreigners to take an interest in the sports'.[49] The contests during the Afghan independence celebrations enabled physical proximity and created a diplomatic site. In colonial contexts, sports provided a domain to challenge the colonisers' authority. As Angela Woollacott has shown, '[f]or men, the evolving and pervasive passion for sport was an arena in which the politics of colonialism were played out overtly, where the colonised or colonials could hope at least symbolically to defeat their imperial superiors'.[50] Sport could be endowed with political significance if it was framed as an anticolonial or anti-imperial act of resistance. The reverse applied to conditions in Kabul, where Afghan independence could be challenged by former imperial masters in the framework of the athletic encounter.

The independence of the Afghan state was an emerging notion and open to qualification for the colonial officers who became British diplomats in Kabul after 1922. For instance, Peter Sluglett suggests that 'Humphrys [the first British Minister in Kabul] seems to have had some difficulty in adjusting to the fact that Afghanistan was no longer a dependency of British India'.[51] Games mirrored the political relations between Afghanistan, India and Britain. A strong legacy was provided by some members of the Legation in Kabul, like William Kerr Fraser-Tytler, who had also been mobilised as officers of the Indian Army during the Third Anglo-Afghan War in 1919. Several encounters in games and sports were framed in militaristic terms; for instance Fraser-Tytler's descriptions of a game of billiards between Amanullah Khan and Richard Roy Maconachie in 1923: 'His Majesty ... challenged Mr Maconachie, whom he defeated by seven points. His Majesty declaring "peace" when his score was at 34.'[52] Sports and games presented an occasion for participants in the Third Anglo-Afghan War, Indian Army officers and Amanullah Khan alike to revisit their shared historical experiences. In 1928, the Legation played an Afghan team at cricket, but lost 'after an interesting game'.[53] The report on the game explicitly noted the athletic quality of the match and the 'thoroughly sporting spirit on the part of the Afghans'.[54] However, Leon Poullada records that the defeat contributed to Humphrys's 'hearty personal dislike' of Amir Amanullah Khan.[55] To set the record straight, the Legation 'took their revenge next day at tennis [which] drew a large and fashionable gallery'.[56]

British diplomats attentively observed their Afghan opponents on the playing field and their adherence to colonial codes of conduct. Sport and games carried powerful messages of good moral behaviour. For instance, when Queen Soraya played a game of tennis with Gertrude Humphrys, the British Minister's wife, at the Legation, the latter pointed out afterwards that:

> Her Majesty, though I think she really tried to play fair, took a much larger number of services than the rules of the game would allow amongst commoners. We played four games, all of which Her Majesty won quite easily, as the spectators gleefully pointed out. Her Majesty however, was good enough to say that I played very well and a great deal better than the Italians. Her Majesty is not a stayer and was very warm and exhausted after so much play.[57]

If a game was lost, the focus on the outcome shifted to other areas beyond the result. In this case, Gertrude Humphrys suggested that Queen Soraya had not followed the rules, was not in good shape and had also exercised too hard on the court. Ultimately,

5.2 Sir Richard Maconachie and Mr Farwell, military attaché, playing tennis

she had not adhered to the 'gentlemanly' ethics of sport common among the Anglo-Indian elite (figure 5.2). Tennis, especially, was framed in terms of British–Indian hegemony, its matches often being a 'fore-gone conclusion' in favour of the Legation teams, as in 1944: 'The only event which the Afghans lost was the tennis match against the British Legation and this, as it took place in the comparative privacy of the Afghan Military Club, was not so serious a set-back.'[58]

The independence celebrations were perceived as a measure by which to estimate Afghanistan's progress, or, as Fraser-Tytler put it, 'each year one sees some little difference … always a little progress; it is most interesting to watch the development of a country practically from its beginning'.[59] State independence equalled the inception of history. Afghanistan was assessed in its ability to provide an adequate, level playing field for encounters in games and sports. For instance, in a game of billiards between the Legation's counsellor and military attaché with 'the other side', the 'disconcerting' conditions in a 'tent, crowded with people' as well as the 'considerable bias' of the table and cues 'like hockey sticks' stood out.[60] Equally, the independence week also came under considerable scrutiny as an indicative representation of Afghanistan's adherence to the 'comity of civilised nations'.[61]

The British–Afghan encounter in sport during Afghanistan's annual independence celebrations presented symbolically charged occasions, both in terms of political and athletic ambitions, because Britain and India played a prominent role in the independence narrative of the Afghan state and its representation in public. Reporting on his journey from the Legation to his accreditation, Humphrys described to George

Nathaniel Curzon, the then British Foreign Secretary and former viceroy of India, the 'monument erected to the "Victory of Thal". Surrounded by chained lions … it affords an apt illustration of the official Afghan attitude towards recent history.'[62] In 1919, Afghan forces commanded by Nadir Khan, the later Nadir Shah, had besieged the British fort in the Kurram valley in India, thereby contributing materially to the outcome of the war of 1919 and, consequently, to Afghan independence. In addition to monuments, the military parade that opened the independence week also commemorated the War of Independence. In 1942, the British Minister in Kabul, Francis Verner Wylie, noticed in his report on the independence week that 'they trundled round an old blow pipe of a gun all decorated with flowers which is alleged to … have been used by Nadir Khan at Thal and to have spread dismay among the ranks of the British there'.[63] When the diplomatic community applauded the procession, Wylie commented in his dispatch that:

> nobody clapped louder than His Britannic Majesty's Envoy Extraordinary and Minister Plenipotentiary in Afghanistan! The next item after the old gun was a battery of artillery pulled by light draught horses just supplied by the British Government to their old and tried friends the Afghans. I could not help thinking that there in the short space of 100 yards or so was a tolerably good pictorial representation of British policy and achievement (?) in this God forsaken granted Kingdom. Gawrr.[64]

British representations of Afghan independence were self-referential. Afghanistan's independence was, in a way, relative. It was understood in reference to the representatives of the colonial state from which Afghanistan had become independent. The same applied to Afghan notions of sport.

During the independence celebrations, the Legation diplomats found themselves 'in their element'.[65] The British Legation in Kabul appeared as a point of reference, not only for Afghanistan's statal independence, but also in terms of its athletic abilities. The contests with 'amateur' Legation diplomats were framed in terms of gauging the Afghan nation's athletic potential. Fraser-Tytler wrote on the 1932 games that 'they beat us at tennis, after a very good match. We didn't expect them to do this, but they beat us fair & square through sheer steadiness. Afghanistan is in fact coming on at games, & there is no reason why in this fine climate they should not produce really good athletes.'[66] The textual renderings of these encounters sought to claim British guardianship over Afghanistan's sport development. The British–Afghan encounter on the tennis court, on this occasion, was conceptualised in the larger history of professional Afghan sport.

Diplomatic discourse was, and is, marked by a significant degree of body-centricity.[67] The independence celebrations were *the* occasion to display the athletic diplomatic body to a wider Afghan public. British diplomats even trained for the occasion, sometimes to the point of injury.[68] Complementing the privacy of writing, in which they challenged Afghanistan's independence, the British Legation in Kabul employed sport as a form of public diplomacy. The diplomat's body transcended the familiarity of the Afghan court and the Legation. Both represented physical boundaries that regimented statal diplomatic practice. On the playing field, by contrast, the British–Afghan encounter was marked by the violent impact of the game on the body owing to advanced age, corporeal dysfunction and limited skills. The Legation's attempt to harness athletic ability in order to compete with Afghan teams in front of Afghan audiences of varying sizes and heterogeneous composition was ultimately marked by a significant degree of failure. A (hockey) match report written by Fraser-Tytler in a letter to his mother illustrates this well:

> We've … been chiefly engaged in trying to efface ourselves as much as possible, as from the athletic point of view we have been unduly in the limelight. … We were … rather horrified to find on arrival on the ground that we had to take on eleven real hockey players recruited from different schools & institutions in Kabul, & that in the presence of the King, the Court, the Corps diplomatique, & about ten thousand spectators. On one side Tiny Farwell [the military attaché] is good, [Arthur Ernest Henry] Macann [the secretary], the Doctor [Henry Hawes Elliot], our office super-intendent [Spinks] & I [William Kerr Fraser-Tytler] had played hockey before, but none of us for many years – in my case for 17 – & we were years older than any of our opponents. However, we played valiantly, & aided by a considerable amount of luck managed to draw with them! But it was the devil of a game for the back, & I haven't recovered from it yet. After the age of forty it is not safe to play a hard game like that without proper training. The Afghan team were very annoyed at not winning, but everybody else was I think pleased that we made a draw of it. The King [Nadir Shah] particularly charming as he always is congratulated Tiny most warmly & enquired tenderly after my hand on which I got an awful smack from our Mr Spinks who, being half blind already & totally so at the end of a hard game, got me & and the ball simultaneously just as I was stopping it. E[ila Fraser-Tytler, William Kerr's wife] told me that during the game H[is] M[ajesty] never once applauded when his own side got a goal & always when we did.[69]

There is a degree of hyperbole in this passage, owing to the private nature of the correspondence from which it is taken, and its humorous dimension cushions the fail-ure of the British athletic display. The contrast to the well-trained Afghan professionals established the Legation diplomats as amateurs, who are consequently distanced from their opponents as followers of 'gentlemanly' notions of sport.[70] Outside of the playing field, Nadir Shah's inquiry into the injuries sustained among the British Legation indicates a degree of physical intimacy in British–Afghan relations and brings to mind images of treating those wounded in battle. The king's applause for the British team can be read as applause for the 'valiant' fight, as Fraser-Tytler claims, or as a genuine expression of relief in view of a level result. Fraser-Tytler's comment that '[t]he whole action was very kingly' shifts the lens away from the game and on to the Afghan king.[71] Nadir Shah's monarchical conduct is judged as appropriate by the amateur hockey player and colonial officer from India. As such, a textual reading of the report serves to illustrate the depth of identities at play in Afghan–British relations.

Despite the risk of injury, limited skills and very good opponents, Anglo-Indian colonial officers of the British Legation continued to compete in the Afghan independence celebrations. In 1939, Fraser-Tytler wrote to his mother:

[A]s usual the British are to the fore. We had our usual beating, the Legation against all Afghanistan, at hockey, and at tennis I brought down the house so to speak by playing myself with [Patrick John] Paddy Keen [the secretary] in an exhibition match, against a very fairly good [*sic*] couple of Afghans in the presence of the entire court and diplomatic corps. We jolly nearly won too, and would have done so but for a rather unnecessary piece of bad play by both of us in the crucial game of a three set match. They won, but actually the difference was only two games, 14 to 12 in three sets. I have got a rather bad tennis elbow and had to go on the court with my arm bandaged in two places, but all that added to the enthusiasm of seeing Methuselah skipping about the court like a two year old. There is no other member of the diplomatic corps who could have done it. But of course the tennis was not what one could call particularly high class.[72]

Results were not all that mattered. The athletic performance of the Legation was measured across several sports, including tennis, hockey, cricket and volleyball. In 1940, for instance, the Legation 'lost at hockey after a good game, both our pairs won at tennis, and at cricket we lost after a very good game. So honour was satisfied.'[73]

Underlying the narratives provided in a range of sources are the meanings attached to the athletic outings. Starting with the 1928 cricket game, which was won by the Afghan side, British–Indian teams emerged on the playing field with a particular purpose that went beyond winning or losing. Humphrys's disappointment at the defeat of the Legation's cricket team originated in the British Minister's own experience of playing the sport as well as in his expectation of showing the 'soft' Afghan king, Amanullah Khan, into his place by means of the 'imperial game'.

Other narratives focused on the idea of fair play. Losing a game was acceptable if it took place within the established norms of sporting behaviour. For instance, Fraser-Tytler alerted his mother to the fact that '[t]hey beat us at hockey by the unfair practice of saying they were playing a departmental [War Office] team & actually playing an all-Afghanistan one'.[74] The defeat of Legation teams at the hands of Afghan athletes was perhaps genuinely unsuspected, but it did give rise to disappointment, which fed on well-established stereotypes.[75]

During the 1930s, the Afghan independence celebrations came to be recognised as an increasingly international platform, and the games pitted the 'Legation against the world'.[76] On the one hand, in a South Asian dimension, teams from India and Afghanistan toured increasingly.[77] For instance, an Afghan hockey team visited Bombay on a north Indian tour in early 1934 and competed in the first Western Asiatic Games in New Delhi.[78] The second round of the event was scheduled to take place in Kabul in 1938, but never materialised. On the other hand, the global context of the Olympic Games expanded the various meanings attached to the athletic encounter of Legation teams beyond the confines of British–Afghan relations. In Fraser-Tytler's perception, the 1936 Olympic Games in Berlin contributed to the manifestation of a physically powerful German nation. British diplomats now had to measure their own athletic exploits against strong Germans and professional Afghan athletes.[79] An Afghan hockey team took part in the Games in Berlin, and Fraser-Tytler thought that the interplay of German propaganda conducted by the 'many well-built, athletic young Germans' who had come to Afghanistan after the Olympic Games to become instructors to King Zahir Shah in 'physical training, swimming and skiing' had had a great effect on 'the impressionable Afghan mind'.[80] Accordingly, the British Legation 'show[ed] increasing signs of vitality by entering Legation teams to play the Afghans at Hockey, Cricket and Tennis' during the independence celebrations.[81] The ageing British diplomat's body in Afghanistan and the 'imperial game' came to be framed in the context of the European crisis of the 1930s:

> A game of cricket with the Afghans on Tuesday in which I, in my insane capacity of wicket keeper caught three men and made 4 runs – why I should suddenly take to cricket at the age of 53, after having shunned it all my life I can't imagine, but it is really a very fine game, if painful at times. We are playing them during the Jashen sports, and also at tennis and hockey. I think this is, besides being amusing, good propaganda. A little time ago when our stock was low the feeling here was 'these poor d--d British, they can do nothing but play games while their country is being destroyed' – German propaganda of course – but we went on playing games, and now people are beginning to ask themselves whether Britain is really going to be destroyed after all, and whether there isn't something in this curious British spirit which just carries on and plays games in bad days as well as in good. We are a very baffling people to foreigners.[82]

From participation to observation: post-colonial nations and the colonial lens

Throughout its history, the Legation's hockey and cricket teams mixed British and Indian players, but the documentary record is notably silent on the contributions of Indians. In most of Fraser-Tytler's renderings, for instance, the 'British' diplomatic mission appears as a European team, although a substantial amount of its team members were Indians. The diplomatic institution, too, relied heavily on Indian administrators, labourers and funding. The exploits of Indians, diplomatic and athletic, were systematically marginalised and underrepresented. The Legation's hockey team, for instance, mixed colonisers and colonised, and colonial officers represented an ageing and diminishing contingent in these teams by the 1930s (figure 5.3). In addition to age and race, class and nationalism provided powerful determinants for the teams' composition. In terms of class, colonial diplomat-athletes rarely engaged in the 'plebeian' contest of football.[83] Different kinds of sport provided opportunities to well-organised and popular Indian teams to project their athletic and political ambitions as well as subvert the authority of British colonial officers through athletic performance.[84]

5.3 The photograph shows the diversity of the 'British' Legation in Kabul in terms of its diplomatic and athletic aspects as well as its European and South Asian composition. The Legation hockey team included officials in athletic clothing (predominantly in the second row) as well as visiting Indian players (in the two rows at the back)

Complementing the 'Indianising' trend of Legation teams were the visits of Indian teams for the occasion of the Afghan independence celebrations. India won three Olympic hockey competitions in succession in 1928, 1932 and 1936. The Legation hosted visiting Indian teams on the Legation grounds, utilising their presence for the benefits of the 'British' Legation's athletic performance while also qualifying Indian nationalism:

> The Legation is so much the finest building and garden in Kabul, and it is right that the young Indians who come up here should see it and take a certain pride in the place. It gives them a chance, if a brief one, to realise that in foreign countries at any rate there is some value in the British connection.[85]

Indian athletes in Kabul provided one of many audiences for the Legation. During their visit to Kabul, they were cast as passive recipients of the Legation's imperialist ambitions that, ironically, were sourced from Indian funds:

> We had one of those awful little ceremonies this morning which keep the Empire together. A team of Quetta people had come up to Kabul to play football and their manager asked if they might pay their respects. So round they came at 11 a.m. 14 tongue tied young fellows with a nice man in charge. We showed them a bit of the

house, and the garden which is at its best and gave them tea and cake and fruit, and they ate with large eyes and looked with awe at our panelled dining room, and silver and things the like of which they had probably never seen before. They left at twelve and we heaved a sigh of relief and returned to our jobs.[86]

As colonial diplomat-athletes retired to the grandstand, their focus on the games shifted from participation to observation. Both South Asian athletes – Indian and Afghan – as well as Afghan statesmen came to be subjected to the steady colonial gaze in dedicated annual despatches on the Afghan independence games.[87] One statesman was Shah Mahmud, the Afghan War Minister, whom Francis Verner Wylie described as 'a baby that had lost its rattle' after visiting Indian hockey and football teams had won their matches, but who looked 'deliciously happy again – just like a babe whose nurse has given it back its rattle', when the Legation's tennis double, including Wylie, lost on the following day.[88] Giles Frederick Squire echoed his predecessor's assessment, but extended it to representatives of the Afghan state in general:

> [I]t is a great pity that he [Shah Mahmud] is such a bad loser and it is difficult to assess the value of the matches owing to the childish desire on the part of all Afghans from the Minister of War downwards that their teams should always win. The results of a defeat at the hands of a visiting team are likely to be very unpleasant for the victors and in fact only one team, the Afghan Fo[o]tball Club from Peshawar, was rash enough to win one of its matches [in 1943], the others were all drawn or discreetly lost.[89]

Squire's passage digs deep into the patriarchal repertoire of colonial rhetoric. Both Afghan sportsmanship and statesmanship were simultaneously questioned. The lack of 'a more sporting spirit' suggested an Afghan reluctance to accept the colonial codes of conduct which framed sport as a moral enterprise as well as a transition of the independent Afghan state from childhood to adolescence. In India, British colonial officers saw themselves as 'diffusers' or 'proselytisers' of games.[90] By contrast, Afghanistan appeared as a place where colonial sport's moral enterprise could be put on display by employing Indians in athletic encounters with Afghans. The responsibility for the failure of sport's moral enterprise did not, however, rest with the colonial masters from India, but with Afghan sportsmen and state representatives.[91] This also distracted from the reality of the defeat of Legation teams. The failure to adhere to the written and unwritten rules of games echoed notions of lawlessness as Wylie referred to the independence celebrations as 'the annual outbreaks'.[92] The games of 1945 were, in G. C. L. Crichton's words, marked by the 'usual over-keenness of the Afghan teams (and their referees!) to win'.[93] The reference by the observing colonial officer negates the impartiality of the Afghan referee. The insinuation of Afghan inability to rule on the playing field also corresponded with Wylie's questioning of the independence of the Afghan state, to which he referred in inverted commas, just like Humphrys had done in the early 1920s. Moreover, Afghan conduct in sport led Squire to make a case for the benefits of colonial rule in India. He moulded the colonial myth of excellence in state building with exemplary gentlemanly sportsmanship, both of which sought to provide positive role models for colonial and, in this case, 'para-colonial' societies:

> No Indian, especially from the North West Frontier Province, who has spent a week in Kabul during the Independence Celebrations in close contact with the Afghans is likely to be so keen on independence for his own country if it is going to mean anything like Afghan conditions for him.[94]

Conclusion

The colonial lens through which Anglo-Indian officers had viewed sport in Afghanistan since 1919 did not change in August 1947. Well-established colonial characteristics framed Afghan society in terms of the 'combative, ill-tempered and excitable Pathan nature'.[95] Having witnessed the end of the Raj in the previous year and now nearing the end of his tenure as Britain's first ambassador in Afghanistan, Squire questioned the usefulness of sport as a channel of international relations among former colonial nations:

> As in all international contests it is doubtful whether these games really help to improve relations and do not rather tend to perpetuate mutual jealousy and ill-feeling. The Afghan desire to win has in the past led to somewhat childish displays of temper on the part of officials from the Prime Minister downwards, and even to the victimisation of any team which has had the temerity to beat its Afghan opponents.[96]

While '[t]he visiting teams from India [we]re well looked after and entertained with true Afghan hospitality' in 1944, the games of 1948 and 1949, according to Squire, did 'little to promote international goodwill' as Pakistani and Indian teams were severely disadvantaged.[97] Whereas the participation of Legation teams was never questioned, the athletic encounter of emerging post-colonial nations appeared counterproductive in the absence of the former colonial master's guiding example on the playing field. Squire's assessment was distorted by a melancholy retrospective on the Indian colonial empire and on the history of the British Legation in Kabul, which concluded in its reshaping as the British Embassy in 1948:

> I have now witnessed six of these affairs but do not think that any marked progress has been made during this time. Of course the British Legation which used to figure so prominently has now completely faded out of the picture. It was we who were formerly responsible in some measure for the hockey and football teams which used to come up from the old undivided India for the occasion; and two of the principal sporting events were tennis and football matches, Afghanistan versus the British Legation. Afghanistan's inability to find tennis players and the increase in the size and number of other Missions led to the former being converted three

years ago into a garden party; and the Legation hockey team inevitably came to an end after the grant of independence to India in 1947.[98]

The missionary element in Squire's statement is unmistakable, though not surprising given Squire's credentials as a facilitator of Christian worship at the Legation.[99] Squire shared an interest in God and games with 'muscular Christians'. His claim that Anglo-Indian colonial officers facilitated athletic contact between India and Afghanistan indicates a reshaping of British diplomats' involvement in the Afghan independence celebrations, which had begun with their active participation. At the end of that development, the conduct of former colonial nations was framed in terms of political legitimacy.

Afghanistan's condition as a state, society and nation was measured against the behaviour of Afghan teams, players and athletes. The reports on the Afghan independence celebrations written at the Legation implied that the Anglo-Indian mission had diffused sport and its moral and ethical codes into independent Afghanistan. The fading of the Afghan 'sporting spirit' on the playing field coincided with the end of the colonial state. The ability to enforce rules of the game equalled the colonisers' doubts regarding the ability of former colonial nations to rule themselves. The colonial framework established and perpetuated by the British Legation in Kabul regarding sport in Afghanistan survived beyond this chapter's other temporal threshold of independence in 1947. In 1973, Louis Dupree, in his widely published monograph on Afghanistan, referred to Afghan conduct in sport in familiar colonial terms: 'in both sports, be they traditional or modern sports introduced from the outside, the Afghan, product of a harsh, inward-looking, group-oriented society, plays to win'.[100] In 2014, Nicholas Barrington, 'Oriental Secretary' in Kabul from 1959, considered the annual tennis tournament as the 'championship of Afghanistan' owing to the scarcity of courts, his claim of choosing 'my areas of prowess well' echoing the hegemonic terms in which Anglo-Indian colonial officers had used the game to balance the Legation's performance sheet during the Afghan independence celebrations before 1947.[101]

Notes

1 British Library, London (hereafter BL), IOR/L/PS/12/1925, no. 96 from A. E. H. Macann, 4 September 1937.
2 Middle East Centre Archive, Oxford (hereafter MECA), GB165–0326, 1/1/10, letter from W. K. Fraser-Tytler, 26 May 1939.
3 BL, IOR/L/PS/10/1207, copies of the diaries of the military attaché, British Legation, Kabul, for the weeks ending 18 August and 25 August 1928; see also D. B. Edwards, *Before Taliban: Genealogies of the Afghan Jihad* (Berkeley, CA: University of California Press, 2002), 1–10.
4 BL, IOR/L/PS/10/1207, copy of the diary of the military attaché, British Legation, Kabul, for the week ending 27 August 1927.
5 MECA, GB165–0326, 8, Kabul Legation diary, 42–9, 132–5; see also 'Afghanistan

news: Independence Day celebrations', *The Times of India*, 14 September 1922; 'Afghanistan's independence week: a care free and confident people', *The Times of India*, 4 September 1935.

6 National Archives of India, New Delhi (hereafter NAI), External Affairs, 1944, 528-F, no. 69 from G. F. Squire, 5 August 1944.

7 The National Archives, London (hereafter TNA), FO 371/10986, N 5349/533/97, no. 70 from F. H. Humphrys, 29 August 1925.

8 BL, IOR/L/PS/12/1841, Intelligence summary no. 22 for the week ending 3 June 1938; MECA, GB165–0326, 1/1/10, letter from W. K. Fraser-Tytler, 2 June 1939.

9 R. T. Stewart, *Fire in Afghanistan, 1914–1929: Faith, Hope and the British Empire* (Garden City, NY: Doubleday, 1973), 385–97.

10 'Afghan jirgha and reforms: independence festival', *The Times of India*, 7 August 1928.

11 MECA, GB165–0326, 8, Kabul Legation diary, 134.

12 For instance TNA, FO 402/18, no. 88, no. 58 from W. K. Fraser-Tytler, 11 June 1937; NAI, External Affairs, 1943, 637-F, D.O. no. 322/41 from G. F. Squire, 4 September 1943.

13 MECA, GB165–0326, 8, British Legation diary, 43.

14 MECA, GB165–0326, 8, British Legation diary, 45.

15 NAI, External Affairs, 1944, 528-F, no. 69 from G. F. Squire, 5 August 1944.

16 A. Saikal, *Modern Afghanistan: A History of Struggle and Survival* (London: I. B. Tauris, 2012), 39.

17 The Indian Political Service was so called only after 1937. It emerged from the Foreign and Political Department of the Government of India.

18 Edward Blunt, *The I.C.S.: The Indian Civil Service* (London: Faber & Faber, 1937), 165.

19 For the various epistemological registers created and circulated to enable the framing of Afghanistan since the nineteenth century, see, among others: M. J. Bayly, *Taming the Imperial Imagination: Colonial Knowledge, International Relations, and the Anglo-Afghan Encounter, 1808–1878* (Cambridge: Cambridge University Press, 2016); B. D. Hopkins, *The Making of Modern Afghanistan* (Basingstoke: Palgrave Macmillan, 2008); see also S. M. Hanifi, *Connecting Histories in Afghanistan: Market Relations and State Formation on a Colonial Frontier* (Stanford, CA: Stanford University Press, 2011).

20 MECA, GB165–0326, 1/1/9, letter from W. K. Fraser-Tytler, 27 May 1938.

21 NAI, External Affairs, 1942, 14-F, D.O. no. 134/41 from F. V. Wylie, 29 August 1942.

22 D. Day and L. Mallam, *Frogs in the Well* (Moray: Librario, 2010), 136.

23 BL, IOR/L/PS/10/1207, copy of the diary of the military attaché, British Legation, Kabul, for the week ending 27 August 1927.

24 See also E. S. Rosenberg and S. Fitzpatrick (eds), *Body and Nation: The Global Realm of U.S. Body Politics in the Twentieth Century* (Durham, NC: Duke University Press, 2014).

25 See also R. Holland, S. Williams and T. Barringer (eds), *The Iconography of Independence: 'Freedoms at Midnight'* (London: Routledge, 2010).

26 J. A. Mangan, *Athleticism in the Victorian and Edwardian Public School: The Emergence and Consolidation of an Educational Ideology* (London: Frank Cass, 3rd edn, 2000).

27 J. A. Mangan and K. Bandyopadhyay, 'Imperial and post-imperial congruence: a challenge to ideological simplification', *International Journal of the History of Sport*, 21:3–4 (2004), 405.

28 J. A. Mangan, *The Games Ethic and Imperialism: Aspects of the Diffusion of an Ideal* (Harmondsworth: Viking, 1986), 18.

29 For a more nuanced approach to the diffusionist model of the history of sports in colonial contexts, see: R. Cashman, 'Cricket and colonialism: colonial hegemony and indigenous subversion?', in J. A. Mangan (ed.), *Pleasure, Profit, Proselytism: British Culture and Sport at Home and Abroad, 1700–1914* (London: Frank Cass, 1988), 258–72; B. Majumdar, 'Imperial tool "for" nationalist resistance: the "games ethic" in Indian history', *International Journal of the History of Sport*, 21:3–4 (2004); B. Majumdar, 'Tom Brown goes global: the "Brown" ethic in colonial and post-colonial India', *International Journal of the History of Sport*, 23:5 (2006).

30 A. Kirk-Greene, 'Badge of office: sport and His Excellency in the British Empire', in J. A. Mangan (ed.), *The Cultural Bond: Sport, Empire, Society* (London: Frank Cass, 1992), 178–200.

31 J. A. Mangan, 'Britain's chief spiritual export: imperial sport as moral metaphor, political symbol and cultural bond', in Mangan (ed.), *The Cultural Bond*, 1–10.

32 Cited in Majumdar, 'Imperial tool "for" nationalist resistance', 384.

33 E. M. Collingham, *Imperial Bodies: The Physical Experience of the Raj, c. 1800–1947* (Cambridge: Polity, 2001), 121, 124.

34 I. Copland, 'The other guardians: ideology and performance in the Indian Political Service', in R. Jeffrey (ed.), *People, Princes and Paramount Power: Society and Politics in the Indian Princely States* (Oxford: Oxford University Press, 1978), 286–7.

35 BL, IOR/R/1/4/1334, application of F. H. Humphrys, 22 September 1903.

36 BL, IOR/R/1/4/1334, application of F. H. Humphrys, 22 September 1903.

37 P. Sluglett, 'Humphrys, Sir Francis Henry (1879–1971): colonial administrator and diplomatist', *Oxford Dictionary of National Biography* (Oxford: Oxford University Press, 2004).

38 'Humphrys, Francis Henry', *1971–1980, Who's Who & Who Was Who 7* (London: A & C Black, 1981).

39 William Kerr Fraser-Tytler, 'In memoriam', *Journal of The Royal Central Asian Society*, 49:2 (1962), 118.

40 'Fraser-Tytler, Lt-Col Sir William Kerr', *Who Was Who* (London: A & C Black, 2007).

41 'Sir G. Squire: ambassador and churchman', *The Times*, 17 April 1959. See also 'Squire, Giles Frederick', *Who's Who 2011 & Who Was Who* (London A & C Black, 2011).

42 NAI, Foreign and Political, 1926, 4(12)-E, application of H. H. Elliot, 8 November 1926.

43 NAI, Foreign and Political, 1931, 49(5)-Est, application of E. S. S. Lucas, 13 April 1931.

44 BL, IOR/R/1/4/1331, application of A. W. Fagan, 11 April 1919.

45 Ian Talbot, 'Cunningham, Sir George (1888–1963): administrator in India', *Oxford Dictionary of National Biography*.

46 For histories of Indian cricket see, among others, R. Guha, *A Corner of a Foreign Field: The Indian History of a British Sport* (London: Picador, 2002); Majumdar,

'Imperial tool "for" nationalist resistance'; B. Stoddart and K. A. P. Sandiford, *The Imperial Game: Cricket, Culture and Society* (Manchester: Manchester University Press, 1998); B. Majumdar, 'The golden years of Indian hockey: "we climb the victory stand"', *International Journal of the History of Sport*, 25:12 (2008); see also S. Pal, '"Legacies, halcyon days and thereafter": a brief history of Indian tennis', *International Journal of the History of Sport*, 21:3–4 (2004).

47 MECA, GB165–0326, 10, note by W. K. Fraser-Tytler on the situation in Afghanistan, 20 August 1941.

48 BL, IOR/R/12/LIB/10, British Legation Kabul game book; BL, IOR/R/12/LIB/11, British Legation Kabul fishing record.

49 BL, IOR/L/PS/10/1207, copy of the diary of the military attaché, British Legation, Kabul, for the week ending 27 August 1927; I. B. Neumann, *Diplomatic Sites: A Critical Enquiry* (London: C. Hurst & Co., 2013).

50 A. Woollacott, *Gender and Empire* (Basingstoke: Palgrave Macmillan, 2006), 81.

51 Sluglett, 'Humphrys, Sir Francis Henry (1879–1971)'.

52 MECA, GB165–0326, 8, British Legation diary, 133.

53 BL, IOR/L/PS/10/1207, copy of the diary of the military attaché, British Legation, Kabul, for the week ending 25 August 1928.

54 BL, IOR/L/PS/10/1207, copy of the diary of the military attaché, British Legation, Kabul, for the week ending 25 August 1928.

55 L. B. Poullada, *Reform and Rebellion in Afghanistan, 1919–1929: King Amanullah's Failure to Modernize a Tribal Society* (Ithaca, NY: Cornell University Press, 1973), 252.

56 BL, IOR/L/PS/10/1207, copy of the diary of the military attaché, British Legation, Kabul, for the week ending 25 August 1928.

57 MECA, GB165–0326, 8, British Legation diary, 86.

58 NAI, External Affairs, 1944, 528-F, no. 69 from G. F. Squire, 5 August 1944.

59 MECA, GB165–0326, 1/1/10, letter from W. K. Fraser-Tytler, 2 June 1939.

60 MECA, GB165–0326, 1/1/5, letter from W. K. Fraser-Tytler, 18 August 1932.

61 TNA, FO 371/8077, N 8493/59/97, letter from F. H. Humphrys, 3 August 1922; TNA, FO 402/3, no. 78, no. 50 from F. H. Humphrys, 8 April 1924.

62 TNA, FO 371/8077, N 3667/59/97, no. 3 from F. H. Humphrys, 25 March 1922.

63 NAI, External Affairs, 1942, 14-F, D.O. no. 134/41 from F. V. Wylie, 29 August 1942.

64 NAI, External Affairs, 1942, 14-F, D.O. no. 134/41 from F. V. Wylie, 29 August 1942.

65 BL, IOR/L/PS/10/1207, copy of the diary of the military attaché, British Legation, Kabul, for the week ending 27 August 1927.

66 MECA, GB165–0326, 1/1/5, letter from W. K. Fraser-Tytler, 18 August 1932.

67 Maximilian Drephal, 'Corps diplomatique: the body, British diplomacy, and independent Afghanistan, 1922–47', *Modern Asian Studies*, 6 July 2017.

68 MECA, GB165–0326, 1/1/8, letter from W. K. Fraser-Tytler, 27 May 1937.

69 MECA, GB165–0326, 1/1/4, letter from William Kerr Fraser-Tytler, 20 August 1931.

70 For further reading on the division into 'amateur' and 'professional' athletes, see H. Perkin, 'Teaching the nations how to play: sport and society in the British Empire and Commonwealth', *International Journal of the History of Sport*, 6:2 (1989).

71 MECA, GB165–0326, 1/1/4, letter from William Kerr Fraser-Tytler, 20 August 1931.

72 MECA, GB165–0326, 1/1/10, letter from W. K. Fraser-Tytler, 2 June 1939.

73 MECA, GB165–0326, 1/1/11, letter from W. K. Fraser-Tytler, 29 August 1940.

74 MECA, GB165–0326, 1/1/5, letter from W. K. Fraser-Tytler, 18 August 1932.
75 Some of these notions, for example 'treachery', were so firmly established in the Indian Army, which supplied parts of the Indian Political Service, by the early twentieth century that they found regular expression in military reports. For instance: TNA, WO 287/22, military report on Afghanistan, 1925, xvii.
76 B. J. Gould, *The Jewel in the Lotus: Recollections of an Indian Political* (London: Chatto and Windus, 1957), 98.
77 See Mangan and Bandyopadhyay, 'Imperial and post-imperial congruence'.
78 B. Majumdar and N. Mehta, *India and the Olympics* (Abingdon: Routledge, 2009), 23–4. For an earlier reference to Theodore Leighton Pennell and Afghan tour football, see J. A. Mangan, 'Soccer as moral training: missionary intentions and imperial legacies', *International Journal of the History of Sport*, 27:1–2 (2010); T. L. Pennell, *Among the Wild Tribes of the Afghan Frontier: A Record of Sixteen Years' Close Intercourse with the Natives of the Indian Marches* (London: Seeley and Co., 1909), 153–67; in 1946, an Afghan football team toured in India: TNA, FO 371/52275, E 2578/66/97, no. 12 from G. F. Squire, 28 February 1946.
79 See also J. A. Mangan, 'Global Fascism and the male body: ambitions, similarities and dissimilarities', *International Journal of the History of Sport*, 16:4 (1999).
80 BL, IOR/L/PS/12/1765, unofficial quarterly letter no. 2 from W. K. Fraser-Tytler, 6 October 1939.
81 BL, IOR/L/PS/12/1765, unofficial quarterly letter no. 6 from W. K. Fraser-Tytler, 1 October 1940.
82 MECA, GB165–0326, 1/1/11, letter from W. K. Fraser-Tytler, 23 August 1940.
83 J. Mills and P. Dimeo, 'Introduction: empire, nation, diaspora', *Soccer and Society*, 2:2 (2001), 148; Perkin, 'Teaching the nations how to play'. See also P. Dimeo, 'Colonial bodies, colonial sport: "martial" Punjabis, "effeminate" Bengalis and the development of Indian football', *International Journal of the History of Sport*, 19:1 (2002).
84 Majumdar, 'Imperial tool "for" nationalist resistance', 398; Perkin, 'Teaching the nations how to play', 148.
85 MECA, GB165–0326, 1/1/8, letter from W. K. Fraser-Tytler, 3 June 1937.
86 MECA, GB165–0326, 1/1/11, letter from W. K. Fraser-Tytler, 23 August 1940.
87 NAI, External Affairs, 1945, 651-F, D.O. no. 322/41 from G. C. L. Crichton, 4 August 1945; NAI, External Affairs, 1946, 540-NWA, no. 57 from G. F. Squire, 3 August 1946; TNA, FO 371/63247, F 12439/9774/97, no. 79 from G. F. Squire, 30 August 1947.
88 NAI, External Affairs, 1942, 14-F, D.O. no. 134/41 from F. V. Wylie, 29 August 1942.
89 NAI, External Affairs, 1943, 637-F, D.O. no. 322/41 from G. F. Squire, 4 September 1943.
90 See A. Guttmann, 'The diffusion of sports and the problem of cultural imperialism', in E. Dunning and D. Malcolm (eds), *The Development of Sport*, vol. 2, *Sport: Critical Concepts in Sociology* (London: Routledge, 2003), 343–56; Mangan (ed.), *Pleasure, Profit, Proselytism*; Mangan, *The Games Ethic and Imperialism*.
91 See also K. Moore, '"The warmth of comradeship": the first British Empire Games and imperial solidarity', *International Journal of the History of Sport*, 6:2 (1989), 246, 248; Majumdar, 'Imperial tool "for" nationalist resistance', 396–7.
92 NAI, External Affairs, 1942, 14-F, D.O. no. 134/41 from F. V. Wylie, 29 August 1942.

93 NAI, External Affairs, 1945, 651-F, D.O. no. 322/41 from G. C. L. Crichton, 4 August 1945.
94 NAI, External Affairs, 1943, 637-F, D.O. no. 322/41 from G. F. Squire, 4 September 1943.
95 J. A. Mangan, 'Christ and the imperial playing fields: Thomas Hughes's ideological heirs in empire', *International Journal of the History of Sport*, 23:5 (2006), 783.
96 BL, IOR/L/PS/12/1669, no. 104 from G. F. Squire, 1 September 1949.
97 NAI, External Affairs, 1944, 528-F, no. 69 from G. F. Squire, 5 August 1944.
98 BL, IOR/L/PS/12/1669, no. 104 from G. F. Squire, 1 September 1949.
99 'Sir G. Squire: ambassador and churchman'.
100 L. Dupree, *Afghanistan* (Karachi: Oxford University Press, 1997), 224.
101 N. Barrington, *Envoy: A Diplomatic Journey* (London: I. B. Tauris, 2014), 22.

6

Friendship is solidarity: the Chinese ping-pong team visits Africa in 1962*

Amanda Shuman

There is great promise in these [Ghanaian] West African players and one day, soon, they'll make the table tennis world sit up and applaud.

Rong Guotuan, China's first ping-pong world champion, following the team's visit to Africa in 1962.[1]

Many people today are aware of the so-called 'ping-pong diplomacy' that helped thaw US–China relations in the early 1970s.[2] Few know that the Chinese leadership already had two decades of experience using sport, including ping-pong, for diplomacy. There had been an official desire in China to see athletes represent the nation through their athletic success on the world stage for several decades prior to the establishment of the People's Republic of China (PRC) in 1949.[3] The PRC leadership, however, was the first to use international sport for its broader foreign and domestic policy goals. In the 1950s, as the PRC battled with the Republic of China (ROC-Taiwan) for international recognition in sport and beyond, sport became a prominent site for legitimising the new socialist state and solidifying its place within the Soviet-led socialist world. Chinese leaders and media touted exchanges that focused on 'learning from the Soviet Union' (*xuexi Sulian*) and the socialist bloc as proof of growing friendship and solidarity between 'fraternal countries' (*xiongdi guojia*).[4]

By the late 1950s, however, the political tides had already begun to turn. When Rong Guotuan won the men's singles title at the 1959 Table Tennis World Championships – the first Chinese athlete to win any major world championship – he became a national and international celebrity at a crucial moment.[5] China was in the midst of the Great Leap Forward, a massive political, economic and social movement that kicked off in 1958 with Mao proclaiming that the nation would overtake UK production in fifteen years.[6] State-sponsored sport in China had proliferated in the second half of the 1950s, culminating with the First National Games held in Beijing in October 1959. These Games, coinciding with national day celebrations, were meant to showcase a decade of progress under Communist Party rule. Chinese sports leaders argued that Rong's win represented a major achievement of the new state sports system. He was, in short, a positive image of socialist success that also extended beyond China's borders.

Less than two years later, in the face of financial disaster and widespread famine, the leadership called off the Great Leap campaign. Mao retreated while Liu Shaoqi (Mao's second in command), Zhou Enlai and Deng Xiaoping undertook a more pragmatic approach to domestic growth.[7] Austerity measures implemented nationwide meant that funding for sports programmes ran out – except, that is, for top athletes like Rong. Major changes in Chinese foreign policy were taking place, including the deterioration of Sino-Soviet relations, the establishment of diplomatic relations with newly decolonised nations, and a rise in participation in various Afro-Asian solidarity movements. Sino-Soviet competition began in the Third World, with both sides determined to influence and gain the upper hand in national liberation struggles worldwide.[8] The country was broke, but Chinese leaders were determined to build relations with new allies while positioning China as the ideologically superior socialist model, and they believed sport could help accomplish this.

PRC leaders thus engaged in a form of sports diplomacy in the 1960s explicitly for the purposes of improving China's image and wielding what in today's terms would be called 'soft power'.[9] The state intended its athletes and sports leaders to deliver a positive image of the nation through 'cultural attraction, ideology, and international institutions' and legitimate its alternative model of socialist development 'in the eyes of others'.[10] Chinese sports diplomacy was also a form of public diplomacy that aimed to spread China's soft power. The leadership believed that foreign media exposure of its sports teams, as well as drawing large audiences of spectators for competitions and exhibition matches, would 'influence broader opinion in foreign societies'.[11] The peak of propaganda efforts came with the Games of the New Emerging Forces (GANEFO) movement, a Sino-Indonesian-sponsored challenge to the International Olympic Committee's dominance in sport that also attempted to solidify China's geopolitical position as a Third World leader.[12]

More typical than such mega-events, however, were state-sponsored sports delegation visits, in which sports leaders and top athletes like Rong served as bona fide diplomats. This was especially true of Chinese involvement in international sport in the 1950s and 1960s, which revolved almost exclusively around smaller sports competitions and delegation visits.[13] At a time when travel for Chinese citizens was severely restricted, the State Sports Commission and the Chinese Foreign Ministry worked together to send Chinese sports delegations abroad and receive foreign delegations in China. The plethora of official documents produced during official sports visits speaks to their broader diplomatic importance to the Chinese state.[14] As far as the leadership was concerned, these could be just as successful or even more successful than larger events in expanding Chinese influence and in gathering leaders together for diplomatic purposes.

Sports delegation visits between China and recently decolonised countries in the 1960s carried out a form of diplomacy that emphasised affective relations. The goal of visits was to build 'friendship' – a code word for cultivating better strategic political relations under the umbrella of 'people's diplomacy'. This entailed making 'as many friends as possible' through direct people-to-people contact, while also exposing enemies and promoting China.[15] These visits sought to reinforce political solidarities by strengthening emotional bonds between those involved, while showcasing a Chinese brand of socialism that leaders hoped would appeal to these new 'friends'. This brand professed, among other things, placing the revolutionary struggle of oppressed peoples against colonialism and imperialism above the struggle against capitalism.[16] PRC leaders firmly believed that underdeveloped African and Asian countries could learn from China's alternative (non-Soviet) socialist path of development. They were, in other words, building personal affect in an effort to take the lead over the Soviet Union in the Third World.

In China, sport delegation visits in the 1960s were also always simultaneously about reinforcing foreign and domestic policies.[17] The official framing of visits in the domestic media – which usually highlighted meetings and receptions with important political leaders and always claimed 'warm' relations between 'friends' – was clearly geared towards a general readership. In the wake of the Sino-Soviet split, such visits were used to teach the Chinese public about the nation's position in the world among new 'friends' and to demonstrate the early successes of China's own socialist path.

Following a brief background to the relationship between sport and the Chinese Communist Party's understanding of the world, the remainder of this chapter provides a case study of the Chinese ping-pong team's tour of several African countries (Ghana, Guinea, Mali, Sudan, and the United Arab Republic (UAR)-Egypt) in spring 1962.[18] Declassified telegrams and reports from the Chinese Foreign Ministry, as well as official media, show how the Chinese leadership utilised this first-ever sports delegation sent to West Africa to strengthen political solidarities and uphold a positive image of China. Some scholars have argued that public diplomacy is distinct from propaganda because the latter is 'uninterested … in any meaningful form of relationship building'.[19] Yet, as this case study demonstrates, the PRC did engage in cultivating 'meaningful' relations through the method of 'finding things in common' with their hosts.[20] The official Chinese media as well as the summary report from the Foreign Ministry on the visit shed light on the ways in which the leadership measured and understood diplomatic efforts through sport – sometimes in very concrete ways, but more often in terms of building affective relations. Furthermore, the Chinese leadership made no distinction between public diplomacy and propaganda. The ping-pong team's popularity abroad and its sports achievements were portrayed officially with an air of superiority, and as evidence of Chinese socialist influence burgeoning in Africa, while the team's exchange of sports skills and participation in non-sports activities was touted as proof of a growing 'friendship' that represented genuine political solidarity. In sum, Chinese leaders considered the visit a resounding diplomatic and propaganda success.

Placing China on the world stage through sport

Sports development in the Mao years (1949–76) was closely connected to the oscillations of official understandings of China's place in the world. Chinese Communist Party leaders understood their nation as belonging to a global community made up of other nations and peoples with similar historical backgrounds, all engaged in a struggle against colonialism and imperialism – a community often described in secondary literature as the 'Third World'.[21] This was especially true after the 1955 Bandung Conference, but the origins of this understanding pre-date the founding of the People's Republic of China.[22]

As early as 1940, Mao Zedong advocated finding a 'third state' of development that could serve former colonial and semi-colonial states in their transition to socialism.[23] This transitional 'new democratic' state would differ from that found in the Soviet Union, by skipping the bourgeois or capitalist dictatorship stage and moving directly into a society headed by a proletarian-led, joint dictatorship of all the revolutionary classes. Mao also argued, however, that the Chinese revolution needed the assistance of the Soviet Union in order to succeed. Thus, in the first few years of the PRC, the Chinese Communist Party carried out a programme of 'New Democracy' at the same time that it also promoted 'learning from the Soviet Union' under the official policy of 'leaning to one side'.[24] The development of Chinese sports programmes and sports exchanges in the first half of the 1950s sought to fulfil the goals of New Democracy, while also adopting Soviet-inspired sports programmes in China.[25] In the late 1950s, as Mao became increasingly disillusioned with Khrushchev's policies of de-Stalinisation, the PRC shifted away from following the Soviet Union and towards creating a Chinese socialist model in the world of sport.[26] By the time the Great Leap Forward began in 1958, although Soviet-inspired models remained, PRC leaders had decided to forge their own path in sport.[27]

Parallel to these developments, the 1955 Bandung Conference gave voice to an emergent global community of recently decolonised and Third World nations. Recent scholarship on this conference has especially emphasised its utmost importance in helping forge solidarities among participants by building on their emotions, creating what Christopher Lee has called a 'community of feeling'.[28] United primarily (and sometimes only) through a sense of shared historical struggle against imperialism and colonialism, leaders of participating nations sought to create new organisations for themselves, such as the Non-Aligned Movement and the Afro-Asian Peoples' Solidarity Organization (AAPSO).[29] The PRC leadership professed an early interest in these developments; Premier Zhou Enlai argued in his closing speech at Bandung that cooperation was possible and achievements could be made simply 'because we peoples of the Asian and African countries share the same fate and the same desires'.[30] In the late 1950s, as Sino-Soviet relations grew tense and the Great Leap Forward began, the Chinese government invested more heavily in building relations with newly independent African states and in supporting various national liberation movements.[31] This included sending official delegations on visits to African countries (especially the UAR and Algeria) and paying for African delegations to come to China to engage in 'people's diplomacy'. Through these visits, the government worked to generate favourable impressions and new contacts that would help the PRC gain further recognition while convincing Africans that Chinese support for their independence was genuine.[32]

Sino-Soviet relations meanwhile deteriorated further after 1960 and culminated in a split. Chinese leaders had come to believe that China, as the greatest underdeveloped nation in the world that had already undergone a social revolution, should lead the rest of the world's revolutionary movements.[33] In their analysis, the Soviet Union had abandoned the international socialist movement and forgotten about oppressed peoples around the world; the PRC should instead set the example. The fundamental ideological difference between the Chinese and Soviet communist parties in these years was in their divergent understandings of the world revolution. Soviet leaders, as they had done for decades, prioritised an anti-capitalist revolution, while Chinese leaders emphasised an anti-imperialist one.[34]

As the two sides competed for influence in the Third World, sport played an increasing role in Chinese efforts to become more involved in burgeoning African and Asian solidarity movements. In fact, the state-sponsored development of elite competitive sport in China in the 1960s existed almost solely for the purpose of propagating the Party's alternative socialist path within the global community – especially to recently decolonised nations in Africa and Asia.

Afro-Asian solidarity and Chinese sports diplomacy in the 1960s

Between 1961 and 1965, when the influence of Chinese leaders vis-à-vis Soviet and Indian leaders in the AAPSO reached its height, sports also played an important role in expanding Chinese influence in Africa.[35] Although in mid-1960 China had diplomatic relations with just five African countries (the UAR, Morocco, Algeria, Sudan and Guinea), by July 1965 it had established relations with twenty.[36] Official sport visits and other cultural exchanges with these nations, which often occurred after the signing of cultural cooperation agreements, helped foster diplomatic relations at a time when prominent international organisations like the United Nations did not recognise the PRC.[37] PRC leaders clearly believed that sending around cultural delegations could and did promote a favourable image of China and Chinese socialism. Moreover, because surprisingly little was known about some of these countries, delegation visits became an avenue for basic knowledge acquisition on new allies.[38] Information gathered during a visit helped provide subject matter for Chinese foreign propaganda during this period, which expanded even as delegation members themselves sometimes helped distribute it.[39]

The production in China of official reports and media on delegation visits also served an important but often overlooked purpose: helping reshape the worldviews of a domestic audience. By employing official reports and media to fashion delegations as expressions of China's solidarity with and guiding role among oppressed peoples in African and Asian nations, the Chinese leadership conveyed to its own citizens a new position in the world for China in the wake of the Sino-Soviet split.[40] As Julia Strauss has argued, the rhetoric used in Chinese publications was not simply 'empty words', but rather a method of legitimating the state's policies and attempting to 'attract, persuade, mobilize or consolidate support within'.[41] Sports interactions with the Soviet Union and the socialist bloc in the 1950s, in fact, had already set a precedent in Chinese official media. Coverage of well-known Soviet and socialist bloc athletes, as well as numerous delegation visits, had helped disseminate to the general public China's geopolitical position vis-à-vis the Soviet Union and its allies.[42] Sport was therefore already a popular and familiar medium for teaching ordinary citizens about their nation's role in the world, but the message in the 1960s was different. Instead of 'friendly' learning from the Soviet Union and socialist bloc, 'friendship' was reserved for those engaged in the worldwide struggle against colonialism and imperialism, and Chinese socialism was the model for oppressed peoples everywhere to follow. Sports exchanges and competitions became sites where Chinese leaders sought to foster affective relations based on these principles.

By the early 1960s, concerted attempts to use international sport to build relations with African and Asian nations and negotiate Afro-Asian solidarities began with ping-pong. China's earlier international success in the sport, as well as the fact that the International Table Tennis Federation (ITTF) was one of the few international sports organisations that consistently recognised the PRC, also meant that the state continued to heavily fund the sport after the Great Leap Forward.[43] Indeed, the ITTF gave the nation its first opportunity to host a major international sporting event, and in April 1961 Beijing was the site of the World Championships. Athletes from more than thirty nations showed up to this event – where they watched Chinese players take home most of the awards.[44]

The ping-pong team's success attracted attention worldwide, and in 1962 it received a request that presented a unique opportunity. In January, the Ghanaian central sports council contacted the Chinese Foreign Ministry, via its embassy in Beijing, to ask for a ping-pong delegation to be sent to Ghana in May or June of that year.[45] Ghana had joined the ITTF in 1961 and was one of only two African nations to send a delegation to the World Championships in Beijing where, according to official results, the players lost every match.[46] The request made in 1962 asked for five players (three male and two female) and for a coach who would then remain in Ghana for a year, all expenses paid, to help train the national team for the upcoming first Pan-African championships to be held in Cairo in September.[47] As was typical for delegation visits, China was responsible for travel costs to and from the country, and then Ghana would take care of lodging, food and in-country transportation. The Chinese side partially agreed to the request, adding another female player, a group leader and a French translator to the delegation.[48] Meanwhile, the *Daily Graphic* reported that the visit would without a doubt 'give a new fillip to the game in Ghana'.[49] The Ghana Table Tennis Federation enthusiastically prepared for the visit by holding interregional championships to select players for further training. The Chinese side revised down the request for a coach to stay a year in Ghana to three months, although the Ghanaian side hoped that one might come in the future for a year and a half to train a new coach.[50] Most importantly, the PRC leadership decided this was an ideal chance for the delegation to visit several additional African countries. At a time in which Chinese leaders had little experience with West Africa, the delegation could at the very least make a good impression and gather information on some of these countries.

So in April 1962, a year after the World Championships held in Beijing and a year and a half before Zhou Enlai's high-profile tour of Africa, the government sent its top ping-pong athletes to the continent.[51] Over the course of two months, the Chinese athletes visited the UAR, Ghana, Guinea, Mali and Sudan. In charge of the ping-pong delegation was Huang Zhong, vice-chair of the State Sports Commission, and a cadre trusted by the Chinese top leadership. The Commission's plan for the visit stated that, since it would be the first time a Chinese sports team was going to West Africa, the team's mission would be to support diplomatic work, hold 'friendship activities' (*youhao huodong*), carry out sports exchanges that would foster understanding and friendship, and 'expand our nation's political influence'.[52] Though not explicitly stated, the leadership believed that the high-profile ping-pong players had the potential to propagate a positive image of China in a way that might appeal to a broader audience, especially in countries like Ghana and the UAR where the sport was already popular.

The Chinese press reported on the delegation's activities during the visit, often delivering timely but brief accounts of where the delegation was and if they had played any matches. Articles in *People's Daily* (for a domestic audience) and *New China News Agency* (for an international audience) rarely mentioned anything further about matches or players, but frequently described the team's effusive welcome everywhere they went and listed the names of any important political leaders they had met. During the visit, *New China News Agency* described the team's reception as 'warm' and 'cordial' – such as being 'warmly welcomed' upon arrival or 'warmly applauded' during a match – no fewer than twenty-two times, while the terms 'friendship' and 'friendly' made at least nineteen appearances.[53] Twenty-five times articles named African sports leaders, finance ministers, presidents and other dignitaries. Though much is missing about the actual activities and meetings, the Chinese message delivered was one of growing friendly relations with Africans.

Articles published in China afterwards and Huang's post-visit summary report sent to the Foreign Ministry provide more details on the nature of the visit. Huang's report begins by summarising the basic facts, including that Coach Wang Chuanyao had remained in Ghana to work.[54] The team had played thirty-four matches and exhibitions, thirteen of which occurred in Guinea and twelve in Ghana, and it had won the vast majority. Huang also estimated a total audience of approximately 15,000 that had come to see the team play. The report then moves straight into outlining the diplomatic efforts, including the ping-pong team's 'warm' reception and courting by leaders at all levels in each country. This included a high-profile meeting with Guinean president Sékou Touré at the Presidential Palace, mentioned not only in Huang's report but also in an article published in the English-language *China's Sports* (an official mouthpiece) that was ostensibly penned by Rong Guotuan himself.[55]

Rong's article and Huang's report both went to great lengths to list the ways in which the delegation had worked to build China–Africa solidarities by developing affective bonds with its hosts. This often had little to do with sport and everything to do with strengthening relations or connections (*guanxi*) as one might find in China, such as in spending time together and exchanging small gifts. Associated with the concept of feelings (*ganqing*), the cultivation of *guanxi* is even today often attached to (and sometimes conflated with) 'friendship'.[56] Thus when Rong states that 'friends' in Mali gifted the team handbags and wallets made of crocodile skin following a sightseeing visit to a crocodile park in Bamako, he calls these 'tokens of the friendship the Mali people have for the Chinese people'.[57] The gift exchange in Sudan was apparently so emotional that everyone was 'moved to tears' (*gandong de liulei*).[58] Rong's article and Huang's report also worked to convince their readers that relations on both sides were profound, authentic and enduring. For example, Ghana's national men's and women's singles champions, E. A. Quaye and Ethel Jacks, who had both attended the 1961 World Championships in Beijing, greeted the team at the airport with a Chinese folk song that was 'moving to hear' from 'Ghanaian friends'.[59] In the UAR, a vice-president of the ITTF invited the players to his home, which was decorated with Chinese paintings, ornaments, and figurines, showing his 'esteem and affection … for our country'.[60] Youth that had studied in China came to greet the team after matches in the UAR, including a young Chinese-speaking couple who spent an evening with the team, gave them a family photo and stated that they wanted to go back to China for a visit. A Chinese folk song, a house decorated in a Chinese style and a Chinese-speaking couple dreaming of China: the article recollected such comments not just as proof of how these people had deeply personal relationships with the country, but also of how their strong admiration for it reflected China's growing influence in Africa.

During the visit, the team's non-sports activities helped reinforce a bond based on narratives of shared historical struggle against colonialism and imperialism. In their meeting with Touré, Rong's article reported, the Guinean president had reiterated that the 'friendship' between the Chinese and Guinean peoples was based on 'our common aim and common anti-imperialist and anti-colonialist sentiments'.[61] Emphasising commonalities was considered essential in creating better relations with Africans.[62] Huang stressed in his report that the team had used all opportunities – from the fourteen official meetings with leaders to numerous other sports and non-sports activities – to express the 'deep camaraderie' (*shenhou qingyi*) between the Chinese and African people (figure 6.1). This included visits to important historic and cultural sites in order to learn about the 'heroic struggle' of African people against imperialism and colonialism.[63] In Ghana, for example, the delegation visited the Cape Coast Castle, a black slave fort that had served as a prison in colonial times, the report noting that slaves from this particular location had also been 'fettered and handcuffed' and then sent to North America.[64] When visiting the UAR, the team made a stop at Port Said, where they saw vestiges of the 1956 Suez Crisis – or, in the words of the report, where the Egypt had resisted 'the attack of English and French imperialism'[65] – such as the tomb of the unknown soldier (figure 6.2).[66] The delegation found a particularly resonant historical thread when they visited the memorial of Khartoum Mahdi in Sudan, where they saw the yellow robe and mandarin jacket presented to British general Charles Gordon by the Qing court for his help in suppressing the Taiping rebellion in the 1860s. Chinese revolutionary leaders, including Mao, admired the Taiping rebels as early heroes in their attempt to overthrow the Qing dynasty, and they viewed Gordon as an interfering British colonialist siding with the Qing. Gordon was later killed during an attempt to suppress Mahdist rebels in Khartoum and with his clothing on display had thus been, according to the report, 'duly punished' in Sudan.[67] Huang concluded from all of these experiences that the team had received a 'profound education'

6.1 'They found friendship warm and deep'. Chinese national team ping-pong players Sun Meiying (left) and Hu Keming (right) with Khadidjata Diallo of Guinea

6.2 Team leader Huang Zhong places a wreath on the tomb of the Unknown Soldier at Port Said

in both patriotism and internationalism,[68] but performing these ritual visits while drawing upon the language of a shared historical struggle against colonialism and imperialism also fell in line with Mao's 1956 pronouncement to 'use the past to serve the present, make the foreign serve China'.[69] Such non-sports sightseeing visits were, in other words, clearly meant to develop affective bonds between Chinese guests and their local hosts that would boost their 'friendship' in a broader sense – and fulfil a PRC political agenda.

Couched in terms of Afro-Asian solidarity, the 1962 sports delegation also went beyond affect by working to promote China's national image and Chinese socialism through the lens of sport. In the UAR, Huang's report noted that the visit was preceded by one week of showing a documentary on Chinese ping-pong in movie theatres, and the Chinese team's first match was broadcast on television.[70] Although Huang does not specify who decided to show the film, where it was shown, or who watched it, the implication throughout the report is that the team's reputation in these countries was already well established and they were very popular. Local media had also helped boost the team's image. Ghana's *Daily Graphic* published a series of articles about the team, including brief biographies on the players and a front-page group photo of the 'Tennis stars' the day prior to their arrival,[71] as well as subsequent reports on exhibition matches that managed to 'thrill the fans'.[72] (The latter included Huang losing in a 'special exhibition match' to Kofi Baako, Ghana's Minister of Defense and Table Tennis Federation chair.) Huang reported that the team had been overwhelmed by fans' requests for autographs and photos after each match held in the UAR, and in every country youth had become 'wildly excited' after seeing the team play.[73] The *Ghanaian Times* meanwhile published an article calling the 1961 World Championship in Beijing a 'milestone' in which it noted that sixteen of the world's best players now came from China. The Chinese report noted that this article attributed China's achievements to an improvement in Chinese peoples' material and cultural lives under socialism. According to Huang, grand receptions given for the ping-pong team in every country were also an indication of respect for China as a whole, as were comments throughout the visit praising China's socialist construction, anti-imperialist position and 'support for all oppressed peoples struggling for independence'.[74] The popularity of this Chinese ping-pong delegation, the report thus insinuated, represented a broader admiration of African peoples towards China and Chinese socialism.

Furthermore, despite public proclamations about shared struggles and the building of 'friendship', what Huang's internal report to the Foreign Ministry clearly indicates is that the PRC leadership never saw relations with African countries as equal. The report constantly attempts to place China and Chinese socialism on a pedestal, and suggests that PRC superiority extended beyond sport. Huang argued that the visit showed African people China's 'vigorous development' across all of society. For example, he noted that female ping-pong players from China, where officially the slogan was 'men and women are equal', had especially drawn attention in Guinea, Mali and Sudan, 'where women have not been fully liberated'.[75] The implication here was that a morally superior society – which China already had but these countries had yet to achieve – included the emancipation of women. Huang cited the Guinean president Touré as having praised the Chinese leadership and socialist system for support of the worldwide people's liberation movement based on a real desire to eliminate the foundation of imperialism. Ghana's national defence leader meanwhile stated that Ghana could learn a lot from China's experience with socialist construction. It probably helped that in the previous year Chinese leaders had already satisfied some Ghanaian ping-pong-related requests, such as providing them with an unspecified number of paddles and issues of the English-language magazine *China's Sports*.[76] The gifting of these shows how, in the eyes of Chinese leaders, an inexpensive request for sports items could easily be fulfilled even when the country was financially strapped – if, that is, it served a strategic foreign policy goal and especially if it included propaganda that might raise China's image and influence in a particular country.

While a major task of this visit was raising or reinforcing China's image through exposure of the ping-pong team, the report also made some general observations on sports programmes in these countries. Huang, for example, commented that sports activities in African countries, especially Guinea, Mali and Sudan, were somewhat 'backward' and their sports programmes 'incomplete', lacking mass participation, appropriate sports facilities and equipment, and (especially) specialised sports talent. The only exception to this was some 'rather good' advances made in sport in the UAR, where the delegation watched the national football team beat the European champions Portugal.[77] The report added with disgust, however, that sport in the UAR was unfortunately 'in the hands of the rich' – a comment that further disparaged President Nasser and the Soviet-leaning UAR leadership while also insinuating that the UAR could not be trusted. Nevertheless, the report noted that the future for all of these African countries was bright because following independence their governments had placed a lot of importance on sports. In Ghana, for example, soccer, ping-pong, field hockey, cricket and boxing were not only widespread, but the government was also ambitious and seeking to lead Africa in them. Guinea was in the middle of building a stadium to seat 25,000 and developing new programmes not just in ping-pong but also in gymnastics. Furthermore, an All-African Sports Federation established earlier in the year had branches in individual sports disciplines, some of which had already held championships.[78] This kind of information gave the Chinese leadership some ideas on the current state of sport that could then be used either for spreading its own influence in specific countries, or in shoring up potential supporters for other battles brewing in the world of international sport.[79]

In fact, the Chinese ping-pong delegation had already begun to spread its influence by concretely engaging with sports development in these countries. Where the skill level was considered 'low', such as in Guinea and Mali, the Chinese delegation helped establish ping-pong associations, visited schools and work units at all levels, and held various exhibitions for the masses. A few months prior to this visit, the Chinese government had already made the decision to send Guinea a modest amount of sports equipment, including a few ping-pong tables.[80] These endeavours also clearly met with some success in Mali, which subsequently set up a national Table Tennis Federation and in 1963 became a member of the International Table

Tennis Federation.[81] In Ghana and Egypt, where the skill level was considered better – Ghanaian E. A. Quaye was West African champion in men's singles and had played in the 1961 ITTF World Championships in Beijing – the focus was on promoting and extending the sport through exhibitions held at, for example, local schools.[82] Several practice competitions were also held with the Ghanaian national team to help improve their skills.

Nevertheless, as the post-visit report indicates, the Chinese leadership measured the success of the 1962 visit less in terms of local sports endeavours and more in terms of what it did to build affective relations with Africans and boost China's image in these countries. Chinese official media wasted no time in delivering the good news to a home audience. The State Sports Commission held a reception on 27 June, less than a week after the delegation had returned to Beijing, to honour the countries for their hospitality. Speaking to a room full of invited envoys and diplomats from these countries, Foreign Minister Chen Yi thanked the African countries for their warm reception of the ping-pong team before then adding that China and these countries found themselves in a similar situation: standing up to oppression from imperialism and colonialism.[83] *People's Daily* also quoted the Ghanaian ambassador to China as having stated that the visit had left a 'deep impression' and encouraged 'friendship' between 'the peoples of China and Africa'.[84] Other leaders from the State Sports Commission, the Foreign Ministry and the Chinese–African People's Friendship Association were also present. And, of course, so were the ping-pong players, who played an exhibition match for these guests following the reception.

Conclusion

Over the course of 1965 and 1966, Chinese politics became increasingly radical and militant. Mao's personality cult gained new traction following his epic swim in July 1966 – an event that included a colour video of Mao bobbing around the Yangzi and was understood in China as a display of the ageing leader's good health – and the subsequent rise of Red Guard factions.[85] African delegations visiting China in the summer and autumn of 1966 experienced some of this first hand when they received a heavy dose of Chinese socialism that emphasised Mao Zedong thought.[86] In late 1966, sports leaders and top athletes came under heavy criticism, and sports activities – including delegation visits – had largely ceased by the end of the decade. Over the course of several months in 1968, three famous ping-pong players, including Rong Guotuan, committed suicide.[87]

In the early 1970s, the leadership revitalised ping-pong and ushered in the adoption of an official sports policy in China known as 'friendship first, competition second'.[88] The policy and accompanying slogan instructed athletes and leaders to put 'friendship' above all else at international sports competitions and during delegation visits, and this was especially true with African and Asian nations. One prominent example was the Afro-Asian Table Tennis Friendship Invitational Tournament held in Beijing in November 1971. The Chinese press emphasised repeatedly that the purpose of the event was 'enhancing friendship' with people from African and Asian countries and promoting table tennis development.[89] The international press often portrayed this approach as a new attempt on the part of the Chinese Party-state to broaden the scope of its amicable foreign relations. 'Ping-pong diplomacy', as it continues to be well known today, helped thaw Sino-American relations – and the PRC joined the United Nations in October 1971. Yet, as I have shown, this official soft power sports policy to create 'friendly' foreign relations with African and Asian nations existed in the previous decade.

For the Chinese leadership, the 1962 visit of the ping-pong team to Africa was clearly considered a successful use of sport for diplomacy. In his 2011 book, Joseph Nye cites a recent book of multinational surveys as having deemed China's soft power efforts 'ineffective'.[90] He argues that although persuasion in soft power can be manipulative, attractiveness ultimately depends on 'emotional appeals and narratives' made by non-elites (i.e. unofficial third parties).[91] Emotion was indeed at the very heart of Chinese sports diplomacy in the 1960s, but it was dictated according to the Chinese leadership and not the masses. This did not make these visits ineffective. On the contrary, Chinese leaders measured the success of a visit both tangibly in terms of numbers or visits with leaders, as well as intangibly in their building of affective relations ('friendship') between delegation members, their African hosts and any other Africans with whom the Chinese team came in contact during a visit. As Anne-Marie Brady has previously noted, China's 'friendship diplomacy is not just cultural diplomacy – it's a remarkably effective way to deal with the outside world'.[92] This was certainly the case with sports diplomacy under Mao.

The long-term political success of the 1960s sports delegation visits might be difficult to assess, but the leadership used the vocabulary, narratives and framework from this visit – and likely others, in combination with the leadership of its embassies in these countries – to aid subsequent efforts at cultivating Sino-African relations. The history of Ghana's Cape Coast castle and Gordon's 'punishment' in Sudan, for example, both made it into speeches given by Zhou Enlai when he visited these countries in January 1964 as part of his high-profile African tour.[93] Such narratives linking China with many African countries based on a colonial past are, in fact, still in use today: visiting the Khalifa museum to see Gordon's infamous 'yellow jacket' continues to be a sightseeing stop for Chinese delegations.[94] Furthermore, the ping-pong team's connections in several African countries clearly helped bolster these countries' participation in later events like the Afro-Asian tournament in 1971.[95] And, as the famous US ping-pong team visit to China indicated, the Chinese leadership knew how to use sports diplomacy to its advantage.

Overall, Chinese leaders used elite sport in the 1960s to accomplish goals directly related to China's international and domestic political agendas. In the aftermath of the Great Leap Forward and Sino-Soviet split, elite sport helped open up new transnational networks and establish foreign relations that reconfigured China's place in the world. Central-level sports policies siphoned limited state resources to athletic superstars with the hope that Chinese athletes would reach and compete at world levels, break world records and win glory for China in the international arena. This, they believed, would truly elevate the nation's image. China's official media coverage of its athletes at mega-events like the GANEFO, as well as during smaller sports delegation visits, was intended to spread a positive national image to recently decolonised Third World nations and a domestic audience. Persuading local Chinese – whether leaders, athletes or ordinary citizens – has always been as important to the Chinese government as reaching foreigners. At a time in which the country was recovering from the Great Leap Forward and the deterioration of Sino-Soviet relations, this method of sports diplomacy helped legitimate the regime's policies and deliver a new understanding of China's place in the world to an international as well as domestic audience.

Notes

* I would like to thank Maggie Greene, Chuck Kraus, Heather Dichter and Simon Rofe for their insightful comments on this piece. A special thank you to Matt Johnson for providing crucial feedback on an earlier draft. I am also grateful for the assistance of Claire Nicolas in locating copies of newspaper articles from Ghana.

1 Rong Guotuan, 'African tour', *China's Sports*, 4 (1962), 8.

2 For a recent account of this famous period, see Nicholas Griffin, *Ping-Pong Diplomacy: The Secret History Behind the Game That Changed the World* (New York: Scribner, 2014), especially 'Part three: East meets West', 165–234.

3 Both Andrew Morris and Xu Guoqi have looked at how Chinese interest in international sport in the first decades of the twentieth century stemmed from a wish to raise national image in the world. Andrew Morris, *Marrow of the National* (Berkeley, CA: University of California Press, 2004); Xu Guoqi, *Olympic Dreams: China and Sport, 1895–2008* (Cambridge, MA: Harvard University Press, 2008).

4 As part of the official policy to 'learn from the Soviet Union', the Chinese sports world frequently interacted with the Soviet Union and the Soviet-led socialist bloc through sports exchanges. Amanda Shuman, 'The Politics of Socialist Athletics', PhD dissertation, University of California Santa Cruz, 2014, 91–112.

5 In addition to the usual claims in the official China media that Rong brought 'glory to the motherland', the *Daily Mirror* in London recognised Rong's achievement as one of those sporting 'miracles' performed by nations 'virtually overnight'. Quoted in Griffin, *Ping-Pong Diplomacy*, 86. However, Rong was no ordinary athlete. Born in Hong Kong to a family originally from a town in nearby Guangdong province, the PRC leadership recruited him 'back' to the mainland in the 1950s exclusively to play ping-pong for the new socialist state. In the 1950s, the designation given to athletes like Rong – of which there were others – was 'returned Chinese'. Rong's decision to play for the PRC was probably influenced by a series of fortuitous events: top leaders He Long and Chen Yi called him to a private meeting to make an offer; Jiang Yongning, another famous player and colleague from Hong Kong, was already in Guangzhou and the two met to discuss the matter; and finally, despite Rong being a top player, the Hong Kong team did not choose him for the upcoming Asian championships. Griffin, *Ping-Pong Diplomacy*, 77–82.

6 R. Macfarquhar, *Origins of the Cultural Revolution Volume 2: The Great Leap Forward, 1958–1960* (New York: Columbia University Press, 1983), 16–17.

7 Lorenz Lüthi, *The Sino-Soviet Split: Cold War in the Communist World* (Princeton, NJ: Princeton University Press, 2008), 194.

8 Jeremy Friedman, *Shadow Cold War: The Sino-Soviet Competition for the Third World* (Chapel Hill, NC: University of North Carolina Press, 2015).

9 The term 'soft power', coined by Joseph Nye in 1990 and elaborated upon in subsequent articles and books, has been used to describe how liberal states with civil societies influence others through 'attraction and persuasion rather than coercion or payment'. However, the term has become popular in recent years in China, and Nye himself describes the Beijing Olympics and programmes such as the Confucius Institutes as forms of Chinese soft power, even while he continues to assert that this soft power cannot be successful without a civil society. Joseph S. Nye, Jr, 'China's soft power deficit', *Wall Street Journal*, 8 May 2012, available at www.wsj.com/articles/SB1 0001424052702304451104577389923098678842 (accessed 13 April 2016).

10 Joseph S. Nye, Jr, 'Soft power', *Foreign Policy*, 80 (1990), 153–71, 167.

11 Jan Melissen, 'Beyond the new public diplomacy', Netherlands Institute of International Relations, Clingendael Papers 3 (October 2011), 9.

12 Amanda Shuman, 'Elite competitive sport in the People's Republic of China 1958–1966: the Games of the New Emerging Forces (GANEFO)', *Journal of Sport History*, 40:2 (2013).

13 Sports visits between China, the Soviet Union and the socialist bloc were prolific throughout the 1950s. In the case of China, the leadership publicised many of these visits in order to promote new domestic sports policies and an image of socialist solidarity for a mainland Chinese audience, in addition to the more common understanding that these were exchanges of technical expertise and knowledge. Amanda Shuman, 'Friendship and fraternal ties: learning from the Soviet Union and building the People's Republic of China through sport in the early 1950s', *The Whole World Was Watching: Sport in the Cold War* (Stanford: Stanford University Press, forthcoming).

14 Some documents – including the ones I use in this chapter – reside in the Chinese Foreign Ministry Archives in Beijing, which following a decade or so of opening some files, has as of 2014 closed its doors to the public once again. This makes it difficult to conduct research on Chinese delegations travelling abroad. However, documents on foreign delegations visiting China can be found in various provincial and municipal archives in areas where delegations travelled.

15 Anne-Marie Brady, *Making the Foreign Serve China: Managing Foreigners in the People's Republic* (Lanham, MD: Rowman & Littlefield, 2003), 1, 23.

16 Friedman, *Shadow Cold War*, 1.

17 Jeanne L. Wilson, 'Soft power: a comparison of discourse and practice in Russia and China', *Europe-Asia Studies*, 67:8 (2015), 1171–202, 1193. As Wilson notes, Nye understands 'soft power as a tool of foreign policy' rather than the Chinese understanding that it is also about domestic policy.

18 Between 1958 and 1971, Egypt was known as the United Arab Republic.

19 Melissen, 'Beyond the new public diplomacy', 8.

20 Brady, *Making the Foreign Serve China*, 14.

21 Alexander Cook, 'Third World Maoism', in T. Cheek (ed.), *A Critical Introduction to Mao* (New York: Cambridge University Press, 2010), especially 288–9; Arif Dirlik, 'Spectres of the Third World: global modernity and the end of the Three Worlds',

Third World Quarterly, 25:1 (2004). Dirlik notes that the term 'Third World' seems to have outlived its Cold War counterpart, the 'Second World' largely because 'the invention pointed to certain realities that endowed the concept with substance' (Dirlik, 'Spectres', 135). Specifically, the use of the term 'Third World' during the Cold War was the product of ideological restructuring based on the teleology of capitalism, where the First World was capitalism, the Second World was socialism, and the Third World was everything else and was set on a path towards reaching the First and Second World. The problem with the Cold War use of such a term, according to Dirlik, is that it did not take into account a 'Third World' concept that consisted of a 'complex history of the search for potential "third worlds" as developmental and utopian projects' ('Spectres', 136). The result was that the term itself marginalised and discounted these searches for alternatives by presuming all societies 'had to be headed towards either capitalism or socialism as it existed' ('Spectres', 136).

22 Cook, 'Third World Maoism', 289.

23 Mao Zedong, 'On new democracy', January 1940, available at, www.marxists. org/reference/archive/mao/selected-works/volume-2/mswv2_26.htm (accessed 1 September 2014).

24 This policy accepted the Soviet Union as the leader of the international socialist movement and provided for a Sino-Soviet alliance in foreign affairs. It also included Soviet assistance to numerous Chinese domestic policies related to the arts, culture, education and sciences. T. P. Bernstein and H. Y. Li (eds), *China Learns from the Soviet Union, 1949–Present* (Lanham, MD: Lexington Books, 2011); Lüthi, *The Sino-Soviet Split*, 31–3; Shen Zhihua and Li Danhui, *After Leaning to One Side: China and Its Allies in the Cold War* (Washington, DC and Stanford, CA: Woodrow Wilson Center Press; Stanford University Press, 2011), 118.

25 Shuman, 'The politics of socialist athletics', 46–51.

26 Lüthi, *The Sino-Soviet Split*, 46–7.

27 Shuman, 'The politics of socialist athletics', 200–34.

28 Christopher J. Lee, 'Introduction: between a moment and an era: the origins and afterlives of Bandung', in C. J. Lee (ed.), *Making a World After Empire: The Bandung Movement and its Political Afterlives* (Athens, OH: Ohio University Press, 2010), 25.

29 Lee, 'Introduction', 25–6; Odd Arne Westad, *The Global Cold War: Third World Interventions and the Making of Our Times* (Cambridge: Cambridge University Press, new edn, 2011), 106.

30 'Speech by Premier Zhou Enlai at the Closing Session of the Asian–African Conference', 24 April 1955, History and Public Policy Programme Digital Archive, Translation from China and the Asian–African Conference (Documents) (Peking: Foreign Languages Press, 1955), 29–31, available at http://digitalarchive.wilsoncenter. org/document/121624 (accessed 26 July 2016).

31 Alaba Ogunsanwo, *China's Policy in Africa 1958–1971* (Cambridge: Cambridge University Press, 1974), 15–60.

32 Ogunsanwo, *China's Policy in Africa*, 31–5. According to Ogunsanwo, these were largely successful politically even though the Chinese did not have the ability to provide economic aid (as compared with the US or the Soviet Union).

33 Mao Zedong, 'Speech at the Tenth Plenum of the Eighth Central Committee', September 24, 1962, available at www.marxists.org/reference/archive/mao/selected-works/volume-8/mswv8_63.htm (accessed 24 November 2014); Franz Schurmann,

Ideology and Organization in Communist China (Berkeley, CA: University of California Press, 1968), 29, 37–43.

34 Friedman, *Shadow Cold War*, 2.
35 Omar Ali Amer, 'China and the Afro-Asian Peoples' Solidarity Organization', PhD dissertation, Université de Genève Institut Universitaire de Hautes Études Internationales, 1972, 10.
36 Bruce Larkin, *China and Africa 1949–1970: The Foreign Policy of the People's Republic of China* (Berkeley, CA: University of California Press, 1971), 66–7. Relations with Burundi had already been suspended, however, by early 1965.
37 Ogunsanwo, *China's Policy in Africa*, 84.
38 Friedman, *Shadow Cold War*, 51. Friedman argues that Chinese expertise on Africa in 1961 was so dismal that it influenced diplomatic efforts. In April 1961 Mao even admitted to a visiting delegation from Africa and Asia that China did not have a 'clear understanding of African history, geography and the present situation' in Africa. Quoted in Li Anshan, 'African Studies in China in the twentieth century: a historiographical survey', *African Studies Review*, 48:1 (2005), 59–87, 62. The Institute of African–Asian Studies (under the Central Party External Ministry and Chinese Academy for Social Sciences) was only founded in July 1961 (Li, 'African Studies', 63).
39 Çağdaş Üngör, 'Reaching the Distant Comrade: Chinese Communist Propaganda Abroad (1949–1976)', PhD dissertation, Binghamton University (SUNY), 2009, 196, 236. Üngör calls the period from the Great Leap Forward to the Cultural Revolution a 'golden age' for Chinese foreign propaganda like Radio Peking and the Foreign Languages Press ('Distant Comrade', 315, 317–18).
40 Zachary Scarlett shows how official media accomplished this by creating new kinds of Maoist taxonomies that 'recategorized, remapped and reordered the rest of the world'. Zachary Scarlett, 'China After the Sino-Soviet Split: Maoist Politics, Global Narratives, and the Imagination of the World', PhD dissertation, Northeastern University, 2012, 48.
41 Julia Strauss, 'The past in the present: historical and rhetorical lineages in China's relations with Africa', *China Quarterly*, 199 (2009), 777–95, 779.
42 Shuman, 'The politics of socialist athletics', 93.
43 The ITTF president at the time, Ivor Montagu, was a staunch communist (a British spy for the Russians) who supported the PRC and did not allow ROC participation. For more on Montagu, see Griffin, *Ping-Pong Diplomacy*.
44 For an account of this event see Griffin, *Ping-Pong Diplomacy*, 120–5. Coincidentally, Beijing held this international event around the same time the central leadership and sports leaders began discussing budget cuts and readjustments across the board following the disaster of the Great Leap Forward.
45 Chinese Foreign Ministry Archives (CFMA) 108–00816-01: telegram sent by the Ghanaian Embassy to the State Sports Committee and International Cultural Affairs Committee, 3 January 1962.
46 'The entire results booklet of the 1961 World Championship can be found online in the ITTF archives available at www.ittf.com/museum/archives/index.html (accessed 18 April 2016). From the main page, select '1961- Peking' from the dropdown and then '37. Programs: Results' to navigate through. The only other participating nation from Africa in 1961 was Nigeria.

47 CFMA 108–00816–01: telegram sent from the Ghanaian Embassy to the State Sports Commission and International Cultural Affairs Committee, 3 January 1962; 'Meet the Chinese stars', *Daily Graphic*, 24 April 1962, 11.

48 CFMA 108–0816–01: Tiwaizi 2010 hao: Guanyu wo pingpangqiudui fangwen Jiana ji qita Feizhou guojia de qingzhi [Instructions concerning our ping-pong team's visit to Ghana and several other African countries] (undated, January or February 1962).

49 'China team to tour Ghana', *Daily Graphic*, 18 February 1962.

50 CFMA 108–0816–01: telegram sent from the Ghanaian Embassy in Beijing to the State Sports Commission and the International Cultural Affairs Committee, 28 March 1962.

51 Strauss, 'The past in the present', 779.

52 CFMA 108–00816–01: Tiwaizi 2030 hao: Zhongguo pingpangqiudui fang Fei huodong jihua [Plan of activities for the Chinese ping-pong team's visit to Africa] (undated, April or May 1962).

53 This is based on my own assessment of more than a dozen *New China News Agency* press releases from late April to early June 1962. I speculate that part of the reason more information was not provided in the releases is because during the actual visit Chinese officials did not yet have a firm grasp on what to expect from their hosts or the visit.

54 CFMA 108–00816–01: Zhongguo pingpangqiu dui fangwen Feizhou baogao [Report on the Chinese ping-pong team's visit to Africa], 1 August 1962.

55 Rong Guotuan, 'African tour', 6.

56 Brady, *Making the Foreign Serve China*, 15.

57 Rong, 'African tour', 7.

58 CFMA 108–00816–01: Zhongguo pingpangqiu dui fangwen Feizhou baogao.

59 Rong, 'African tour', 7.

60 Rong, 'African tour', 8.

61 Rong, 'African tour', 6.

62 Anne-Marie Brady argues that the PRC leadership has always sought to find 'things in common' when developing *guanxi* with non-Chinese. Brady, *Making the Foreign Serve China*, 14.

63 CFMA 108–00816–01: Zhongguo pingpangqiu dui fangwen Feizhou baogao.

64 CFMA 108–00816–01: Zhongguo pingpangqiu dui fangwen Feizhou baogao.

65 CFMA 108–00816–01: Zhongguo pingpangqiu dui fangwen Feizhou baogao.

66 Rong, 'African tour', 8. The tour also included the pyramids, sphinx and the Suez Canal.

67 CFMA 108–00816–01: Zhongguo pingpangqiu dui fangwen Feizhou baogao.

68 CFMA 108–00816–01: Zhongguo pingpangqiu dui fangwen Feizhou baogao.

69 Quoted in Brady, *Making the Foreign Serve China*, 1.

70 CFMA 108–00816–01: Zhongguo pingpangqiu dui fangwen Feizhou baogao.

71 'Chinese due on Saturday', 9 May 1962, 11; 'Tennis stars from China', *Daily Graphic*, 11 May 1962, 1.

72 'Chinese thrill the fans', *Daily Graphic*, 16 May 1962, 10.

73 CFMA 108–00816–01: Zhongguo pingpangqiu dui fangwen Feizhou baogao.

74 CFMA 108–00816–01: Zhongguo pingpangqiu dui fangwen Feizhou baogao.

75 CFMA 108–00816–01: Zhongguo pingpangqiu dui fangwen Feizhou baogao.

76 CFMA 108–00251–07: Guanyu Jiana zuqiudui he pingpangqiudui fanghua shi

[Concerning the visit of Ghana's soccer team and ping-pong team to China], 1–24 March 1961. Not all requests were fulfilled. A request to see the blueprints for the Beijing workers' stadium, built for the first National Games held in 1959, was denied; the Foreign Ministry noted they were 'classified' (*jimi*).
77 From this, Huang concluded that the Chinese national soccer team was only as good as those in Ghana, Guinea and Nigeria; in other words, soccer in the UAR was better than in China.
78 CFMA 108–00816–01: Zhongguo pingpangqiu dui fangwen Feizhou baogao.
79 This post-visit report was produced a few weeks before the opening of the 1962 Fourth Asian Games held in Jakarta, which themselves turned into a fiasco and eventually led to the creation of the Games of the New Emerging Forces. Stefan Hübner, 'The Fourth Asian Games (Jakarta 1962) in a transnational perspective: Japanese and Indian reactions to Indonesia's political instrumentalisation of the Games', *International Journal of the History of Sport*, 29:9 (2012), 1295–1310; Shuman, 'Elite competitive sport in the People's Republic of China 1958–1966', 265–6.
80 CFMA 108–00723–07: Guanyu zengsong Jineiya yaoqiu yuanzhu tiyu yongpin qicai shi [Concerning presenting as a gift Guinea's request for sports goods and equipment]. Sent from the State Sports Commission to the International Cultural Affairs Committee, 20? November 1961. China sent about 21,000 RMB worth of sports goods. The original request was from the Guinean government for over 180,000 RMB worth of equipment, but the Sports Commission suggested sending a much smaller amount, fearing that other countries might also make similar requests.
81 'Mali and Olympism', *Olympic Review*, 134 (December 1978), 695–9, 698; 'Minutes of the Biennial General Meeting, Prague, April 9th and 14th 1963', 2, ITTF Archive, available at www.ittf.com/museum/archives/ (accessed 31 March 2016).
82 'Chinese are here', *Daily Graphic*, 14 May 1962, 10; '39. Results: Swaythling A' in '1961 – Peking', ITTF Archive, available at www.ittf.com/museum/archives/index.html (accessed 19 April 2016).
83 'Daxie dui wo guo pingpangqiudui de reqing jiedai, guojia tiwei zhaodai Feizhou guojia shijie, Chen Yi fu zongli chuxi zhaodaihui bing zai hui shang jiangle hua' [Thanks for the warm reception of China's ping-pong team, State Sports Commission entertains envoys from African countries, Vice-Premier Chen Yi attended the reception and spoke at the meeting], *People's Daily*, 28 June 1962.
84 'Daxie dui wo guo pingpangqiudui de reqing jiedai, guojia tiwei zhaodai Feizhou guojia shijie, Chen Yi fu zongli chuxi zhaodaihui bing zai hui shang jiangle hua'.
85 Red Guards were youth groups of Mao supporters who heeded his call to 'rebel against the system' in 1966. Initially, these were primarily students in Beijing, but grew to include rebels of various backgrounds and ages. 'Living Revolution: Red Guards' on Long Bow Group, Inc., *Morning Sun: A Film and Website About Cultural Revolution*, available at www.morningsun.org/living/redguards/redguards.html (accessed 16 May 2016). The most detailed account of the Cultural Revolution, which includes the rise of the Red Guards, can be found in R. MacFarquhar and M. Schoenhals, *Mao's Last Revolution* (Cambridge, MA: Harvard University Press, 2006).
86 Shuman, 'The politics of socialist athletics', 386–8.
87 Wang Youqin, 'Chinese Holocaust memorial: China's national ping pong team', available at hum.uchicago.edu/faculty/ywang/history/bj_pp_qd.htm (accessed 13 May 2016).

88 Wei Jingyu, 'Youyi di yi, bisai di er' [Friendship first, competition second], *People's Daily*, 2 April 1971.

89 'Afro-Asian Table Tennis Friendship Invitation Tournament: gala opening in Peking', *Peking Review*, 45 (5 November 1971), 10–12.

90 Joseph S. Nye, Jr, *Future of Power: Its Changing Nature and Use in the Twenty-first Century* (New York: Public Affairs, 2011), 89.

91 Nye, *Future of Power*, 93.

92 Brady, *Making the Foreign Serve China*, 23.

93 'Premier Chou En-lai's Speech at the State Banquet given by President Kwame Nkrumah (January 13, 1964)' and 'Premier Chou En-lai's Speech at the State Banquet Given by President Ibrahim Abboud (January 27, 1964)', in *Afro-Asian Solidarity Against Imperialism: A Collection of Documents, Speeches, and Press Interviews from the Visits of Chinese Leaders to Thirteen African and Asian Countries* (Beijing: Foreign Languages Press, 1964), 137, 227–8.

94 Strauss, 'The past in the present', 784.

95 One example is Mali, which apparently received Chinese coaches before its heyday in the sport in the 1970s and 1980s. 'Revival of table tennis in West Africa, Kaka Lawson visits Mali', 10 December 2014, available at (www.ittf.com/_front_page/ittf_full_story1.asp?ID=38020&Category (accessed 19 April 2016).

7

Barnstorming Frenchmen: the impact of Paris Université Club's US tours and the individual in sports diplomacy

Lindsay Sarah Krasnoff*

The young men of Paris Université Club (PUC), France's elite basketball team of the mid-1950s, rocked back and forth across the chilly Atlantic waters. It was supposed to be a joyous five-day journey from Le Havre to New York. Instead, most players remained in bed, too seasick to leave their bunks aboard the *America*. Nobody ate in the dining room; instead sandwiches were placed on cabin floors so that the Frenchmen could roll off, eat, then roll back on to their berths without having to stand up.

Thus began the trip by the first French basketball team to the United States after 1945. In a series of exhibition games, they barnstormed their way through the Midwest and mid-Atlantic. Despite the ominous start, PUC's December 1955–January 1956 tour was a success on many levels. Athletically, it introduced the team to the US style of play and the place basketball – and sports in general – occupied in American culture. The experience also opened the Frenchmen's eyes to what the United States was really like for, with the exception of PUC's American player and voyage organiser Martin Feinberg, it was the first time that any of them had set foot on US soil. The team returned in January 1962, another seminal experience that demonstrated the power of basketball, imparted US culture, and portrayed the verities of racial attitudes and the Jim Crow segregation of whites and blacks in the pre-Civil Rights United States.

The two trips broke ground for the amateur club. Neither was sponsored by the US government, although they occurred as the US Department of State began to organise goodwill tours for its athletes and coaches. Nor were they part of any French government plan to exhibit athletic prowess abroad or improve performances – such official use of sport to cultivate soft power via victories started after the 1960 Olympics: the 'zero hour' of the country's sports crisis, a failure to win many accolades or titles that lasted until the mid-1970s. Instead, these jaunts were the brainchild of a tall young man from Cleveland, Ohio, who wanted his teammates to see his homeland and learn about its culture, society and basketball.

PUC's experience of the United States influenced the Frenchmen's views and understanding of the country through the opportunity to travel and interact with everyday American citizens. Effectively, the trips presaged one of the major ideas that underwrites official US government sports diplomacy today: that through the universal power of sport, citizens from different countries can learn more about the United States and people in ways that policy speeches or press accounts cannot convey. Interactions with private individuals can be potent tools, a window into a society, an up-close personal exchange of ideas that can cut through officially disseminated information.

The PUC tours were thus sterling examples of the merits of sports exchanges as elements of diplomacy, even though they were not government-sponsored or even public–private partnerships. Rather, Feinberg's organisation proved the power of the individual, what Giles Scott-Smith calls the 'new diplomacy', in which private citizens can informally play diplomatic roles.[1] Today one would refer to this as people-to-people diplomacy, but back then the concept had yet to be coined; it was merely a goodwill gesture instigated by one individual. That the PUCists, as PUC players and alumni were called, later drew upon their US experiences to help remedy French basketball during the sports crisis testifies to the importance of sport as a diplomatic tool, even the unofficial, grassroots-level variety.

The new power of sport

France had to recalibrate itself for the realities of the post-1945 world. Its Great Power status was superseded by new superpowers, the United States and the Soviet Union, and the *hexagone*, as the country is sometimes called in reference to its shape, adjusted – but not easily. Caught between Moscow and Washington, Paris sought to re-establish itself via the influence it carried through its overseas holdings. Unfortunately for the Élysée Palace, Indochina's fight for independence (1946–54) followed by the start of Algeria's struggle to throw off the yoke of empire (1956–62) toppled the Fourth Republic and brought General Charles de Gaulle back to power as president of the Fifth Republic in 1958. Within a few short years, its holdings in Africa declared full sovereignty from the republic (1960), while other overseas possessions became direct administrative departments, such as Martinique and Guadeloupe (1964).

It was not just the geographical make-up of France that fluctuated during this time. The demographic composition of the mainland also changed as workers from former imperial holdings in North and Sub-Saharan Africa, as well as the Antilles, arrived to fuel the thirty 'glorious years' of post-war economic recovery. They staffed factories, took menial jobs that metropolitan workers did not want, and put down roots. As they did, the notion of who was French started to change.

The concept of French citizenship is one firmly entrenched in *jus soli* – citizenship of the soil – one that dates back to the French Revolution of the late eighteenth century. This means that anyone can become French if they are born on its territory, or become naturalised citizens through an examination and assimilation into the national fabric via speaking the language, adhering to secularisation in the public sphere (since 1905), respecting republican ideals set forth in the Declaration of the Rights of Man and Citizen, service to the state, adapting French-style dress, and so on. Like the United States on the other side of the Atlantic, France had thus been an immigrant destination for centuries, a place where one could theoretically advance based on merit and ability if one inserted oneself fully into public life. By the post-war period, France had assimilated waves of Jews and others from Eastern and Central Europe, particularly Poland, Spain, Italy and, by the late 1950s and 1960s, Portugal, as citizens. While some subjects of the French Empire in Africa attained citizenship prior to the Second World War, the majority only did so after the passage of the 1946 Fourth Republic constitution.

Sport was one of the easiest ways for generations of immigrants, citizens and subjects from all backgrounds to assimilate into French life and solidify their 'French' identity. Players of colour represented France in international competition, such as Senegal-born Raoul Diagne and Moroccan-born Labri Ben Barek in football in the 1930s, as did players of Polish, Spanish and Italian descent, such as Raymond Kopa in the 1950s. Sport thus helped reinforce national identity, regardless of skin colour or religious background. This trend continued in the post-war period, as the sons, daughters, grandsons and granddaughters of immigrants represented France at the highest levels of athletic competition.

Such rapid changes in the composition of 'who was French' initially paled in the 1950s and 1960s in comparison to the larger anxiety over 'what was French?' This predicament was inflamed by the large number of children born in the 1940s and 1950s, an unprecedented swelling of the demographic bulge, who started to come of age and challenge parental authority. This generation, known as the baby-boomers, started to strain the schools and challenge long-held social norms.[2] The baby-boomers embraced US cultural imports, to the horror of many elders and opinion makers. From drinking Coca-Cola to listening to Elvis to watching 'spaghetti western' television shows, young French of the 1950s turned to the United States as the cultural capital of cool.[3]

Youth's embrace of all things American fed into the start of a cyclical period of anti-Americanism. Such proclivities peppered French discourse dating back to the late eighteenth century. What began as a rejection of US culture morphed, as Philippe Roger argues, into a conduit of dissatisfaction with the politics and policy of France's sister republic.[4] By the twentieth century, the *hexagone*'s anti-Americanism coincided with periods of waning hegemony or anxiety about the country's soft power influence.[5] Parents and grandparents need not have worried excessively; once the baby-boomers matured in the 1960s, anti-Americanism began to emerge more profusely as the youth started to protest escalating US intervention in Vietnam and overwhelmingly took their cultural cues from Britain.[6]

De Gaulle thus confronted a multitude of issues when he resumed the reins. Counteracting global images of an old, defeated France invaded by sugary sodas and hip-swivelling rock 'n' rollers was ever more important under his presidency. Revival was the message the Élyssée wished to impart to the world, a rejuvenated France buoyed by its newfound youth and vigour, free of empire, and a leader for those seeking an alternative path to Washington and Moscow's Cold War clout. Just as French power was conveyed through its world-renowned leadership in the arts, literature, gastronomy and cinema, sport was another domain that could be deployed to the republic's advantage. Thanks to a new era of communications, namely the growth of television and the first satellite-diffused broadcasts into private homes, images of athletes collecting accolades held new potency. Thus, in many ways, the power of media amplified that of sport and provided new ways for athletes to embody the nation.

The French government was not unique in turning to sport as a soft power tool. Major international competitions were quickly politicised in the early twentieth century, an action that nulled their original intention to promote peace and harmony. Subsequently, countries hijacked the high-profile stage such tournaments provided to assert primacy, such as Nazi Germany in 1936. The Soviet Union's 1952 entry into the Olympic movement upped the Cold War ante and forced its nemesis in North America to integrate sport into its diplomatic toolbox, albeit slowly.

The US government began limited cultural exchange programmes in the early 1950s.[7] According to Roy Clumpner, the US Department of State was keyed into the importance of sport before mid-decade, prodded by the Soviet sport 'offensive'.[8] This perceived onslaught included deployment of several USSR teams abroad, a powerful move that swayed Foggy Bottom and resulted in President Dwight Eisenhower's authorisation of limited funds to send US teams abroad.[9] Yet convincing the US Congress of the need to sponsor international athletic endeavours remained a tricky task. As Rachel Vaughan points out in this volume, the years leading up to the 1960 Winter Games, held at Squaw Valley, were pivotal in swaying the legislative branch to open the coffers for sports diplomacy.[10]

Sport was used not only to counterbalance the East versus West Cold War dynamic, but also by other states to cultivate soft power. Amanda Sherman's chapter in this book examines how the People's Republic of China (PRC) used sports exchanges and visits in the 1950s and 1960s to build friendly ties with countries within the Eastern bloc, as well as newly decolonised Africa. Such missions, she argues, served to shore up the PRC's legitimacy in the eyes of the international community at a time when it vied with the Republic of China (Taiwan) to be viewed as the internationally recognised government of China.

There was thus a conscious shift by many governments to incorporate sports exchanges, visits and competitions to cultivate their power via global public opinion. The general concept of 'nation branding', or creating an identity via projection of a country's image to foreign publics, was not new. This was particularly the case for France, which Jan Melissen argues did so as early as the *ancien régime* under Louis XIV.[11] But the post-war international order gave impetus for countries to deploy new tactics in their quest to influence societies around the world. By this era, Melissen notes, such image cultivation extended to groups not officially affiliated with a government, thus giving more power to non-state actors.

Some of the key organisations that recognised the potency of sport after the war included the international athletic governing federations. The post-war era was one in which many of the world's largest, most popular sports reorganised. That they did so outside of the new bipolar particulars of the geopolitical scene gave them degrees of autonomy from the larger diplomatic transformations that shaped the international arena. Grégory Quin, Nicola Sbetti and Philippe Vonnard note the case of the

Fédération International de Football Association (FIFA), which they argue became a new environment for diplomacy.[12] Thus, the definition of who was an arbiter of diplomacy began to shift as the new era of public diplomacy enabled athletes to serve as more potent diplomatic ambassadors.

Grasping at sports for cultural influence was not a far stretch of the imagination for France. One of its citizens, Baron Pierre de Coubertin, birthed the modern Olympics in 1896. Through the mid-twentieth century, Frenchmen led the development of international athletic governing bodies. The *hexagone* was a founding member of FIFA in 1906 and two of its citizens played outsized roles in moulding the world's largest, most powerful sports entity.[13] France was a founding member of the Fédération International Medico-Sportive in 1928 and joined the nascent Fédération International de Basketball Amateur (FIBA), the second-largest federation by mid-century, a year after that body's 1932 establishment.

French sports leadership also played out on the field. The nation's Olympians garnered enough medals at the first ten Olympiads to be placed in the top five in the overall medal counts seven times. The men's basketball team, *Les Tricolores*, today known as *Les Bleus*, won the bronze medal at the 1937 European Championship, while the women's team were fourth at the 1938 tournament.[14] After the war, France continued to lead. At the 1948 London Games, France came third in the overall medal count with its underfunded but relatively large contingent, a *fait accompli* facilitated by *Les Tricolores*.

Basketball, despite its US roots, was a point of pride for the French and enjoyed a long history dating to the game's 1893 European début in a Paris gymnasium at 14, rue de Trévise.[15] Despite its early introduction to France, the round ball's association with the Protestant-affiliated Young Men's Christian Association (YMCA), whose instructors taught the sport, hindered its initial popularity during a time of fierce debate over the secular nature of republican public life. Basketball gained traction by the presence of YMCA foyers and US doughboys during the First World War and spread during the interwar years through the French Army and Catholic Church, which viewed it as a tool to revitalise a youth devastated by the conflict.[16] Yet this era was one in which the game's ties with the United States were severed as the *hexagone* developed its own coaches, stars and styles of play. The national teams gained acclaim in the 1930s and helped lead the Europeanisation of the sport.[17] It was the post-1945 years, however, that ushered in the first 'golden era' of French hoops, a sport that many still associated with the Army, the Church and the schools.[18]

Les Tricolores' silver medal finish at the 1948 Olympics, a David versus Goliath fight against the United States, was instructive.[19] While the French had played against US GIs in the last years of the war – the first basketball game held on liberated Parisian soil occurred in the autumn of 1944 – and picked up some American forms of play, the London Games began to change the French style. The national sports daily, *L'Équipe*, reported at the Games that the French lacked precision against their competitors, though they learned US tactics, a key takeaway.[20]

In this sense, the diffusion of basketball skills after the war was similar to what occurred within the realm of football. British football coaches during the late nineteenth and early twentieth century were viewed as leaders in the field, linked not only to their role as originators of the game, but also, as Matthew Taylor points out, reflective of the United Kingdom's role as a global leader. As the British spread the game across Europe through its workers and coaches, Europeans assimilated and bettered UK tactics, such as the defeat of England by Hungary's 'Magical Magyars' at Wembley Stadium in November 1953. This is a phenomenon that Taylor calls a 'cross-cultural transfer of knowledge', one in which reworked national games sometimes outflanked that of the original diffusers.[21] A similar transaction occurred with American-style basketball after 1945, a period of unprecedented US military, diplomatic and cultural power on the international stage.

French hoops thus benefited from the transfusion of US skills. *Les Tricolores* won bronze medals at the European Championship (1949, 1953, 1959), fourth place at FIBA's 1954 World Basketball Championship and fourth place at the 1956 Olympic Games. Many members of *Les Tricolores* played for PUC, an amateur team. The club, which called Stade Charléty at the southernmost point of Paris's 13ème *arrondisement* home, won the French Championship twice (1947, 1963), often played in the league's finals and won four French Cup trophies (1954, 1955, 1962, 1963). The PUCists were aided first by Martin Feinberg starting in 1955, then 'Gentleman' Henry Fields, an African American recruited to the team by Feinberg in 1962. As PUC teammate Michel Rat recalled decades later, Feinberg played an important role as a teacher who imparted US-style tactics and thus helped the club improve.[22] Fields played a similar role, introducing the defensive style and techniques of US basketball legend Bill Russell, one of the game's modernising tacticians, to France, an element that helped PUC overcome arch-rival Bagnolet to win the 1963 title.

By the mid-1950s, French confidence in their basketball ability was justifiably high. In a report issued by the Institute National de Sport (INS) following the 1956 Olympic Games, officials argued that all resources possible should be given to the sport, even though it was not as popular as football or rugby. The study pointed out that, 'our basketball players are among the best in the world'.[23] The logical conclusion was that investment in the round ball would be a good bet to produce more medals, thus shoring up the image of the country as an athletic, youthful, wining one to counter the setbacks suffered by the defeat at Dien Bien Phu (1954), the Suez Canal crisis (1956) and the outbreak of the Algerian War (1956).

Intriguingly, the INS report included further rationale behind French hoops prowess. 'Our favourable [Olympic] sports are fencing and basketball', it stated, reasoning that these were the most intelligent individual and team sports, thus well suited to the national psyche.[24] Players past and present relay that succeeding at the sport's highest levels requires a lot of thought and mental calculation, that it is indeed one of the more cerebral sports.[25] Yet at the time the statement may also have sought to couch basketball as a 'French' endeavour. Despite cyclical anti-American sentiment, France had previously embraced American cultural constructs, such as jazz, and reworked them into something distinct in their own right. The same could be said of basketball in the first part of the twentieth century.

The 1950s and 1960s, however, were different as American players entered French leagues and introduced US-style techniques and tactics on the hardcourt. Adaption of transatlantic hoops finesse started to be blended into the playbook. This coincided with a similar cultural transmission that occurred within the sphere of music. As Jonathyne Briggs argues, in the 1950s and 1960s the French took American rock 'n' roll and turned it into their own genre, illustrated most vividly by Johnny Hallyday and the Yé-Yés.[26] For most in the *hexagone*, basketball was already conceived of as 'French'. Yet the increased 'Americanisation' of basketball allowed for the same creation of multiple spaces of culture that Briggs argues music provided, which 'permitted new possibilities of social interaction'.[27]

New spaces for social interaction were indeed found within the realm of basketball. PUC coach Emile Frézot, himself a former *Tricolore*, was ecstatic to recruit Feinberg during the autumn of 1955.[28] Feinberg was a novelty, even though another American had played for PUC a season earlier. It was not just his style of play that made Feinberg so legendary, but the way he taught his new teammates American techniques, as well as his camaraderie. Feinberg quickly became an invaluable asset.

Paris Université Club's First US Tour

Feinberg organised one of the earliest post-war sports exchanges between France and the United States, albeit an unofficial one. He grew up in Depression-era Cleveland playing basketball, and represented the University of Michigan Wolverines on court while training there with the Navy Air Corps in 1944. Feinberg arrived in Europe in January 1954 after service in the Korean War, toured the countryside, then enrolled at university in Paris to study international relations on his GI Bill benefits (tuition and a $75 per month stipend). 'I did not go to France to play basketball', Feinberg maintained decades later.[29] But two sisters (twins) convinced him to try out for PUC that year. French players were typically not tall – or not as tall as Feinberg. 'The men's coach was thrilled to have a six-foot-three American', he recalled. The twenty-six-year-old Ohioan was considerably older than most other players on the team, and he had more on-court experience.

The American found that the French treated basketball differently. 'I didn't see real concern about basketball being as major of a sport', as in the United States, he recalled. It remained a niche endeavour in a country that favoured British sports. Even Roger Antoine, Feinberg's teammate and long-serving captain of *Les Tricolores*, loved football first and foremost.[30] Moreover, basketball was a sport of the provinces and mid-sized urban areas, domains of the bourgeoisie. It was far removed from the boisterousness of working-class (football) or upper-class (rugby) sports and was one of the few disciplines incorporated into the physical education programme in the country's *collèges* and *lycées*.[31] Basketball was thus associated with the middle classes or schools, but also embraced by some of the elite. Future prime minister Lionel Jospin played during his university and military service years and continued to be a regular in local leagues into his sixties.[32]

The sport's infrastructure confirmed that at times it was an afterthought. 'The stadiums were horrible', Feinberg said; most of them had been constructed before the war. 'Invariably, we played in places with slippery floors.' There was 'absolutely no comparison' between his experience playing for the Wolverines and what he encountered in France. 'That's one of the reasons why I wanted to bring the PUC to see this [*sic*] wondrous of stadiums to play basketball in', he explained of the team's first US trip. Another consideration was to introduce his teammates to his homeland, so that they could see for themselves what the United States was actually like – and how it differed from the version portrayed to the French public by its media and government.

Working with Dan Fearis, general secretary of the American Athletic Union (AAU), then responsible for organising US amateur basketball, Feinberg pieced together a short tour through the Midwest.[33] The French government and the University of Paris pledged money to underwrite the trip, and part of the proceeds from ticket sales would defray costs. The players also contributed $70 each to participate.[34] But the plan was more than just to play basketball; the young Frenchmen also wanted to learn and see everything they could about the United States. As *L'Équipe* noted in its special coverage of the team's tour to US shores, 'the PUCists, desirous to enrich their cultural plan, demanded that they be accorded visits to the grand American hospitals'.[35]

The front page of *L'Équipe*'s 21 December edition featured a photograph of the team departing aboard the *America* for New York.[36] It was thanks to a small miracle that two teammates, Antoine and Jacques Owen, made the trip, their visas coming through at the very last minute.[37] Thus, that chilly December morning, Feinberg, seven of his teammates and Frézot sailed to New York. Quipped *L'Équipe*, 'Martin Feinberg was particularly over-playful! The prospect of a return to his homeland exhilarated the American to such a degree that we were unable to recognise this shouting friend as the great lethargic boy who we knew!'[38] Excitement permeated the air. Frézot noted that a pilgrimage to the basketball mecca of America was one not only of athletic significance, but also one of cultural importance. 'This initiative should have been taken a while ago', he said, so that coaches responsible for the future of the French game could go, observe and 'bring back the truths that American basketball has become!'[39] Once on board, however, enthusiasm gave way to sea sickness for most of the rough Atlantic passage. The team arrived in New York, then boarded a flight to Chicago on 28 December, even while some still suffered from *mal de mer*.[40]

It was the first time that a French basketball team played on US soil after 1945 – *Les Bleus* did not do so until a 1965 friendly match in New York against Poland. Moreover, aside from Feinberg, it was the first time that any of the PUCists had visited the United States. They survived on a tight per diem allowance of $6 and camped out at a YMCA to save money.[41] Such frugalness did not dampen the group's excitement. They wished to compete against US teams and see how they fared. Yet, as Feinberg explained to a reporter, 'mostly I'm very much interested in them liking America. That, for me, is the idea.'[42]

All were eager to learn and soak up the myths of 'America'. Feinberg recalled a night spent with his Chicago friends and several teammates at the exclusive Pump Room restaurant. The Frenchmen took in the glamorous nightlife. Teammate Jacques

Huguet, the group's comic and a medical student, entertained the entire room with an impromptu monologue.[43] Another, Roger Zagury, a French Jew from Casablanca, was impressed by it all: the lights, the construction, the newness. 'It gives the impression that the country isn't finished yet', he told a reporter, 'not like Europe.'[44]

PUC's road record was mixed. The team's first stop was Wheaton, Illinois, where they lost their first game (29 December, 43–68). They then won two matches, one against Lake Forrest College (2 January 1956, 69–64) and the other versus North Central of Iowa (3 January, 67–58). US reporters critiqued their style of play. *Sports Illustrated* remarked that the Frenchmen, 'played a game that looked absurdly old-fashioned', and 'concentrated on ball control, an occasional well-executed fast break, and set plays off the double-pivot offense'.[45] After a 43–74 loss to Marquette University, the *Milwaukee Sentinel* reported that, 'what the Parisians lacked in cage know-how and finesse they tried to make up with *ésprit de corps*'.[46] Another loss to DePaul University in Chicago (5 January, 45–71) and then to University of Baltimore in Baltimore (9 January, 68–76) served up further fodder for critique. As *Sun* reporter Walter Herman noted, 'Baltimore, like most United States college teams, utilizes the shoot-and-run offense and zone defense. Paris, on the other hand, has a tight and very effective man-for-man defense and, in spite of a height deficiency, grabbed more than its share of rebounds.'[47]

By the end of their tour, the team was exhausted and nearly broke. Feinberg remained behind in a Cleveland hospital with a torn Achilles tendon; thus the Frenchmen were left without an interpreter.[48] They showed up to their 9 January game in Baltimore soaking wet after getting caught in the rain and hungry as they only ate a light breakfast that day.[49] Living on such a tight budget showed its mark.

While the Department of State had begun to organise athletic exchanges by this point, the US government did not officially sponsor PUC's 1956 or 1962 tours.[50] The Department, however, was reportedly interested in the initiative and dispatched Voice of America staff to broadcast the January 1956 Baltimore game to France.[51] Feinberg and his teammates returned home, alongside the fond memories and impressions of what they saw.

The return

Feinberg's role at PUC changed in the early 1960s, after he had finished his studies, from player to coach. He continued to serve as a mentor on the court and made friends with new teammates, such as Rat, a Parisian-area native who had joined PUC in 1959. In 1962, Feinberg recruited 'Gentleman Fields', as the six-foot-five New York native was known, from the US military airbase in Orléans.[52] Upon his release from service that year, Fields joined PUC on the court.[53] Both Rat and Fields were part of the December 1962 tour Feinberg organised for the team.

The goal that winter, just as for the previous trip, was not necessarily for PUC to play games. Instead, it was about taking it all in – at heart, the ultimate goal of any sports exchange. 'I loved the United States', Feinberg said, 'and wanted them to learn about basketball and Americans.' That they did, as the team was exposed to the complex race issues that shaped US society.

PUC set out for the United States that December by air. They won their first game against Gallaudet University in the Baltimore–Washington corridor (18 December, 42–39). They then lost to Oglethorpe (20 December, 37–87) and Brownston, an AAU team (2? December, 66–68). The record was not ideal, but the PUCists certainly learned a lot about the United States.

Along the way, the barnstorming Frenchmen were baptised into the bliss of American-style basketball shoes. At the time, the French called any type of sneaker a 'tennis shoe'. According to Feinberg, the ones available in France were heavy and not ideal for playing basketball. There was nothing on the market akin to the US-produced Converse basketball sneakers that Feinberg wore. PUC was once again on a shoe-string budget, but Feinberg devised a tactic: he arranged a radio interview for the team, after which each player received a pair of Converse sneakers.[54] 'They were very generous, the Americans', Feinberg said, 'wherever we asked for the tennis shoes [basketball sneakers], we got them.' Rat related how important such gestures were for the Frenchmen. 'We had French sneakers, like the Busnel', he said of the model named after *Les Tricolores'* coach during its golden heyday, Robert Busnel.[55] Yet 'everyone was crazy for Converses', raved Rat, 'because they were American products'.[56]

The Frenchmen were also introduced to Jim Crow segregation in which blacks had supposedly 'separate but equal' public spaces from whites, whether it be drinking fountains, restaurants, schools or where to sit on the bus. Unlike the 1956 trip through the Midwest, in 1962 the team played teams in the South. Following the Gallaudet game, the team boarded a bus bound for Atlanta, where they would play Oglethorpe. En route, their clothes were lost, according to Fields, so the team played the game in what they wore on the trip.[57] While in the Atlanta area, the bus stopped to refuel and the PUCists took advantage of the break to grab refreshment at the roadside restaurant. The team entered but were stopped in their tracks. Fields recollected that, 'The lady [owner or server] said nicely, "I'm sorry we can serve you [referencing the white players] but we can't serve him," talking about me. So, we left and went somewhere else. That's the only time that there were any difficulties.'[58] Feinberg told his teammates that he didn't wish to eat there, and they left. 'I was embarrassed', he remembered, 'that was very embarrassing for me.'

Rat recalled that that incident was the first time most of the French players had encountered Jim Crow. 'We were profoundly shocked at that', he said. Not that there wasn't discrimination against non-Caucasians in France – there was. Feinberg noted that French attitudes towards blacks at the time were 'more hidden, a lot deeper than in the United States'. Feinberg recalled that when travelling through France with PUC, he roomed with Antoine, son of a Caucasian French mother and black African father. 'I can't ever remember being refused a hotel', he said.

Fields helped explain the context of the era. At the time, he said, the government in Paris 'made the French people believe that you aren't racist, you don't have any problem against the coloureds, that only Americans are racist'. It was the Cold War, he noted. There were still old grievances that the old bipolar configuration exacerbated. 'I suffered from it', he said, because the French thought that they were not racist.

This attitude, in part at least, can be attributed to the French concept of citizenship. Under the republican model, anyone can become French if they speak the language, adopt the customs and styles of dress, and adhere to society's mores (though these 'standards' were set by the French establishment). There was some comfort that other 'outsider' groups, such as the Polish, Italian and Portuguese immigrants who settled in France, also experienced discrimination for several generations until their offspring assimilated into society. Yet black French and those from the Maghreb had to work harder than their white counterparts to prove their abilities, whether it was on the court, in school or in life.[59]

Despite the incident, Fields thought the trip was fantastic and helped prove that not all Americans were racist. 'They were expecting to see people saying "you can't be together"', he said of his French teammates. 'They were expecting blacks on one side of the street and whites on the other. That's what you read about. But, the only time they saw that there was a problem was in Georgia.' Fields noted, 'that was the only time that there was any difference' in how he was treated. Based on what his young French teammates saw on television back home, 'they expected that to be happening all the time'.

The trip was thus a potent illustration of the power of sports exchanges as a means to learn more about a different society based on such people-to-people interactions. The young PUC players who travelled to the United States were not necessarily the typical representatives of their generation. They favoured basketball, a sport not part of the cultural mainstream, and had high regard for the United States. Many of the PUCists came away with favourable impressions of France's sister republic in most matters, save that of race relations. Decades later, they recalled these experiences and incorporated elements of the American game (training, tactics, gear) in their efforts to reverse the French basketball catastrophe.

Basketball in the sports crisis

By the time the team returned from its second US romp, the sports situation in France had drastically changed. The 1960 Rome Olympics lifted the veil on the notion that France could lead through athletic prowess. That summer, French Olympians came twenty-fifth in the medal table, with two silvers and three bronzes. The basketball team, expected to do well, was quickly eliminated from the tournament, piercing the belief that they were the best in the world. The Games were an embarrassment and demonstrated that sport was trickier to deploy as a soft power tool than foreseen by the French government.

At the instigation of de Gaulle, the government launched an inquiry and found several explanations for the poor showing: a youth that preferred other leisure time activities to practising sports, a long school day that prohibited youth athletics in any serious way, sports facilities that were old, out of date and/or difficult to access.

With regard to the nation's elite athletes, who held regular full-time jobs and trained on weekends or at night, a lack of sufficient time to prepare was cited. More importantly, government and press reports alike highlighted the larger issue: France lacked a national sports culture to foster athletic achievement.[60]

The quickly coined 'sports crisis' took *Les Tricolores* hostage; the team did not qualify for another Olympic Games until 1984, and after 1963 France was absent from the World Championship until 1986. Combined with the lack of accolades in other major sports events, including football, the image of a France in flux was augmented and exacerbated by the *événements* of May 1968.

Change came in the 1970s after a series of four-year sports plans in the 1960s failed to remedy the situation. The 1975 Mazeaud Law legislated for the first time a place for sport within the national culture, devoted funds to develop it, and established programmes to detect and train the next generation of elite athletes. Basketball benefited. The French Basketball Federation (FFBB) led efforts to reverse that sport's decline, informed by officials who had observed the sport in the United States twenty years earlier, an important testimony to the importance of sports exchanges, even the unofficial, grassroots-level variety.

Attempts were made to improve the physical bodies that competed on the hardcourt. The FFBB's head doctor Jacques Huguet – the PUC comic who entertained Chicago's Pump Room – pushed for better diet and nutrition for basketball players, especially those at the elite level, as more nutritious food could produce healthy players and – eventually – taller players, a key tool to winning games in Cold War Europe.[61] He also introduced better physical conditioning so as to strengthen players and help protect them from injury. Huguet was inducted in the Academy of French Basketball in 2012 as a legend who helped change the sport.

Efforts were made to improve results through better coaching and opening the game up to international players. 'Gentleman' Henry Fields coached generations of youths after finishing a long career as a semi-professional player at Monaco and Antibes. Through his drills, young *basketteurs* practised the impeccable defensive tactics of Bill Russell and produced new waves of technically proficient players. Fields was far from the only American player-coach to leave his mark in the *hexagone*; he was however one of the earliest and most respected.[62] He was inducted into the Academy of French Basketball in 2014 for his devotion to the game.

New structures were deployed to train the nation's most promising athletes from an early age. The Mazeaud Law created the Institute National de Sport, de l'Expertise et de la Performance (INSEP), the national sports institute, in Paris's Bois de Vincennes, where elite athletes could train under specialised coaches, earn a subsidy and not have to worry about a full-time job.[63] In 1984, the FFBB created the Centre Fédérale de Basket-Ball (CFBB) at INSEP. This entity formed and nurtured elite youth talent by congregating the nation's best players together to finish their athletic and academic training under the watchful eyes of sports experts. One such authority was Michel Rat, the PUC player aghast at the treatment accorded Fields in Georgia. Under Rat's tutelage, the first generation of French players to be drafted into the NBA directly from France was formed: Tony Parker, Boris Diaw and Ronny Turiaf (who attended INSEP before playing at Gonzaga and being drafted). In 2014, Rat was inducted into the Academy of French Basketball for his life's work, and in 2015 he was named president of the CFBB.

All of these measures in which PUC alumni played crucial roles helped the fortunes of French basketball. For Rat, the influence of American players in France, especially Feinberg and Fields at PUC, helped to improve the game. 'They brought us the tactics', Rat said.

Conclusion

PUC's barnstorming tours were influential. Through sport, these Frenchmen saw the United States, learned about its political, economic and social system, met everyday Americans and returned with mostly favourable impressions of their host country, an important consideration given cyclical French anti-Americanism. The two trips would not have occurred without the foresight and drive of Martin Feinberg.

The basketballer from Cleveland had a front-row seat from which to evaluate the changes in the French sport. Today, 'I see a lot more technical training', he said, 'a lot more defence, attack and shooting particularly. So much more concentration on the basics.' Indeed, it is these very things, the basics and technicalities of the game, that French players are known for today, an odd reversal of fate from the era of PUC.

The informal nature of the trip ensured that the players viewed the United States uncoloured by any official information programme. In showing his friends around the country, Feinberg relayed the many attributes – and some negatives – that made the United States. These early French–American basketball exchanges created lasting impressions on young players in ways traditional diplomacy and diplomats rarely could. Set against the larger context of post-war French anxieties and reconstruction, a French–American Cold War diplomacy that was often fraught with tension over international influence, and race relations in both countries, these trips are noteworthy. Alumni of PUC's US trips matured and entered the rungs of basketball coaching and officialdom. Importantly, the PUC cohort orchestrated France's late twentieth century basketball renaissance, one that was uniquely 'French' but heavily informed by their US experience. The PUC's barnstorming tours of the United States had many short-term dividends, as well as longer-term ones that still play out on the court – and at the podium. Today *Les Bleus* accumulate medals and international titles, and are a leading supplier of *basketteurs* to the world's elite league, the NBA, a twenty-first-century version of the original PUC barnstormers.

Notes

*   Portions of this chapter form the basis for elements of the forthcoming book, Lindsay Sarah Krasnoff, *French cagers*.

1 Gilles Scott-Smith, 'Introduction: private diplomacy, making the citizen visible', *New Global Studies*, April 2014, 2–3.

2 For more on the baby-boomers, their importance in portraying a rejuvenated France, and the 'youth crisis' that started in the late 1950s, see Lindsay Sarah Krasnoff, *The Making of Les Bleus: Sport in France, 1958–2010* (Lanham, MD: Lexington Books, 2012), 25–33; Kristin Ross, *Fast Cars, Clean Bodies: Decolonization and the Reordering of French Culture* (Cambridge, MA: MIT Press, 1995); Richard Ivan Jobs, *Riding the New Wave: Youth and the Rejuvenation of France After the Second World War* (Stanford, CA: Stanford University Press, 2007).

3 See Krasnoff, *The Making of Les Bleus*; see also Richard Kuisel, *Seducing the French: The Dilemma of Americanization* (Berkeley, CA: University of California Press, 1993) and Victoria de Grazia, *Irresistible Empire: America's Advance Through Twentieth Century Europe* (Cambridge, MA: Harvard University Press, 2006) for more on American cultural trends and impacts in mid-century France.

4 See Philippe Roger, *The American Enemy: A Story of French Anti-Americanism* (Chicago: University of Chicago Press, 2005).

5 Other works that chronicle and examine the history of French anti-Americanism include Richard F. Kuisel, *The French Way: How France Embraced and Rejected American Values and Power* (Princeton, NJ: Princeton University Press, 2012) and *Seducing the French*; Seth D. Armus, *French Anti-Americanism (1930–1948): Critical Moments in a Complex History* (Lanham, MD: Lexington Books, 2007); and David Strauss, *Menace in the West: The Rise of French Anti-Americanism in Modern Times* (Westport, CT: Greenwood Press, 1978).

6 See Krasnoff, *The Making of Les Blues*.

7 The US Department of State, through provisions of the Fulbright Act and the Smith–Mundt Act, which provided funding for cultural diplomacy and information programmes, began to send a few coaches and players abroad.

8 Roy A. Clumpner, 'American Federal Government Involvement in Sport, 1888–1973', PhD Thesis, UIniversity of Edmonton, Alberta, Spring 1976, 316.

9 President Dwight Eisenhower's 1954 Emergency Fund for International Affairs provided substantive financial support for cultural diplomacy programming but sports exchanges did not get more substantively underway until later in the decade. For more details on the evolution of US government sports exchanges and diplomacy initiatives, see Clumpner, 'American Federal Government Involvement in Sport', Chapter XIII, 'Federal Involvement to Promote American Interests or Foreign Policy Objectives, 1950–1973'.

10 Rachel Vaughan, 'Two Chinas diplomacy and the 1960 Squaw Valley Winter Olympics', paper presentation at SOAS, University of London, 'Message, Mode and Metpahor' Sport and Diplomacy conference, July 2015, 15.

11 Jan Melissen, 'The new public diplomacy: between theory and practice', in Jan Melissen (ed.), *The New Public Diplomacy: Soft Power in International Relations* (Basingstoke: Palgrave Macmillan, 2005), 3–6.

12 Grégory Quin, Nicola Sbetti and Philippe Vonnard, 'FIFA's reconstruction after the Second World War: a matter of diplomacy?', draft paper, SOAS, University of London, 'Message, Mode and Metpahor' Sport and Diplomacy conference, July 2015, 3.

13 French nobleman Pierre de Coubertin pushed for the first modern Olympics, held

in Athens in 1896. The event showcased the ideals of amateurism and promoted international peace. Frenchman Jules Rimet had an outsized role within FIFA, starting with his organisation of the first World Cup in 1930 during his long tenure as FIFA president from 1921 to 1954. Rimet and fellow countryman Henri Delaunay were also driving forces in the creation of the European Championship of football, a concept both advocated for decades prior to its 1960 inception. See UEFA, 'UEFA European Football Championship origins', available at www.uefa.com/uefaeuro/history/background/index.html (accessed 26 April 2017).

14 Certain sports in France were viewed as more suitable for men or for women. For example, football was considered too violent and physical for women to play until the late twentieth and early twenty-first centuries. Basketball, on the other hand, was perceived to be well suited to the female physique as early as the 1890s. Thus, women's basketball has a long, strong history and the national team excelled at international competitions. For further background, see Mary Lynn Stewart, *For Health and Beauty: Physical Culture for Frenchwomen, 1880s–1930s* (Cambridge, MA: Harvard University Press, 2000), and for the wider European context in the late nineteenth and early twentieth centuries, Davia Majauskieine, Vilma Cingiene and Mindaugas Bobikas, 'Traits caractéristiques de l'évolution du basket-ball féminin en Lituanie (1920–1940)', in Fabien Archambault, Loic Artiaga and Gérard Bosc, *Le Continent basket: L'Europe et le basket-ball au XXe siècle* (Brussels: PIE Peter Lang, 2015).

15 The rue de Trévise facility is today the oldest original basketball court in the world, constructed out of wood imported from North America in 1893. French Basketball Federation, 'Visitez la plus ancienne salle de basket', available at www.ffbb.com/visitez-la-plus-ancienne-salle-de-basket (accessed 26 April 2016).

16 For more on the sport's early phases in France, including its popularisation, see Gérard Bosc in Fabien Archambault, Loic Artaga and Gérard Bosc, *Double Jeu. Histoire du basket-ball entre France et Amérique* (Paris: Vuibert, 2007).

17 As Sabine Chavinier-Réla argues, French rules were adopted in many parts of Europe during the interwar period until the later 1930s, when more American rules were instituted. Sabine Chavinier-Réla, 'Les règles du basket français dans l'entre-deux-guerres, entre dimension nationale et continentale', in Archambault *et al* (eds), *Le Continent basket*, 30.

18 *Les Bleus* won the silver medal at the 1947 European Basketball Championship.

19 The 1948 London Games were the second time that basketball had been included in the Olympics, the first was Berlin 1936.

20 'L'Attaque des Tricolores enervée a manqué de raisonnement', *L'Équipe*, 14 August 1948, 4.

21 Matthew Taylor, 'Football's engineers? British football coaches, migration and intercultural transfer, c. 1910–c. 1950s', *Sport in History*, 30:1 (2010), 156.

22 Michel Rat, interview with the author, 29 June 2015.

23 'Notes soumises à Monsieur le Difrom Général de la Jeunesse et des Sports à propos de la preparation aux JO 1960', Institut National du Sport, undated, Centre of Contemporary Archives (CAC) 19780586, Article 100 JO Rome.

24 'Notes soumises à Monsieur le Diror Général de la Jeunesse et des Sports à propos de la preparation aux JO 1960'.

25 Michel Rat and Jean-Marie Jouaret, interviews with the author, 29 June 2015; Jacques Cachemire, interview with the author, 8 July 2015; Nicolas Batum, interview with the

author, 4 February 2015; Kévin Séraphin, interviews with the author, 23 February 2015 and 11 March 2015; Evan Fournier, interview with the author, 10 May 2016.

26 Jonathyne Briggs, *Sounds French: Globalization, Cultural Communication & Pop Music, 1958–1980* (New York: Oxford University Press, 2015), 5.

27 Briggs, *Sounds French*, 4.

28 Martin Feinberg, interview with the author, 7 December 2014.

29 All Feinberg quotes: Martin Feinberg, interview with the author, 7 December 2014, 13 December 2014 and via email to the author, 2 December 2014.

30 Pierre Tessier, 'Roger Antoine successeur désigné de André Buffière au capitnnat de l'équipe de France', *L'Équipe*, 20 September 1955, 5.

31 While the French school system did not incorporate school athletics in the way that American and British schools do, there was a regular PhysEd period.

32 Today, Jospin does not stray too far from the court. In February 2016 he was a guest on one of France's Sunday night basketball programmes. Information about Jospin's basketball career extracted from interviews with Feinberg and Rat and 'Basket: Lionel Jospin sur BeIn Sports Pour Comenter sur le basket', *Le Dauphine*, 27 February 2016, available at www.ledauphine.com/france-monde/2016/02/27/basket-lionel-jospin-sur-bein-sports-pour-commenter-la-nba (accessed 26 April 2016).

33 Pierre Tessier, 'Le PUC s'embarquera le 21 décembre pour les États-Unis…', *L'Équipe*, 6 December 1955, 8.

34 'Events and discoveries: French fried', *Sports Illustrated*, 16 January 1956, available at www.si.com/vault/1956/01/16/604289/events--discoveries (accessed 1 August 2017).

35 Tessier, 'Le PUC s'embarquera le 21 décembre', 8.

36 'Les basketteurs du PUC embarquent les 'Kiwis' Débarquent', *L'Équipe*, 21 December 1955, 1.

37 'Les basketteurs du PUC embarquent les 'Kiwis' Débarquent', 1.

38 Gérard Edelstein, 'Le PUC est parti pour les États-Unis', *L'Équipe*, 21 December 1955, 5.

39 Edelstein, 'Le PUC est parti pour les États-Unis', 5.

40 Robert Chromie, 'Paris athletes say oui oui on Chicago visit', *Chicago Tribune*, 29 December 1959, 25.

41 'Events and discoveries: French fried'.

42 Chromie, 'Paris athletes say oui', 25.

43 Feinberg, interview with the author, 7 December 2014.

44 Chromie, 'Paris athletes say oui', 8.

45 'Events and discoveries: French fried'.

46 Rel Bochat, 'Marquette routs Paris 'Five', 74–43', *Milwaukee Sentinel*, 5 January 1956, 11.

47 Walter F. Herman, 'Baltimore U. holds off late rally to top Paris, 76–68', *Baltimore Sun*, 10 January 1956, 19.

48 Feinberg, interview with the author, 7 December 2014.

49 Feinberg, interview with the author, 7 December 2014.

50 Feinberg, interview with the author, 7 December 2014.

51 Patrick Skene Catling, '"Foul" situation fails to slow French team of "only seven"', *Baltimore Sun*, 10 January 1956, 36.

52 'Henry Fields, le basket de New York à Auterive', *La Croix*, 18 September 2009,

available at www.la-croix.com/Actualite/Sport/Henry-Fields-le-basket-de-New-York-a-Auterive-_NG_-2009-09-18-539439 (accessed 26 May 2017).

53 Henry Fields, interview with the author, 30 June 2015.

54 Feinberg, interview with the author, 7 December 2014.

55 Robert Busnel also served as coach of the national women's team, 1948–60. He was named president of the FFBB in 1966, a position he held until his 1984 election as president of FIBA. In 1990 he stepped down from the presidency after steering the sport through a phenomenal period of international growth, driven by the rise of the NBA.

56 All Rat quotes: Michel Rat, interviews with the author, 22 October 2014, 29 June 2015 and 20 October 2015.

57 Henry Fields, interview with the author, 30 June 2015.

58 All Fields quotes: Henry Fields, interview with the author, 30 June 2015.

59 Lindsay Sarah Krasnoff, 'Can football save France in a post-Charlie Hebdo world?', *CNN International Sport*, 13 March 2015.

60 See Krasnoff, *The Making of Les Bleus*.

61 Jean-Yves Guincestre, interview with the author, 16 July 2008.

62 A 1968 rule change by the FFBB allowed each team to field two foreign players, a move then-FFBB president Busnel made to force the French game to assimilate new styles of play and thus improve. Despite the subsequent 'American colonisation' of the 1960s and 1970s and the at times negative press discourse that covered it, Fields remained an icon.

63 INSEP was originally named the Institute National de Sport et d'Éducation Physique; over the years its name went through several transformations in recognition of the changing attitudes and foci vis-à-vis sport.

8

Football, diplomacy and Australia in the Asian century

David Rowe

Admitting and expelling Australia?

On the eve of the final of the 2015 AFC (Asian Football Confederation) Asian Cup final between host nation Australia and South Korea, the host city's major newspaper, the *Sydney Morning Herald*, carried a story about a move among some of the west Asian (especially Gulf) nations to expel Australia from the Asian Football Confederation.[1] For those among the hosts who believed that securing the event had cemented the place of Australia in Asian football and in Asia in general, this would have been something of a shock. Although AFC president Sheikh Salman Bin Ibrahim Al-Khalifa (from the Gulf state of Bahrain) claimed that his reported comments to the Dubai-based *Al Ittihad* newspaper had been 'manipulated' and that 'To read a story like this is really sad because there's no truth in it', there were clearly undercurrents of the opposition to Australia that preceded and followed its entry to the Confederation on 1 January 2006.[2]

Australia had only joined the AFC in 2006 after many years of manoeuvring to leave the Oceania Football Confederation (OFC), the smallest regional member of the Fédération Internationale de Football Association Federation (FIFA).[3] This was more than a mere bureaucratic re-alignment of Australia in the world of football, but constituted both a symbolic and pragmatic integration of the nation into the dynamic region in which its future lay.[4] Football would operate as a vehicle for closer contact between the peoples of Asia and Australia, and for regular, relatively informal connections between government and business elites. Yet Australia moving into the AFC was clearly not universally welcomed. Les Murray, a long-time commentator and former sports director of the Special Broadcasting Service (SBS, the multicultural public service broadcaster most closely associated with televising football in Australia) and a former member of FIFA's Ethics Committee, has described the reasons for the resistance to Australia joining the AFC.[5] He notes, like Ben Weinberg,[6] that prior to the 2001 election of the Qatari Mohamed bin Hammam (who was banned for life from FIFA in 2012 for 'conflicts of interest' while AFC president):

The prevailing attitude in Asian football circles towards Australia was at best deeply suspicious and at worst one of downright contempt. The reasons were perverse but, in a way, understandable. The Asians saw Australia as a powerful football nation, one capable of winning in the region. And they dreaded the thought of a white, blue-eyed nation – reminiscent of the colonial era – dominating Asia.[7]

This resistance was overcome when bin Hammam combined with fellow businessman Frank Lowy, chairman of Football Federation Australia (FFA), in overseeing the admission of Australia to the AFC. Indeed, Murray represents their relationship as an instance of football diplomacy in itself when recalling Australia's AFC installation at its 2005 Congress in Marrakech: 'As Lowy and bin Hamman – a Jew and an Arab – embraced, I reflected on football's extraordinary capacity to catalyse deténte and uproot divisive wedges. I was never more proud to be a football man.'[8]

Subsequently, various reasons were canvassed for expelling Australia, including that it was benefiting from the arrangement but contributing little to the AFC's greater good, and that its success in gaining entry to the FIFA World Cup in 2010 and 2014 (it had already qualified for 2006 through the OFC) had denied one of the AFC's four allocated places to a pre-2006 AFC member. Bin Ibrahim Al-Khalifa, elected in 2013, noted in the *Al Ittihad* story that he was not in office at the time of Australia's admission, and implied that, if he had been, a review process concerning the decision would have been mandated. Above all, there was the matter of 'fit' – Australia was not felt by some AFC members to be a legitimate part of an Asian organisation. Yet, in 2013 it had also become a full member of the ASEAN (Association of Southeast Asian Nations) Football Federation (AFF), a regional grouping of AFC members located in south east Asia,[9] and by unanimous vote of its eleven member associations. As was reported in an official AFC media release on the extraordinary AFF Congress in Dili, Timor-Leste (East Timor) at which the decision was made:

> FFA Director, AFC Vice President and FIFA Executive Committee Member Moya Dodd looked to the future, saying: 'Whilst this could be seen as the final piece in Australia's integration into AFC, it is more appropriate to say this is the beginning of a mutual commitment to the advancement of football in South East Asia.'
>
> The decision was welcomed by Lt General Dato' Azzuddin Ahmad, general secretary of AFF. 'FFA today joins the other 11 countries of AFF as an equal, and we look forward to working closely with Australia in the years to come", said Ahmad.[10]

The irony of the subsequent agitation to remove Australia only nine years after admission to the AFC and five months after joining the AFF is that the new member championed the move not only to improve its football, but also to provide strong impetus to what has been described as 'football diplomacy' in government, business and sporting circles.[11] As it turned out, the story about moves to oust Australia from the AFC quickly disappeared from the news media – its ejection would seem, in any case, to be unlikely on constitutional grounds.[12] The incident does, though, throw into sharp relief the rhetorical claims made on behalf of sport diplomacy, and notably that enhanced sporting ties are organically linked to improved political, economic, social and cultural relations. It is necessary, then, to divine lessons from the case of Australia that may apply in informative and useful ways to the wider analytical field of sport/football diplomacy, while recognising Australia's specific geopolitical context and its historical relationship with sport. It is argued here that historical ambivalence towards football in Australia is mirrored to some degree by ambivalence regarding Australia's place in Asia. As a consequence, football diplomacy is fertile ground for the exploration of contemporary Australia–Asia relations, and notably so when analysing contending discourses surrounding Australia's hosting of Asia's largest and most prestigious football tournament.

(Re)Positioning Australia

As a settler-colonial nation in the southern hemisphere, Australia's geopolitical positioning is consistently questioned. Its foundational connection is to Great Britain through its establishment in the late eighteenth century of a series of penal and free-settler colonies that eventually formed the Commonwealth of Australia as an independent nation state in 1901. Integral to this colony and nation formation was the subjugation of its Indigenous population and assertion of the doctrine *terra nullius*,[13] the legal repudiation of which has produced, after the introduction of 'native title', continuing demands for full reconciliation, a formal treaty and recognition of Indigenous people in Australia's constitution. Although the 'Aboriginal question' is not the focus of this chapter, this does not mean that it is irrelevant to sport diplomacy in Australia. For example, in the lead-up to the 2000 Sydney Olympics there were protests by some Aboriginal groups and intimations of a 'sympathy' boycott by African nations, but the former were generally muted and the latter did not eventuate. The strong representation of Indigenous culture in the Cultural Olympiad and Opening and Closing Ceremonies helped to assuage concerns about the negative relationship between the Games and Aboriginal Australians.[14] With regard to Australia's relationship with Asia, there has been a predominant concern with the dominant 'Britishness' that founded Australia as a nation state. This Anglophile national identity extended across the twentieth century to a more generalised association with the 'West' as Australia developed other important affiliations, especially with the USA through military alliance and economic exchange, alongside the non-British sources of its post-Second World War immigration, notably from southern and northern continental Europe.

Australia's close ties with the USA include the use of the Northern Territory's Pine Gap and other Australian locations for the purpose of global communications surveillance; US Marine Corps rotation through Darwin since 2012; membership of the ANZUS defence cooperation alliance (also including Aotearoa/New Zealand); and involvement in US-led military action in Afghanistan and Iraq (and in Vietnam before it). They have marked the country clearly as a Western ally, if not as a transplanted

Western nation itself. A particularly memorable image, derived from comments made by US president George Bush (although he was not the first to use the 'Sheriff' metaphor), is that of Australia as the US's 'Deputy Sheriff' in the Asia Pacific region.[15] Remarks by Australian prime minister John Howard after the 2002 Bali bombings (in which eighty-eight Australians were killed) canvassing the possibility of pre-emptive attacks in the region, prompted criticisms at the time, such as those by Malaysian prime minister Mahathir Mohamad: 'Australia has to choose whether it's an Asian country or a western country', he told the newspaper *The Australian* in November 2002. 'If you take the position of being a deputy sheriff to America, you cannot very well be accepted by the countries of this region.'[16]

Such resentment towards Australia was also felt by Indonesia through the former's military role in organising and leading the multinational peacemaking taskforce International Force East Timor (INTERFET) in 1999, as Indonesia withdrew from Timor-Leste/East Timor after a long guerrilla war and sustained repression of the local population.[17] Apart from these specific geopolitical tensions in the Asia Pacific region, a more wide-ranging grievance could be discerned by means of the historical legacy of the White Australia Policy. Immediately following Australian nationhood in 1901 (superseding various colonial restrictions on non-White entry to the continent), the Immigration Restriction Act was passed as an explicitly racialised exclusionary provision with regard to Asians (especially the Chinese) and those from the Pacific Islands (Polynesia, Melanesia and Micronesia, although not the *Pakeha* – Anglo-Celtic people from Aotearoa/New Zealand). Support for White Australia spanned the major political parties with, for example, the Australian Labor Party expressing concern about the importation of cheap Asian and Islander labour. This policy was maintained and strengthened until the Second World War (in which Australia's most direct military conflict was with Japan), after which the immigration of displaced persons and a series of liberalising reforms (culminating in the 1975 Racial Discrimination Act) saw the end of a racially based, and Asia focused, national immigration policy.[18] The arrival of 90,000 South Vietnamese refugees (about 2,000 of whom were so-called 'boat people') by the mid-1980s in the wake of the Vietnam War (in which, as noted, Australia was a combatant) was a conspicuous indication of the passing into history of White Australia.

Of course, legal changes did not mean an end to public debates and ideological undercurrents surrounding Australia's positioning in an Asian context, especially given long-standing anxiety over what had often been described as the 'Yellow Peril'. The 'Australia for the White Man' banner of the politically influential and popular *Bulletin* magazine (which opened in 1860 and closed in 2008) was displayed on its front cover from 1886 until as late as 1961, when it was removed by its then-editor Donald Horne. In the early 1980s renowned historian Geoffrey Blainey sparked considerable controversy after expressing concern about levels of Asian immigration and projections of an 'Asia Australia', a view shared by various members of the Liberal–National Coalition Opposition (including future prime minister John Howard).[19] The emergence and brief flourishing of the anti-Asian immigration, One Nation party under Pauline Hanson in the following decade (since re-born in 2016 in anti-Islamic guise) signalled the strain placed on the long-standing bi-partisan national policy of multicul-turalism.[20] In this period, especially during a prime ministership (1996–2007) which was 'characterized by an increasing attempt to distance himself from multiculturalism as official policy',[21] Howard 'barely uttered the "m" word in his early years as prime minister'.[22] In later years he was openly critical of what he saw as its detrimental impact on 'Anglo-Saxon culture as the "core culture" in Australia into which other cultures ought to "blend"'.[23] This ideological position is especially important given that, as is discussed below, Australia's commitment to multiculturalism was the cornerstone of what, in contrast with its more formal and institutional form, is described here as the 'popular' public diplomacy surrounding the 2015 AFC Asian Cup. Following the Iraq, Afghanistan and Sri Lankan wars, there was an increase in asylum seeking to Australia, including by those who undertook hazardous voyages originating in Indonesia and Sri Lanka. The 2001 'Tampa affair', in which the eponymous Norwegian vessel was refused entry to Australian waters after rescuing 438 mainly Afghani asylum seekers at sea, saw the issue of 'border protection' become prominent, notably in the context of that year's (by then post-9/11) federal election. There followed the progressive refinement of the 'Pacific Solution' that excised many islands from Australia's migration zone; detained those who had arrived 'unauthorised' by boat in neighbouring Nauru and Papua New Guinea; and refused settlement to 'unauthorised arrivals by boat' in Australia even if granted refugee status.[24] Aggressive 'stop the boats' and 'turn back' (intercept and return) policy campaigning in successive elections by the Liberal–National Coalition in the current decade, and the Labor Party's eventual acceptance of it, highlight the persistence of an exclusionary strain running through Australian politics with regard, in particular, to the Asia Pacific region.

These and other developments triggered vigorous debates over Australia's humanitarian and international treaty obligations, and it would be misleading to present anti-immigration and anti-Asian political positions as dominant in Australia. However, for the purposes of this chapter such discursive conflicts over Australian demography and identity demonstrate importantly how Australia's positioning as in or alongside Asia – or, more vividly, diagnoses of the 'Asianisation of Australia'[25] – are crucial to understanding sport's role as an arm of the nation's diplomacy. They should be seen as the counterpoints to the 'turn to Asia' in a world where China and Japan are Australia's major trading partners, with Korea, Singapore, Thailand and Malaysia also in the top ten of two-way trading partners,[26] and India and Indonesia being cultivated as major future export markets. Furthermore, the top ten countries providing permanent migrants to Australia in 2013–14 was headed by India and China, with the Philippines, Pakistan, Vietnam, Nepal and Malaysia also in that group.[27] It is for this reason that the Australian Labor government (1997–2013) published the *Australia in the Asian Century White Paper*,[28] with claims in its executive summary such as:

The Asian century is an Australian opportunity. As the global centre of gravity shifts to our region, the tyranny of distance is being replaced by the prospects of proximity. Australia is located in the right place at the right time – in the Asian region in the Asian century...[29]

The White Paper continues to reinforce this theme of needing 'to strengthen Australia's deep and broad relationships across the region at every level' involving 'links [that] are social and cultural as much as they are political and economic'. Thus, stronger relationships 'will lead to more Australians having a deeper understanding of what is happening in Asia', while in turn 'more of our neighbours in the region will know us better than they do today'.[30] The section on 'Sport' in *Australia in the Asian Century* points to the significance of Australia hosting the 2015 AFC Asian Cup. It briefly outlines how, 'Our sporting connections can open doors and create links between people in the region'[31] and places specific emphasis on 'football diplomacy' and Australia's membership of the AFC, which meant that, 'for the first time Australia had a significant, ongoing sporting relationship with a large number of Asian and Middle Eastern countries, complementing our diplomatic and other links'.[32]

Australia's deep connections with Britain help to explain the importance of sport to its historically Western-oriented national culture and stimulated its own influential local adaptations and innovations. Its extensive involvement in international sport (such as its unbroken participation in the Summer Olympics since their revival in 1896 and hosting of them in 1956 and 2000) provides many opportunities to engage diplomatically with Asian nations.[33] However, in most cases Australian sport has been governmentally separated from Asia: hence the above-mentioned importance of its admission to the Asian Football Confederation in 2006. The opportunities for football diplomacy are greatly enhanced when a common continental or regional governance structure allows Australia to be defined as an Asian sporting nation and so to host and participate in major regional events like the 2015 AFC Asian Cup. Here, as in all sporting events, nations engage in overt competition, but this re-positioning of Australia for a sporting purpose is symbolically unifying in continental terms, and may signify a new mode of integration and collective identification that situates Australia *within* Asia in the Asian century. The turn to Asia has tended to display a rather instrumental, technocratic emphasis on economic and political integration. The sphere of bilateral trade agreements and political accords is limited in terms of fostering networks of cross-national/cultural engagement. For this reason, sport, among other cultural forms such as the visual and performing arts, has been championed in the White Paper and elsewhere as a promising domain of diplomacy (broadly defined as encompassing political, economic, social and cultural exchange in both formal and informal environments).[34] The place of sport within Australian diplomacy of different kinds now requires more detailed exploration.

Sport and diplomacy in Australia

In seeking to capture an elusive concept there is a significant and growing body of literature on public diplomacy that can only be touched on lightly here. For example, Nicholas J. Cull, in a special issue on the subject in the*Annals of the American Academy of Political and Social Science*, has proposed a 'basic taxonomy' of types: 'Listening', 'Advocacy', 'Cultural diplomacy', 'Exchange diplomacy' and

'International broadcasting'.[35] Jan Melissen, in a similar vein, conceives of a 'new public diplomacy' that 'is aimed at foreign publics',[36] echoing Paul Sharp's emphasis on the role of direct relations in the contact of a country's people by another being represented.[37] Public diplomacy is therefore characterised by the involvement of non-governmental actors and emphasises civil-societal relationships that are relatively autonomous from the state – or are designed to appear so. At issue is the extent to which public diplomacy can be detached from more conventional pursuits of national interest and its state-based orchestration. Sport, as a major form of popular culture, is a domain where the state is not generally in the foreground, meaning that sport diplomacy is well suited to the task of connecting the citizens of different countries on ostensibly neutral ground. As Pigman and Rofe have argued in the introduction to a special issue of *Sport in Society* addressing sport and diplomacy,[38] sport's international visibility is powerfully connected to the rise of soft power strategies in international relations. Among sports, football's global reach is unmatched, leading, for example, to Japan, South Korea and China all using football diplomacy to break out of international isolation.[39] Football diplomacy is, then, an important subset of sport diplomacy which, in turn, has an increasingly well-articulated relationship to public diplomacy.

In the Australian context sport is principally treated as 'public diplomacy' within the Department of Foreign Affairs and Trade (DFAT) under the umbrella of 'Sport for Development' and its Australian Sports Outreach Program (ASOP), including Pacific Sports Partnerships (PSP), which are funded by DFAT and managed by the statutory authority the Australian Sports Commission (ASC). Sport's public diplomacy relevance is clarified in its 'Development-through-sport' strategy:

> AusAID[40] and the ASC recognise that sport is [also] a 'natural fit' for public diplomacy and that public diplomacy benefits will be enhanced when development-through-sport activities contribute effectively to positive social change.
>
> With a reputation as a sporting nation, and with sport playing an important role in Australian communities, Australia is well placed to use sport to contribute to the government's public diplomacy objectives.[41]

The strategy attributes a range of functions to sport, including that it 'promotes a positive image of Australia internationally' and demonstrates Australia's 'commitment to and engagement with the region'.[42] Sport's public diplomacy role is more ambitiously affirmed in DFAT's 49th edition of *Australia in Brief*, which claims that 'Australia is regarded as a world leader in using sport to assist developing countries to achieve positive societal outcomes' in melding sport's role in public diplomacy and development aid.[43] The following (50th) edition of *Australia in Brief*, though, removed any reference to sport and development aid, and Australia's 'world leader' role in it.[44] This excision may have been because of substantial cuts to the overall foreign aid budget by the Liberal–National government,[45] revealing that sports diplomacy rhetoric may be disconnected from its support with public material resources. Sport also figures extensively in DFAT's *Public Diplomacy Strategy 2014–16*, being named alongside cultural diplomacy and science diplomacy as an effective way 'to promote Australia's diplomatic, development and economic interests'.[46]

With regard to budgetary and strategic matters, Murray has criticised the confinement of sport to the public diplomacy remit of DFAT, complaining that, 'Sports-diplomacy could and should have great potential for Australia', taking advantage of the fact that its regional neighbours are 'sports mad' and 'its remarkable sporting success'.[47] It is notable that most of the 'regional neighbours' that Murray mentions are not, apart from Indonesia, in Asia. But, in any case, hosting mega sport events such as the 2015 AFC Asian Cup – the football diplomacy case study in focus here – is a very different mode of sport diplomacy from development aid. As Ang, Tambiah and Mar note in their report on 'smart engagement' with Asia:

> there are major differences between development-oriented projects seeking to alleviate social, health and economic problems, and business networking efforts around major sporting events that build on the prestige of these occasions. These divergent elements may be difficult to unify in a coherent sports diplomacy framework.[48]

Although development aid is not merely altruistic and humanitarian in intent, it nonetheless involves the transfer of resources from the 'donor' to the 'recipient'. In the case of major sport tournaments, the host is donating its spaces and services in the expectation that there will be tangible material benefits in employment and tourism alongside the intangible advantages of prestige, profile and diplomatic opportunity. These tensions between philanthropy, diplomacy, soft power and economic interest are apparent in the Australian government Department of Foreign Affairs and Trade's *Australian Sports Diplomacy Strategy 2015–18*, which states in its introduction that:

> Planning and delivering major sporting events is a global growth sector and Australia's enviable track record in creating and hosting successful, premier sporting events means the country is well-placed to take advantage of this. Real opportunities exist for Australian expertise and capability in all stages of the major sporting event life-cycle, including: bidding; planning; event staging services; operations and management; cultural ceremonies; and venue design and construction.[49]

Here the emphasis on Australia's 'potential to capitalise further on its full suite of sporting credentials by engaging with neighbouring countries' is explicitly articulated with 'achieving public diplomacy outcomes in the Indo-Pacific region and beyond' as they relate to the 'export' of sports industry services.[50] Examining the 2015 AFC Asian Cup – and sport event hosting, management and related commercially hosted service activities in general – reveals, then, the co-existence of multiple agenda that can be complementary, inconsistent or even contradictory in the sphere of football diplomacy.

Australia as Asian football host

A substantial element of the 2015 AFC Asian Cup event agenda was directly or indirectly economic – the attraction of sports tourists and the use of coverage to expose Australia to other potential tourists and to raise its international profile. Apart from the business and political networking that the event afforded, a more diffuse form of football diplomacy – described earlier as 'popular' – sought to use the tournament as a symbolic expression of Australia's ease with other cultures, not least because, as an immigrant nation committed to multiculturalism, many (originary) compatriots of visiting and remote-viewing sport fans are *already* deeply connected to Australia through citizenship, residency, extended kinship, friendship and professional network ties. The explicit encouragement of Australia-based national-ethnic groups to follow visiting teams, and for others to 'adopt' one, can be regarded as more than just astute event marketing.[51] It is also an encouragement of a fan-to-fan mode of popular public diplomacy that is quite different from the elite networking that is commonly foregrounded as sport diplomacy practice. There is, therefore, a difficult balancing act involving various levels of the state and commerce facilitating without overly manipulating or forcing sport fan interaction. As Steven Jackson has argued:

> Arguably, we should neither overstate nor understate the diplomatic potential of sport, but rather seek to understand the nature and effects of its use with respect to diplomacy. This challenges us to consider diplomacy *within* sport, diplomacy *for* sport and diplomacy *through* sport. Moreover, it is important to recognise that these 'types' of diplomacy do not operate in distinct and mutually exclusive ways, but rather tend to work in tandem, adopting a range of configurations depending on the context.[52]

As a recent special issue of *Diplomacy and Statecraft* on sport and diplomacy has amply demonstrated, scholarship on the many forms of sport diplomacy has expanded alongside its object of inquiry.[53] All these iterations of sport diplomacy are evident regarding the 2015 AFC Asian Cup, as are those that rely on highly mediated forms of communication.[54] Securing the AFC Asian Cup (in 2011) as hosts (unanimously supported as the sole bidder) so soon after Australia's admission to the Confederation was heralded as a significant advancement of its football diplomacy capacity, and substantial public funds from the federal government and the host state governments of New South Wales, Victoria, Queensland and the Australia Capital Territory were expended on hosting the event. According to Smith, the estimated exposure of the participating governments to the financial shortfall of the event was US$46.55m (€15.65m).[55] This very large public investment followed Australia's disastrous attempt to host the 2018 and 2022 FIFA World Cups, which led to it withdrawing from the first and gaining only one vote for the second, at an estimated cost to the nation of US$32.05m (€ 28.58m).[56] This failure should be viewed in the context of the previously articulated somewhat ambivalent history and position of football in Australia which would question, to some degree, its public diplomatic credentials, but also the scandal surrounding the bidding process itself.[57] Although it is 'the most popular team sport in Australia', with 'almost two million participants outnumbering the other football codes combined', football is in historical terms institutionally and economically the weakest of those codes.[58] This disadvantage has been ascribed to the game's primary association with the aforementioned large post-Second World War wave of southern European immigration to Australia and an ethnocentric response among the dominant Anglo-Celtic Australian population, as well as to a degree of inter-ethnic conflict and non-cooperation.[59] Its otherness – ethnic, gendered and sexual – in Australia was graphically described in the title of a book by the late leading player, coach, administrator, broadcaster and writer, Johnny Warren: *Sheilas, Wogs & Poofters: An Incomplete Biography of Johnny Warren and Soccer in Australia*.[60] Indeed, as Neilsen has pointed out, Warren argued in the book that even the enlistment of the Australian national team, the Socceroos, to serve the interest of football diplomacy during the Vietnam War, was an indication of the lowly status of the game in Australia.[61] No other sport in the country, Warren suggested, would be put in harm's way in a war zone and so cynically exploited in the propaganda supporting an unpopular war.

There is, then, something of an irony that football in Australia should be held out as an ideal vehicle for public diplomacy in Asia, when it had long been resisted and even lampooned in the country for its ethnic 'otherness' and after its own administration, abetted by the federal government, had implemented a systematic policy of 'de-ethnicisation' that had banned ethnic organisational structures and signification from the A-League on its founding in 2004.[62] A further irony is that the game is better established in Asian countries such as Japan and Korea, which had (albeit uneasily) co-hosted the FIFA World Cup in 2002. A substantial element of the popularity of the 'world game' in Asia, though, is derived from the major European leagues, especially through the cultural imperialism of the English Premier League.[63] Nonetheless, according to the AFC the event was 'a stunning success' by a range of measures. These include it being 'the most watched AFC Asian Cup ever, marking the 2015 tournament as a milestone event in Australian and Asian sporting history' that 'set new benchmarks for colour, passion, inclusiveness and exemplary crowd behaviour'. Its aggregate attendance was 'a staggering 650,000' and 'a worldwide TV audience in excess of one billion', almost a fifth of whom were in China, while 'the event's official #AC2015 Twitter hashtag reach was 2.69 billion at the end of the semi-finals'. Among the event's extra-sporting legacies was 'an ongoing education program which has already helped more than 50,000 primary school students learn more about Asia' through football-themed units of study.[64]

The familiar ensemble of benefits is presented, including nation building, tourism, increased economic activity and business contact, but public diplomacy is given particular prominence both through the use of 'community ambassadors' and engagement with 'Australia's diverse multicultural communities' who, along with Socceroo supporters, were encouraged to 'adopt' a second, visiting team. According to Local Organising Committee (LOC) CEO Michael Brown, the AFC Asian Cup 'significantly reinforced the positive perceptions about Australia throughout Asia, attracted tens of thousands of tourists and delivered an estimated \$A23 [\$US17.55, €15.65] million boost to Australia's GDP'.[65] With the business matching programme 'opening many new doors for Australian companies throughout Asia', Brown was 'proud of our star-studded team of ambassadors, and of our fabulous team of 1,300 volunteers for giving such a great Aussie welcome to the whole of Asia'. This was *in situ* football diplomacy, the LOC making 'great efforts to engage Australia's diverse multicultural communities' who, having 'embraced the event', led a 'number of teams [to] have commented that the crowd support in Australia made them feel like they were playing at home'.[66]

The community ambassador scheme, led by 200 Asian Australians, was designed to capitalise on the 'close to two million people of Asian heritage calling Australia home' as part of 'expat communities' using the event as a 'celebration of multiculturalism in Australia and an exhibition of supporter culture from across the continent'.[67] Apart from its key football legacies, the 'national legacy' counted among areas of focus 'strengthening diplomatic relations across Asia', 'furthering business and trade links', 'increasing tourism through football', 'deepening relations with Asian communities' and 'improving social outcomes through community social responsibility activities'.[68] This interweaving of legacy elements exposes the ways in which football diplomacy works on behalf of dedicated national interests while, at the same time, obscuring them in trans- or supranational discourse.

Exhibited among the pro-tournament rhetoric there is an evident insider/outsider dynamic concerning Australia's relationship to Asia, producing some uncertainty as to whether Australia is a part of Asia and so hosting fellow Asians, or is external to Asia and thereby welcoming visiting 'others'. Similar ambiguity applies to residents – Australians of Asian heritage being interpellated as 'expats' whose primary affiliation is elsewhere – either in another nation or a different region/continent – even if born in Australia. The complex social subjectivities found in transnational environments, not least in relation to sport, tend to be obscured in such representations of the Asian other.[69] Of more direct relevance here is the constant evocation of Australian multiculturalism in the light of both wider political proclamations of the failure of the multicultural project in Western liberal democracies and of the structural de-ethnicisation of football in Australia.[70] The former is rather more concerned with Australia's relation to Asia than the latter as the White Australia Policy was mainly addressed to Asia, while the de-ethnicisation of football principally concerned migrants from southern Europe, including Greece, Macedonia, Italy, Croatia and Serbia.[71] It is for this reason that Australia's main popular public diplomatic symbols circulated via the 2015 AFC Asian Cup, and as a counter to its continued identification by some within and without as a 'White Nation', were dedicated to de-Westernisation and non-Whiteness.[72]

Conclusion: the diplomatic game

Asia features strongly in the FFA's *We Are Football: This is Our Vision: Whole of Football Plan* that was released a few months after the AFC Asian Cup. Under 'Challenges', in noting that 'Australia is one of the most multicultural nations in the world', it is proposed that, 'Football will become more than just a sport. It will have an increasingly important role to play in social cohesion, community integration, physical health and well-being, and international relations and economic development, particularly in Asia.'[73] The quasi-diplomatic discourse evident here is reinforced through an almost *de rigueur* referencing of the 'Asian Century' in which 'The rise of Asia will mean changes to who populates Australia, who we trade with and where we source capital from, an evolution that will change everyday life in Australia.'[74] Under 'Targets', the ambitious aim is 'Embrace Asia. Football will lead Australia's sporting and social engagement with our neighbours across Asia. Football will provide a platform for both commercial partners and government to build meaningful relationships with our Asian neighbours.'[75] The proposition in this instance is that football has the capacity to take a vanguard role in advancing Australia's engagement with Asia because of the regional popularity of the game, and that the successful hosting of the 2015 AFC Asian Cup and membership of the AFC provide both the exemplar and the governmental means of doing so. This claim is audacious; not least in the light of the aforementioned uneasiness among some other AFC members concerning Australia's presence among them. Indeed, Australia's isolation in the AFC was highlighted even more when FFA chairman Frank Lowy declared its board's support in the FIFA presidential election on 29 May 2015 for the Jordanian prince Ali bin Hussein – only a day after the AFC reaffirmed its commitment to the long-serving and highly controversial Swiss president Joseph S. Blatter.[76] The arrest of several FIFA officials on corruption charges in Zurich just before the 65th FIFA Congress in that city, and Blatter's subsequent re-election victory and announcement four days later of his intention to resign amid widespread opposition to his continuation, have exposed further divisions within the AFC that, it should be acknowledged, go well beyond the position of Australia within it.

With Blatter being subsequently investigated by Swiss prosecutors and, along with his possible successor, UEFA (Union of European Football Associations) president Michel Platini, examined by FIFA's Ethics Committee over 'disloyal payments' by the former to the latter, the position of the AFC on the FIFA presidential election in February 2016, and Australia's relationship to it, had the potential to be a further source of tension.[77] Although the AFC stated that 'Any association who wishes to support a specific candidacy – or to announce their own candidate – is free to do so', the same announcement noted that 'The AFC President is, according to the AFC Statutes, responsible for relations with FIFA and other Confederations, and has already expressed his personal preference for the candidacy of Michel Platini, as quoted in the statement of 30 July', and that 'A growing majority of AFC Member Associations have also expressed their support for Mr Platini's candidacy, based on his credentials to lead world football, whilst others have expressed an interest for other candidates, have expressed no interest at all, or are waiting before making up their minds'.[78] Australia's positioning with regard to publicly announced voting blocs (for a technically secret ballot) had wider significance for its regional assimilation or integration. The eventual outcome was that Platini was not permitted to stand and, despite the AFC declaring its support for the candidature of Salman,[79] Australia voted again for Hussein in the first round, with UEFA general secretary Gianni Infantino winning the second round against Salman.[80] In not supporting the current AFC president for the FIFA presidency, the FFA once again subordinated intra-Federation football diplomacy to a commitment to wider FIFA reform.

Although football is the most popular sport in Asia, it by no means monopolises the field of sport diplomacy. As noted earlier, the Olympics is an important area of sport diplomacy that also offers benefits and risks in international relations. Cricket 'diplomacy' is routinely deployed in Australia–India relations,[81] although the 2008 'Monkeygate affair' involving the accusation of racial abuse by Indian cricketer Harbhajan Singh of the Australian Andrew Symonds caused political tensions between the countries.[82] Sport diplomacy also does not operate evenly and consistently, taking place variously at country-to-country, regional, intra/intercontinental and global levels. As a consequence, rather artificial constructions are articulated for the purposes of sports governance, such as in the case of Australia and the AFC, where the concept of 'Asia', a vast, populous and diverse continent, is a flexible governmental construct that is available to be mobilised as essentialist rhetoric by various parties. Indeed, symbolic mobilisations of the idea of Asia in such instances are frequently redolent of Edward Said's critique of 'Orientalism' and its imaginary conceptualisation of a West/East binary and hierarchy.[83]

In addressing the Australian context with regard to football and a specific tournament – the 2015 AFC Asian Cup – it has not been possible to discuss in any detail the sport/football diplomacy strategies of other nations or with regard to other sports. However, there are some general lessons that may be drawn from this example. First, and most obviously, the success or failure of football diplomacy is necessarily conditioned by the historical legacy and *status quo* of international relations, not least with regard to imperialism and colonialism. There are also different modes of football diplomacy, especially elite political and business networking as opposed to more popular diplomatic and less easily choreographed relationships between the peoples of different nations, located in different and frequently fluid national spaces, and with a diverse range of social subjectivities. The cultural specificity of football is also significant for public diplomacy in view of its reliance on often-ruthless competition, and vulnerability to exploitation for xenophobic and racist purposes. Conflicts may arise in the form of violence among rival spectators or through on-field controversies with international political ramifications, and through antagonistic media commentary. Sport's competitive logic may symbolically concentrate tensions around border issues involving the passage of players and spectators who may seek asylum or overstay visas (especially from war or economically depressed zones); disputes over national representation (such as North/South Korea; Palestine/Israel; China/Taiwan; East Timor/

Indonesia; Ireland/United Kingdom); or campaigns over human rights issues (e.g., protests over Darfur and Tibet prior to the Beijing 2008 Olympics, and over gay rights regarding the 2014 Sochi Winter Olympics and the 2018 Russia and 2022 Qatar FIFA World Cup, with the last also raising questions concerning the conditions of migrant workers). Aggressive competition among nations to host major sport events can lead to conflict over 'dirty tricks', while alliances and rivalries among nations in peak sporting organisations (like the various voting blocs and geopolitical spheres of influence in the International Cricket Council, IOC, AFC and FIFA) can exacerbate – or at least crystallise – rather than assuage tensions between nation states.

Such conflicts and difficulties are unsurprising, but it is important that they are considered in the face of some of the more anodyne claims of football's unproblematic relationship with public diplomacy founded on exaggerated and inaccurate assumptions of universal football-based amity. Events such as the 2015 AFC Asian Cup may be caught up in events of wide-ranging significance over which they have little control. The 2015 Asian Cup took place during an intense period of diplomatic activity concerning Australia's attempt to dissuade Indonesia from executing two Australian citizens (Andrew Chan and Myuran Sukumaran) for drug smuggling. The executions went ahead less than three months after the Final, leading Australia to withdraw its ambassador to Indonesia for consultation.[84] Indonesia failed to qualify, but had it done so its team would have been in Australia for the tournament, providing both opportunities for football diplomacy on a government-to-government basis, and also for the application of pressure through institutional sport and media channels. It would also – as had occurred, for example, in the protests to China over Tibet during the Torch Relay in the lead-up to the 2008 Beijing Olympic Games[85] – have facilitated multiple, international media-covered protests at football grounds around Australia at matches involving the Indonesian national team, as well as affording many other opportunities for popular public diplomatic representations, both mediated and in physical locations such as a stadium or team hotel. The possibilities afforded to multiple modes of football diplomacy surrounding mega-events, and their likely amplification via large co-present crowds, cohorts of journalists and multi-media platforms, may be as 'spectacular' as the games themselves, but with correspondingly uncertain outcomes.

Notes

1 Sebastian Hassett, 'Angry Gulf nations leading charge to kick Australia out of Asian Football Confederation', *Sydney Morning Herald*, 29 January 2015, available at www.smh.com.au/sport/soccer/afc-asian-cup/angry-gulf-nations-leading-charge-to-kick-australia-out-of-asian-football-confederation-20150129-131e5g.html (accessed 11 May 2015).

2 Quoted in 'AFC chief slams Australia expulsion claims', *SBS*, 30 January 2015, available at http://theworldgame.sbs.com.au/article/2015/01/30/afc-chief-slams-australia-expulsion-claims (accessed 11 May 2015).

3 Chris Hallinan and Tom Heenan, 'Australia, Asia and the new football opportunity', in Younghan Cho (ed.), *Football in Asia: History, Culture and Business* (London: Routledge, 2015), 173–90.

4 Anthony Bubalo, *Football Diplomacy (Policy Brief)* (Sydney: Lowy Institute for International Policy, 2005), available at www.lowyinstitute.org/files/pubfiles/ Bubalo,_Football_diplomacy_stripe.pdf (accessed 11 May 2015).

5 Les Murray, *By the Balls: Memoir of a Football Tragic* (Sydney: Random House, 2006).

6 Ben Weinberg, *Asia and the Future of Football: The Role of the Asian Football Confederation* (London: Routledge, 2015).

7 Murray, *By the Balls*, 279.

8 Murray, *By the Balls*, 280.

9 AFC (Asian Football Confederation), 'Australia admitted as AFF member', 26 August2013, available at www.the-afc.com/australia/australia-admitted-as-aff-member (accessed 11 May 2015).

10 AFC, 'Australia admitted as AFF member'.

11 Anthony Bubalo, *Football Diplomacy Redux: The 2015 Asian Cup and Australia's Engagement with Asia (Policy Brief)* (Sydney: Lowy Institute for International Policy, 2013), available at www.lowyinstitute.org/files/bubalo_football_diplomacy_redux_ web.pdf (accessed 11 May 2015); Bubalo, *Football Diplomacy (Policy Brief)*.

12 The terms 'soccer' and 'football' are used interchangeably here. The former has tended to be used in Australia in differentiating association football from the three other major football codes (Australian rules, rugby league and rugby union). However, in 2005 the newly established Football Federation Australia, consistent with the removal of 'soccer' from the nomenclature of the national governing body, stipulated that 'football' should be used in accordance with the dominant terminology across the world. This chapter uses the term 'football', except where 'soccer' is specifically named by others. Under the AFC constitution, a member association can only be expelled on a minimum of one of four proven grounds by a 75 per cent majority vote at its annual Congress. These grounds are: 1. failing to fulfil financial obligations to the AFC; 2. seriously violating its own statutes, codes, rules, regulations and standing orders or those of the AFC or FIFA; 3. ceasing to be the legal football association in its own country; 4. ceasing to be a member of FIFA (for reference, see note 2 above). Clearly, none of these grounds currently applies to Australia.

13 This doctrine of 'empty land' was overturned by the so-called 'Mabo judgment' in 1992, in which the High Court of Australia recognised 'native' title in common law. See Peter Butt, Robert Eagleson and Patricia Lane, *Mabo, Wik and Native Title* (Sydney: Federation Press, 4th edn, 2001).

14 David Rowe, 'The bid, the lead-up, the event and the legacy: the global cultural politics of awarding and hosting the Olympics' (Special Issue: 'Olympic and World Sport: Making Transnational Society'), *British Journal of Sociology*, 63:2 (2012); Peter Christian Wejbora, *The Sydney 2000 Olympics Bid and its Impact on the Process of Redefining Australian National Identity* (Sydney: University of Technology, Sydney, 1996), available at https://opus.lib.uts.edu.au/bitstream/2100/1111/2/02whole.pdf (accessed 28 September 2016).

15 Robert Manne, *Making Trouble: Essays Against the New Australian Complacency* (Melbourne: Black Inc. Agenda, 2011), 21.

16 Quoted in David Fickling, Australia seen as "America's deputy sheriff"', *The*

Guardian, 10 September 2004, available at www.theguardian.com/world/2004/sep/10/indonesia.australia (accessed 11 May 2015).

17 James Cotton, *East Timor, Australia and the Regional Order: Intervention and its Aftermath in SouthEast Asia* (London and New York: Routledge Curzon, 2004).

18 Laksiri Jayasuriya, *Transforming a 'White Australia': Issues of Racism and Immigration* (New Delhi: SSS, 2012).

19 Andrew Markus and M. C. Ricklefs (eds), *Surrender Australia? Essays in the Study and Uses of History: Geoffrey Blainey and Asian Immigration* (Sydney: Allen and Unwin, 1985).

20 Michael Leach, Geoff Stokes and Ian Ward, *The Rise and Fall of One Nation* (St Lucia: Queensland University Press, 2000).

21 John William Tate, 'John Howard's "Nation": multiculturalism, citizenship and identity', *Australian Journal of Politics and History* 55:1 (2009).

22 Wayne Errington and Peter van Onselen, *John Winston Howard* (Carlton: Melbourne University Press, 2007), 222; Tate, 'John Howard's "Nation"', 112.

23 Tate, 'John Howard's "Nation"', 109.

24 Jon Stratton, *Uncertain Lives: Culture, Race and Neoliberalism in Australia* (Newcastle: Cambridge Scholars, 2011).

25 Tim Soutphommasane, *The Asianisation of Australia?* (Sydney: Australian Human Rights Commission, 2014), available at www.humanrights.gov.au/news/speeches/asianisation-australia (accessed 11 May 2015).

26 Australian Government Department of Foreign Affairs and Trade, *Australia's Top 10 Two-Way Trading Partners* (Canberra: Australian Government, 2014), available at http://dfat.gov.au/trade/resources/trade-at-a-glance/Pages/default.aspx (accessed 13 May 2015).

27 Australian Government Department of Immigration and Border Protection, 'Country profiles' (2015), available at www.immi.gov.au/pub-res/Pages/statistics/country_profiles/country-profiles.aspx (accessed 13 May 2015).

28 Australian Government, *Australia in the Asian Century White Paper* (Canberra: Department of the Prime Minister and Cabinet, 2012), available at www.murdoch.edu.au/ALTC-Fellowship/_document/Resources/australia-in-the-asian-century-white-paper.pdf (accessed 13 May 2015).

29 Australian Government, *Australia in the Asian Century White Paper*, 1.

30 Australian Government, *Australia in the Asian Century White Paper*, 3.

31 Australian Government, *Australia in the Asian Century White Paper*, 268.

32 Australian Government, *Australia in the Asian Century White Paper*, 268.

33 Jared van Duinen, 'Playing to the "imaginary grandstand": sport, the "British world", and an Australian colonial identity', *Journal of Global History*, 8:2 (2013).

34 Ien Ang, Yudhishthir R. Isar and Phillip Mar, 'Cultural diplomacy: beyond the national interest?', *International Journal of Cultural Policy*, 21:4 (2015).

35 Nicholas J. Cull, 'Public diplomacy: taxonomies and histories', *ANNALS of the American Academy of Political and Social Science*, 616:1 (2008), 35.

36 Jan Melissen, 'The new public diplomacy: between theory and practice', in Jan Melissen (ed.), *The New Public Diplomacy: Soft Power in International Relations* (Basingstoke: Palgrave Macmillan, 2005), 13.

37 Paul Sharp, 'Revolutionary states, outlaw regimes and the techniques of public diplomacy', in Melissen (ed.), *The New Public Diplomacy*, 106–23.

38 Geoffrey A. Pigman and J. Simon Rofe, 'Sport and diplomacy: an introduction', *Sport in Society* (Special Issue on Sport and Diplomacy), 17:9 (2014).

39 Wolfram Manzenreiter, 'Football diplomacy, post-colonialism and Japan's quest for normal state status', *Sport in Society* (Special Issue on Sport and Foreign Policy in a Globalizing World), 11:4 (2008).

40 In late 2013 the Australian Agency for International Development (AusAID), which previously funded the programmes, was absorbed by DFAT.

41 Australian Sports Commission (ASC) and the Australian Agency for International Development (AusAID), *Development-through-Sport* (Canberra: ASC/AusAID, 2013), 3–4, available at https://secure.ausport.gov.au/__data/assets/pdf_file/0007/636883/Development_through_Sport_Strategy_2013-2017.pdf (accessed 13 May 2015).

42 ASC and AusAID, *Development-through-Sport*, 3–4.

43 Australian Government Department of Foreign Affairs and Trade, *Australia in Brief* (49th edition) (Canberra: DFAT, 2012), 47.

44 Australian Government Department of Foreign Affairs and Trade, *Australia in Brief* (50th edition) (Canberra: DFAT, 2014), available at http://dfat.gov.au/about-us/publications/Documents/australia-in-brief.pdf (accessed 13 May 2015).

45 Karen Barlow, 'Budget 2014: axe falls on foreign aid spending, nearly AU$8 [US$61.04, €8.54] billion in cuts over next five years', *Australian Broadcasting Corporation*, 13 May 2014, available at www.abc.net.au/news/2014-05-13/budget-2014-axe-falls-on-foreign-aid-spending/5450844 (accessed 13 May 2015).

46 Australian Government Department of Foreign Affairs and Trade, *Public Diplomacy Strategy 2014–16* (Barton: Department of Foreign Affairs and Trade, 2016), available at http://dfat.gov.au/people-to-people/public-diplomacy/Documents/public-diplomacy-strategy-2014-16.pdf (accessed 26 September 2016).

47 Stuart Murray, 'Sports diplomacy in the Australian context: a case study of the Department of Foreign Affairs and Trade', *Sports Law eJournal* (ISSN 1836–1129, 2013), 15, available at http://epublications.bond.edu.au/cgi/viewcontent.cgi?article=1017&context=slej (accessed 13 May 2015).

48 Ien Ang, Yasmin Tambiah and Phillip Mar, *Smart Engagement with Asia: Leveraging Language, Research and Culture*, Report for the Australian Council of Learned Academies (ACOLA) (Melbourne: ACOLA, 2015), 130, available at www.acola.org.au/PDF/SAF03/SAF03%20SMART%20ENGAGEMENT%20WITH%20ASIA%20-%20FINAL%20lo%20res.pdf (accessed 13 May 2015).

49 Australian Government Department of Foreign Affairs and Trade, *Australian Sports Diplomacy Strategy 2015–18*, 2015, available at http://dfat.gov.au/about-us/publications/Documents/aus-sports-diplomacy-strategy-2015-18.pdf (accessed 4 August 2015).

50 Australian Government Department of Foreign Affairs and Trade, *Australian Sports Diplomacy Strategy 2015–18*.

51 AFC Asian Cup, 'Adopt a team', 2015, available at http://adoptateam.com.au/ (accessed 29 September 2015).

52 Steven Jackson, 'The contested terrain of sport diplomacy in a globalizing world', *International Area Studies Review*, 16:3 (2013), 276.

53 J. Simon Rofe (ed.), 'Sport and Diplomacy', *Diplomacy and Statecraft* special issue 27:2 2016.

54 Geoffrey A. Pigman, 'International sport and diplomacy's public dimension:

governments, sporting federations and the global audience', *Diplomacy & Statecraft*, 25:1 (2015).

55 Commonwealth of Australia, *Building Australia's Football Community: A Review into the Sustainability of Football* (authored by W. Smith) (Canberra: Commonwealth of Australia, 2011), 38, available at www.ausport.gov.au/__data/assets/pdf_file/0020/624161/FFA_sustainability_report.pdf (accessed 16 May 2015).

56 'Own goal', Australian Broadcasting Corporation, 13 September 2011, available at www.abc.net.au/4corners/stories/2011/09/08/3313323.htm (accessed 13 May 2015).

57 Heidi Blake and Jonathan Calvert, *The Ugly Game: The Qatari Plot to Buy the World Cup* (London: Simon and Schuster, 2016).

58 Football Federation Australia, *We Are Football: This is Our Vision: Whole of Football Plan* (Sydney: Football Federation Australia, 2015), 28, available at www.wholeoffootballplan.com.au/pdfs/Whole_of_Football_Plan.pdf (accessed 11 May 2015).

59 Chris Hallinan and John Hughson (eds), *The Containment of Soccer in Australia: Fencing Off the World Game* (London: Routledge, 2010).

60 Johnny Warren with Andy Harper and John Whittington, *Sheilas, Wogs & Poofters: An Incomplete Biography of Johnny Warren and Soccer in Australia* (Sydney: Random House, 2002).

61 E. Nielsen, 'Sheilas, wogs and poofters in a warzone: the "Socceroos" and the 1967 Friendly Nations Tournament in Vietnam', in Heather L. Dichter (ed.), *Soccer and Diplomacy* (Ithaca, NY: Cornell University Press, 2017, forthcoming).

62 See various contributions to Hallinan and Hughson (eds), *The Containment of Soccer in Australia*.

63 David Rowe and Callum Gilmour, 'Sport, media and consumption in Asia: a merchandized milieu', *American Behavioral Scientist*, 53:10 (2010); Ben Weinberg, '"The future is Asia?" The role of the Asian Football Confederation in the governance and development of football in Asia', *International Journal of the History of Sport*, 29:4 (2012).

64 Alison Hill, 'Asian Cup a stunning success', 2 February 2015, available at www.afcasiancup.com/news/en/asian-cup-a-stunning success/13ctjghssat6j16duu2o7sy0le (accessed 29 September 2015).

65 Hill, 'Asian Cup a stunning success'.

66 Hill, 'Asian Cup a stunning success'.

67 'Legacy', AFC Asian Cup, 2015, available at www.afcasiancup.com/about/en/1ef1k4z3frqfr1j5l306k3izi0 (accessed 29 September 2015).

68 'Legacy', AFC Asian Cup.

69 Matthew Klugman and Brent McDonald, 'Australians taking sides in the Asian Cup, but for which team?', *The Conversation*, 16 January 2015, available at https://theconversation.com/australians-taking-sides-in-the-asian-cup-but-for-which-team-36221 (accessed 18 May 2015); David Rowe, 'The mediated nation and the transnational football fan', *Soccer and Society*, 16 (2014). doi: 10.1080/14660970.2014.963315.

70 Stephanie A. Baker and David Rowe, 'Mediating mega events and manufacturing multiculturalism: the cultural politics of the world game in Australia', *Journal of Sociology*, 50:3 (2014).

71 Loring M. Danforth, 'Is the "World Game" an "Ethnic Game" or an "Aussie Game"?

Narrating the nation in Australian soccer', *American Ethnologist*, 28:2 (2001); Phillip Mosely, *Ethnic Involvement in Australian Soccer: A History 1950–1990* (Belconnen: Australian Sports Commission, 1995).

72 Ghassan Hage, *White Nation: Fantasies of White Supremacy in a Multicultural Society* (Annandale, NSW: Pluto, 1998).

73 Football Federation Australia, *We Are Football*, 21.

74 Football Federation Australia, *We Are Football*, 21.

75 Football Federation Australia, *We Are Football*, 23.

76 Scott McIntyre, 'Australia's move against Sepp Blatter in FIFA vote is honourable – but risky', *The Guardian*, 29 May 2015, available at www.theguardian.com/football/2015/may/29/australias-move-against-sepp-blatter-in-fifa-vote-is-honourable-but-risky (accessed 4 August 2015).

77 BBC, 'FIFA: Sepp Blatter & Michel Platini investigated by Ethics Committee', 26 September 2015, available at www.bbc.com/sport/0/football/34371697 (accessed 28 September 2015).

78 'AFC statement on FIFA presidential election', AFC, 3 September 2015, available at www.the-afc.com/media-releases/afc-statement-on-fifa-presidential-election (accessed 28 September 2015).

79 'AFC Member Associations reiterate support for Shaikh Salman', AFC, 18 February 2016, available at www.the-afc.com/afc-president/afc-member-associations-reiterate-support-for-shaikh-salman (accessed 27 September 2015).

80 Tom Smithies, 'FIFA presidential elections: FFA Chairman Steven Lowy expects no backlash despite backing third Man', *Daily Telegraph*, 27 February 2016, available at www.dailytelegraph.com.au/sport/football/fifa-presidential-elections-ffa-chairman-steven-lowy-expects-no-backlash-despite-backing-third-man/news-story/50b26b055a848d07f7658c6e351af0f4 (accessed 27 September 2016).

81 Brian Stoddart, 'The centrality of cricket in Indo-Australian relations: India, Australia and the "cricket imaginary"', *International Journal of the History of Sport*, 25:12 (2008).

82 David Rowe, 'Spinning out of control: Harbhajan Singh, postcolonial cricket celebrity and the "revenge narrative"', in Lawrence A. Wenner (ed.), *Fallen Sports Heroes, Media, and Celebrity Culture* (New York: Peter Lang, 2013), 251–63.

83 Edward W. Said, *Orientalism* (London: Penguin, 2003).

84 Julian Bajkowski, 'Australia recalls Ambassador over Indonesian executions', *GovernmentNews*, 29 April 2015, available at www.governmentnews.com.au/2015/04/australia-recalls-ambassador-over-indonesian-executions/ (accessed 13 May 2015).

85 David Rowe and Jim McKay, 'Torchlight temptations: hosting the Olympics and the global gaze', in John Sugden and Alan Tomlinson (eds), *Watching the Games: Politics, Power and Representation in the London Olympiad* (London: Routledge, 2012), 122–37.

Part III

'No sport' as diplomacy

9

Boycotts and diplomacy: when the talking stops*

Carole Gomez

'All of this is politics and we are not concerned with politics', said Avery Brundage, president of the International Olympic Committee (IOC), in response to a question about Rhodesia's participation in the 1972 Summer Olympics in Munich.[1] A few days later, following the Munich massacre, Brundage declared, '[T]he Games must go on and we must continue our efforts to keep them clear, pure and honest and try to extend sportsmanship of the athletic field to other areas.'[2] Several decades later, on the eve of the opening of the Olympic Games in Rio in August 2016, in the middle of a sport and political crisis on the potential exclusion of Russian athletes following Russia's doping scandal, IOC president Thomas Bach said, 'This decision is about justice. Justice has to be independent from politics. Whoever responds to a violation of the law with another violation of the law is destroying justice.'[3]

Whatever the occasion, sport – and the Olympic movement in particular – has tried to assert the apolitical nature of sport.[4] This premise is included in the Olympic Charter and prominently brandished in front of every person or institution that may express doubt. Despite repeated and constant efforts by the Olympic movement and sports federations to affirm that sport is, and must remain, independent of politics, it is clear that the apolitical nature of sport can be nothing but a chimaera, a relic of a distant time. In high politics perhaps the last person to believe that sport did not impact politics was US president Herbert Hoover, who did not attend the 1932 Summer Olympic Games in Los Angeles. He skipped the Olympics to instead focus on his re-election, believing that to 'be away from Washington for three weeks would be a national disaster'.[5] Perhaps as a consequence, he lost the state of California and the presidential election to Franklin Delano Roosevelt. On the other hand Maurice Herzog, the 1958–66 French Minister of Youth Affairs and Sport, understood the relationship between sport and politics, declaring that 'sports, being outside of politics, gives it an eminently political factor'.[6] Thanks to its economic impact and to the development of sport as a tool of diplomacy, it has been an essential element of international relations since the late 1970s.[7] With the contemporary sport market worth an estimated €650 billion and the organisation of mega sport events costing tens of billions of dollars, sport has considerable relevance to contemporary consideration of diplomacy and international politics.[8] Sport has a long heritage of being used by states; representatives of city states in ancient Greece were the founding participants of the Olympic Games. More recently, during the Cold War between the Soviet bloc and the US-led 'West', both sides used international sporting events, most notably the Olympic Games, to advance their respective agendas.[9] Sport was a way to influence opinion domestically and internationally. In this way it has often been linked to the concept, discussed elsewhere in this volume, of 'soft power': that it is possible to achieve one's national interest through attraction.[10] To borrow from Carl von Clausewitz's famous maxim, sport could be considered to be the continuation of politics by other means.[11] Sport is part of the discussion: for example interest in and competition over medals tallies illustrate the importance of sport beyond the track or arena. It is no little surprise to say that sporting competition is prime territory for political exploitation, with the sanction of a boycott a much-vaunted tool. Nonetheless, the conceptual underpinnings of boycotts are not always well understood. This chapter outlines the discourse on boycotts, their parameters and examples from both the Cold War and post-Cold War, while posing the overarching question of the effectiveness of a sporting boycott. The outcome is a complex picture that does not conform to clear-cut bilateral divisions: boycotts have a Gordian quality.

The analysis begins here in presenting two types of sport sanctions: sport-associated international sanctions and sport boycotts. Despite the prevalence of the term, international sanctions taken by the UN and sport boycotts have only been imposed twice: against apartheid-era South Africa after 1960 and against Yugoslavia (Serbia and Montenegro) in 1992. Sport boycotts, however, have more commonly been used, during the Cold War particularly, and it is on this dimension that the chapter focuses. Boycotts of the Olympic Games in Montreal (1976), Moscow (1980) and Los Angeles (1984) – the last two explored in the chapters in this volume by Joseph Eaton and Umberto Tulli – were important and symbolic events. While such practices may seem to belong to a different era, threats of boycotts against Beijing 2008 and Sochi 2014, and the FIFA World Cups in Russia in 2018 and Qatar in 2022, highlight the continued relevance of this practice.

A definitional starting point

Boycotts have a long heritage, having existed since Antiquity.[12] The eponymous, if possibly apocryphal, tale of Charles Cunningham Boycott being forced to leave Ireland in the late nineteenth century speaks to the resonance that the lexicon 'boycott' has in the contemporary world. Equally, writing in 1933 in the *British Year Book of International Law*, Hersch Lauterpacht, who would go on to be knighted in 1956 while serving as a Justice in the International Court of Justice, noted that boycotts were 'not a new phenomenon in international life', having been 'resorted to on a number of occasions in the last thirty years'.[13] Thus to engage in a boycott is to notify to a polity, by refusing to acknowledge or engage with it, that its behaviour is considered unacceptable. Simply put, a boycott as a form of international sanction is an organised mechanism designed to change the behaviour of its target.[14] Francesco Giumelli considers three dimensions to studying international sanctions: as a 'signal of dissatisfaction with certain policies targeting foreign countries or domestic audiences, forcing the target country or its leaders to discontinue certain actions in the future or compel a government to change or reverse existing policies'.[15] This analysis is supported by the work of Barry Burciul, who considers the effort to change the behaviour of an entity as having 'a symbolic importance and psychological impact'.[16] Thus, by deciding to boycott an actor in global affairs, a state or non-state actor refuses to deal with it, to support it or to endorse its policies until the object of the boycott changes the behaviour that is deemed unacceptable. An important dimension to this is the subject and object of the boycott. There is a quality of one polity doing something to another. Thus boycotts, and sports boycotts in particular, may appear to be tools of punishment; of a tit-for-tat or zero-sum equation that brings a sense of justice to any particular dispute.[17] What is also important to this discussion is the way this plays into the recent literature on public diplomacy (discussed elsewhere in this volume) which considers the role of the audience. As such one needs to consider here those to whom any boycott is being portrayed. While there are undoubtedly multiple audiences or publics, a binary analysis sees a 'domestic' audience on whose behalf the boycott is in operation, and a 'target' audience who will feel the impact of the boycott. While this may seem straightforward there is a duality at work also, for boycotts have a Janus-faced quality. This is evident in that the 'domestic' audience, that is, the one impacted by the sanctions, might welcome their imposition given a disconnect between themselves and their government.[18] The example of the black South African population supporting international sanctions against the government in South Africa is a case in point.[19] Finally, there is a paradox one can observe in discussing sport boycotts. This is thatBoycotting is based on exclusion, while one of sport's main characteristics, and why it holds such universal appeal, is that it is focused on inclusion. These seemingly irreconcilable features of sport boycotts illustrate the complexity of their consideration.

A typology of sport boycotts

Jean-François Revel considers a boycott, or the threat of a boycott, to embrace several realities, responding to specific economic objectives and policies.[20] On this basis, Éric and Catherine Monnin,[21] and Éric Monnin and Christophe Maillard have constructed a typology of three types of sport boycotts (figure 9.1).[22]

The first is binary: with one party failing to participate in an event in another territory. This boycott is the most well known, with the examples of the Moscow and the Los Angeles Olympics being prominent. These boycotts demonstrate how the United States and the Soviet Union sought to gain the upper hand in their Cold War contest and present this to both domestic and international audiences. Following the 1979 Soviet invasion of Afghanistan, President Jimmy Carter stressed, 'it is very significant for the World to realise how serious … a threat the Soviet invasion of Afghanistan is'.[23] Carter, bedevilled by domestic political troubles, issued an ultimatum to the

Boycott 1:

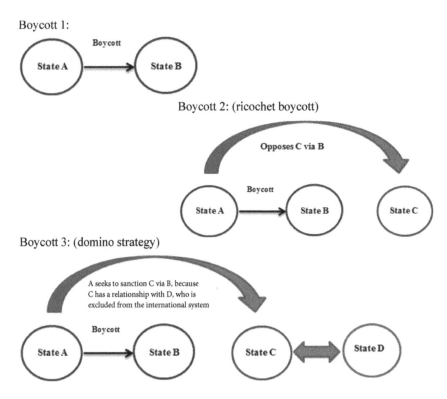

Images Carol Gomez, 2016.

9.1 Taxonomy of boycotts

USSR, urging Soviet troops to withdraw from Afghanistan, threatening that he would seek the cancellation or transfer of the 1980 Olympics away from Moscow. The threat of cancellation or transfer ultimately failed given the events that took place in the Luzhniki Stadium in the summer of 1980, but the United States followed up by leading a boycott of fifty-one national delegations from the Moscow Games.[24] The boycott of the Los Angeles games is typically viewed as the Soviet bloc's response to the 1980 boycott.[25] Countries largely tied to the Soviet bloc cited lack of security and non-compliance with the Olympic Charter, including the 'all-private' character Tulli's chapter in this volume considers, as their rationale for the Los Angeles boycott. On the former critique the Soviet international news agency *Novosti* stated that 'at least 100 terrorist organisations planned to kill or kidnap the Soviets'.[26] The Soviet statement on the boycott said that from the earliest 'days of preparations for the present Olympics, the American Administration has sought to set course at using the Games for its political aims … [C]hauvinistic sentiments and an anti-Soviet hysteria are being whipped up in the country.'[27] The bipolar nature of the world at that time explains the apparent success of the boycotts' implementation.

Yet, returning to Brundage's reasoning, sport sought a way to operate outside the global political conflict. Although inspired by a variety of factors, the establishment of the World Athletics Championships in 1983 was a direct response to the boycotts of the era. Denied the opportunity to showcase competition at the highest level, the International Association of Athletics Federations used the boycotts to justify a global championship which would see athletes from both East and West compete (7–14 August 1983 in Helsinki, Finland). Further, both the United States in 1980 and the Soviet Union in 1984 were keen to offer boycotting nations an alternate venue for sporting competitions. The Liberty Bell Track and Field Classic hosted in Philadelphia in July 1980 and supported to the tune of $10 million by Congress, saw twenty-nine nations' athletes participate; athletes from nations which had been amongst those who had supported the Carter administration's boycott.[28] Equally, in 1984 the Soviet Union sponsored the Friendship Games, where athletes of forty-nine nations met at venues across the Soviet Union and Eastern Europe in what was seen as the Eastern bloc's 'alternate Olympics'. The question arises as to whether by aping the event being boycotted one actually reinforces the sanctity of that original event. Jimmy Carnes, the coach of the 1980 US Olympic track and field team, stated of the 'alternate' Liberty Bell Classic, 'We can't call this the alternative Games. There's no alternative.'[29]

The second type of boycott Monnin *et al.* identified is a triangulate one. Examples centre on two polities' refusal to engage on a third polity's territory. This was the case of the 'triple boycott' of the 1956 Summer Olympics in Melbourne. The boycott was spurred by three separate incidents. On the eve of the Melbourne Olympics, the Suez Crisis broke out in October 1956 between Egypt and France, the UK and Israel. In light of this conflict and to protest the advance of Israeli positions into the Sinai, Egypt, followed by Lebanon and Iraq, refused to send sports delegations to Australia to take part in competitions against British, French and Israeli athletes. The same year, the Soviet Army violently suppressed demonstrations in Poland and Hungary in the Budapest Uprising. Faced with this violent repression, Spain, the Netherlands and Switzerland refused to let their delegations participate in the Games alongside Soviet athletes. China also decided to cancel its participation in the Games to protest the presence of a delegation from Taiwan. The People's Republic of China would only return to the Games in 1980 at the Lake Placid Winter Olympics, seven years after having taken its place in the United Nations Security Council at the expense of Taiwan, and having secured from the IOC that the Taiwanese team would be known as Chinese Taipei. Analysing the 1956 boycotts, Lara Killick cites a 'desire for change' as critical to these countries' decision making.[30] The Melbourne triple boycott illustrates how three distinct incidents prompted particular responses from a range of states that had a collective manifestation in a sporting area. Éric Monnin calls this a 'ricochet boycott'.[31]

The typology identifies a third type of boycott as 'quadrangular'. The aim is to demonstrate, through an event, one entity's disapproval of the presence of another country in the competition, because of the latter's behaviour towards a third country. The Montreal Olympic Games in 1976 can be cited in this instance, with over twenty mainly African countries refusing to participate because of New Zealand's involvement. New Zealand was accused of failing to comply with the isolation of apartheid South Africa.[32] The following year the Gleneagles Agreement confirmed the Commonwealth's unanimous opposition to sporting ties with South Africa, while providing a reference point to the cause for the years ahead. While the boycott of South Africa is regularly cited as an example of a boycott that worked, such an assessment should be treated with caution. Sanctions against the apartheid regime undeniably helped to raise public awareness and to call the international community's attention to the situation. However, there is considerable debate as to the degree to which these sporting and diplomatic actions contributed to South Africa's long walk to freedom, as seen in the plethora of sources on the subject.[33]

The question of effectiveness

The effectiveness of sanctions in diplomacy is a perennially difficult issue to address. States utilise many forms of sanctions, including boycotts, as an important form of political pressure before resorting to military force as a measure of last resort. The international community's response to post-1991 Iraq under Saddam Hussein illustrates the evolution from economic sanctions to 'smart' or 'targeted' sanctions.[34] Under this new framework, the older, blanket type of sanctions are replaced by specific sanctions to pressure regimes to change. Yet recent studies of international sanctions reveals that have found that the effectiveness of international sanctions ranges between 5 and 40 per cent.[35] Thus we return to the question of effectiveness of the use of any sanction given its limited or marginal success, particularly the increased awareness of the negative impact of sanctions upon the broader population.

In this light the chapter posits that an effective sport boycott requires the gathering of three elements: broad-ranging national or international support, a strong information operation and the ultimate compliance of the boycotted entity. Most important is the first of these related elements, as all networks, civil society stakeholders and government actors must have a high degree of unity of action in supporting the boycott. That said, there needs to be acknowledgement that boycotts have levels of adherence along a spectrum from compliance to wholesale adoption. In part this recognises the difficulty of hermetically sealing the subject from the object of boycott but also that a degree of compliance may provide a platform for the protagonist to serve their interests. As an example, Dick Palmer as the secretary of the British Olympic Association entered the Olympic Stadium in Moscow alone – that is, without members of the British team. He, and representatives of fifteen other of the eighty-one participating nations, would use the opportunity of the Opening Ceremony in 1980 to make a silent protest concerning the Soviet presence in Afghanistan.[36] Palmer's and his contemporaries' actions were not the first or the last protests at an Olympic Opening Ceremony. As just one example, in 1906 the United States team did not dip its flag – the Star Spangled Banner – to King Edward VII at the Opening Ceremony, and acted as a catalyst to Anglo-American tensions throughout the Games.[37] More broadly, the case of using the Olympic platform raises an essential question surrounding the deployment of a boycott. That is whether using the opportunity of the Olympics to make a point, or make that point in absentia, is more effective.[38]

The threat of a wholesale boycott of the Beijing Olympics failed in large part due to a diversity of the rationale to boycott. Opposition to the Beijing Games came from those concerned with the lack of respect for human rights and the violent repression of Tibet, as well as Beijing's tolerance of high levels of pollution in China with associated health risks for athletes and spectators.[39] Despite calls and concerns on these grounds, Beijing's opponents found it difficult to send a clear, united message to the world's public, and so the Olympics proceeded as what one commentator called a 'triumph of cynicism'.[40]

There can be a negative, potentially counterproductive, consequence of considering sanctions, as John Galtung illustrates in his study of sanctions against Rhodesia.[41] Galtung draws upon John Mueller's concept of 'rally round the flag' to analyse why a population might support its government despite sanctions.[42] According to Jay Gordon, the rally-round-the-flag effect takes place 'when the population at large is subject to deprivation by a foreign nation':

> They respond to it as they would a form of attack, with increased nationalism and support of their political leadership. Thus, while the intent of the nation imposing the sanctions might be to 'send a message' of the wrongfulness of the target State's actions, the effect is to consolidate support for the leadership, and its legitimacy is enhanced rather than undermined.[43]

The rally-round-the-flag effect is exacerbated in countries where the government can control the flow of information to its population, thus portraying the sanctions as targeting the population as well as or instead of the regime. This was the case in the 1990s with respect to Saddam Hussein's response to the UN sanctions, where Hussein's regime carefully portrayed the impact of the sanctions on Iraqis to its domestic, and the international, audience. In the realm of sport and diplomacy, proposals for a boycott of the 2008 Beijing Games rested on a number of drivers, as previously stated. Buoyed by additional issues surrounding the Olympic Torch relay, in London, Paris and San Francisco in particular, critics of the Beijing Games were portrayed by the Chinese government to its citizens as being against the Olympic spirit, and played to the PRC's previously held view that the West failed to understand China. Hundreds of people demonstrated in several cities in China to show support for Chinese policies and to express their anger against the West. When confronted with Free Tibet protestors in London, who forced the PRC's ambassador to the United Kingdom to carry the torch on a secure bus, the Xinhu state news agency responded by 'strongly condem[ing] this vile behaviour'.[44] In response to protests in Paris, protestors gathered outside outlets of French supermarket Carrefour and even outside French schools and embassies, calling for a boycott of French products such as wine and cheese.[45] Ultimately, only a few heads of state boycotted the opening ceremonies, which were, in the end, attended by heads of state of Russia, the United States and France.[46] This again demonstrates the need to act collectively in a boycott for it to have a chance of succeeding. Otherwise singular boycott efforts stand little chance of impacting their external target.It is worth noting, however, that the Janus-faced quality of a boycott means that this may never have been the sole aim of those proposing the sanction.

In short, the effectiveness of sporting boycotts has a mixed record. The Olympic boycotts of Moscow and Los Angeles were deeply vested in the bipolar Cold War. Yet, as will be discussed in greater depth by Eaton and Tulli in the pages that follow, even under those circumstances they were not wholesale successes for either state, let alone associated governments, a generation of athletes or spectators expecting to see the world's best competition.

The symbolic value of a sport boycott

Beyond all techniques and outcomes that can be quantified and measured, a boycott in sport is also based on something intangible and difficult to discern: its symbolic value. Indeed, beyond its economic and political impact, a sport boycott carries a symbolic weight. Sanctioning a state through a boycott seeks to shape its image. A nation state of course has multiple identities but one of the goals of a boycott in seeking to change behaviours is to influence the perception of the recipient to a wider audience. Put simply, a goal can be to question their honour and hence their ability to operate in international affairs.[47] Boycotting a nation means to exclude it from the international game and doubly reinforces the symbolic aspect of the sanction. Consider the system of sanctions taken against Yugoslavia in May 1992 through Resolution 757 of the United Nations Security Council: 'all States shall take the necessary steps to prevent the participation in sporting events on their territory of persons or groups representing the Federal Republic of Yugoslavia (Serbia and Montenegro)'.[48] This meant, on the eve of the UEFA European Football Championships in Sweden, Yugoslavia was disqualified, and Denmark's players famously came back from their holidays to win the tournament. Yugoslavia was also prevented from sending its team to the 1992 Barcelona Olympics (though Yugoslav athletes did compete under special designation as Independent Olympic Participants).[49] As Loïc Trégourès highlights, the decision taken by the United Nations was perceived by swathes of the Yugoslav public as an unfair and gratuitous punishment, and 'popular opinion is that Yugoslavia was excluded because it was too strong rather than to send a signal of disapproval towards its government'.[50] The symbolism of the ban to deprive a national team of its opportunity to compete in international competitions may well have been counterproductive. The Yugoslavs' cause garnered some sympathy from others in the international community. Though failing to utilise the French veto to prevent UNSCR 757, the French ambassador to the United Nations did poignantly remark 'sporting sanctions are unnecessarily vexatious'.[51]

Emergence of civil society: the key for a successful sport boycott

In the post-Cold War environment the focus on the salience of boycotts has shifted. Debates around the pre-eminence of the nation state abound among scholars of International Relations, but what is agreed upon is the emergence of a new type of non-state actor on the international stage: civil society.[52] While the term 'emergence' may be contemporary, civil society actors were already important during the Cold War period.[53] The 1978 FIFA World Cup in Argentina serves as a pertinent example. Argentina was selected as the host nation by FIFA in London, England on 6 July 1966; a few days afterwards Dr Arturo Umberto Illia was ousted from office by a military coup. Argentina experienced ten years of political crisis, torn between a military junta and democratic presidents. Two years before the World Cup, in 1976, the junta secured the *Casa Rosada* – the seat of executive government in Buenos Aries. International debate ensued over whether participating in the World Cup would mean the implicit support of Argentina's repressive military junta.[54] Thanks to well-mobilised civil society groups, who learnt from the way groups had shaped debates about the Helsinki Accords and apartheid South Africa by organising public debates and contemplating a boycott of the event, the international community in both politics and sport was forced to address the question.[55]

As such the 1978 World Cup became the first occasion that a non-state actor was involved in the potential deployment of a boycott, to call attention to the junta's objectionable human rights policies. Civil society activists (led by the troika of General Jorge Videla, Admiral Emilio Massera and Brigadier-General Orlando Agosti) published cartoons denouncing the junta, including ones depicting the brutal dictator's widespread oppression and extrajudicial killing. These groups provided a platform for political refugees to highlight their cause. Sport contributed to the movement. Prominent Dutch players Johan Cruyff and Willem van Hanegem, the former among the best players in the world, refused to travel to Argentina, while other European players and trainers questioned their participation in the competition as well.

Despite these substantive efforts, paralysis prevented a widespread boycott from taking shape. The Videla regime and Argentinian diplomacy remained emboldened with support from the United States through football fan Secretary of State Henry Kissinger. The World Cup took place without major incident and Argentina's national team duly won the trophy. These efforts did, nonetheless, herald a key marker in the rise of civil society in the relationship between sport and diplomacy.

Civil society actors were also evident in relation to a potential boycott surrounding the 2014 Winter Olympics in Sochi, Russia. The Russian president had a clear interest in securing the Games, having attended the IOC meeting in Guatemala that awarded the Games in July 2007 to the Black Sea resort. Olympic scholar Jules Boykoff notes, '[f]or Putin and his Russian allies, winning the Olympics was pure-grade political grist'.[56] *New Yorker* editor David Remnick noted in the *Huffington Post* in the days immediately preceding the Opening Ceremony that 'What's happening at the Olympics is that Russia is self-presenting, in the contemporary terminology', before continuing that Russian authorities wanted 'to put forward some notion of what Russianness is and Russian history and what Russia is in the 21st century'.[57] Nonetheless, the first calls for a boycott of the Sochi Games date back to August 2008, when the Georgian government in Tbilisi denounced Russia's involvement in the second war in South Ossetia.[58] The initial wave was followed by a lull in calls to boycott, until June 2013 when Russia banned the dissemination of homosexual 'propaganda' to minors. The move was denounced by human rights associations, as well as by Amnesty International and All Out and other LGBT rights associations.[59] The call to boycott on this basis was disseminated quickly via social media following the publication of reports concerning the considerable expenditure related to the Sochi Games's organisation and allegations of corruption over the course of their preparation.[60] As a result, a variety of civil society actors, including freedom of expression advocates, campaigners for the abolition of the anti-homosexual legislation, environmental activists and anti-corruption activists, were united in offering opposition to the Sochi Games on economic, environmental and political grounds. Importantly, they were able to gather considerable Western media attention.[61] Indeed, media outlets followed one civil society actor with particular relish. Pussy Riot, a disruptive punk-art collective, adeptly blended their own – anti-Putin – agenda with critique of the Putin regime on the platform the Olympics provided. Boykoff recorded that 'Pussy Riot's ... public actions and statements generated substantial press attention'; while *Guardian* journalist Shaun Walker entitled his article, 'Short detention in Sochi gives Pussy Riot pair what they wanted – a media frenzy'.[62] At the same time the Russian authorities saw predominantly Western media coverage of the boycott as unhelpful agitation. Indeed, they thought it was a particularly 'unfriendly and provocative gesture'.[63] Nonetheless, on the one hand it is possible to view discussion of a boycott with a degree of success, given it focused attention from a broad range of stakeholders utilising the platform provided by the Sochi Winter Olympics. However, on the other hand, drawing upon the previous Cold War framework, the absence of a state-sponsored boycott of Sochi would suggest the age of the boycott passed with the fall of the Berlin Wall. The relationship between boycotts and the nation state, with civil society non-state actors exerting greater influence, remains worthy of further research.

Conclusion: what is the future of sporting event boycotts?

The transition from Cold War to the post-Cold War environment would seem to suggest the era of the sporting boycott has passed. However, consideration of the use of boycotts has evolved. The direct involvement of nation states in calls for boycotts has decreased. The ideological structure of the Cold War meant blocs of states acted with greater harmony (albeit not always with common purpose, as Joseph Eaton considers in these pages). Equally, both the United States and Soviet Union devoted energies to sport as part of the ideological struggle. The classic cases of the 1980 and 1984 Olympic Games boycotts illustrate a state's willingness to suffer – through sacrificing profile, national pride and potential medals – in order to pursue its national interests. These two classic cases, along with the boycott of apartheid South Africa, represent the high point of state-based sporting boycotts. A proliferation of calls to boycott over a variety of lesser issues, and a subsequent reduced effectiveness, led to a degree of weariness among Western publics for calls to boycott. Thus by the time of the Beijing Olympics, while many news outlets and non-governmental organisations reported on the situation in Tibet, placing the PRC's human rights abuses under persistent media spotlight, a number of heads of state questioned the relevance of boycotting the Games or its opening ceremonies. Does this mean that boycotts are now defunct? Non-state actors and civil society would seem to offer opportunities to breathe life into the concept, with the support of the twenty-first-century infrastructure that social media provides. Boycotts of particular practices have been influential in recent times in the commercial realm. The call in November 2012 by senior British parliamentarian Margaret Hodge to boycott Starbucks and Amazon in the United Kingdom over their legal tax avoidance practices garnered widespread coverage and both companies altered their stance.[64] What is notable here is that, while Hodge, as chair of the Public Accounts Committee, held a state role, her call was not the UK government's official policy.

In the years ahead, the FIFA World Cups in Russia and Qatar, in 2018 and 2022 respectively, will provide another platform for sport and politics to mix in ways that Brundage would have found troubling. Diplomacy's tripartite qualities of negotiation, communication and representation will facilitate such a mix. While critics have called for a boycott against both locations since the decision was announced in December 2010, preparations for both tournaments have proceeded, with fundamental changes to the annual global football calendar being undertaken to facilitate the November–December schedule for Qatar 2022.[65] At the same time, the international community has pressed Qatar through diplomatic means, and through a number of non-governmental organisations in particular, to improve its labour laws, particularly after reports in *The Guardian* newspaper over the conditions – including many deaths – of workers building the competition stadiums.[66] To this end, civil society has had, and will continue to have, influence in how these football tournaments areperceived. Within this realm of influence, boycotts and the possibility of boycotts will continue to evolve and reinvent themselves away from state-based enterprises to those facilitated by civil society. This returns us to the overarching question of the chapter on the effectiveness of a boycott. In offering the analysis here, the consideration of sanctions – of which a boycott is just one dimension – is intrinsically linked to their effectiveness. For sport boycotts to be effective sanctions, it is clear that they must continue to evolve. While the direct influence of boycotts on state policy is not always evident, in a world of diffuse state power they represent a potentially powerful tool for civil society.

Notes

* My thanks to J. Simon Rofe and Heather Dichter for their helpful comments on my paper and to Simon for organising the 'Sport and Diplomacy: Message, Mode and Metaphor' colloquium in July 2015.

1 'Le mouvement de protestation des pays africains contre la participation de la Rhodésie s'amplifie', *Le Monde*, 17 August 1972.

2 David Binder, 'The Munich massacre', *New York Times*, 5 September 1972, available at www.nytimes.com/packages/html/sports/year_in_sports/09.05.html (accessed 23 September 2016).

3 Michael Powell, 'IOC chief Thomas Bach supports a peculiar form of justice on doping', *New York Times*, 4 August 2016, available at www.nytimes.com/2016/08/05/sports/olympics/ioc-thomas-bach-russian-doping-rio-games.html (accessed 23 September 2016).

4 See for example the Olympic Charter statement, Fifth fundamental principle of Olympism, available at www.olympic.org/Documents/olympic_charter_en.pdf (accessed 23 September 2016).

5 John Sayle Watterson, *The Games Presidents Play: Sports and the Presidency* (Baltimore, MD: The Johns Hopkins University Press, 2006).

6 Maurice Herzog interview, *Abidjan Matin*, 9 May 1960.

7 See the Special Forum on 'Sports diplomacy' in *Diplomatic History*, 40:5 (November 2016).

8 Janis Osenieks and Girts Jansons, 'The impact of sports on the economy', *Lase Journal of Sport Science*, 2012, available at www.lspa.eu/files/research/Journal_of_Sport_Science/2012_3_1/2012_3_1_9.pdf (accessed 20 September 2016).

9 The Woodrow Wilson Center's Cold War International History Project provides the most comprehensive resource on sport in the Cold War: 'Global history of sport in the Cold War', available at http://digitalarchive.wilsoncenter.org/theme/sport-in-the-cold-war (accessed 16 August 2017).

10 Joseph S. Nye, Jr, 'Public diplomacy and soft power', *Annals of the American Academy of Political and Social Science*, 'Public diplomacy in a changing world', 616:94 (2008).

11 For example, during the Peloponnesian War, 431–404 BC Carl von Clausewitz, *On War* (Oxford: Oxford University Press, 2008).

12 Evans Clark (ed.), *Boycotts and Peace: A Report by the Committee on Economic Sanctions* (New York: Harper & Bros., 1932).

13 Hersch Lauterpacht, 'Boycott in international relations', *British Yearbook of International Law*, 125 (1933), 126.

14 Carole Gomez and Bastien Nivet, 'Sanctionner et punir. Coercition, normalisation et exercice de la puissance dans une société internationale hétérogène', *Revue internationale et stratégique*, 97:1 (2015).

15 Francesco Giumelli, 'How EU sanctions work: a new narrative', *EUISS Chaillot Paper*, no. 129, 13 May 2013, available at www.iss.europa.eu/uploads/media/Chaillot_129.pdf (accessed 22 September 2016).

16 Barry Burciul, *Report on the Seminar on United Nations Security Council Sanctions*, Canadian Centre for Foreign Policy Development, Ottawa, 17 July 1998, available at http://publications.gc.ca/collections/Collection/E2-338-1998E.pdf (accessed 23 September 2016).

17 Gomez and Nivet, 'Sanctionner et punir.'.

18 See, for example, Jennifer Parks, 'Welcoming the "Third World": Soviet sport diplomacy, developing nations, and the Olympic Games', in Heather L. Dichter and Andrew L. Johns (eds), *Diplomatic Games: Sport, Statecraft, and International Relations since 1945* (Lexington, KY: University of Kentucky Press, 2014).

19 Literature on the sporting boycott of South Africa is plentiful; see, for example, David
     R. Black, '"Not cricket": the effects and effectiveness of the sport boycott', in Neta C.
     Crawford and Audie Klotz (eds), *How Sanctions Work: Lessons from South Africa*
     (Basingstoke: Palgrave Macmillan, 1999), 219; Rob Nixon, 'Apartheid on the run: the
     South African sports boycott', *Transition*, 58 (1992).

20 Quoted in Fernand Landry, 'Olympisme, politique et éducation', in *Académie
     olympique internationale*, Athens, Twentieth Session, June 1980, Hellenic Olympic
     Committee, 1980, 155.

21 Éric Monnin and Catherine Monnin, 'Le boycott politique des Jeux olympiques de
     Montréal', *Relations internationales*, 2/2008 (No. 134).

22 Éric Monnin and Christophe Maillard, 'Pour une typologie du boycottage aux Jeux
     olympiques', *Relations internationales*, 2/2015 (No. 162).

23 Terence Smith, 'The President said nyet', *New York Times*, 20 January 1980, available
     at www.nytimes.com/packages/html/sports/year_in_sports/01.20.html (accessed 20
     September 2016). For an account of the Olympic boycott in Carter's presidency, see
     Nicholas Evan Sarantakes, *Dropping the Torch: Jimmy Carter, the Olympic Boycott,
     and the Cold War* (Cambridge: Cambridge University Press, 2011).

24 The fifty-one countries, plus territories were: Albania, Antigua and Barbuda,
     Argentina, Bahamas, Bahrain, Bangladesh, Barbados, Belize, Bermuda, Bolivia,
     Canada, Cayman Islands, Central African Republic, Chad, Chile, China, Egypt, El
     Salvador, Fiji, Gabon, Ghana, Haiti, Honduras, Hong Kong, Indonesia, Iran, Israel,
     Ivory Coast, Japan, Kenya, Liberia, Liechtenstein, Malawi, Malaysia, Mauritania,
     Mauritius, Monaco, Morocco, Netherlands Antilles, Niger, Norway, Pakistan,
     Panama, Papua New Guinea, Paraguay, Philippines, Qatar, Saudi Arabia, Singapore,
     Somalia, South Korea, Sudan, Suriname, Swaziland, Chinese Taipei, Thailand, The
     Gambia, Togo, Tunisia, Turkey, United Arab Emirates, United States, Uruguay,
     Virgin Islands, West Germany and Zaire.

25 The boycotting countries were Afghanistan, Angola, Bulgaria, Cuba, Czechoslovakia,
     East Germany, Ethiopia, Hungary, Iran, Laos, Libya, Mongolia, North Korea, Poland,
     the Soviet Union and Vietnam.

26 *Herald Journal*, 18 May 1984.

27 John F. Burns, 'Moscow will keep its team from Los Angeles Olympics', *New York
     Times*, 8 May 1984, available at www.nytimes.com/1984/05/09/world/moscow-will-
     keep-its-team-los-angeles-olympics-tass-cites-peril-us-denies-it.html (accessed 23
     September 2016).

28 See also Nicholas Sarantakes, 'The White House Games: the Carter administration's
     effort to establish an alternative to the Olympics', in Dichter and Johns (eds),
     Diplomatic Games, 349–50.

29 Craig Neff, '… and meanwhile in Philadelphia', *Sports Illustrated*, 28 July 1980.

30 Lara Killick, *The Bloody Olympics Down Under: Sport, Politics and the Melbourne
     Games*, 2010, available at www.bl.uk/sportandsociety/exploresocsci/politics/articles/
     melbourne.pdf (accessed 23 September 2016).

31 Éric Monnin and Catherine Monnin, *Le boycott politique des Jeux olympiques de
     Montréal*, Relations internationales, 134 (Paris: Presses Universitaires de France,
     2008), 93–113.

32 Literature on Montreal includes Courtney W. Mason, 'The bridge to change: the 1976
     Montreal Olympic Games, South African apartheid policy, and the Olympic boycott

paradigm', in *Onward to the Olympics: Historical Perspectives on the Olympic Games* (Waterloo, Ontario: Wilfred Laurier, 2007).

33 Nelson Mandela's autobiography is ambivalent on the impact of the sports boycotts on the end of the apartheid regime. More broadly on South Africa's apartheid regime and the opposition to it, see H. Thörn, *Anti-apartheid and the Emergence of a Global Civil Society* (Basingstoke: Palgrave, 2006); Ryan M. Irwin, *Gordian Knot: Apartheid and the Unmaking of the Liberal World Order* (New York: Oxford University Press, 2012).

34 Joy Gordon, 'Smart sanctions revisited', *Ethics and International Affairs*, 25 (2011).

35 Robert A. Pape, 'Why economic sanctions do not work', *International Security*, 22:2 (1997); Gary Clide Hufbauer, Jeffrey J. Schott and Kimberly Ann Elliott, *Economic Sanctions Reconsidered: History and Current Policy* (Washington, DC: Peterson Institute for International Economics, 1990).

36 Ron Fimrite, 'Only the Bears were bullish' *Sports Illustrated*, 28 July 1980. The British Olympic Association had come under considerable pressure from the Thatcher government to stand with the United States and avoid British participation; see Kevin Jefferys, *Sport and Politics in Modern Britain: The Road to 2012* (Basingstoke: Palgrave Macmillan, 2012), 149–71.

37 See J. Simon Rofe and Alan Tomlinson, '"Strenuous competition on the field of play, diplomacy off it" – the 1908 London Olympics, Theodore Roosevelt, Arthur Balfour, and transatlantic relations', *Journal of the Gilded Age and Progressive Era*, 15:1 (2016).

38 Tanya Domi, 'Send athletes to the Sochi Olympics, but boycott the Games', *New York Times*, 6 February 2014, available at www.nytimes.com/roomfordebate/2014/02/06/when-should-countries-boycott-the-olympics/send-athletes-to-the-sochi-olympics-but-boycott-the-games (accessed 23 September 2016).

39 *Les jeux olympiques. Un enjeu de consécration*, La documentation française, 7 August 2008, available at www.ladocumentationfrancaise.fr/dossiers/chine-jeux-olympiques-pekin-2008/jo-enjeu.shtml (accessed 23 September 2016).

40 Marie Bénilde, 'Le boycott des Jeux olympiques n'a pas eu lieu', *Le Monde diplomatique*, 21 August 2008, available at http://blog.mondediplo.net/2008–08–21-Le-boycott-des-JO-n-a-pas-eu-lieu (accessed 23 September 2016).

41 Johan Galtung, 'On the effects of international economic sanctions, with examples from the case of Rhodesia', *World Politics*, 19:3 (1967). See also the discussion by Ivan Eland, 'Economic sanctions as tools of foreign policy', in George A. Lopez and David Cortright (eds), *Economic Sanctions: Panacea or Peacebuilding in a Post-Cold War World?* (Boulder, CO: Westview, 1995).

42 John Mueller, 'Presidential popularity from Truman to Johnson', *American Political Science Review*, 64:1 (1970).

43 Jay Gordon, 'When economic sanctions become weapons of mass destruction', 26 March 2004, available at, http://conconflicts.ssrc.org/archives/iraq/gordon/ (accessed 23 September 2016).

44 Richard Edwards and David Thomas, 'China condemns "vile" Olympic Torch protests', *Daily Telegraph*, 7 April 2008, available at www.telegraph.co.uk/news/uknews/1584224/China-condemns-vile-Olympic-torch-protests.html (accessed 26 April 2017).

45 'Carrefour faces China boycott bid', 15 April 2008, *BBC News*, available at http://news.bbc.co.uk/2/hi/asia-pacific/7347918.stm (accessed 23 September 2016).

46 Only the presidents of Estonia, Poland, Austria and the Czech Republic were absent from the Beijing ceremony.

47 For an ecletic discussion of honour, see Laurie M. Johnson and Dan Demetriou, *Honour in the Modern World – Interdisciplinary Perspectives* (Lanham, MD: Lexington Books, 2016), esp. ch. 12: Richard Ned Lebow, 'The Ancient Greeks on taming honor and appetite', 239–56.

48 Security Council Resolution 757 Re Bosnia Herzogovina 30 May 1992, available at https://undocs.org/S/RES/757 (accessed 26 May 2017); Martin-Bidou Pascale, 'Les mesures d'embargo prises à l'encontre de la Yougoslavie', *Annuaire français de droit international*, 39 (1993).

49 The designation Independent Olympic Participant allows individual athletes from states that are not fully recognised by the international community to participate in competition. Athletes from, but not representing, Kosovo were given this status in the 2016 Rio Olympic Games. For further information on Kosovo and the role sport can play in international recognition, see Dario Brentin and Loïc Tregoures, 'Entering through the sport's door? Kosovo's sport diplomatic endeavours towards international recognition', *Diplomacy and Statecraft*, 27:2 (2016).

50 Loïc Trégourès, 'L'embargo sportif de la Yougoslavie en 1992, ou la diplomatie du symbole', Annual Conference of the French Association of Political Science (AFSP), Strasbourg, France, 2 September 2011, available at www.afsp.info/congres2011/ sectionsthematiques/st51/st51tregoures.pdf (accessed 23 September 2016).

51 Document S/PV.3082, 30 May 1992, available at www.un.org/en/ga/search/view_doc. asp?symbol=S/RES/757(1992) (accessed 23 September 2016).

52 For further discussion of non-state actors, see J. Simon Rofe, 'It is a squad game: Manchester United as a diplomatic non-state actor in international affairs', *Sport in Society*, 17:9 (2014).

53 The relevance of civil society actors in human rights debates are discussed in Sarah B. Snyder, *Human Rights Activism and the End of the Cold War: A Transnational History of the Helsinki Network* (Cambridge: Cambridge University Press, 2011).

54 Jean-Gabriel Contamin and Olivier Le Noé, 'La coupe est pleine Videla! Le Mundial 1978 entre politisation et dépolitisation', *Le Mouvement Social*, 1/2010 (No. 230), available at www.cairn.info/revue-le-mouvement-social-2010–1-page-27.htm (accessed 23 September 2016).

55 Luiz Carlos Ribeiro, 'Futebol e ditadura na América Latina: a experiência do C.O.B.A', Twenty-seventh National History Symposium, July 2013, available at www.snh2013. anpuh.org/simposio/view?ID_SIMPOSIO=997 www.snh2013.anpuh.org/resources/ anais/27/1364915151_ARQUIVO_FuteboleditaduranaAmericaLatina, Ribeiro_1_.pdf (accessed 23 September 2016).

56 Jules Boykoff and Matthew Yasuoka, 'Media coverage of the 2014 Winter Olympics in Sochi, Russia: Putin, politics, and Pussy Riot', *Olympika*, XXIII, (2014), 28.

57 Michael Calderone, 'How Russia is censoring reporting on Sochi Olympic controversies', 28 January 2014, *Huffington Post*, available at www.huffing tonpost.com/2014/01/28/media-sochi-olympics-russia_n_4670600. html?ncid=engmodushpmg00000004 (accessed 26 September 2016).

58 Luke Harding, 'Georgian president urges US and EU to boycott Russia's Winter Olympics', *The Guardian*, 26 August 2008, available at www.theguardian.com/ world/2008/aug/26/georgia.russia (accessed 23 September 2016).

59 All Out Association, http://allout.org/en (accessed 22 September 2016).

60 Report published by Boris Nemtsov and Leonid Martynyuk 'Winter Olympics in the sub-tropics: corruption and abuse in Sochi', 2013, available at www.putin-itogi.ru/cp/ wp-content/uploads/2013/05/Report_ENG_SOCHI-2014_preview.pdf (accessed 22 September 2016).

61 Boykoff and Yasuoka, 'Media coverage of the 2014 Winter Olympics in Sochi, Russia', 27–55.

62 Boykoff and Yasuoka, 'Media coverage of the 2014 Winter Olympics in Sochi, Russia', 3.

63 'Boycotter ou pas les JO de Sotchi, le dilemme des Occidentaux', *Le Monde*, 16 December 2013, available at www.lemonde.fr/sport/article/2013/12/16/le-debat-fait-rage-sur-le-boycottage-des-jo-de-sotchi_4335268_3242.html (accessed 23 September 2016).

64 Jeff Jarvis, 'Should we boycott Google, Starbucks and Amazon?', *The Guardian*, 17 November 2012, available at www.theguardian.com/commentisfree/2012/nov/17/ should-boycott-google-starbucks-amazon (accessed 23 April 2017).

65 Rowena Mason, 'England should boycott 2018 World Cup', *The Guardian*, 31 May 2015, available at www.theguardian.com/football/2015/may/31/england-boycott-2018-world-cup-andy-burnham (accessed 23 September 2016).

66 Robert Booth, 'Qatar World Cup construction "will leave 4000 migrant workers dead"', *The Guardian*, 26 September 2013, available at www.theguardian.com/global-development/2013/sep/26/qatar-world-cup-migrant-workers-dead (accessed 23 April 2017).

10

'Chinese rings': the United States, the two Chinas and the 1960 Squaw Valley Winter Olympics

Rachel Vaughan

It is only relatively recently that scholars have begun to recognise the centrality of sport to the public diplomacy and soft power strategies of governments within the international arena.[1] To a degree, this was partly the reluctance of Western governments to acknowledge the role of sport within their diplomatic arsenal. In contrast, the West's Cold War adversary, the Soviet Union, began to engage with sport as a facet of wider political and ideological strategies after the Second World War.[2] In 1949, the State Department outlined the American position thus: '[T]h[e] [United States] government does not inject itself into questions of policy and management within either the [I]nternational [Olympic Committee] or the [United States] National [Olympic Committee]'.[3] Secretary of State Dean Acheson elaborated: '[an] Olympiad is not held under Government supervision and the question of its site does not involve International Relations between Governments'.[4] Crucially, however, despite long-standing official non-involvement in international sporting matters, hosting the 1960 Games focused US diplomatic attention on the opportunities and problems presented by the Olympics within the wider Cold War.

This chapter argues that the deep (but unofficial) involvement of the State Department in the planning and staging of the Squaw Valley Games demonstrates the extent to which it regarded sport as an important part of wider Cold War cultural and propaganda concerns. Furthermore, it illustrates the manner in which US diplomats sought to use the public diplomacy platform that the Olympic movement provided, not merely for reasons of US 'national projection', but in the interests of another country, in this case Nationalist China, whose desire for international recognition and legitimacy very much tallied with American Cold War interests.

In the years between 1896, when the first 'modern' Olympics were held in Athens, Greece, and the onset of the Cold War, the Olympic movement continually asserted its separation from the broader international political arena. Avery Brundage – president of the US National Olympic Committee (NOC) 1928–53 and president of the International Olympic Committee (IOC) 1952–72 – for one, was a dedicated advocate of the absolute separation of the sporting and political realms. Ultimately such a position was untenable: the Olympic Games, in contrast to Pierre de Coubertin's late nineteenth century concept, became inextricably linked with aspects of sovereignty and nationalism as a result of being based on national teams, with the associated trappings of statehood such as national flags and anthems. Equally the Olympics became a 'safe' platform on which to demonstrate national strength and vitality.

The division of China from 1949 into the Communist People's Republic (PRC) on the mainland, and the exiled Nationalists – the Republic of China (ROC) – on the island of Taiwan/Formosa, came to symbolise the ideological division between East and West. Simultaneously, issues of recognition associated with divided states including China (but also Germany and Korea[5]) were inextricably inter-related with broader questions of Cold War alliances and the conflict between the superpowers, both generally and in specific relation to the Olympics. It is within this context that this chapter is located, through its examination of the behind-the-scenes involvement of State Department officials – and in turn the US government more broadly – in the organisation and staging of the 1960 Winter Games in order to facilitate and promote American public diplomacy towards the legitimacy and primacy of the Nationalist Chinese regime.

The two Chinas

American diplomatic involvement in the supposed sanctity of the Olympics in 1960 was the consequence of over ten years of complicated and at times confusing political developments emanating from what emerged as the two entities of 'China'. In October 1949, following its success in the Chinese Civil War, the communist regime announced the creation of the PRC and claimed jurisdiction over both the mainland and the outlying islands, including what remained of the ROC on Taiwan/Formosa.[6] From the perspective of Beijing, the Nationalists' island base was simply the one province of the PRC currently controlled by Chiang Kai-shek's Guomintang (GMT) Nationalist Party.[7] Indeed, this status of the ROC as simply a province of 'China' prevailed when Chiang Kai-shek became a signatory to the United Nations, receiving a permanent seat on the Security Council in 1947.[8] The ROC enjoyed a disproportionately privileged position because of it having been recognised as *the* legitimate government of China in 1945 by the wartime allies (including the USSR), and through the continuing patronage of the United States.[9] Yet the denial of the existence of the PRC was to become increasingly difficult to sustain (although US policy attempted to do so, until recognising the PRC under Nixon), especially when the regime targeted bodies like the IOC in manoeuvring against its isolation.

The relationship between China and the IOC began as early as 1915, although the latter did not recognise the China National Amateur Athletic Federation (CNAAF) as constituting a Chinese NOC until 1931.[10] Following the communist takeover, two of the three Chinese IOC officials (along with the CNAAF) fled to Taiwan/Formosa.[11] The IOC upheld recognition of the ROC as the Chinese NOC, with Brundage suggesting that really the Chinese NOC had simply changed its address.[12] The PRC formed its own governing body, the All-China Federation for Physical Culture (ACFPC) almost immediately,[13] but the IOC heard nothing more until 1952, when the PRC sought Olympic recognition to enable a team to compete at the Helsinki Games. Mirroring their respective governments, both the CNAAF and the ACFPC claimed jurisdiction over sport throughout the whole of China.[14] As such, the civil war had effectively given rise to 'China' possessing two NOCs.

At the Helsinki Session held just prior to the opening of the 1952 Games, IOC members voted on whether to grant either of the Chinese teams affiliation at the Summer Games. Neither of the rival Chinese NOCs was willing to accept even a whisper of recognition to the other. It was decided by 29 votes to 22 that both NOCs should be allowed entry,[15] with subsequent participation conditional on which of the NOCs had affiliation from the relevant international federation for each event in which it wished to compete.[16] The PRC declared the whole IOC debate as irrelevant, intimating that recognition of the mainland regime was inevitable. On hearing about the IOC's decision to allow dual Chinese representation, the Nationalists immediately withdrew their single Olympic athlete. Ironically, no mainland athletes competed in Helsinki either – they arrived only after their events had concluded. In 1954, the IOC decided to admit the mainland regime by twenty-three votes to twenty-one at its Session in Athens[17] as constituting the 'Olympic Committee of Democratic China'; the Nationalist NOC was allowed to keep its previous title of 'Chinese Olympic Committee'.[18] Unfortunately, the situation was never tenable. As David Kanin wryly observes, 'such a policy was as unrealistic in the Olympic movement as in the rest of international politics'.[19]

In contrast to Richard Espy's opinion that the decision to recognise the communist NOC was apolitical and that, as such, the Committee remained within both the remit of the Olympic Charter and the historical foundations of the organisation, it is clear that in fact the IOC decision was *expressly* political, although this had not been the intention.[20] The organisation attempted to uphold its apolitical status by 'introducing the idea of recognising territories under the control of an NOC, rather than insisting that an NOC have a nation behind it'.[21] This became the adapted basis, in fact, of Coubertin's original concept of sporting geography, supposedly transcending state boundaries in the light of the moral primacy of sport.[22]

The communist Chinese eventually announced the withdrawal of their delegation from the Melbourne Games by telegram to the IOC on 6 November 1956.[23] Although Brundage and Tung Shao-yi – the one pre-1949 Chinese member of the IOC remaining on the mainland – were in communication during 1957–58, relations deteriorated and ultimately the PRC withdrew from the Olympic movement and from the eight international federations that recognised both Chinas as members.[24]

Before 1960, Chinese Olympic participation did not appear to have caused the US diplomatic community much concern. Unsurprisingly, American relations with the Far East were dictated by more traditional foreign policy concerns, including the non-recognition of the PRC as a state.[25] But in the aftermath of the 1956 Olympic Games, attention became increasingly focused on the ultimately successful bid from Squaw Valley California to host the 1960 Winter Olympics. The American position was based on three inter-related concerns relating to ideas of soft power, public diplomacy, national vitality and prestige. On the one hand, once the United States had been designated host, a further 'ratcheting-up' of engagement with issues relating to hosting the Olympics was necessary. Quite simply, it was impossible not to engage on some level with the issue in hand. Secondly, and inter-relatedly, United States policy towards sport and diplomacy was also evolving as a specific response to what it saw as Moscow's deliberate politicisation of the Olympic arena.[26] Finally, and crucially in relation to this chapter, the Squaw Valley Games became a context within which the State Department chose to push the wider policy of the primacy of Nationalist China.

State Department approval for the 1960 Winter Games was forthcoming as early as 1957: '[t]hat Squaw Valley was awarded the opportunity of serving as host ... is considered by the Department to be a splendid opportunity for the state of California to demonstrate its munificent hospitality'.[27] The State Department made considerable behind-the-scenes efforts both before and during the Games in an attempt to ensure ROC participation, concentrating on two, inter-related diplomatic objectives. First, to facilitate a mutually acceptable name for the Nationalist NOC – the nomenclature issue. Neither the US nor the Nationalists were prepared to accept a designation of 'Taiwan', for example. Secondly, to smooth over (or even sidestep entirely) the IOC's standard qualification requirements to enable the handful of Chinese Winter athletes to actually compete, which would send an important diplomatic message to the world regarding US support of the Nationalist regime.

Officially, the US government had no specific organisational role: responsibility lay instead with the Squaw Valley Olympic Committee (SQOC) led by Prentis C. Hale, and the Games were privately sponsored and supported. Similarly, State Department involvement was also unofficial, but its close involvement in the 1960 San Francisco IOC vote prompted wider Departmental reappraisal of governmental interference in international sporting matters.[28] An internal memo wondered: 'In view of the questions which have arisen with regard to the 1960 Olympics ... it would seem wise for the Department to decide whether they are issues in which ... [it] has strong contingent if not direct interest.'[29] Crucially, and as this chapter demonstrates, the State Department did indeed use hosting the Games to promote more general American policy vis-à-vis the primacy of the ROC regime. However, the exact nature of Departmental involvement did cause some concern internally. One option, 'to defend and advocate the interests of the Republic of China NOC',[30] based on 'interests ... [being] ... political matters of importance' – as such constituting quasi-official involvement in the Games – was suggested, but with the cautionary observation that both the Department in general, and the Secretary of State in particular, might be subjected to public scrutiny. Overall, despite many assurances of the positive impact the Olympics would have on the United States, diplomatic opinion remained somewhat ambivalent: 'The Secretary feels that in relation to the existing policy of the United States and the obvious problems presented by admission of Red Chinese, that it would have been better if the Games had not been invited or assigned here.'[31] This was a telling prediction of the problems that were to beset the staging of the Games, and the conflicting pressures of attempting to demonstrate independence of the US political establishment from the Olympics on the one hand, and fundamental aims of American foreign policy on the other.

Politically, US prestige would be under scrutiny during the two weeks of the Olympics. The White House regarded federal involvement as vital and emphasised the need for an outstanding organisational job.[32] Similarly, the Eisenhower administration viewed hosting the Games as a fantastic opportunity for the domestic implementation of its 'People-to-People' programme, and hoped that parallel events would signal propaganda victories in the broader Cold War. White House engagement with the problem of Chinese participation emerged during the preparation of the president's message of good wishes to the team and Kenneth 'Tug' Wilson (president of the United States Olympic Committee (USOC)) for the programme. John Calhoun, director of the Executive Secretariat, advised the White House that 'it would be desirable for the President to defer sending the message for a few days so as to avoid the possibility that his action might be misinterpreted as condoning developments on the Chinese participation issue at Squaw Valley and at the IOC meeting in San Francisco'.[33] Unsurprisingly, both the Squaw Valley Organizing Committee (SVOC) and State Department deemed a sound financial base essential. Furthermore, US military expertise and assistance would be indispensable in staging the skiing events. Specific federal funding had also been requested relating to the construction of the main ice-skating arena on land that was already owned by the US government.[34]

What's in a name? The nomenclature issue

The actual name by which the Nationalist/ROC Olympic team was known had been a relatively long-running problem within Olympic circles and came to severely exercise the State Department, as well as the Chinese themselves in relation to the Squaw Valley Games. While this might seem to be a relatively minor concern, the nomenclature issue took on significance within the context of the China problem, as it directly contributed to perceptions of legitimacy and recognition of the Nationalist/ROC regime (versus that of the PRC) as to what constituted the one designation of 'China'. From the American perspective, facilitating a team name which was acceptable (or even favourable) to the ROC was key – and a central tenet of ongoing wider US policy.

From the Olympic perspective, it was far from clear as to whether the PRC would even seek to compete in the Squaw Valley Games. From 1957 onwards, Beijing had repeatedly demanded that the IOC expel the Nationalists from the Olympic movement.[35] In turn, the IOC reiterated that it was neither willing nor able to make political decisions, and that as two NOCs existed governing two apparently separate geographical areas, both should be recognised and allowed to send representatives to the Games. The PRC's response was to accuse Brundage of imposing politics into the sanctity of the IOC, label him a lackey of the United States and promptly announce the withdrawal of communist China from the Olympic movement.[36] The situation was made significantly worse by a letter from Otto Meyer (chancellor of the IOC) to Marcello Garroni (secretary general of the Italian NOC) concerning the reorganisation of NOCs along territorially representative grounds. This communication was an attempt to implement the previously proposed amendment from October 1959, listing NOCs territorially rather than on a political basis. It had been preceded by the decision of the Executive Committee (in May of the same year) to remove the name of the Chinese NOC from its list of recognised national bodies, and require that the ROC body reapply for affiliation under a name more reflective of the area within which it controlled sport.[37]

The IOC called a vote on the issue at its 55th Session in Munich in May 1959. Lord Burghley's suggestion that the Nationalists be recognised but not be allowed to assert they had control over sport on the mainland, was finally carried by 48 to 7.[38] The ROC was informed that it was no longer recognised as the 'Chinese National Olympic Committee' but was free to reapply with a name that more accurately reflected the territory over which it had control. This IOC ruling was inherently flawed – athletes from Singapore, Macao and Hong Kong were also eligible to compete for 'Taiwan' – and widely misinterpreted. Brundage also appeared to be contravening more general US policy in at least partial deference to the British, through Burghley's suggestion of the ballot in Munich. Just as Moscow had resolutely backed the PRC, to all intents and purposes the US took the opposing position and had thrown in its lot with Chiang Kai-shek.[39]

The IOC request that the Nationalists reapply under a different name threatened to have serious repercussions in terms of the Squaw Valley Olympics. Both the ROC and the US hoped that the conciliatory approach of the former, in deferring to the Munich decision, would have resulted in the new name under which it was proposed the team would compete – the 'Republic of China Olympic Committee' – being accepted at the following October IOC meeting and that, as such, the matter would be closed.[40] However, this was not to be the case. Initially the Nationalists reapplied to the IOC as per the United Nations Security Council, but the IOC rejected it.[41]

In a pre-press conference briefing in June 1959, a lengthy statement was prepared in response to anticipated questions concerning ROC participation. It was noted here that Eisenhower viewed as 'ridiculous' the decision to expel the Nationalist Chinese as not legitimately constituting 'China'.[42] Eisenhower went on to explain that the whole thing was simply like a man using his own name, 'and he added that the most trouble-some problems came from things like this, or things that [Syngman] Rhee,[43] Chiang [Kai-shek] or Greece started all on their own and manage to make us look so illogical as to be ridiculous'.[44] The IOC appeared unwilling to take a decisive stance until the last possible moment before the Summer Games in Rome. Until then, they worked to the interim ruling from the Munich Session: the ROC would be able to compete as the 'Republic of China' because it had been invited in that specific capacity.[45] Until the Rome Olympic Organizing Committee had received confirmation of the IOC posi-tion, there were a number of attempts to include 'Taiwan' in the official programmes, although such allegations were later disputed.[46] The potential for the IOC to change the nomenclature stipulation and insist that the Nationalist team was designated as 'Republic of China – Taiwan' (or similar) caused the State Department significant anxiety. 'Mr Parsons explained that the matter has significant political implications which concern the Department for reasons of United States foreign policy, and that it is important as a precedent for the Rome Games.'[47] Prentis C. Hale, Douglas Roby

(US member of the IOC), representatives from the Nationalist NOC and various State Department officials debated at length whether to press for a postponement of the decision. The prevailing view of the last two was to play it by ear, work towards a speedy resolution and rely on Roby's ability to persuade Brundage to go along with this view.[48] Unfortunately, Edwin Martin (the State Department's director of Chinese Affairs) was informed that: 'the voting situation did not look good now ... [Roby] had been over the most recent list of members expected to attend ... and had found that the Soviet bloc would be heavily represented, whereas a great many IOC members who could be expected to take a favourable position ... would not'.[49]

The State Department noted with approval the conciliatory gesture by the Nationalist NOC in agreeing to abide by the IOC directive and reapplying under the new name 'Republic of China Olympic Committee'.[50] However, the IOC rejected this concession because the name was still based on the word 'China'. The only solution for the Nationalists was to defer to the concept of 'sporting geography' and have its representation based on the territorial area of 'Taiwan/Formosa' instead – regarded by the IOC as the area over which it actually controlled sport.[51] The IOC had aired a possible resolution along these lines the previous year.[52] The idea of being designated as 'Taiwan' had not been favourably received by either the Nationalist Chinese or the State Department, with the latter opining quite simply: 'the Republic of China is not "Taiwan"'.[53]

Perhaps surprisingly, Gunson Hoh of the ROC NOC still viewed Brundage as being a 'friend of China'. Furthermore, he regarded the IOC president as being resolutely anti-communist and at odds with the British lord Burghley.[54] Under Burghley's IAAF[55] leadership, Nationalist athletes had been forced to participate in the athletics events at the 1956 Olympics and the 1958 Asian Games as 'Taiwan/Formosa', potentially setting a precedent for an alternative resolution of the Chinese problem. As early as 1956, the IAAF Congress approved the affiliation of the Nationalist Chinese Athletic Federation as 'Taiwan' rather than the 'Republic of China' or similar variant.[56] The IAAF was able to avoid accusations of incorporating a dual China approach through viewing the mainland regime as 'China' and the Nationalist enclave as 'Taiwan'.[57] This provided the IOC with a potential territorially based precedent concerning its own resolution of the problem through the use of the principle of 'sporting geography'. However, this ruling was only possible in the IAAF because of the agreement of the Nationalist Chinese Athletic Association; a similar solution within the Olympic context remained unsanctioned. Moreover, the IAAF resolution was not without its problems: despite the proffered territorial basis of the arrangement, Beijing threatened to withdraw as a result of the admission of Taiwan and the associated implication of a 'two Chinas' solution. However, the PRC was discouraged from going through with its threat because with the removal of its affiliation within the governing international federation, any national team with which it subsequently had a bilateral athletics meeting could have faced serious sanctions from the IAAF.[58] As such, it would have rapidly run out of teams to face in competition.

The 1960 San Francisco Session of the IOC tentatively accepted the proposed name change of the Nationalist Chinese NOC from 'Chinese National Olympic Committee' to 'Republic of China National Olympic Committee', although it deferred making a final and binding decision on the matter. Brundage himself had complicated things further, by, on his own volition, inserting an additional requirement that Nationalist athletes should specifically compete under the name 'Taiwan'.[59] In something of the tradition of the IOC's tendency to procrastinate, as relatively few members were in attendance in San Francisco, it decided to postpone a final ruling until later that year. However, as an interim measure and in order that Nationalist athletes might have the opportunity to compete in the Squaw Valley and Rome Olympics, the Executive Board would 'permit entries for Taiwan from the organisation which at present calls itself "The Olympic Committee of the Republic of China"'.[60] A week or so before the official opening of the Winter Games, Secretary of State Christian Herter gave a useful summary of the political implications of the situation in a letter to the USOC. Herter stressed that the Nationalist NOC had been a long-standing Olympic member, 'recognized by the IOC for nearly forty years and had participated faithfully in the Olympic movement',[61] before being required to re-register by the IOC because of the Munich decision.

The final decision of the IOC on the nomenclature issue – albeit taken after the conclusion of the Squaw Valley Games – effectively confirmed the original ruling of Meyer and Brundage, despite the best attempts of Roby, other sympathetic Committee members and the State Department. At the 1960 Summer Olympics the ROC would be *listed* as the 'Republic of China Olympic Committee' but they would *compete* under the listing of 'Taiwan'. Roby reported that the outcome was partially the result of 'aggressive tactics of the British delegation, led by Lord Burghley, who asserted that no matter what the Committee decided, the Chinese would have to use the name Taiwan in track and field events' – the latter a consequence of the IAAF decision to recognise the ROC as 'Taiwan'.[62] Despite earlier discussion as to whether the Nationalist athletes should actually participate in the Rome Opening Ceremony parade, the team took up their place under the banner of 'Formosa'. However, as the group passed the dignitaries' viewing stand, about half way down the home straight of the stadium track, the first official following the banner unfolded a sign reading 'Under protest'. A despatch from the American Embassy in Rome elaborated: 'he carried this for about one hundred yards and then folded it up and put it away, to the cheers of persons in that part of the stands'.[63] After all the energy expended in relation to the nomenclature issue, the American Embassy in Rome noted with disappointment: 'The designation of the Republic of China team as Formosa … has unfortunately been regarded as a somewhat natural development by most uninformed people.'[64]

That the name of the ROC team took on such significance for the State Department (as well as the Nationalist Chinese themselves) exemplifies one aspect of the validity of the Olympics within the context of public diplomacy and the projection of wider American policy through the lens of sport.

The problem of participation

By the opening of the Squaw Valley Games in February 1960, the nomenclature issue seemed to have been resolved (albeit rather messily), but the prospect of whether any Nationalist athletes would actually compete remained far from certain. With little interest in winter sports in the ROC, the pool of potential Olympians was relatively low. The situation was further complicated because of the routine Olympic requirement for individual national sporting federations to be affiliated with their international counterpart. Unfortunately, the two main sports in which the Nationalists hoped to have Olympic representation – skiing and figure skating – had failed to do this.[65] The very real possibility emerged that, after all the efforts to secure an acceptable name for the Nationalist NOC, there might not actually be a team at all. It was a difficult issue to resolve, not least for the State Department. On the one hand was the supposed independence of the Olympic movement and universal access to international sport. On the other, a central tenet of American foreign policy – the recognition of the Nationalist regime on Taiwan/Formosa as the 'Republic of China' – could not be seen to be compromised. Prentis Hale emphasised to the State Department, surely somewhat unnecessarily, that if events were to proceed in an unfavourable manner, the less publicity on the matter, the better.[66]

At the beginning of February 1960, the International Skiing Federation (FIS) informed the ROC that it was not possible to grant special dispensation to facilitate Olympic participation and that the next opportunity for membership requests would be in 1961.[67] The FIS explained that the only way the skiers might take part would be through an appeal direct to the IOC under Rule no. 34, designed to allow exceptional participation of athletes who had no access to an affiliated national federation for their sport.[68] Through his personal friendship with Marc Hodler, FIS president, Hale all but guaranteed to both the ROC NOC and the State Department that the Chinese skiers would be allowed to take part.

As a direct result of the publicity surrounding the skiers' situation, Congressman Walter Judd requested State Department confirmation on the status of the Chinese Olympic team.[69] The State Department assured him that the skiers' plight was causing both the Department and the Chinese delegation immense concern. Edwin Martin explained: 'I felt that even more important than the actual participation of the Chinese skiers in the games was the principle of the thing and the question of their status in the IOC.'[70] Increasing political pressure was also emerging from Congress in relation to whether the disbarring of the Chinese athletes was contrary to the Appropriations Bill, providing operational and maintenance funds for the Games.

Raymond Hare (deputy under secretary for Political Affairs) reiterated that it was highly desirable for the Chinese skiers to compete in the Games, no matter how this was achieved. Indeed, Hare specifically warned that if no mechanism for Chinese participation was found, the US government and its policy on China would find itself in a 'difficult and embarrassing position'.[71] By 11 February there was still no decision, and the individuals involved had taken up residence in the Olympic Village. However, this was also causing problems – the Nationalist team were unable to hoist their flag in the Village until the FIS granted them official permission to compete, prompting further State Department concern.[72] However, Hale explained that he had already overstepped his authority in allowing the Chinese skiers to remain in the Village pending the FIS ruling on their eligibility, and felt unable to take further action. Authorities had told the team that should they be deemed ineligible to compete, they would have to leave the Village immediately and that political intervention in the matter was impossible due to the independent nature of both the USOC and the SVOC. Informally, the State Department confirmed it would do its best to ensure a favourable outcome.[73]

As late as 17 February – the day before the Olympics officially began – the status of the skiers was still not finalised, to the consternation of the State Department. The latter was also becoming agitated over the apparent incompetence of Hale, who had previously assured all parties that there would be no problem ensuring the skiers' participation.[74] Hale was left in no doubt as to the frustration he was causing in governmental circles: 'the Department had been working on the matter actively because of the great political importance and also because it would seem most unfortunate if athletes from a country with which our relations are as close as in the case of the Republic of China should be subject to what might appear to be unsympathetic treatment'.[75] In desperation, the State Department appealed to Roby for last minute assistance on the issue, although it became increasingly apparent that the matter was likely to end unfavourably:

> In agreement with Hale, we had hitherto endeavored to work on this matter as quietly as possible and, even now, we had no intention of initiating publicity. However, an adverse decision would generate reaction and, in the foreseeable event that the Department were queried, we would certainly not hesitate to make it clear where our sympathies lay, what we had done about it and how disappointed and distressed we were that the matter had turned out negatively.[76]

Interestingly, the State Department subsequently disputed this position. Citing an unnamed but reliable source, the Department noted that it had been informed on good authority that Hodler had been happy to go along with the Rule 34 resolution and that the final decision to exclude the skiers was down to Brundage and Hale. Raymond Hare's response was unapologetic and did not gloss over the role of the State Department in the matter – here at least, the playing out of issues at the heart of US foreign policy objectives was deemed too important either to ignore or deny.

On 19 February the Nationalist Chinese Embassy transmitted final confirmation to the State Department that the skiers were unable to compete. The announcement, jointly released by the SVOC and the ROC NOC, explained the skiers were ineligible because of the 'failure of their Skiing Association to comply with all of the requirements for competition'.[77] They constructed the note carefully to avoid any accusations that the skiers had been 'banned' because of problems with the status of the NOC. As a concession to ROC pride and sensibilities, they allowed the skiers to stay in the Olympic Village for the period of the Games. In addition, the one healthy skier (the other was injured) would be used as a forerunner to test the downhill course prior to the start of the racing.[78] Rosen explained that the State Department had done all it reasonably could to facilitate the entry of the athletes, and inferred that the blame probably lay with Hale and his misleading assurances that the team would be free to compete. 'Mr Hale had come to the Department in early January to talk with Mr Hare about this situation and the Department's concern was made emphatically clear. Hale had assured us that everything would work out all right if only the Chinese would produce a skier.'[79]

Conclusion

While the State Department was only too aware of the general politicisation of sport emanating from the Soviet bloc, the practicalities of the US hosting the 1960 Winter Games in Squaw Valley marked somewhat of a watershed in terms of the juxtaposition of American political and sporting diplomatic concerns. Hosting the Games pushed international sporting issues up the American political agenda, especially those connected with the problem of the recognition status of the ROC. The extensive involvement, albeit unofficially, of American diplomats in the planning and execution of the Games not only demonstrated an increased realisation of the value of the Olympics as a public diplomacy platform, but was also directly linked with demonstrating US policy with, and towards, the ROC. This was central to wider American policy within the Cold War – the promotion of Nationalist China as constituting the 'legitimate' China, at the expense of the PRC. Unfortunately, in reality it was rather more complicated despite the absence of the PRC team – the Olympic Games were supposedly non-political and the practicalities of trying to ensure ROC involvement and in a favourable guise were far from straightforward. A State Department memo summarised:

> The United States, as host country, is deeply involved in the political issues here. We are the major ally of the embattled Republic of China; refusal to permit athletes of the Republic of China to compete in this international tournament on American soil would be interpreted abroad as a rebuff to our allies and would suggest that the US is less than firm in implementing its stated policy of support for the international position of the Republic of China.[80]

The period between the end of the Winter Games and the opening of the Rome Olympics saw continued State Department interest in international sport, much of which focused on the China problem. From the American perspective, the crux of the issue was pushing for full Olympic participation by a team from Nationalist China under terms acceptable to the Chinese themselves, the Italian organisers (both sporting and political) and the United States. [81] Soon after the conclusion of the Winter Olympics, the State Department issued a number of recommendations regarding American objectives towards the Rome Games.[82] Ultimately, far from bringing states together, the Olympics seemed to mirror the increasingly acrimonious disputes between the 'two Chinas' in the Cold War itself.

Notes

1 For more on this, see especially Heather L. Dichter, H-Diplo Essay No. 122, 'Sport history and diplomatic history', available at https://issforum.org/essays/PDF/E122.pdf (accessed 2 November 2016); Andrew L. Johns, 'Competing in the global arena: sport and foreign relations since 1945', in Heather L. Dichter and Andrew L. Johns (eds), *Diplomatic Games: Sport, Statecraft and International Relations since 1945* (Lexington, KY: University of Kentucky Press, 2014), 1–15. Richard Arndt is among those who have stressed the importance of including sport within the wider context of US public diplomacy as it developed through the second half of the twentieth century: Richard T. Arndt, *The First Resort of Kings: American Cultural Diplomacy in the Twentieth Century* (Washington, DC: Potomac Books, 2005), 402.

2 See, for example, Richard B. Walsh, 'The Soviet athlete in international competition', *Department of State Bulletin*, 24 December 1951, 107–10; Evelyn Mertin, 'Steadfast friendship and brotherly help: the distinctive Soviet–East German sport relationship within the socialist bloc', in Dichter and Johns (eds), *Diplomatic Games*, 53–84; Jenifer Parks, 'Welcoming the "Third World": Soviet sport diplomacy, developing nations and the Olympic Games', in Dichter and Johns (eds), *Diplomatic Games*, 85–114; and the writings of James Riordan, particularly 'Rewriting Soviet sports history', *Journal of Sport History*, 20:3 (1993).

3 National Archives College Park [hereafter NACP]: State Dept. files [hereafter RG 59], Central Decimal Files [hereafter CDF] 1945–49, file: 811.4063/ 3-2549, Memo from Department of State, 20 April 1949.

4 NACP: RG 59, CDF 1945–49, file: 811.4063/ 2-2649, Letter from Dean Acheson to Charles Eaton, 26 March 1949.

5 John J. Metzler, *Divided Dynamism: The Diplomacy of Separated Nations: Germany, Korea, China* (Lanham, MD: University Press of America, 1996); Udo Merkel, 'Sport, politics and reunification: a comparative analysis of Germany and Korea', *International Journal of the History of Sport*, 23:4 (2009). For discussion on divided Germany, see for example, Carolyn Eisenberg, *Drawing the Line: The American Decision to Divide Germany, 1944–1949* (Cambridge: Cambridge University Press, 1996); Margarete Myers Feinstein, *State Symbols: The Quest for Legitimacy in the Federal Republic of Germany and the German Democratic Republic, 1949–1959* (Boston: Brill, 2001); William Glenn Gray, *Germany's Cold War: The Global Campaign to Isolate East Germany, 1949–1969* (Chapel Hill, NC: University of North Carolina Press, 2001). In specific relation to Germany and sport, see especially Heather L. Dichter, 'Sporting relations: diplomacy, small states, and Germany's postwar return to international sport', *Diplomacy & Statecraft*, 27:2 (2016); R. Gerald Hughes and Rachel J. Owen '"The continuation of politics by other means": Britain, the two Germanys and the Olympic Games, 1949–1972', *Contemporary European History*, 18:4 (2009)4; Rachel J. Owen, 'The Olympic Games and the Issue of Recognition: Anglo American Perspectives, 1944–1972', unpublished PhD thesis,

University of Wales, Aberystwyth, 2006. In relation to Korea, see for example, Won S. Lee, *The United States and the Division of Korea, 1945* (Seoul: Kyung Hee University Press, 1982); William Stueck, 'The United States, the Soviet Union and the division of Korea: a comparative approach', *Journal of American–East Asian Relations* 4:1 (1995).

6 David Reynolds, *One World Divisible: A Global History since 1945* (London: Penguin, 2000), 54–8.

7 Dong Jinxia, *Women, Sport and Society in Modern China: Holding up More than Half the Sky* (London: Frank Cass, 2003), 32.

8 Christopher R. Hill, *Olympic Politics Athens to Atlanta 1896–1996* (Manchester: Manchester University Press, 2nd edn, 1996), 44.

9 Statement by Truman, 15 December 1945, *Department of State Bulletin*, 16 December 1945, 945.

10 Fan Hong and Xiong Iaozheng, 'Communist China: sport, politics and diplomacy', in J. A. Mangan and Fan Hong (eds), *Sport in Asian Society: Past and Present* (London: Frank Cass, 2003), 319–20. For discussion of China in international sport before 1949, see for example, Xu Guoqi, *Olympic Dreams: China and Sports 1895–2008* (Cambridge, MA: Harvard University Press, 2008), 12–34, 40–8, 61–9; Fan Hong and Lu Zhouxiang, 'Politics first, competition second: sport and China's foreign diplomacy in the 1960s and 1970s', in Dichter and Johns (eds), *Diplomatic Games*, 385–408; Susan Brownell, *Beijing's Games: What the Olympics mean to China* (Lanham, MD: Rowman & Littlefield, 2008), 73–88.

11 Xu Guoqi, *Olympic Dreams*, 77.

12 Allen Guttmann, *The Olympics: A History of the Modern Games* (Urbana, IL: University of Illinois Press, 2nd edn, 2002), 145.

13 Fan Hong, 'The Olympic movement in China: ideals, realities and ambitions', *Sport in Society*, 1:1 (1998), 154.

14 Xu Guoqi, *Olympic Dreams*, 76–7; Brownell, *Beijing's Games*, 130.

15 Unfortunately, it is not clear exactly how the vote was split. Xu Guoqi, *Olympic Dreams*, 83.

16 Public Record Office/National Archives, Kew, UK (hereafter PRO/NA): FO 371/ 100898 [not numbered] TASS, 'On the eve of the Olympics', Extract from *Pravda*, 18 July 1952 (translation); PRO/NA: FO 371/ 100898 [not numbered] TASS, 'On Chinese participation in the Olympics', Extract from the Hsinhua News Agency, 16 July 1952; Richard Espy, *The Politics of the Olympic Games, with an Epilogue, 1976–1980* (Berkeley, CA: University of California Press, 1981), 37

17 *The Times*, 14 May 1954.

18 Brownell, *Beijing's Games*, 132.

19 David B. Kanin, *A Political History of the Olympic Games* (Boulder, CO: Westview Press, 1981), 75. See also Brownell, *Beijing's Games*, 132.

20 Richard Espy, *The Politics of the Olympic Games, with an Epilogue, 1976–1980* (Berkeley, CA: University of California Press, 1981), 66.

21 Hill, *Olympic Politics Athens to Atlanta*, 45.

22 Coubertin's influence on the modern Olympic movement was pivotal at the outset, with Hill citing him as its instigator (Hill, *Olympic Politics Athens to Atlanta*, 5). His long association with the movement from the late nineteenth century until his death in 1937 allowed for the evolution of his views. *Olympism: Selected Writings of*

Pierre de Coubertin 1863–1937, ed. Norbert Muller (Lausanne: International Olympic Committee, 2000). For further detail, see John MacAloon, *This Great Symbol: Pierre de Coubertin and the Origins of the Modern Olympic Games* (Chicago: University of Chicago Press, 1981) and its second edition in the *International Journal of the History of Sport*, 23:3–4 (2006).

23 Xu Guoqi, *Olympic Dreams*, 85; Brownell, *Beijing's Games*, 132–3. Somewhat ironically, there were reports that when the Nationalist team first arrived, the organisers mistakenly raised the communist Chinese flag in their honour; however, this was promptly removed by the ROC delegation and their own was hoisted in its place. *New York Times*, 30 October 1956.

24 Football, athletics, weightlifting, swimming, basketball, shooting, cycling, wrestling and the Asian Table Tennis Federation.

25 See Dwight D. Eisenhower Presidential Library, Abilene, Kansas (hereafter DDE): Papers as President, Ann Whitman File (hereafter PaPAWF), Dulles-Herter Series, Box 4, 'Dulles, John Foster – July 54 (3)', Memorandum from Eisenhower, 6 July 1954.

26 Kanin, *A Political History of the Olympic Games*, 249.

27 NACP: RG 59, CDF 1950–54, folder: 811.453/ 1–1855 to 811.46/ 6–3055, file: 811.4531/ 6–1857, Letter from Robert C. Hill, State Department to Senator William Knowland, 27 June 1957.

28 NACP: RG 59, Miscellaneous records of the Bureau of Public Affairs [hereafter MRBPA] 1944–62, Lot 65D472, Subject Files of the Policy Plans and Guidance Staff 1946–62, file: 'Winter Olympics 1960', State Department internal memorandum, 3 February 1960. The Bureau of Public Affairs 'engages domestic and international media to communicate timely and accurate information with the goal of furthering U.S. foreign policy and national security interests as well as broadening understanding of American values.' See www.state.gov/r/pa/ (accessed 15 December 2015).

29 NACP: RG 59, MRBPA 1944–62, Lot 65D472, Subject Files of the Policy Planning and Guidance Staff 1946–62, file: 'Winter Olympics 1960', State Department memorandum, 11 February 1960.

30 NACP: RG 59, MRBPA 1944–62, Lot 65D472, Subject Files of the Policy Planning and Guidance Staff 1946–62, file: 'Winter Olympics 1960', State Department memorandum, 11 February 1960.

31 DDE: John Foster Dulles Papers, General Correspondence and Memoranda Series, Box 5, Miscellaneous Correspondence 16 May 1957–59 August 1957, Memorandum from Robert Cartwright, SCA to William B. Macomber, Secretary of State, 9 August 1957.

32 DDE: PaPAWF, Central Files, Official File, Box 734, '143D Olympic Games (2)', Memorandum from Bob King, Federal Assistance – 1960 Olympic Winter Games, 'Reasons Why', n. d., 1957.

33 NACP: RG 59, CDF 1960–63, folder: 800.453/ 2–361 to 800.4531/ 8–1660, file: 800.4531/ 1–160, paper: 800.4531/ 2–1960, State Department Memorandum from John A. Calhoun to Frederic E. Fox, White House, 19 February 1960.

34 Some confusion remained as to the exact extent of federal financial assistance which was being requested. DDE: PaPAWF, Central Files, Official File, Box 734, '143D Olympic Games (2)' Memorandum for Brundage, 27 November 1957.

35 See Brownell, *Beijing's Games*, 133.

36 PRO/NA: FO 371/ 150557 [FCN 1801/ 1] Translated extract from *Hsinhua*, 29
    February 1960; Hong and Xiaozheng, 'Communist China: sport, politics and
    diplomacy', 326.
37 For a useful summary of the background to the China situation see NACP: RG
    59, Bureau of Far Eastern Affairs [hereafter BFEA], Assistant Secretary for Far
    Eastern Affairs; Subject, Name, Country Files 1960–63, 1960 Subject Files, Folder:
    from 'Memorandum of Conversation – Australia' to 'Interparliamentary Union,
    Tokyo', file: '1960 Olympics', 1960, Bureau of Far Eastern Affairs Memorandum:
    'Background', 8 April 1960.
38 Guttmann, *The Olympics*, 93.
39 For more on the US and China in the Cold War, see for example, Gordon H. Chang,
    Friends and Enemies: The United States, China and the Soviet Union, 1948–1972
    (Stanford, CA: Stanford University Press, 1990); Evelyn Goh, *Constructing the US
    Rapprochment with China 1961–1974: From 'Red Menace' to 'Tacit Ally'* (Cambridge:
    Cambridge University Press, 2004).
40 NACP: RG 59, MRBPA 1944–62, Lot 65D472, Subject Files of the Policy Planning and
    Guidance Staff, 1946–62, Department of State Memorandum from Andrew Berding,
    Political Affairs to Christian Herter, Secretary of State, 19 January 1960.
41 PRO/NA: FO 371/ 150699 [FK 1801/ 2] Note to file from Dalton, Foreign Office, 3
    February 1960.
42 DDE: PaPAWF, Press Conference Series, Box 8, '6/17/59', Pre-Press Conference
    briefing, 17 June 1959, 2.
43 Syngman Rhee was president of the Republic of Korea ROK, more commonly known
    as South Korea (1948–60).
44 DDE: PaPAWF, Press Conference Series, Box 8, '6/17/59', Pre-Press Conference
    briefing, 17 June 1959, 2.
45 NACP: RG 59, MRBPA 1944–62, Lot 65D472, Subject Files of Policy Planning and
    Guidance Staff 1946–62, Department of State Memorandum, 19 January 1960.
46 NACP: RG 59, CDF 1960–63, folder: 800.453/ 2–361 to 800.4531/ 8–1660, file:
    800.4531/ 1–160, paper: 800.4531. 4531/ 1–1560, Department of State Memorandum
    of Conversation, participants: Prentis C. Hale, president Squaw Valley OCOG,
    Raymond A. Hare, Deputy under secretary for Political Affairs, J. Graham Parsons,
    assistant secretary for Far Eastern Affairs, John S. Hoghland II, deputy assistant
    secretary for Congressional Relations, Edwin M. Kretzmann, deputy assistant
    secretary for Public Affairs, 15 January 1960.
47 NACP: RG 59, CDF 1960–63, folder: 800.453/ 2–361 to 800.4531/ 8–1660, file:
    800.4531/ 1–160, paper: 800.4531. 4531/ 1–1560, Department of State Memorandum
    of Conversation, participants: Prentis C. Hale, president Squaw Valley OCOG,
    Raymond A. Hare, deputy under secretary for Political Affairs, J. Graham Parsons,
    assistant secretary for Far Eastern Affairs, John S. Hoghland II, deputy assistant
    secretary for Congressional Relations, Edwin M. Kretzmann, deputy assistant
    secretary for Public Affairs, 15 January 1960.
48 NACP: RG 59, CDF 1960–63, folder: 800.453/ 2–361 to 800.4531/ 8–1660, file:
    800.4531/ 1–169, paper: 800.4531/ 2–460, State Department Memorandum of
    conversation between Shao-chang Hsu and Edwin W. Martin, director, Chinese
    Affairs, 4 February 1960.
49 NACP: RG 59, CDF 1960–63, folder: 800.453/ 2–361 to 800.4531/ 8–1660, file:

800.4531/ 1–160, paper: 800.4531/ 2–460, State Department Memorandum of conversation between Roby and Martin, 4 February 1960.

50 NACP: RG 59, CDF 1960–63, folder: 800.453/ 2–361 to 800.4531/ 8–1660, file: 800.4531/ 1–160, paper: 800.4531/ 2–260, Letter from Macomber, to Dorn, House of Representatives, 12 February 1960.

51 NACP: RG 59, MRBPA 1944–62, Lot 65D472, Subject Files of Policy Planning and Guidance Staff 1946–62, Department of State Memorandum, 19 January 1960.

52 NACP: RG 59, CDF 1960–63, folder: 800.453/ 2–361 to 800.4531/ 8–1660, file: 800.4531/ 1–169, paper: 800.4531/ 2–260, Letter from Macomber to Dorn, Member of the House of Representatives, 12 February 1960.

53 NACP: RG 59, CDF 1960–63, folder: 800.453/ 2–361 to 800.4531/ 8–1660, file: 800.4531/ 1–169, paper: 800.4531/ 2–260, Letter from Macomber to Dorn, Member of the House of Representatives, 12 February 1960.

54 Lord Burghley, the sixth marquis of Exeter, was a British member of the IOC, became president of the International Amateur Athletic Association (IAAF) in 1946 and was a vice-president of the IOC from 1952 to 1966. NACP: RG 59, CDF 1960–63, folder: 800.453/ 2–361 to 800.4531/ 8–1660, file: 800.4531/ 1–169, paper: 800.4531/ 1–2260, Memorandum of conversation between Shao-chang Hsu, Chinese Embassy, Gunson Hoh, Josiah W. Bennett, Office of Chinese Affairs, and Arthur Rosen, Office of Chinese Affairs, 22 January 1960.

55 'International Amateur Athletic Federation', renamed 'International Association of Athletic Federations' in 2001.

56 PRO/NA: FO 371/ 150557 [FCN 1801/ 6] Letter from Pain, Hon. Secretary-Treasurer, IAAF, to Mr Teng Chuan-kai, China National Amateur Athletic Federation, 9 August 1960.

57 PRO/NA: FO 371/ 145547 [W 1801/ 1] 'The Olympic Games – Political Problems', FO Intel. No. 85, 16 July 1959.

58 PRO/NA: FO 371/ 150557 [FCN 1801/ 3] Letter from Dalton, FO to Stewart, British Embassy Peking, 13 April 1960.

59 NACP: RG 59, CDF 1960–63, folder: 800.453/ 2–361 to 800.4531/ 8–1660, file: 800.4531/ 1–160, paper: 800.4531/ 4–860, State Department Memorandum of conversation between Minister Carlo Perrone-Capano, Italian Embassy, Parsons, assistant secretary, BFEA, Ruth Bacon, BFEA, and Paul K. Stahnke, BFEA, 8 April 1960.

60 PRO/NA: FO 371/ 150557 [FCN 1801/ 3] Extracts from the Minutes of the 56th Session of the IOC, San Francisco, February 1960.

61 NACP: RG 59, MRBPA 1944–62, Lot 65D472, Subject Files of the Policy Planning and Guidance Staff 1946–62, 'Winter Olympics 1960', Letter from Herter, to Asa S. Bushnell, Secretary, USOC, 11 February 1960.

62 NACP: RG 59, CDF 1960–63, folder: 800.453/ 2–361 to 800.4531/ 8–1660, file: 800.4531/ 8–1660, paper: 800.4531/ 8–2360, Incoming telegram no. 721 from Zellerbach to Secretary of State, 23 August 1960.

63 NACP: RG 59, CDF 1960–63, folder: 800.453/ 2–361 to 800.4531/ 8–1660, file: 800.4531/ 8–1660, paper: 800.4531/ 8–2760, Incoming airgram no. G-150 from Zellerbach, Rome, 27 August 1960.

64 NACP: RG 59, CDF 1960–63, folder: 800.453/ 2–361 to 800.4531/ 8–1660, file: 800.4531/ 8–1660, paper: 800.4531/ 8–3060, Foreign Service Despatch no. 222 from H. G. Torbert, Rome to State Department, 30 August 1960.

65 From the outset the prospect of participation in the figure skating was bleak due to the attitude of the relevant international federation, the International Skating Union (ISU). See NACP: RG 59, CDF 1960–63, folder: 800.453/ 2–361 to 800.4531/ 8–1660, file: 800.4531/ 1–160, paper: 800.4531. 4531/ 1–1560, Department of State Memorandum of Conversation, participants: Hale, Hare, Parsons, John S. Hoghland II, deputy assistant secretary for Congressional Relations, Kretzmann, 15 January 1960; NACP: RG 59, CDF 1960–63, folder: 800.453/ 2–361 to 800.4531/ 8–1660, file: 800.4531/ 1–160, paper: 800.4531/ 2–1260, State Department Memorandum of conversation between Hale and Rosen, 12 February 1960; NACP: RG 59, CDF 1960–63, folder: 800.453/ 2–361 to 800.4531/ 8–1660, file: 800.4531/ 1–160, paper: 800.4531/ 2–1960, State Department Memorandum from John Calhoun to Frederic Fox, White House, 19 February 1960; NACP: RG 59, CDF 1960–63, folder: 800.453/ 2–361 to 800.4531/ 8–1660, file: 800.4531/ 1–160, paper: 800.4531/ 2–2460, State Department Memorandum of conversation between Laird and Rosen, 24 February 1960.
66 NACP: RG 59, MRBPA 1944–62, Lot 65D472, Subject Files of the Policy Planning and Guidance Staff, 1946–62, file: 'Winter Olympics 1960', Letter from Hale to Hare, 18 January 1960.
67 NACP: RG 59, CDF 1960–63, folder: 800.453/ 2–361 to 800.4531/ 8–1660, file: 800.4531/ 1–160, paper: 800.4531/ 2–260, State Department Memorandum of conversation between Shao-chang Hsu, Chinese Embassy and LaRue R. Lutkins, Deputy Director for Chinese Affairs, 2 February 1960.
68 NACP: RG 59, CDF 1960–63, folder: 800.453/ 2–361 to 800.4531/ 8–1660, file: 800.4531/ 1–160, paper: 800.4531/ 1–1360, Letter from Macomber to Dorn, House of Representatives, 13 January 1960.
69 Judd represented Minnesota in the House of Representatives, an outspoken anti-communist and advocate of the primacy of the ROC.
70 NACP: RG 59, CDF 1960–63, folder: 800.453/ 2–361 to 800.4531/ 8–1660, file: 800.4531/ 1–160, paper: 800.4531/ 2–360, State Department Memorandum of conversation between Dr Walter Judd, House of Representatives and Martin, 3 February 1960.
71 NACP: RG 59, CDF 1960–63, folder: 800.453/ 2–361 to 800.4531/ 8–1660, file: 800.4531/ 1–160, paper: 800.4531/ 2–360, State Department Memorandum of conversation between Hale, Hare and Lutkins, 3 February 1960.
72 NACP: RG 59, CDF 1960–63, folder: 800.453/ 2–361 to 800.4531/ 8–1660, file: 800.4531/ 1–160, paper: 800.4531/ 2–1160, State Department Memorandum of conversation between Hsu and Martin, 11 February 1960.
73 NACP: RG 59, CDF, 1960–63, folder: 800.453/ 2–361 to 800.4531/ 8–1660, file: 800.4531/ 1–160, paper: 800.4531/ 2–1260, State Department Memorandum of conversation between Hale and Rosen, 12 February 1960.
74 NACP: RG 59, BFEA, Assistant Secretary for Far Eastern Affairs, Subject, Name, Country Files 1960–63, 1960 Subject Files, folder: 'Memorandum of Conversation – Australia' to 'Interparliamentary Union, Tokyo', file: '1960 Olympics', State Department Memorandum from Parsons, Far Eastern Affairs to Hare, 18 February 1960.
75 NACP: RG 59, BFEA, Assistant Secretary for Far Eastern Affairs, Subject, Name, Country Files 1960–63, 1960 Subject Files, folder: 'Memorandum of Conversation

     – Australia' to 'Interparliamentary Union, Tokyo', file: '1960 Olympics', State Department Memorandum from Parsons, Far Eastern Affairs to Hare, 18 February 1960.

76 NACP: RG 59, CDF 1960–63, folder: 800.453/ 2–361 to 800.4531/ 8–1660, file: 800.4531/ 1–160, paper: 800.4531/ 2–1760, State Department Memorandum of conversation between Hale and Hare, 17 February 1960.

77 NACP: RG 59, CDF 1960–63, folder: 800.453/ 2–361 to 800.4531/ 8–1660, file: 800.4531/ 1–160, paper: 800.4531/ 2–1960, State Department Memorandum of conversation between Hsu and Martin, 19 February 1960.

78 NACP: RG 59, CDF 1960–63, folder: 800.453/ 2–361 to 800.4531/ 8–1660, file: 800.4531/ 1–160, paper: 800.4531/ 2–1960, State Department Memorandum of conversation between Hsu and Martin, 19 February 1960.

79 NACP: RG 59, CDF 1960–63, folder: 800.453/ 2–361 to 800.4531/ 8–1660, file: 800.4531/ 1–160, paper: 800.4531/ 2–1960, State Department Memorandum of conversation between Hsu and Martin, 19 February 1960.

80 NACP: RG 59, BFEA, Assistant Secretary for Far Eastern Affairs, Subject, Name, Country Files 1960–63, 1960 Subject Files, folder: 'Memorandum of Conversation – Australia' to 'Interparliamentary Union, Tokyo', file: '1960 Olympics', State Department Memorandum from Parsons, Far Eastern Affairs to Hare, 18 February 1960.

81 NACP: RG 59, CDF 1960–63, folder: 800.453/ 2–361 to 800.4531/ 8–1660, file: 800.4531/ 1–160, paper: 800.4531/ 2–560, Outgoing Telegram from Herter to US Embassy Rome, 11 February 1960.

82 NACP: RG 59, BFEA, Assistant Secretary for Far Eastern Affairs; Subject, Name, Country Files 1960–63, 1960 Subject Files, Folder: from 'Memorandum of Conversation – Australia' to 'Interparliamentary Union, Tokyo', file: '1960 Olympics', 1960, Memorandum 'The Olympics and the GRC', 4 April 1960.

11

Decentring US sports diplomacy: the 1980 Moscow boycott through contemporary Asian–African perspectives*

Joseph Eaton

The boycott of the 1980 Moscow Olympics is commonly described as having been a fiasco. The titles of books on the boycott tell of President Jimmy Carter's failed response to the Soviet invasion of Afghanistan – *Dropping the Torch: Jimmy Carter, the Olympic Boycott, and the Cold War* by Nicholas Evan Sarantakes (2010) – and the unfair treatment given athletes, denied their chance to compete at Moscow – *Boycott: Stolen Dreams of the 1980 Moscow Olympic Games* by Jerry Caraccioli and Tom Caraccioli (2008). The wrong nations boycotted, the Olympic movement was damaged and the athletes suffered, while the Soviets remained in Afghanistan. The boycott's legacy – and lesson for possible future boycotts – is best summed up in the cliché, 'Olympic boycotts do not work.'[1] This chapter deals with the places where American diplomacy on the boycott did work. All of the examples examined are from the Global South: either East Asian or African nations that joined the boycott. Yet the story of the American diplomatic effort becomes more complicated as understandings of the meaning of boycott were reinterpreted to suit local perspectives.

The Olympic boycott – at the nexus of international sport and diplomacy – was the most visible manifestation of opposition to the Soviet Union. In early 1980, the reaction of non-aligned nations to the Soviet invasion had been immediate and nearly united. A United Nations General Assembly resolution condemning the Soviet invasion was approved on 14 January by a vote of 104 to 18 (with 18 abstentions).[2] The *Washington Post* described the vote as 'Moscow's most stunning diplomatic defeat since the world condemned its 1956 invasion of Hungary'.[3] As a writer for the *Christian Science Monitor* noted at the time, calls for an Olympic boycott made from the developing world – including that from the 28 January Islamabad meeting of the Islamic Conference – were more prone to resonate in some European capitals than President Carter's haranguing.[4]

As Jenifer Parks has shown, Soviet authorities, fearful of a repetition of previous boycotts, worked assiduously to include as many nations as possible at Moscow. The USSR, long the champion of involving developing nations in international sport, faced a global boycott in 1980. The sixty-five-nation boycott denied the Soviets their long-awaited sport diplomacy triumph.[5]

However, judging the success of American sport diplomacy in 1980 also demands scrutiny of how 'Carter's boycott' was interpreted by participating nations. Within East Asia and Africa, the boycott was read to suit local perspectives, co-opted by national authorities and media. There was no single boycott, as re-examination of the boycott within different national contexts shows a complicated variety of purposes for joining the boycott, ranging from public display of governmental fiscal austerity by corrupt regimes, to support for a growing pan-Islamic movement, to reinvigorating the non-aligned movement in order to punish a belligerent superpower, to enforcing authoritarian rule at home. The 1980 boycott also resonated with the memory of previous Olympic protests, particularly Indonesia's attempt to create an alternate Olympiad in 1963 and the twenty-two-nation boycott of the 1976 Montreal Olympics made in response to the New Zealand rugby All Blacks' tour of South Africa.

Reappraisal of the 1980 boycott also necessitates taking a fresh look at the alternative sporting events that were created for the athletes from boycotting nations, particularly the Liberty Bell Classic, a two-day track meet held in Philadelphia on 16 and 17 July, just days before the Moscow Games began. These forgotten sporting diplomatic initiatives proved effective for how they were interpreted alongside the national boycotts of some nations in Asia and Africa. However, the boycott overshadowed other American foreign policy objectives as the human rights-conscious Carter administration settled for Olympic non-participation as the measure of successful diplomacy.

Indonesia's boycott and the non-aligned movement

Indonesia's role in the 1980 Olympic boycott was especially symbolic, not for Indonesia's role in international sport (Indonesia did not win an Olympic medal until 1988), but as a continuation of the nation's historical commitment to the non-aligned movement and tradition of rebellion against Olympic authorities. In 1962, under pressure from Arab states and the People's Republic of China (PRC), the Indonesian Olympic Committee (Komite Olahraga Nasional Indonesia) prevented athletes and officials from both the Republic of China (ROC) and Israel from receiving visas to attend the fourth Asian Games. The International Olympic Committee (IOC) responded by suspending Indonesia, the first suspension in that governing body's history. The Indonesian rejoinder far outweighed the nation's miniscule Olympic profile. President Sukarno retaliated by creating an 'alternative Olympics', the Games of the New Emerging Forces (GANEFO), first held in 1963 in Jakarta.[6] GANEFO – given the revolutionary motto 'Onward, No Retreat!' – was established for post-colonial and socialist 'emerging nations'. Sukarno, in the tradition of the 1955 Bandung Conference, relished the chance to challenge the neo-colonialism of the Olympic movement: 'Let us declare frankly that sport has something to do with politics. And Indonesia now proposes to mix sport with politics.'[7] A writer for *Sports Illustrated* described the games – held in a Soviet-built 103,000 seat arena and funded by the People's Republic of China – as perhaps the 'most completely disorganized sports event of which history has any record'.[8] Yet the GANEFO episode, if dubious from the standard of international athletic competition, illustrated the potential for a large-scale boycott or even a permanent, competing Olympiad for non-aligned nations.

Soon afterwards, the IOC – threatened by the creation of a non-aligned rival games – welcomed Indonesia back into the Olympic fold. However, the federations for some specific sports banned Indonesian athletes from competition, provoking an Indonesian boycott of the 1964 Summer Olympics. While Indonesia had never won an Olympic medal, the young nation had boxed above its weight, forging an important symbolic role in international sporting politics.

In 1980, Indonesian leaders again perceived more benefit from a boycott than from competition and the dubious chance of earning Olympic medals. The boycott served to cement the alliance with the US but also highlighted the cause of non-aligned/Islamic solidarity. As a vital US ally in East Asia, major oil producer and most populous Muslim nation, the importance of Indonesia's boycott to the Carter administration's global effort should not be discounted. Yet Indonesian authorities publicly framed their boycott around anticolonial, non-aligned themes reminiscent of President Sukarno's Indonesia of the 1950s and 1960s, ironically, the lowest point in US–Indonesian relations.

In early January, the chairman of the Indonesian Olympic Committee (KONI), Major General Gatot Suwagic Kubuwono, declared the probability of joining Saudi Arabia in boycotting the Moscow Games. After meeting with President Suharto, Suwagic declared that 'KONI is waiting for the government decision whether or not to boycott the Olympic Games.'[9] A week later, in Bandung, West Java, demonstrators belonging to an Islamic youth group burnt a Soviet flag in protest against the Soviet invasion of Afghanistan. The demonstrators demanded that the Indonesian government sever relations with Moscow and rescind the Soviet boxing team invitation to an international boxing tournament to be held in Indonesia. The location of the protests, Bandung, the site of the seminal non-aligned conference a generation before, fittingly symbolised Indonesia's renewed interest in challenging a global superpower. Similar demonstrations occurred in Jakarta, despite an official ban on public protests.[10]

In 1980, Indonesia once again used international sporting competition to take a stand in international politics. Indonesia – under scrutiny in Western media for atrocities in East Timor – used the Olympic boycott to change the subject while reclaiming status in the non-aligned movement.[11] Suharto's Indonesia – an ally and major oil supplier to the US – reclaimed the nationalist/non-aligned sporting rhetoric developed under the nation's first president, Sukarno.

The Philippines in crisis

Boycotting came at some cost to the Philippines. In contrast to Indonesia, the Philippines enjoyed a strong Olympic tradition, having sent the first team from Southeast Asia to the Olympics (1924), being the first to medal (1928), and being the first tropical nation to compete in the Winter Olympics (1972). Yet in 1980, the

Philippines' participation in the Olympic boycott brought a net gain to the Philippine government. By joining the American boycott, President Ferdinand Marcos embraced a national security agenda that was favourable to continued support from the United States while distracting from accusations of corruption and human rights abuses against his authoritarian regime.

Late 1979 and early 1980 was a turbulent time for Marcos and the Philippines. The Philippines' economy was in a downward spiral, suffering from the dual burden of high petroleum prices and low prices for its primary export products: coconut oil and sugar.[12] Marcos had been rebuked publicly by Jaime L. Cardinal Sin, leader of the Catholic Church in the Philippines, for his personal extravagance and outlandish spending priorities, criticisms that echoed widely in the nation of forty million Catholics.[13] On New Year's Eve, government officials announced the discovery of a plot to kill Marcos and other Philippine officials.[14] A month later, Filipinos experienced their first elections for provincial and municipal offices since the declaration of martial law in September 1972, though critics doubted the results.[15]

Moreover, Americans had grown weary of their long-time ally. Marcos was routinely scrutinised by the American media for human rights abuses. In February, the House of Representatives heard testimony about his regime's abuse of political prisoners. A movement was afoot to trim military aid to Marcos, while some in Congress had contemplated moving American bases out of the Philippines. Even the most sympathetic assessments of the Marcos regime doubted whether it could survive should the Soviet Union choose to support the anti-Marcos insurgency.[16] Marcos also questioned the American commitment to the Philippines, the Iranian crisis being an indicator of the fainthearted aspirations and diminished power of the US.[17]

On 28 March, Marcos made the announcement that the Philippine team would not go to Moscow. Marcos's appearance on Philippine television came after a week-long absence from public view and several days after the eleventh-hour cancellation of a meeting with Chilean president Augusto Pinochet. Pinochet, accused of the murder of political opponents in the wake of his 1973 coup, was an unwelcome guest for Marcos, under the microscope of the international media for his own abuses.[18]

In his pronouncement to the Philippine public, Marcos framed his decision around themes of domestic crisis and not the Soviet invasion of Afghanistan, declaring that the boycott served the purpose of fiscal austerity, helping to meet his goal of cutting government expenditures by 15 per cent.[19] Yet the spendthrift Marcos's claim that the Moscow boycott served austerity was deceptive. The Philippines turned down Soviet financial incentives to fund travel to the Moscow Games.[20] Moreover, the Philippines found the financial resources to send a team to Philadelphia to participate in the Liberty Bell Games, making Marcos's previous pronouncement of austerity doubtful.

The Philippines' participation in the boycott earned Marcos a consequential diplomatic reward – renewal of trust from the Carter administration. Just weeks after announcing his nation's boycott, Marcos travelled to Hawaii, his first visit to the US since taking power, to address a group of American newspaper publishers. Marcos protested what he claimed to be the distortions of his regime in the American press, declaring that his one-man rule was 'authoritarian' but not 'tyrannical'.[21] President

Carter did not travel to Hawaii, but instead dispatched Assistant Secretary of State for East Asian and Pacific Affairs Richard Holbrooke and former Secretary of State Dean Rusk. While Carter kept his distance from Marcos, the Philippine dictator received a significant reward from Rusk and Holbrooke, a letter from Carter offering thanks for the Philippines' support of the boycott.[22]

After his meetings with Carter's emissaries and Pentagon officials, Marcos crowed that the US was once again 'a dependable ally' and that he had 'less fears of Asia being abandoned' if war were to break out in Europe or the Middle East. Marcos praised the Olympic boycott and other anti-Soviet initiatives of the Carter administration, continuing his calls for the US to assume even stronger leadership while assailing 'the reservations of the European countries' regarding the US response to the Soviet invasion of Afghanistan.[23] Under siege at home and in danger of losing American support, Marcos understood that participation in the boycott was helpful to his hold on power. By the spring of 1980, the Carter administration's focus on a human rights agenda for the Philippines had drifted far beyond the horizon as a national security agenda – manifest in the Olympic boycott – came to dominate Philippine–American relations.

China's boycott: 'Out of Asia, into the World'

Chairman Mao Zedong's death and the end of the Gang of Four's reign over China in 1976 brought a more favourable official attitude concerning sport. As a part of China's post-Mao opening to the world, the Chinese Communist Party embraced again international sport as a means and measure of national greatness. Not coincidentally, the PRC's new 'paramount leader', Deng Xiaoping, had orchestrated national sports policy before the Cultural Revolution. In 1979, China's National Sports Commission embraced an 'Olympic Model'. That year's national games carried the theme 'The New Long March', reflecting the work needed to bring Chinese sport to international prominence.[24] 1980 brought a new slogan that might have served as a generic theme for Deng's China: 'Out of Asia, into the World'.[25] As a *Christian Science Monitor* headline noted on the eve of the 1984 Los Angeles Olympics, 'Friendship no longer ranks ahead of winning for Chinese Olympians.'[26]

In retrospect, China's support of the 1980 boycott was a sacrifice of some magnitude. Having re-entered the Olympic fold in December 1979, the PRC was certain to win its first medals at the Moscow Games. Nevertheless, for one more time, chances for Olympic glory would be subordinate to geopolitics.

The PRC's boycott alongside the US was symbolic of a convergence of interests and deepening of cooperation. Upon taking office, the Carter administration imagined improved relations with the PRC through cultural diplomacy, with athletic exchanges being a key component.[27] The White House also welcomed a transformed China as a balance to the Soviet Union's growing military power, a goal that became more vital after the Soviet invasion of Afghanistan.[28] The emphasis on sport as a diplomatic tool was not surprising given the apparent successes of 'ping-pong diplomacy'.

While many allied governments and media resisted President Carter's pressure to boycott, the PRC government and media showed no hesitation in staying away from Moscow. The degree to which China embraced the boycott shows the significance of the momentous geopolitical shifts of the 1960s and 1970s, of the PRC's move away from the USSR and towards the US. The PRC welcomed the end of détente between the US and USSR, of which the Moscow boycott was the denouement. The Xinhua news agency praised the American 'rethinking' of the Soviet Union's motives, warmly reporting the aggressive statements of US State Department and Carter administration officials.[29] Xinhua eagerly reported the US Senate's affirmation of the Olympic boycott and embargo on selling advanced-technology products to the USSR.[30] PRC media portrayed the global boycott in common terms with the national boycott, stressing the shared dangers from the USSR. Xinhua reported the forty-two-nation Islamic Council's boycott efforts within the context of the Soviet Union's threat to both Pakistan and China, but not through the lens of pan-Islamism, a potentially dangerous movement given separatist movements in the western province of Xinjiang.[31]

The boycott also allowed for the PRC to imagine an enhanced role within Asia through sports diplomacy. In early April, Chinese Olympic authorities called for a joint meeting of the Malaysian, Japanese and PRC national Olympic committees in the hope of influencing Japan to support the boycott.[32] The notion of the PRC and Malaysia, neither of which had ever won an Olympic medal, trying to influence Japan – the nation with the most glorious Olympic history in Asia – to boycott was ironic. It was also telling of China's new aspiration to regional power.

PRC sporting officials never wavered in their support of a boycott. On 8 January 1980, just four days after the White House made its first public statements on the possibility of a boycott, officials at the Physical Culture and Sports Commission expressed the probability that China would boycott.[33] These sentiments were soon echoed by Zhong Shitong, the head of the Chinese Olympic Committee.[34] A few weeks later, Chinese Olympic Committee officials repeated these themes of China participating in a global boycott in the spirit of Olympic 'peace and friendship'.[35] In the closing days of the Moscow Olympics, the official Beijing *Renmin* (*People's Daily*) reported on the willing sacrifice of China's highly rated gymnastics teams, whose athletes embraced the boycott with altruism and patriotism.[36]

To perhaps a greater degree than any other nation, Chinese officials welcomed American efforts to organise substitute games.[37] While, from a contemporary perspective, the People's Republic of China's participation in the Liberty Bell Classic appears trivial, in 1980 the two-day mini-Olympiad was proportionate to the PRC's sporting profile. The PRC had competed in just one Summer Olympics: in the 1952 Helsinki Games where, having arrived late for the competition, only one Chinese athlete participated. The ROC's participation at the Melbourne 1956 Olympics prompted a PRC boycott, beginning a generation of exile from the Olympic movement. The PRC sent a team of twenty-four athletes to Lake Placid but none medalled.

The PRC media eagerly welcomed the Liberty Bell Classic, praising the strength of the competition, noting that the event was the largest track and field meet in the United States since the 1932 Los Angeles Olympics.[38] In a front-page article on 19

July, at the close of the games, the *Renmin* gave a glowing account of the Chinese athletes' performance in Philadelphia. As the article described, the American crowd had hailed the PRC's ten medal winners (five gold) at University of Pennsylvania's 'huge' Franklin Field. Most significantly, the *Renmin* announced the PRC's participation in the Liberty Bell Classic within the context of the new national sports motto, 'Out of Asia, into the World'.[39]

The Liberty Bell Classic gave visibility to the PRC's growing relationship with the US, institutionalised sporting relations between the two nations, and allowed for international competition for the Chinese national teams at an international track meet in the United States – all significant achievements. In contrast, while the Philippines participated in the Liberty Bell Classic, their national efforts produced no enthusiasm within the local media. The US-led sporting diplomacy initiatives of 1980 – the Olympic boycott and Liberty Bell Classic – suited both the PRC's penchant for 'friendship first' in international sport and a newly rediscovered taste for athletic competition.[40]

In late March 1980, as other nations wavered in their support of the boycott, American officials noted after Secretary Vance's meeting with Vice-Minister, Ministry of Foreign Affairs, Zhang Wenjin that, 'China's support is total, both for the boycott and alternative games.'[41] As American diplomatic cables noted at the time, the Olympic boycott provided a favourable topic within Sino-American diplomatic conversations, helping to increase the pace of normalisation between the US and PRC.[42] Quite fittingly, the PRC's participation 'saved' the 1984 Los Angeles Olympics in the wake of the announced boycott of the USSR and most of the Soviet bloc.[43] The Los Angeles Games also saw the PRC's first Olympic medals ('breaking the big duck egg' in reference to China's previous count of zero medals).[44]

The significance of China's boycott was noted by National Security Adviser Zbigniew Brzezinski; an advocate of stronger ties with the PRC. In a memo to Carter, Brzezinski rated the impact of the PRC's boycott with that of a strategic core of countries:

> The four most important nations in the world in Soviet eyes – i.e., the United States, China, Germany, and Japan – are not attending. Even if all other nations had decided to participate, the fact that these four nations were not attending was enough to get the political message across to Moscow.

Brzezinski proclaimed to Carter that the boycott had been 'totally successful in East Asia'.[45]

Contemporary Chinese historical memory struggles to understand the logic of the 1980 boycott. Accustomed to seeing Chinese athletes vying for top honours at international sporting competition and instinctually suspicious of American foreign policy, the notion that the PRC ever welcomed an Olympic boycott in connection with Washington is perplexing.[46] A six-volume history of Chinese sports published on the eve of the Beijing Games failed to even mention the 1980 boycott or the Liberty Bell Classic.[47] While the PRC and US were of one team in 1980, their diplomatic and sporting glories of that year were the product of a unique, and fleeting, convergence of interests.[48]

Egypt's boycott: the Soviet threat and Arab solidarity

Like the PRC, President Anwar Sadat's Egypt offered strong, early support for a boycott of the Moscow Olympics as part of a strategy to challenge the Soviet Union in coordination with the United States. Egypt's response to the Soviet invasion of Afghanistan was vociferous, unlike that of many American allies. From an Egyptian perspective, the Soviet invasion was the first move in a Soviet offensive to control the Middle East's energy resources. For some countries, such as Egypt, joining the boycott in 1980 was a cheap substitute for a robust anti-Soviet policy. Particularly in Western Europe (West Germany, Norway, Thatcher government) and Japan – where economic sanctions and increased military build-up were unpalatable – the Olympic boycott served as a low-cost, high-profile symbol of cooperation with the US.[49] In the case of Egypt, the concern was reversed, as editorials urged the US to go beyond boycotting the Olympics. Just weeks after the Soviet invasion, the Egyptian media prodded the US to take an assertive role in forming a Western bloc to confront the Soviets by various means of which Olympic boycott was just a beginning.

In calling for a robust US response to Soviet encroachment upon the Persian Gulf Region, Egypt foreshadowed themes from President Carter's 23 January State of the Union Address, the 'Carter Doctrine', advocating an activist, forceful US policy in the Middle East. The emphatic Egyptian embrace of the Olympic boycott signifies how the de-Sovietisation of the past several years had been exacerbated by the Soviet move on Afghanistan, suggesting possibilities for further American cooperation with their new ally in the Middle East.[50] As was also clear, Egyptians doubted Carter's capacity to orchestrate a forceful challenge to the USSR.

Egypt's boycott also served to end that nation's estrangement from other Arab nations.[51] In the wake of the March 1979 signing of the Israel–Egypt Peace Treaty, other Arab states ostracised Egypt, diplomatically and economically.[52] The Arab League moved its headquarters from Cairo to Tunis, and the Persian Gulf Organization for Development in Egypt disbanded.[53] Olympic boycott put Egypt in alignment with its biggest benefactors: the United States and Saudi Arabia.[54]

An 11 January 'Voice of the Arabs' radio commentary advocated the creation of a strong Islamic bloc (*tajam'in*) against the USSR – with a capable military component as well as direct military assistance to the Afghan people. The Islamic bloc would demonstrate that 'the Islamic states are not morsels which it can swallow piecemeal once its appetite is whetted'.[55]

Into the spring, the Egyptian media framed the boycott around their nation's role in the non-aligned movement. As the government-run Middle East News Agency explained, the Egyptian stance served the causes of 'justice, fraternity and peace'. The boycott was a step in combatting 'ideological' and 'colonialist' domination.[56] In 1976 Egypt had been hesitant to join the anti-apartheid boycott in protest of New Zealand's rugby tour of South Africa. Not until competing for three days (with no medals) did the Egyptian team grudgingly leave Montreal. In 1980, Egypt never vacillated in its support for a boycott. In January, the chairman of the Egyptian Olympic Committee announced that body's support for the boycott if the USSR did not withdraw from Afghanistan.[57] Egyptian media reported on further meetings between the heads of Egyptian sporting associations and government officials after Sadat's announcement, yet no dissent by athletes or sporting officials was ever mentioned. Sadat's authoritarian Egypt – eager to join with the US and other Arab/Muslim nations – spoke with one voice in 1980.[58]

Sub-Saharan Africa: a boycott of austerity

In sub-Saharan Africa, the Olympic boycott offered the US the possibility to connect with a rich heritage of activist sports diplomacy. Kenya welcomed a boycott in response to the Soviet invasion of Afghanistan from the first mention of the idea at a NATO summit meeting in early January.[59] The significance of Kenya's boycott should not be underestimated. Kenya was the first nation to officially join in the boycott that had ever won an Olympic medal (twenty in total, with nine in both 1968 and 1972).[60] At a White House meeting in late February 1980, Kenya was mentioned as one of a group of five nations that, from an international sporting perspective, were vital to the boycott.[61]

As was the case with Egypt, Kenya's boycott alongside the US was a certainty. Less predictable was how Kenyan officials explained the boycott. President Daniel arap Moi, hesitant to publicise his nation's increasing military ties with the US, explained Kenya's boycott within the context of the country's history in the non-aligned movement.[62] While crises with Iran and the Soviet Union had spurred US–Kenyan cooperation in a range of areas, including military matters, Kenyan officials preferred to cast the boycott in terms of their nation's post-colonial and 'small nation' status. In making his announcement to join the boycott, Moi declared that 'It would be most inappropriate for any non-aligned nation to attend the Moscow Olympics while Soviet troops are in Afghanistan.'[63]

While Moi claimed that Kenya did not wish any harm to the Olympic movement, the threat to 'small nations' represented by the Soviet invasion of Afghanistan was impossible to ignore. Moi reminded his audience that Kenya's foreign policy was based on non-alignment and the territorial integrity of all nations, support for other small nations being key to that doctrine.[64] Given Kenya's international sporting presence and leadership within Africa, it is not surprising that, as a *New York Times* article noted, after Moi's announcement Kenya's commitment to a boycott immediately 'appeared to be having an impact across Africa'.[65]

In 1980, two significant factors contributed to Kenya's positive view of the Olympic boycott. Most significantly, in its short history Kenya had produced Olympic medal-winning boxers and distance runners but also national leaders who understood the potency of Olympic boycotting. A young nation, independent since December 1963,

Kenya had built a tradition of boycotts and, importantly, threatened Olympic boycotts. In 1963 Kenya refused to issue a visa to a South African official for an IOC meeting. The IOC moved the meeting out of Nairobi to Baden-Baden. In response, President Jomo Kenyatta threatened to lead an African boycott to protest South African and Portuguese participation at the Tokyo Olympics, precipitating a crisis that resulted in South Africa's ban from the Olympic movement.[66] In 1968, Kenya was at the head of an anticipated African boycott of the Mexico City Olympics should South Africa participate.[67] In response, the IOC backed down from readmitting South Africa. Four years later, a Kenyan-led threatened boycott pressured the IOC to expel Rhodesia just four days before the Munich opening ceremonies.[68] Kenya was at the core of nations promoting the 1976 African boycott that exposed the continuing apartheid in South Africa.[69] For Kenya, the lesson was clear – boycott and the threat of boycott worked. Not surprisingly, Moi continued to blend the approach to sport and diplomacy of Kenya's founding father, President Jomo Kenyatta (d. 1978).

Since-forgotten American plans for substitute sporting competitions also played a substantial part in creating a successful boycott in connection with Kenya. Kenyan diplomats and sporting officials welcomed the American sponsorship of a boxing tournament to be held in Kenya, in lieu of Olympic competition. In June, Harrison Kilonzo, the secretary of Kenya's Amateur Boxing Association, announced that the US had pledged US $469,000 to support the event, which was expected to involve athletes from at least forty nations.[70]

The 'Gold Cup of Kenya' (6–13 September 1980) included medallists from the US, Thailand, Dominican Republic, Kenya, South Korea, Israel, Great Britain and Puerto Rico.[71] The tournament captured the original spirit of the boycott, when the US government envisioned replacement events in several countries on different continents.[72] Kenya suited the need to connect with non-aligned countries and, from a sporting perspective, the choice of boxing was appropriate, as Kenyan boxing, and African boxing generally, was strong (seven medals as a continent in 1972 with three for Kenya).[73] Kenya also sent the second-largest contingent (thirty-four athletes, second only to the United States) to the Philadelphia Liberty Bell Classic, winning a total of four medals.[74]

With Kenya, one also sees a connection with the People's Republic of China's efforts to expand the boycott of the Moscow Games. In early March, the Kenyan Minister of Foreign Affairs, Dr Robert Ouko, reinforced the Kenyan government's policy on non-interference in the internal affairs of other states together with the Chinese ambassador to Kenya, the boycot serving as a symbol of mutual cooperation against the USSR.[75]

In another victory for American diplomacy, Kenya represented a 'turning point' in Muhammad Ali's February 1980 trip to Africa in support of the boycott. Carter had sent the celebrated American boxer on a goodwill tour of Africa to win African leaders' support. After being snubbed by Tanzanian president Julius Nyerere, Ali's trip received a boost when Kenyan president Daniel arap Moi warmly greeted Ali and reiterated his support of a boycott of the Moscow Games. Dogged by questions about American policy on South Africa and the failure of the US to support the

1976 African Olympic boycott, Kenya's support was the pinnacle of Ali's five-nation trip.[76]

Ghana's boycott of Moscow, in contrast to Egypt and Kenya, was shaped by particular national circumstances. Early discussion of the possibility of Ghana's participation in a boycott recalled the limited effectiveness of the 1976 African boycott of Montreal, a *Ghanaian Times* editorial pointing out that the African boycott was depicted as irresponsible in the Western press. The editorial proclaimed that Ghana should not be used 'as a pawn in the cold war'.[77] Yet in 1980, Ghana's decision would not come down to negative perceptions of the 1976 Montreal boycott, and had nothing to do with the Soviet Union, the US or the politics of race in Africa. The first nation in sub-Saharan Africa to achieve independence after World War II in 1957, Ghana was struggling as an independent nation. Ghana's participation in the boycott was a symbol of the severity of the crisis facing the country in early 1980.

Ghana president Hilla Limann, a respected career diplomat, took office in October 1979 in an election that had followed a military coup by the charismatic Flight Lieutenant Jerry Rawlings and the executions of three former Ghanaian leaders. Rawlings forced government and military leaders to repay money they had embezzled. Facing a billion-dollar foreign debt, unstable economy (with cocoa production at a twenty-year low and industry running at 25 per cent capacity due to a shortage of spare parts) and growing famine, Limann had scarce time to reform the nation's economy.[78] Rawlings had warned Limann that he was 'on probation' and that economic recovery and continuation of the anti-corruption campaign were to be priorities.[79]

So it is perhaps no surprise that Ghanaian Olympic participation fell victim to public perceptions of profligate government spending. In late April, the Christian newspaper *The Believer* decried the expense of sending an Olympic team to Moscow. 'Instead of spending any money on the games', the editorial suggested, 'we should prudently utilize the funds to boost our agriculture and industry.' 'One may ask', the author added in a refrain that is often repeated in discussing publicly funded sport and sport and diplomacy generally, 'that even if Ghana earns a gold medal at the games, does it really benefit us?'[80]

Less than a week before the opening of the Olympics, the Ghanaian government warned against stray athletes making their way to Moscow: 'The committee's decision of last May not to participate in the Moscow Olympics and any major international games outside Africa stems from the realization that Ghana's sportsmen and women are not sufficiently prepared for such major competitions.'[81] In fact, Ghana had won medals (one each in 1960, 1964 and 1972, all in boxing), unlike many nations that had sent teams to multiple Olympics. Nonetheless, in 1980 domestic politics trumped sport.

Symbolic austerity in the form of an Olympic boycott was not enough to save Limann, as the perception grew that his government was inept and corrupt. On 31 December 1981 Lieutenant Rawlings struck again in a coup (his 'Second Coming' and Ghana's fourth coup in fifteen years), jailing Limann and making himself Ghana's leader.

The boycott by Ghana alongside eighteen other African nations was an undeniable blow to Soviet prestige in the developing world. As a *Washington Post* reporter explained in a June 1979 article on the build-up to the Summer Games, 'What the Soviets fear most of all is a boycott by black African teams similar to the 1976 Montreal Games.'[82] During the July–August 1979 Spartakiade – an eighty-four-nation 'dress rehearsal' for the Moscow Olympics – Soviet officials diligently worked to avoid offending African nations, promising that 'The doors to Olympic Moscow will be tightly shut to the advocates of racism and apartheid.'[83] Despite these efforts, the Soviet Union – long an advocate of African nations in international sport, instrumental in pushing the IOC towards anti-racist/anti-apartheid policies – suffered from a large-scale African boycott in 1980. As such the invasion of Afghanistan squandered years of Soviet sport diplomacy.

While the African boycott was impressive, the Carter administration's ignorance of international sport nearly doomed the boycott in Africa. As Peter Ueberroth noted, during a March meeting at the White House South Africa was listed as a possible participant for an American-led alternative games.[84] As seen above, South Africa was the scourge of international sport, having been banned from the Olympics beginning in 1964 and then expelled from the Olympic movement by the IOC in 1970. South Africa had been the focus of the African boycott of the 1976 Summer Olympics, and the target of threatened boycotts in 1964, 1968 and 1972.[85] The Carter White House – apt at counting anti-Soviet allies but blind to the racial component of international sports diplomacy – nearly fumbled away its boycott, at least in Africa. The US was nearly on the wrong side of the Olympic colour line in Africa, again. As Umberto Tulli describes elsewhere in this volume, the Reagan administration – keen to prevent still another African boycott in 1984 – was more attuned to the South African problem in the build-up to the Los Angeles Olympics.

Conclusion: a decentred boycott

In the days leading up to the opening of the Moscow Olympics, a *New York Times* headline proclaimed, 'For Africans, yet another year of Olympic sacrifice.' Some athletes had missed their second, or even third Olympic Games.[86] The same was true for some Asian athletes. Yet, despite the common sacrifices of athletes, the Moscow boycott served disparate purposes, as leaders and media reinterpreted the meaning of boycotting the Moscow Olympics to suit tradition and necessity.

In Indonesia, the People's Republic of China and Kenya, boycotting was part of a long-standing national tradition of using sporting boycott to challenge the colonial, Western-dominated international order. The PRC and Egypt welcomed the end of détente and the Carter administration's increasing focus on a national security agenda. Egyptian protests against the Soviet Union also echoed those in other Arab and Muslim nations, a consequential gesture in the wake of Egypt's peace treaty with Israel. Ghana and the Philippines exploited the symbolism of a sacrificial boycott to show dedication to trimming government expenditures. In addition, the Philippines publicly exploited the boycott to steady relations with the US.

The boycott provided a chance for the US to cooperate with nations that had been vital to the non-aligned/'small nation'/'emerging nation' movements – China, Ghana, Kenya and Indonesia. The Islamic component of Egypt and Indonesia's boycotts was similarly intriguing for offering the US a chance to connect with those nations alienated by the Soviet Union's attack on a predominately Muslim nation. These were no small accomplishments considering recent American foreign policy setbacks in Southeast Asia and the Middle East. While President Carter failed to recruit several close allies into the boycott, it was the Soviet Union – and not the United States – that was increasingly isolated.

Similarly, while the Liberty Bell Classic is usually dismissed as having been a failure, as told by a contemporary *Montreal Gazette* article headline, 'Philly meet poor substitute for Olympics', the Philadelphia gathering, as well as other substitute sporting events, satisfied the need for athletic competition for some boycotting nations, as seen above.[87] These alternative games deserved to be judged not by the times and scores of the athletes but for the positive images the competitions provided for boycotting nations as well as their impact on relations with the US. Such positive viewpoints increased the 'attraction' of the United States at a time when Cold War divisions were prominent, and are perhaps a potent example of sport diplomacy as soft power.

Examination of various national contexts of the 1980 boycott in Asia and Africa also reminds us that 1980 was a difficult time in many nations' political and economic histories. Developing nations struggled with high oil prices and foreign debt. The authoritarian Philippine government struggled violently with internal dissent amid recession. Egypt had made peace with Israel at the cost of losing Arab patrons. Ghana, formerly the pride of post-colonial countries, struggled to stay afloat both economically and politically. 1980 was a terrible year for human rights, both in *and* outside the Soviet bloc. Soviet authorities were not wrong in their description of the strong support for the boycott among 'dictatorial' regimes.[88]

While deemed successful from various Asian and African perspectives, the boycott may not have suited real, long-term US foreign policy interests. As seen in local views of the boycott, an anti-Soviet national security perspective was not always apparent within national boycotts. The boycott was read into existing nationalistic, non-aligned and even pan-Islamic strains of international sporting diplomacy, advancing powerful rhetoric that strengthened dictatorial governments at the expense of national Olympic committees and sporting institutions.[89] Still more troubling is the probability that the boycott – a negative act of simple non-participation in a sporting event – substituted for either substantive cooperation in other American-led initiatives to advance anti-corruption/good governance, or obscured other troubles in those nations' relations with the US, for example human rights abuses. The 1980 boycott – meant to punish the misdeeds of the USSR – suited the authoritarian, parochial and chauvinistic rhetoric common to the developing world without advancing long-term democratic or economic development.

Notes

* My thanks to J. Simon Rofe, Heather Dichter, William Gouveia and David Rowe for their comments on my paper and to Simon for organising the 'Sport and Diplomacy: Message, Mode and Metaphor' colloquium at SOAS University of London in July 2015. My gratitude as well to Jerry Hsaio and Jue Wu for help in finding research materials. A research grant from the Taiwan Ministry of Science and Technology (the former National Science Council) made this research possible (grant NSC 100–2410-H-004-118). Portions of this chapter were the basis for an article published in *Diplomatic History*, 450:5 (2016).

1 Quoted in Howard Berkes, 'Talk of boycotting Russian Olympics stirs emotions' NPR (National Public Radio),17 July 2013, available at www.npr.org/blogs/thetwo-way/2013/07/17/203067633/talk-of-boycotting-russian-olympics-stirs-emotions (accessed 23 April 2015).

2 J. Bruce Amstulz, *Afghanistan: The First Five Years of Soviet Occupation* (Washington, DC: National Defense University Press, 1988), 329–31. As President Carter noted in his memoir, even Cuba, a Soviet client state, worked to distance itself from the Soviet invasion. Jimmy Carter, *Keeping Faith: Memoirs of a President* (Fayetteville, AK: University of Arkansas Press, 1995), 479–80; as Derick L. Hulme Jr notes, Japan was 'careful to act [regarding a boycott] only in concert with a significant number of Third World nations'. Hulme, *The Political Olympics: Moscow, Afghanistan and the 1980 US Boycott* (Westport, CT: Praeger, 1990), 67.

3 Karen DeYoung, 'Overwhelming U.N. vote condemns Soviets', *Washington Post*, 15 January 1980, A1.

4 Jonathan Harsch, 'Olympic boycott issue tests strength of European community', *Christian Science Monitor*, 31 January 1980, 4.

5 Jenifer Parks, 'Welcoming the "Third World": Soviet sport diplomacy, developing nations, and the Olympic Games', in Heather L. Dichter and Andrew L. Johns (eds), *Diplomatic Games: Sport, Statecraft, and International Relations since 1945* (Lexington, KY: University of Kentucky Press, 2014). As Baruch Hazan remarks, the non-aligned boycott deprived the USSR of 'one of the most effective instruments of the Soviet propaganda machine'. Hazan, *Olympic Sports and Propaganda Games: Moscow 1980* (New Brunswick, NJ: Transaction Books, 1982), 5, 125–6.

6 The term 'New Emerging Forces' came from a book by an American, Vera Micheles Dean, *Builders of Emerging Nations* (New York: Holt, Rinehart & Winston, 1961). For an examination of the geopolitics of GANEFO, see Russell Field, 'Re-entering the sporting world: China's sponsorship of the 1963 Games of the New Emerging Forces (GANEFO)', *International Journal of the History of Sport*, 31 (2014).

7 Richard Espy, *The Politics of the Olympic Games: With an Epilogue, 1976–1980* (Berkeley, CA: University of California Press, 1979), 81.

8 T. Peter Ross, 'Sukarno's lavish Ganefo was mostly Snafu', *Sports Illustrated*, 2 December 1963, 28–31.

9 'Consideration of Olympic boycott', Hong Kong Agence France-Presse (AFP) in English, 9 January 1980, Indonesia Daily Report. Asia & Pacific, FBIS-APA-08–006 on 1980–01–09 Readex: Foreign Broadcast Information Service (hereafter FBIS).

10 'Demonstrations in Bandung, Jakarta', FBIS Hong Kong AFP in English, 16 January

1980, Indonesia Daily Report. Asia & Pacific, FBIS-APA-80-011 on 1980-01-16.

11 'No bleep on the moral radar', *Washington Post*, 2 February 1980, A10.

12 Jennifer Conroy Franco, *Elections and Democratization in the Philippines* (London: Routledge, 2001), 190 n.115.

13 'Philippine Cardinal sees civil war', *Washington Post*, 5 September 1979, A14.

14 'Manila reports uncovering plot to kill Marcos and other aides', *New York Times*, 1 January 1980, 3.

15 Henry Kamm, 'Marcos's political scheming leaves opposition rudderless', *New York Times*, 3 February 1980, E3.

16 Frank Mount, 'The Philippines, 1980', *Asian Affairs*, 8 (1980), 122–3; Jack Anderson, 'Philippines: another Iran?', *Washington Post*, 20 April 1980, D7.

17 'Marcos questions Carter on Iran', *New York Times*, 20 April 1980, 15.

18 'Chilean cancels tour after abrupt Marcos rebuff', *New York Times*, 23 March 1980, 3.

19 'Marcos tells Press Philippines to boycott Moscow Olympics'; FBIS Hong Kong AFP in English Daily Report Asia & Pacific, FBIS-APA-80-065 on 1980-04-02. 'Chilean cancels tour after abrupt Marcos rebuff', 3.

20 Hulme, *Political Olympics*, 77.

21 'Marcos, in Hawaii, gets a mixed Filipino reception', *New York Times*, 22 April 1980, A8.

22 Sara Steinmetz, *Democratic Transition and Human Rights: Perspectives on U.S. Foreign Policy* (Albany, NY: SUNY Press, 1994), 169; Peter Tarnoff to Zbigniew Brzezinski, 'Proposed Presidential Letter to Philippine President Marcos on the occasion of his visit to Honolulu April 1980. United States', PH01646, Department of State. Executive Secretariat, 16 April 1980.

23 Frederic A. Moritz, 'Marcos tries to polish tarnished human rights image, boost US ties', *Christian Science Monitor*, 29 April 1980, 6.

24 Susan E. Brownell, 'Sports', in Dingbo Wu and Patrick D. Murphy (eds), *Handbook of Chinese Popular Culture* (Westport, CT: Greenwood Press, 1994), 126.

25 Xu Guoqi, *Olympic Dreams: China and Sports, 1895–2008* (Cambridge, MA: Harvard University Press, 2008), 197.

26 Julian Baum, 'Friendship no longer ranks ahead of winning for Chinese Olympians', *Christian Science Monitor*, 26 July 1984, 3.

27 'Memorandum from the President's Assistant for National Security Affairs (Brzezinski) to President Carter', Washington, 14 June 1977, *Foreign Relations of the United States, 1977–1980* volume XIII, China, Document 31.

28 In prior discussions with Deng Xiaoping, President Carter expressed his desire for the United States to have better relations with developing nations, in hopes that China could help to produce global stability, particularly in Southeast Asia and Africa. 'Memorandum of Conversation', Washington, 29 January 1979, *Foreign Relations of the United States, 1977–1980* Volume XIII, China (Washington, DC: Department of State, 2013), Document 202. For a survey of increasing PRC–US military relations, including cooperation in covert wars in Cambodia and Afghanistan, see James Mann, *About Face: A History of America's Curious Relationship with China from Nixon to Clinton* (New York: Knopf, 1999), chapter 5, 'Carter's Cold War'. For a contemporary depiction of growing US–PRC military relations in the wake of the Soviet invasion of

Afghanistan, see Bernard Gwertzman, 'Arms not included: in Congress, Peking gets most-favored-nation status in trading', *New York Times*, 25 January 1980, A1.

29 'Hodding Carter assesses Soviet goals', FBIS Beijing Xinhua in English 3 April 1980 FBIS-CHI-80–066 1980–04–03.

30 'U.S. reaffirms opposition to Soviet invasion of Afghanistan', FBIS Beijing Xinhua 25 June 1980 B1 Daily Report. People's Republic of China, FBIS-CHI-80–125.

31 'Islamic Council official on Soviet threat', FBIS Beijing Xinhua in English 24 January 1980 page 1 Daily Report FBIS-CHI-80–018 on 1980–01–25.

32 'JOC in dilemma over PRC proposal for sports meeting', FBIS Tokyo KYODO C1 Daily Report, ASIA & PACIFIC, FBIS-APA-80–067 on 1980–04–02.

33 'PRC may reconsider participation in Moscow Olympics', FBIS Tokyo *Kyodo* in English 8 January 1980 China Daily Report FBIS-CHI-80–006 on 1980–01–09.

34 'PRC supports idea of Olympic boycott', FBIS Tokyo *Kyodo* in English 22 January 22 1980 China Daily Report FBIS-CHI-08–016 on 1980–01–23.

35 'PRC Olympic official holds press conference on boycott', FBIS Beijing Xinhua in English 25 January 1980 Daily Report A3 FBIS-CHI-80–018 on 1980–01–25.

36 Yan Nai Hua, 'After deciding not to participate at the Moscow Olympics – an interview with the Chinese gymnastics team', *Renmin Ribao*, 29 July 1980, 3.

37 'China will participate in alternative Olympic Games', FBIS Beijing Domestic Service in Mandarin 27 March 1980 Daily Report A3 FBIS-CHI-80–065 on 1980–04–02. 'Alternative sports events', FBIS Xinhua in English 19 June 1980 FBIS-CHI-80–121.

38 'Hundreds of athletes boycotting the Moscow Olympics gather in Philadelphia for the opening of the "Liberty Bell" track and field meet', *Renmin Ribao*, 18 July 1980, 6.

39 'Our athletes "Out of Asia, Into the World"', *Renmin Ribao*, 19 July 1980, 1; Xinhua also expressed optimism that an alternative swimming and diving competition could be arranged in Hawaii. 'Water sports events', Beijing Xinhua in English, 19 June 1980, A2 Daily Report FBIS-CHI-80–121 on 1980–06–20. The Liberty Bell Classic was seen as just a beginning, as increased visits from US sport teams to China were discussed at meetings between Vice-Foreign Minister Zhang Wenjin and Secretary of State Cyrus Vance. 'Document 303 Telegram from the Department of State to the Embassy in China', *Foreign Relations of the United States, 1977–1980 Volume XIII, China, September 1979–1981*, 1099.

40 Fan Hong and Lu Zhouxiang note that the PRC followed the US (both the 1980 boycott and the 1984 Los Angeles Games) for 'political, diplomatic, economic, and strategic reasons', 'Politics first, competition second: sport and China's foreign diplomacy in the 1960s and 1970s', in Dichter and Johns (eds), *Diplomatic Games*, 403.

41 'Document 304 Information Memorandum from the Assistant Secretary of Defense for International Security Affairs (McGiffert) to Secretary of Defense Brown', *Foreign Relations of the United States, 1977–1980 Volume XIII, China, September 1979–1981*, 1101.

42 'DAS Armacost call on Han Xu: Iran, Japan, Afghanistan, and the Olympics', United States Embassy, China. Confidential Cable. 19 April 1980. Proquest Digital National Security Archive.

43 Lynn Zinser, 'Phone call from China transformed '84 Games', *New York Times*, 14 July 2008, D1; Bin Zhang, '1984: China saved the Olympics', *Success*, 9 2008, 20–22/.

44 Brownell, 'Sports', 127.

45 Zbigniew Brzezinski to President Carter, 6 June 1980, Memorandum, subject: NSC Weekly Report #144. The *Washington Post*'s Robert G. Kaiser made the same point: 'A serious Soviet student of world affairs who was asked to name the four countries outside the Soviet empire that are most important to the U.S.S.R. would list China, the United States, West Germany and Japan.' Kaiser, 'Counterfeit Olympiad', *Washington Post*, 4 June 1980, A19.

46 See http://simonhuanghe.bokee.com/6677168.html (accessed 23 April 2015); Chinese participation in the 1980 boycott is similarly confounding from contemporary American perspectives. See 'U.S. organizer of 1980 boycott talks about politics and the Olympics', Radio Free Europe, Radio Liberty, 28 March 2008, available at www.rferl.org/content/article/1079699.html (accessed 23 April 2015).

47 Hao Qing, *A General History of Chinese Sport*, 8 vols (Beijing: People's Sports Press, 2008).

48 Sino-American cooperation on sport was short-lived. In April 1983, the PRC severed all sport and official cultural exchanges in retaliation for the US decision to grant political asylum to Chinese tennis player Hu Na. 'China suspends cultural, sports links with U.S.', *Washington Post*, 8 April 1983, A1.

49 Michael Getler, 'Crises put new strains on alliance', *Washington Post*, 24 May 1980, A1, A12; Minton F. Goldman, 'President Carter, Western Europe, and Afghanistan in 1980: inter-allied differences over policy towards the Soviet invasion', in Herbert D. Rosenbaum and Alexej Ugrinsky (eds), *Jimmy Carter: Foreign Policy and Post-Presidential Years* (Westport, CN: Greenwood Press, 1994), 19–34. Daniel James Lahey, 'The Thatcher government's response to the Soviet invasion of Afghanistan', *Cold War History*, 13:1 (2013); Paul Corthorn, 'The Cold War and British debates over the boycott of the 1980 Moscow Olympics', *Cold War History*, 13: 1 (2013).

50 For contemporary perspective on broadening US–Egyptian military cooperation, see John M. Goshko, 'Egypt to get best weapons as U.S. hunts Arab support', *Washington Post*, 10 February 1980, A18; Edward Cody, 'Egypt says it trains Afghan rebels', *Washington Post*, 14 February 1980, A1.

51 George C. Wilson, 'Egypt base could cost $400 million: Pentagon planning staging facility for Fast Reaction Force', *Washington Post*, 26 August 1980, A1.

52 'Economic boycott of Egypt imposed by Arab countries', *Washington Post*, 1 April 1979, A1.

53 'Tunisia breaks with Egypt; aid fund abolished', *Washington Post*, 28 April 1979, 21.

54 The Saudi announcement of a boycott was ironic given that, in 1979, they had already told the Soviets that they were not going. As a Soviet official noted, 'I think it is impossible to twice reject proposals of marriage. One time is enough.' Kevin Klose, 'Soviets assail Olympic boycott idea, accuse U.S. of "political blackmail"', *Washington Post*, 15 January 1980, A12.

55 'Commentator urges action of counter Soviet aggression', FBIS LD111643 Cairo Voice of the Arabs in Arabic 11 Jan 80 D11 Middle East and North Africa FBIS-MEA-80–010 1980–01–15.

56 'Sports groups to boycott Moscow Olympics', FBIS NC131806 Cairo MENA in Arabic 13 Apr 80 D11 Daily Report Middle East and Africa, FBIS-MEA-80–077 1980–04–18.

57 'Egypt to boycott Moscow Olympics unless troops withdraw', FBIS NC200635 Cairo MENA in Arabic 19 Jan 80 D1 Daily Report, Middle East and North Africa, FBIS-MEA-80–014 on 1980–01–21.

58 Egypt earned one medal at the Liberty Bell Classic: Nagui Asaad Youssef's gold in the shot put. The event only had two competitors.
59 John Vinocur, 'Few support idea of Olympic boycott', *New York Times*, 4 January 1980, A7.
60 'Kenyan urges Olympic boycott', *New York Times*, 3 February 1980, 10. Sarantakes lists Albania, Honduras, Kenya, Malawi, Paraguay and Saudi Arabia as the first commitments to the boycott. *Dropping the Torch*, 215.
61 The list included Kenya, France, West Germany, the United Kingdom and the PRC. 'Summary of conclusions of a Special Coordination Committee meeting'; *Foreign Relations of the United States 1977–1980 Volume VI Soviet Union* (Washington, DC: Department of State, 2013), 755.
62 'Summary of conclusions of a Special Coordination Committee meeting', *Foreign Relations of the United States, 1977–1980 Vol. XVIII Middle East Region; Arabian Peninsula*, 283.
63 Barry Lorge, 'Kenya joins campaign to move Olympics from Moscow', *Washington Post*, 3 February 1980, A12.
64 'President urges change of venue for Olympic Games', FBIS LD022107 Nairobi Domestic Service in English 2 Feb 80 B2 Daily Report Sub-Saharan Africa, FBIS-SSA-80–024 on 1980–02–04. Kenya had been one of four nations at the core of the 1976 African boycott. See Steve Cady, '22 African countries boycott Opening Ceremony of Olympic Games', *New York Times*, 18 July 1976, 1.
65 Pranay B. Gupte, 'Kenya will boycott Olympics in Moscow', *New York Times*, 4 February 1980, A10.
66 Robert Conley, 'Kenya threatens Olympic boycott', *New York Times*, 21 August 1963, 2.
67 'Kenya, Sudan and Iraq join boycott of Summer Olympics', *New York Times*, 21 February1968, 39.
68 Neil Amdur, 'Kenya threatens to boycott Olympics if Rhodesia is allowed to compete', *New York Times*,17 August 1972, 45.
69 President Moi recalled the 1976 boycott of Montreal in positive terms. Recent assessments of the Montreal boycott are also positive. See www.theatlantic.com/international/archive/2012/08/the-olympics-used-to-be-so-politicized-that-most-of-africa-boycotted-in-1976/260831/ (accessed 23 April 2015); and Courtney W. Mason, 'The bridge to change: the 1976 Montreal Olympic Games, South African apartheid policy, and the Olympic boycott paradigm', in Gerald P. Schaus and Steven R. Wenn (eds), *Onward to the Olympics: Historical Perspectives on the Olympic Games* (Waterloo, Ontario: Wilfred Laurier, 2007). As Mason notes, 'The 1976 Olympic African boycott generated considerable international interest in the South African apartheid policy, and contributed to the evolving campaigns of opposition to it' (292).
70 'Kenyan boxing tourney', FBIS Beijing Xinhua in English 18 Jun 80 A1 Daily Report People's Republic of China FBIS-CHI-80–121 1980–06–20; 'Kenya to hold boxing meet for boycotting countries', *Chicago Tribune*, 28 May 1980, Sports section, 4. Early in the process of planning the boycott, American diplomats had even mentioned Nairobi as a possible site for alternative games. 'Alternate Olympics talks attract small turnout', *Washington Post*, 18 March 1980, A16.
71 'Cup of Kenya, September 6–13', available at http://amateur-boxing.strefa.pl/Tournaments/GoldCupofKenya1980.html (accessed 23 April 2015).
72 Chris Hastings, 'Secret US plot to steal Moscow's Olympic flame', *Telegraph*,

29 August 2004, available at www.telegraph.co.uk/news/worldnews/europe/
russia/1470489/Secret-US-plot-to-steal-Moscows-Olympic-flame.html (accessed 23
April 2015).

73 Josephine Opar, 'Why Kenya became a country of marathoners, not boxers',
Christian Science Monitor, 27 April 2015, available at http://search.proquest.com/
docview/1675987643?accountid=14576 (accessed 23 April 2015); 'When Kenyan
boxers were kings', available at http://kenyapage.net/commentary/teams/when-
kenyan-boxers-were-kings/ (accessed 23 April 2015).

74 '28 national teams in Liberty Bell Track Meet', *New York Times*, 13 July 1980, S6.

75 'Foreign Minister reiterates decision to boycott Olympics', FBIS LD061202 Nairobi
Domestic Service in English 6 March 80 Kenya Daily Report Sub-Saharan Africa,
FBIS-SSA-80-047 on 1980-03-07.

76 Stephen R. Wenn and Jeffrey P. Wenn, 'Muhammad Ali and the convergence of
Olympic sport and U.S. diplomacy in 1980: a reassessment from behind the scenes at
the U.S. State Department', *Olympika: The International Journal of Olympic Studies*,
2 (1993), 54. As the headline of a *Chicago Tribune* article read, 'Sending Ali to Africa
was a gain – for Moscow', *Chicago Tribune*, 9 February 1980, 10.

77 'Paper discusses U.S. call for Olympic boycott', FBIS AB071845 Accra Domestic
Service in English 7 Feb 80 Ghana Daily Report Sub-Saharan Africa, FBIS-
SSA-80-029 on 1980-02-11.

78 Leon Dash, 'Ghana's new chief vows to continue war on corruption', *Washington
Post*, 12 July 1979, A28.

79 Darko Kwabena Opoku, *The Politics of Government–Business Relations in Ghana,
1982–2008* (New York: Palgrave Macmillan, 2010), 27.

80 'Commentary urges Olympic boycott for economic reasons', FBIS AB301815 Accra
Domestic Service in English 30 April 80 T1 Daily Report Middle East and Africa
FBIS-MEA-80-086 on 1980-05-01.

81 'Olympic Committee states boycott decision "still stands"', FBIS AB151410 Accra
Domestic Service in English 15 Jul 80 T1 Daily Report Middle East and North Africa,
FBIS-MEA-80-138 on 1980-07-16.

82 Kevin Klose, 'Boycott by Blacks feared', *Washington Post*, 22 June 1979, C1.

83 Barry Lorge, 'Spartakiade closes: "Olympics are next"', *Washington Post*, 6 August
1979, D1.

84 In Ueberroth's words, 'South Africa stood out like a beacon. Damn it, I thought,
Carter, Cutler, and the rest of them didn't have a clue … The slightest hint of contact
with South Africa on this issue would jeopardize everything the president was trying
to do, and the gesture would offend almost every nation.' Peter Ueberroth, *Made in
America: His Own Story* (New York: Wm. Morrow, 1985), 70.

85 Muhammad Ali's reassurance that the US would not invite South Africa to
any alternative games was a crucial part of his trip to Africa. Pranay B. Gupte,
'Muhammad Ali stumps for Olympic boycott in Kenya', *New York Times*, 6 February
1980, 8; Sarantakes, *Dropping the Torch*, 140.

86 Pranay Gupte, 'For Africans yet another year of Olympic sacrifice', *New York Times*,
13 July 1980, S1. Egyptian shot putter Nagui Asaad Youssef's team withdrew in 1972
after the Munich massacre, was denied in 1976 when Egypt joined the anti-New
Zealand boycott, and then again in 1980.

87 Michael Farber, 'Philly meet poor substitute for Olympics', *Montreal Gazette*,

16 July 1980, 92. In the 1984 Friendship Games, the boycotting Soviets seemed to have achieved what American diplomats had aspired to: a multi-nation series of competitions (the USSR and eight other socialist nations) lasting from July to September. Without mentioning the Liberty Bell Classic by name, Nicholas Evan Sarantakes notes that, 'A track-and-field event eventually [took] place in Philadelphia, but it hardly compared to the gathering in the Soviet Union.' Sarantakes, 'The White House Games: the Carter Administration's effort to establish an alternative to the Olympics', in Dichter and Johns (eds), *Diplomatic Games*, 349–50.

88 'Israel's Olympic Committee votes for boycott of Moscow Games', *Washington Post*, 23 May 1980, A25.

89 The usurpation of sport diplomacy for other purposes was not unique to the US experience. As Jenifer Parks explains in her analysis of Soviet frustrations in trying to gain leadership of the international sport anti-apartheid movement, 'developing nations used sport for their own national and regional interests, which did not always match the goals of their Cold War patrons', 'Welcoming the "Third World"', 103.

12

'They used Americana, all painted and polished, to make the enormous impression they did': selling the Reagan revolution through the 1984 Olympic Games[1]

Umberto Tulli

On 10 December 1984, Ronald Reagan welcomed Peter Ueberroth, the former president of the Los Angeles Organizing Olympic Committee (LAOOC), to the White House for the inception of the president's citation programme for private initiative. In awarding him this honour, the president remarked that Ueberroth had succeeded in organising 'the greatest Olympic Games of all times' without any support from the federal, state or local governments. To Reagan and many others, Ueberroth personified not only the imaginative, individual capabilities that a good entrepreneur should possess, but also the spirit, the discipline and the virtues that drove a free society to the peak of world power. Ueberroth's Games were so successful that *Time* magazine proclaimed him 'Man of the Year' and the White House toyed with the idea of having him as a candidate for the Senate.[2] Abroad, public opinion was equally enthusiastic. 'Los Angeles', a Swiss newspaper solemnly proclaimed, 'gave the world super Games, a sports festival the like of which has not been for a long time and one that was urgently needed to assure the survival of the Olympic movement.'[3]

Historians of the Olympic movement have presented the 1984 Los Angeles Games as the last Cold War Games or, alternatively, as a harbinger of a new era for the Olympic movement, an era in which corporate sponsorship, international audience, global markets and TV broadcasting envisaged large margins of profit and made the Olympic bandwagon truly global.[4] Quite correctly, it has been argued that the Los Angeles Olympic Games rescued the Olympic movement from a decade-long decline, marked by the explosion of security concerns, political boycotts, racial protest and financial troubles. In this sense, the 1984 Los Angeles Olympic Games turned from being the 'Games that nobody wanted' into an unexpected triumph of *Olympic* proportions, which *inter alia* produced a quarter of a billion surplus and represented one of the greatest spectacles ever staged.[5] The key to this success has been identified in the all-private formula of the Organising Committee which, for the first (and last) time in Olympic history, financed and managed the Games without any subsidy from the government.[6] Yet there was a political dimension to the 1984 Olympic Games that remains understudied. A recent work on the 1984 Soviet-led boycott, an article which challenges the idea that the boycott was planned already in 1980 as a retaliation for the

American-led boycott against the Moscow Games, tends to dismiss the White House involvement in the organisation of the Games.[7] Contrary to these analyses, this chapter suggests that the White House was not a passive spectator of the 1984 Los Angeles Olympic Games. Rather, it undertook many initiatives both to support Ueberroth's efforts to stage a perfect edition of the Games and to present a positive image of the United States to the world. In this sense, not only did the federal government coordinate LAOOC's actions, but it also followed assertive politics to maximise the impact of the Games both at home and abroad. The White House played a major role in, at least, three areas. First, the White House assured the security of the Games and all the necessary bureaucratic support. Quite naturally, only the federal government could provide for these tasks. Yet these actions are generally forgotten by historians. Secondly, the White House played a major role during the boycott crisis. Finally, it developed some specific actions to promote abroad a positive image of the Los Angeles Games and their all-private formula. To Reagan's White House, it was immediately clear that the Games could become a global showcase on American capitalism and on Reagan's proclaimed revolution aimed at reducing the state's interference in economy. The importance the White House attributed to the Games was probably the major difference between the 1932 Los Angeles Games and the 1984 edition. Indeed, there were many similarities between the two editions but, in 1932, President Hoover did not recognise the political opportunity offered by the Games and snubbed them while, in 1984, Ronald Reagan was an enthusiast supporter of the Games and tried to capitalise on them.[8]

Thus, the aim of this chapter is threefold. First, at an overarching level, it will highlight how the 1984 Olympic Games was as politicised as other editions of the Olympic jamboree, and the White House was committed to its success. Secondly, it will detail how the Olympic mega-event was imagined as a propaganda and public diplomacy initiative to increase the attractiveness of Ronald Reagan's ideas about the United States and the limited role the federal government should play. This point deserves particular attention since, in recent years, scholars have been debating the relationship between public and private sectors in public diplomacy initiatives. As Wally Olins has argued:

> If the national brand embraces tourism, foreign direct investment, brand exports, sport, the arts, cultural activities and so on, who runs it? Private sector or public sector – or both? Who in the public sector is in charge – the foreign ministry, the industry ministry, tourism, or the Prime Minister's office? Who pays for it? How are the different activities coordinated?[9]

This chapter will argue that the White House imagined the Games as a tool for the promotion of a specific national brand, which was associated more with private, than public, sector – although the federal government was never absent. This leads us to the third and final point. The chapter will address a paradox: the White House contributed to the promotion of a political message in which the success of the Games – which epitomised the success of Reagan's America – was based on the absence of political interference.

The capitalist Games and their triumph

The selection of Los Angeles as the host city for the 1984 Olympics was deeply rooted in the sense of crisis which pervaded the 1970s. The global appeal of the Games was fading dramatically, plagued by political demonstration and violence, boycotts, national rivalries, exorbitant costs and fears about the financial sustainability of the Olympic machinery. Pleading the cause of the Los Angeles bid, Executive Director of the Presidential Committee on Olympic Sports Michael T. Harrigan pointed out the crisis created by the political intervention in Olympic sports: 'the Games must die if politics continue to raise their ugly spectre'. To rescue the Games only the United States 'could turn the clock back to a Games that is free from politics ... by hosting the 1984 Games'.[10] However, it was the financial sustainability which posed the major threat. Since the end of the Second World War, large subsidies from national government had been the main financial tenet for organising and staging the Games. As Rick Gruneau and Robert Neubauer note, 'state sponsorship of the Olympic Games was easily integrated into a quasi-Keynesian political discourse that legitimized government expenditures in pursuit of activities that seemed to serve the public interest'.[11] Yet facing the deep economic crisis of the 1970s, states' financial backing of the Games was now under question. In a period when inflation exploded and tax revenues faded, governments were incurring record levels of public debt to maintain their social services and meet the expectations of their citizens. The 1976 Montreal Games occurred at the height of this economic transformation and were severely affected by it: for the Olympic family, they became synonymous with 'fiscal tragedy' whose legacy was a billion-dollar debt; for Canadians they represented a nightmare (only in 2006 did the city of Montreal completely clear the Olympic debt, and it was estimated that Montreal taxpayers had spent more than $2 billion for the Games). Looking ahead from 1977, details about the 1980 Moscow Games pointed to an ever darker deficit.[12]

Given all these problems, it is not surprising that in 1978, when the bid process for the 1984 Olympic Games closed, Los Angeles was the only bidding city. The Organising Committee had to struggle both internationally and domestically to be recognised as a legitimate host. Internationally, given this victory by default, the International Olympic Committee (IOC) had no choice but to allow the city of Los Angeles to breach Rule 4 of the Olympic Charter, which entrusted the financial responsibility of hosting an Olympic Games to the city itself, and to accept, although with major reservation, that a private company with no link to the government would be responsible for staging the Games. The all-private formula became a new contentious issue on a longer list of IOC complaints towards the United States. Since the mid-1970s, American influence and prestige within the Olympic movement had been rapidly declining. The first problem emerged in 1972. Worried about environmental and economic issues, citizens from Colorado rejected the 1976 Winter Games by a referendum, although the IOC had already attributed the Games to Denver. A new tension arose in 1978, when a campaign against the 1980 Moscow Olympic Games developed in the United States and to a lesser extent in Western Europe. Given the repressive nature of the Soviet regime, many human rights activists began to question the appropriateness of having the Games in Moscow.[13] When Jimmy Carter announced his Olympic boycott, American status within the Olympic movement definitely collapsed. Carter's boycott, proposal to host a counter Olympics for freedom-loving nations and his absence at the Opening Ceremony of the Winter Olympic Games in Lake Placid had insulted the IOC.

Furthermore, the boycott reinforced anti-American sentiments within the Olympic movement and gave momentum to a plethora of appeals to remove the Games from Los Angeles. A further new problem arose at the Moscow Games, when international sports federations agreed on reducing the number of athletes any nation could send to compete in a sport event, thus going against the interest of large athletic powers such as the United States. The largest blow to the American role in the Olympic movement, however, came on the eve of the 1984 Winter Games in Sarajevo, when the Soviets and their allies succeeded in excluding Radio Free Europe and Radio Liberty from the accredited broadcasting networks for the Games. The ban provoked an indignant reaction in the United States. Journalists and conservative congressmen urged the IOC to sanction Soviet behaviour. Dante Fascell (D. Florida), president of the congressional commission to monitor the Helsinki Agreements, denounced the ban as a clear violations of the human rights provisions of the 1975 Helsinki Final Act.[14]

Yet it was the economic plans which caused major tensions between Los Angeles and Lausanne. During the bid process, the mayor of Los Angeles promised 'Spartan Olympics'. The fact that Los Angeles had organised the Games in 1932 allowed it to cut several expenses that other cities had incurred, since many of the sports facilities were in good condition. UCLA and the University of Southern California offered their dormitories, thus erasing the need for a new Olympic Village. As the complexity of the preparations increased, the LAOOC recruited an army of volunteers. These measures were not opposed by the IOC. Yet differences and divisions emerged on how to achieve financial sustainability of the Games. The IOC was angered at plans to have all television rights kept by the city and the Organising Committee to cover the cost of staging the Games. An IOC official deemed this point as 'arrogant – even insulting'.[15]

Domestically, fears about the growing costs were echoed in the United States both locally and at the federal level. Locally, the Games had to struggle against a strong anti-tax movement. Although the Los Angeles bid was backed by a long-standing Olympic dream dating back to 1939, when a group of local entrepreneurs started to work to this end, public support was never strong. Rather, since the early bid process in 1977/78, local newspapers and radio harshly criticised the attempt to bring the Games to California.[16] Opinion polls reported that 65 per cent of Californians supported the Games on the condition there would be no public expenses on taxpayers.[17] The fear of increased taxes and expenditures was extremely high and an anti-tax movement spread through the State. A 1978 referendum (the well-known Proposition 13) which put a ceiling on property taxes had also the effect of making State expenditures for the Games impossible. The same year, Los Angeles citizens took a similar stance with a referendum which approved an increase in tax on tickets to entertainment events and did not allow the city to incur deficits for the Games.

Federal economic support was out of the question. An early attempt to obtain federal support from the Carter administration was a failure. Given the harsh economic difficulties the US was facing in 1979, Carter turned down Los Angeles mayor Bradley's request for economic aid, although the federal government had a positive record of financial support of international sports events which took place in American territory.[18] The Reagan administration was even less accommodating. Since the electoral campaign, President Reagan had promised to redefine the American economy, definitely abandoning the Keynesian model in favour of neoliberalism. Tax reduction, spending cuts, a hard-line monetary policy to fight inflation, and economic deregulation were not only incompatible with federal spending for the Olympic Games but they also provoked a terrible recession between 1981 and 1982, thus making it harder for the federal government to finance the Games.[19]

With no funding from the public sector, the LAOOC was literally forced to turn to the private sector and private capital. This idea resonated with LAOOC president Peter Ueberroth's *weltanschauung*. A self-made millionaire, a proponent of free enterprise and a loyalist Republican, Ueberroth believed that private entrepreneurship was the best solution for the organisation of the Games. Writing in 1985, he made it clear 'that there are many important programmes much more deserving of government support than a sports event, even one as special as the Olympic Games'.[20]

Ueberroth and the LAOOC soon realised the existing infrastructure and sport facilities in the Los Angeles area offered a good chance to contain the costs associated with the Games.[21] They also studied the fiscal mistakes of Montreal and commissioned some studies to define a strategy different from that of the Canadian city. Ueberroth and his staff wanted to avoid what they identified as the two main shortcomings of the Montreal Organising Olympic Committee. First, with 628 sponsors, partners and licensees which generated only $48 million, the Organising Committee received too many official sponsors which contributed too little to the Games.[22] Secondly, according to the LAOOC, the Montreal Organising Committee underestimated the revenue from the sale of TV rights and, rather than summoning an auction among TV companies, it directly sold them to ABC for the moderate price of $25 million.[23]

Under Ueberroth's leadership, the LAOOC not only avoided these mistakes but also launched an aggressive marketing strategy. By July 1981, it was clear that the Games would end with some margin of profit.[24] The first area of action was the sale of TV rights. Negotiations for the sale of TV rights for the American market began in April 1979 and concluded in September, when ABC agreed to pay the LAOOC $100 million for TV rights and $125 million for technical services. Although the IOC received a $25 million payment, IOC president Lord Killanin and IOC executive officer Monique Berlioux criticised Ueberroth's actions. Not only did the LAOOC make premature and bombastic announcements on the TV deals, violating the Olympic Charter that specifically stated that an Organising Committee cannot make public announcements before the Closing Ceremony of the previous Games, but it also reduced the IOC's role. Since the Rome Games in 1960 the IOC had been the leading actor behind TV rights negotiations.[25] Globally, Los Angeles TV negotiations granted revenues close to $300 million, three times the revenue obtained by the Soviets for the Moscow Games and four times those obtained by the Montreal Organising Committee.[26] Meanwhile, the LAOOC defined a plan which aimed at restricting the number of official sponsors to a maximum of fifty (then thirty), asking them for a minimum contribution of $4 million in exchange for exclusive rights in their own market sector. Eventually, this strategy worked out well. Los Angeles raised a whopping $130 million from such companies as Anheuser-Busch, Coca-Cola, McDonald's, Buick, M&M Mars and IBM. Another forty-three companies were licensed to sell 'official' Olympic products. In the end, despite the Soviet-led boycott, the LAOOC turned a $215 million surplus. In addition, several sponsors not only contributed to the economic sustainability of the Games but also paid for the renovation of existing sports facilities. This was the case, for example, with 7-Eleven, which sponsored the creation of the velodrome, and McDonald's, which built the (McDonald's) Olympic Swim Stadium.[27]

The success of private sponsorship triggered criticism. On the eve of the Games, Ralph Nader denounced the ongoing transformation of the United States as a victim of what he labelled 'the megacorporate world of Ronald Reagan'.[28] More cynical critics went so far as to rename the Los Angeles Games the 'Hamburger Olympics', where the only thing that was missing was the hamburger-shaped Olympic swimming pool.[29] Yet to the LAOOC, the vast coalition of corporations was a godsend and assured it an immense profit, where other Organising Committees – regardless of ideology, and depending on government funding – had not. Even President Reagan celebrated the importance of private contribution for staging the Games. As he remarked in March 1983,

> next year's games will show the world what Americans without government subsidy can accomplish. These games will reflect the excellence, the hospitality, and the spirit of accomplishment that are so much a part of our way of life. ... The corporate community, as evidenced by you who are here today, has stepped forward in a big way in, among other things, financing specific construction projects needed for the games. And I think we're all grateful for this example of corporate citizenship.[30]

Private sponsors had a long record within the Olympic movement and especially with the United States Olympic Committee (USOC) but, for the first time, they were the only financial partner of the Games and their presence was more visible than ever. Corporations' slogans and their Olympic connections occupied the pages of major American newspapers and magazines. In some cases, they proposed similar slogans for the European and Japanese markets, too. Through a peculiar mix of patriotism and internationalism, their advertisements produced a positive and dynamic perception of the Los Angeles Olympic Games, thus contributing to the success of the LAOOC. Canon, for example, was selected as 'the official 35mm Camera of the Games' and the company invited photographers all over the world to 'Go for the Gold, with Canon'.[31] Oil company Arco became an official partner as early as 1980. In one of its commercials, a quintessential mix of nationalism and internationalism, Arco proudly claimed its contribution to the LAOOC and to the Olympic movement: 'We're making

12.1 ARCO was a $9 million donor to the 1984 Olympic Games in Los Angeles and its advertisements reflected its commitment to the Games

tracks for the Olympics' (figure 12.1). Not only was the company refurbishing the Los Angeles Memorial Coliseum and its track to create 'a world-class environment for the world-class athletes who will compete there in the 1984 Olympic Games', but it was also building seven practice tracks at schools in and around Los Angeles and supporting the Arco Jesse Owens Games, a track programme for teenagers. 'We, at Arco', the advertisement concluded, 'are putting our time, effort, money and energy into America'.[32]

The greatest commercial partners were McDonald's and Coca-Cola. Both were transnational companies with their headquarters and core business in the US. Both had symbols and logos which were (and still are) among the best known in the world. Both stood for America in the world. Finally, both could be proud of a long partnership with the Olympic movement. As 'official partners' of the LAOOC, McDonald's and Coca-Cola obtained the right to use the Olympic rings, the 'star in motion' logo adopted by the LAOOC and the official mascot, Sam-the-Eagle, worldwide. Through their advertisements and commercial initiatives, they promoted a dynamic and colourful image of the United States on the eve of the Los Angeles Games. They also publicised the achievements of the LAOOC and its symbols worldwide, above all the friendly mascot Sam-the-Eagle which became itself a component of Los Angeles's triumph (figure 12.2).

The mascot was a quintessential patriotic symbol. Although the LAOOC claimed

12.2 The ubiquitous mascot, Sam-the-Eagle, featured here on a postcard, was part of the 1984 Olympic Games success. It inspired a series of dolls, hats, keyrings and mugs, and many other merchandising products.

in one of its official flyers that it 'expresses the cheerful optimism of the Olympic spirit [and] embodies the ideals of the Olympic motto Swifter, Higher, Stronger', Sam was an American eagle, whose name suggested a kinship with Uncle Sam, with a stars-and-stripes Lincoln-style hat.[33] Not surprisingly, Sam became extremely popular in the US, with sales of the mascot and related merchandising exceeding expectations. As he passed by in parades and other public events, children went crazy, urging him to remain with them. Some private citizens wrote to the *Los Angeles Times* to show their support for the mascot. From Glendale, California, Frank Guerra confessed to 'be offended when Sam the Eagle is criticized' and to be 'proud to have Sam the Eagle as our mascot'.[34] In Europe, Sam was acclaimed as the best mascot ever. Sam's popularity reached its peak in Japan, where DAX International produced a fifty-one-episode television show on the mascot (figure 12.3). It ran between 1983 and 1984, and in every episode the optimistic, resourceful, although muddling Sam-the-Eagle helped the police to solve mysteries and the local community to face daily problems. Just when it seemed that Sam could not face the challenge, five Olympic rings appeared on his stars-and-stripes hat, giving him some kind of superpower.

Promoting Los Angeles: the White House and the staging of the Games

Not surprisingly, Sam was not so popular in the Soviet Union, where the press showed the true face of the eagle: an avid profit-making American capitalist (figure 12.4). The Soviet cartoon in figure 12.4 was part of a larger campaign aimed at denouncing

イーグル サム

まほうの つばさに おのりよ プリーズオン！

12.3 Sam-the-Eagle also inspired a Japanese cartoon produced by DAX international (1983)

12.4 Sam-the-Eagle as seen by Soviet press. In this cartoon, Sam is portrayed as a quintessential capitalist symbol

the over-commercialisation of the American Games and the disruptive capitalist bias shown by the LAOOC. The Soviets were hardly alone, however. IOC executive officer Monique Berlioux complained about the over-commercialisation of the Games and American chauvinism. From Greece, Olympia mayor Spyros Fotimos harshly criticised LAOOC's decision to establish a sponsorship programme for the Olympic Torch Relay because – he declared – 'The Olympic flame is not a dollar sign.'[35] Soviet and Greek claims about rampant commercialisation were not off the mark. True, commercialism was already a driving force behind the Olympic Games and the Los Angeles Games were no more commercialised than previous ones. Yet consumers across the world were flooded with advertising from official Olympic sponsors and other companies hoping to link their products with the Games. Also importantly, the commercialisation of the Games was crucial in the financial success of Los Angeles. Not only did Los Angeles become a new model for cities preparing Olympic bids but it also created an effective worldwide advertisement for capitalism, a showcase for America and for what America could offer to the world.

While the LAOOC was defining its strategy to stack up profits, the White House developed an initial plan to support and coordinate LAOOC's actions. The aim was to justify the all-private formula, demonstrating that the free market – not the government – could reach unprecedented goals. Although denying any direct financial support, the White House was immediately involved in the organisation of the Games since it was immediately clear that the Games represented incredible public diplomacy opportunities.

The success of the Games – wrote the State Department to all diplomatic posts in November 1982 – was an issue of importance at the highest levels in the US government: 'please note, however, that the LAOOC will be the official host of the Games. The LAOOC is a private sector initiative, receiving no public monies ... this effort has full administration support and is regarded as something of a model.'[36]

To the White House, diplomatic posts abroad should reply to international criticism towards the all-private nature of the Organising Committee and what was denounced as incoherent political support from the American government.[37] Executive branch involvement officially began in 1981, when President Reagan assured Ueberroth and IOC president Juan Antonio Samaranch that the administration would do everything within its power to provide safety of the athletes, officials, journalists and visitors to the Summer Games. In early 1982, a White House task force was established under the direction of Michael Deaver and Michael McManus to coordinate 'the federal effort in support of the Games'. A few months later, Kenneth Hill and Ed Derwinski joined the team.[38] One of the major initiatives undertaken by the White House task force on the Olympics was to coordinate its actions with the United States Information Agency (USIA), which established its own 'Olympic team' in August 1983. In a few months, the USIA became a fundamental partner to promote the LAOOC abroad, spreading information on the Olympic Games and prioritising the private sector initiatives to organise them. It also reprinted and distributed copies of USOC bulletins *Stars in Motion* and *The Olympian*. A few days before the Games, Charles Z. Wick reported that USIA had assured the publication of ten magazines and commercial bulletins in eighteen languages which prioritised articles and photos in connection with the Games.[39] When the Games closed, Kenneth Hill reported in a balance memorandum that federal agencies had contributed $79 million to the organisation of the Games, although no direct transfer had been made to the LAOOC.[40] The LAOOC, too, was aware of the Games' political importance. Writing just a few months before the Games, LAOOC officer Bill Hussey admitted, 'we are representing the best in our national traditions and ideals. In a real sense we are now serving in the first line of diplomacy and influence abroad. However, in the end, it is the US government, not the LAOOC, which will be judged by world opinion.'[41] Foreign press – especially in Western Europe and Japan – reported the important success that the LAOOC had achieved before the opening of the first all-private Games.[42]

The White House and the Soviet-led boycott

The executive branch's involvement in the organisation and staging of the Games became even more crucial regarding international affairs and the issue of the Soviet boycott. After Ronald Reagan entered the White House, Ueberroth invited the new president to reassure the IOC about the American commitment to welcome athletes from every country. In May, Reagan wrote to Samaranch to 'reiterate the assurance of the American people to welcome the Olympic Games in Los Angeles' and 'to state that the Olympic Charter will be enforced'. In the following month, during an interview for Swedish TV, the President pledged to welcome the athletes of the world.[43] Both the White House and the LAOOC realised that they should cooperate to create a positive image of the city of Los Angeles abroad, since Soviet criticism of the organisation of the Games was growing. In late 1982, the Soviet press reported several shortcomings in the LAOOC's planning for security, and in a number of articles the Soviets denounced many problems with the Los Angeles area: surprisingly the growing commercialisation of the Olympics no longer figured prominently, with an emphasis on poverty, corruption, racism, smog and pollution.[44] Picking up a suggestion from the White House task force, Ueberroth invited an official delegation from the USSR to inspect the infrastructure and the measures taken by the LAOOC to face these problems. The visit by a seven-member delegation from the USSR seemed to bring about the expected results, since the Soviet Sports Minister sent a telegram to congratulate Ueberroth.[45]

IOC president Samaranch warned Ueberroth about some specific Soviet complaints, including entry procedures, custom regulations and regulations for importing horses for the equine events.[46] In the following months, three points became extremely controversial, provoking confusion and tension among Washington, Los Angeles, Lausanne and Moscow. First, the Soviets urged the United States government to authorise landing rights for Aeroflot airplanes during the Games, as an Olympic waiver to Carter's 1980 decision to restrict flights from the Soviet Union. In the original request, the Soviets specified that the flights would carry Soviet and other Eastern European athletes and Olympic officials.[47] The Soviets also proposed to harbour a

Soviet ship in Los Angeles for the duration of the Games. The ship had two main aims: it would deliver part of the sport inventory, equipment, materials and food for Soviet athletes; and it would host Soviet athletes and officials, given Soviet fears over a (proclaimed) lack of security and anti-Soviet demonstrations.[48] Finally, they requested the possibility of having a Soviet Olympic attaché in Los Angeles.

According to historian Brad J. Congelio, these requests arrived at a time when the White House was considering a reversal in its approach to the Soviet Union.[49] In early January 1983, the president approved National Security Decision Directive n. 75 on 'US relations with the USSR'. The Directive did not represent a step back from Ronald Reagan's firm anti-communism, since it reiterated that official American tasks were 'to contain and over time reverse Soviet expansionism' and 'to promote, within the narrow limits available to us, the process of change in the Soviet Union'. Yet, for the first time since entering the White House, Reagan accepted that the United States should also 'engage the Soviet Union in negotiations to attempt to reach agreements which protect and enhance US interests and which are consistent with the principle of strict reciprocity and mutual interest'.[50]

This renewed dialogue could develop through the Olympic Games. Yet the Soviet shooting of Korean Airlines (KAL) Flight 007 further complicated the decision regarding the change in bipolar politics and, more specifically, its requests for the Olympic Games. Soon after the KAL incident, many grassroots organisations in the United States, like the bellicose Ban the Soviet Coalition, began to question the appropriateness of having the Soviets in the United States for the Olympic Games.[51] Trying to capitalise on this renewed public anti-Sovietism, the White House began to consider an Olympic ban on the Soviets. According to National Security Council officer (and future Assistant Secretary for Defense) Robert Sims, the administration should 'watch closely' the impact of the KAL incident on the Los Angeles Games because 'there are potential propaganda pluses for the Soviets if they participate' and given the 'location of the Games in Los Angeles, in an electoral year … there will be major West Wing interest'.[52] Officials from the State Department were more cautious. Robert M. Kimmitt, for example, invited the administration to 'approach this matter very carefully, given all the criticism the Carter Administration had on the Olympic Games'.[53] Counsellor Derwinski, who was in charge of Olympic affairs at the State Department, took a similar stance: 'barring Soviet athletes from participating is a non-issue'. The president had agreed 'to respect the Olympic Charter and welcome athletes from all nations'. So far, the president's handling of the KAL incident had dealt a sharp blow to Soviet prestige. Moving to bar the Soviets from Los Angeles would hand them exactly the kind of propaganda card they were now looking for: 'I believe the US has much to gain by being the perfect host of the Olympics. We should encourage as many people to come as possible and see the wonders of the US. If anything, we should upgrade our role as Olympic hosts in the eyes of the world.'[54]

To maintain and eventually increase the public diplomacy advantage the United States was enjoying, the administration would welcome Soviet and world athletes. Welcoming the Soviets, however, did not imply accepting their requests. After an intense debate within the administration, the Olympic task force dictated the line vis-à-vis Soviet requests: the US government would accept both the Aerflot flights to Los Angeles and the docking of a Soviet ship. It would also accept an Olympic attaché – but not Oleg Yrsmishkin, an alleged KGB agent proposed by the Soviet Union.[55]

On 1 March, the State Department officially refused a visa for Yrsmishkin. On 11 April, USSR NOC president Marat Gramov sent a telegram to Samaranch to denounce the growing interference of the American government within the Olympic movement and the organisation of the Games. It also claimed that 'a large-scale campaign against the Soviet Union's participation in the Olympic Games has been mounted in the United States'. Finally, he complained about the role of Radio Free Europe–Radio Liberty: to the Soviets, the American intelligence-sponsored radios' only scope was to engage in subversive activities in the Soviet Union, and they had nothing to do with the right to information or the Olympic spirit. Accordingly, he urged the IOC to summon a special meeting in Lausanne to solve these problems.[56]

The Soviets made their definitive announcement on 8 May: the 'participation of Soviet sportsmen in the Games [was] impossible' because of 'chauvinistic sentiments and an anti-Soviet hysteria'.[57] The announcement – it is worth noting – occurred the same day that the Olympic torch arrived in New York to start its journey through America. Samaranch immediately deplored the boycott. The LAOOC defended its security measures and confirmed that the Soviets were more than welcome. On 9 May Samaranch and Ueberroth went to the White House. They urged Reagan to publicly reiterate his commitment to enforce the Olympic Charter, to assure protection to Soviet athletes and to meet their requests. Ueberroth even suggested that the president officially invite Chernenko to the opening of the Games. Secretary Shultz and Reagan firmly rejected Ueberroth's advice. However, the president addressed a letter to Samaranch to reiterate American commitment to respect the Olympic Charter.[58] Within a few days, Bulgaria, East Germany, Vietnam, Afghanistan, Czechoslovakia, North Korea, Hungary and Poland joined the Soviets. In a desperate attempt to have the Soviets in Los Angeles, Samaranch flew three times to Moscow while LAOOC officials tried to convince Eastern Europeans to reconsider their decisions. On the contrary, the White House decided to stay out of this campaign. It soon realised it had nothing to lose from the Soviet boycott: it was immediately clear that 'the losers in the boycott were the Russians'.[59]

Containing the boycott, isolating the Soviets

The White House's dismissive approach to the Soviets should not obscure its role in limiting the success of the boycott. Working in close connection with the LAOOC, the administration soon defined a damage control strategy to face the Soviet threat and, eventually, to multiply the divisions within the Soviet bloc.[60]

The first important victory came from Africa. During the preparations for the Games, participation from African athletes was disputed for a number of reasons. First, in 1981 a South African national rugby team had toured the United States. Although rugby is not an Olympic sport, a rugby match between New Zealand and apartheid South Africa triggered the 1976 boycott of the Montreal Games. Accordingly, from Lausanne, Berlioux warned the USOC that the 'tour may have very important and negative consequences upon the staging of the Games'.[61] Secondly, given the Olympic ban on South African athletes South African athlete Zola Budd had applied to be a British citizen in order to participate in the Games. When Budd's request was approved, many sports officials and politicians from Africa vehemently protested, threatening to boycott the Games.[62]

When the Soviets announced their boycott, many in Los Angeles and Washington feared that African NOCs could join it. Not only were they waiting for the official confirmation of participation from twenty-three countries, but many African embassies in Washington had also received alleged Ku Klux Klan leaflets warning about African participation in the Games. Soviet press and TV recalled the alleged threat repeatedly. On 22 May, a special meeting on African participation took place at the White House and a plan of action was adopted. As a result, the State Department was active in pursuing African participation although it 'intentionally avoided overt lobbying effort which may have been seen as an attempt to politicise the Games and would have been counterproductive in Africa'. Through the State Department, the administration reiterated its commitment to welcome athletes from every country and, at the same time, denounced the alleged Ku Klux Klan threat as a Soviet plot. At Ueberroth's proposal, the State Department cabled diplomatic posts and NOCs in Africa, encouraging attendance of the Olympic Games. The Department also urged Ueberroth's staff to 'take steps to encourage African participation: send a representative to a meeting of the Supreme Council for Sport in Africa (SCSA), grant additional press accreditation to African journalists, accommodate ticket requests from African heads of state or other senior officials even if made at the last minute, contribute to the costs of African Olympians' participation in the Atlanta training camp'.[63] USIA launched a $58,900 programme to bring Third World track athletes to the United States for a month-long training camp prior to the Olympics. At the State Department's initiative, USIA hosted Ueberroth for a conference to defuse Soviet propaganda through WORLDNET, its satellite television network.[64] Ueberroth's conference then became three separate one-hour press conferences with Ueberroth, Mayor Bradley and LAPD chief Darrell Gates, broadcast in more than twenty countries in Africa, Asia and Latin America. They assured the international public about their commitment to abide by the Olympic Charter and to protect the security of athletes, sport officials and tourists in Los Angeles. To stress this point, USIA produced two short documentaries, *Hello, Los Angeles* and *Sharing the Dream*, and distributed them to diplomatic posts around the world to clear doubts about security in Los Angeles.[65] Ueberroth even flew to Cuba, where Castro reassured him that Cuba would not interfere with African NOCs' decision over participation.[66]

The most important success, however, came from Eastern Europe. After many communist countries had joined the boycott, Romania was still considering its participation. Radio Free Europe and the Western press reported that the Romanian government was under immense pressure from Moscow. Both the LAOOC and the White House identified Ceacescu's regime as a special target for their damage limitation strategy. Accordingly, Ueberroth flew to Lausanne for a special meeting with Alexander Siperco, IOC vice-president from Romania, on 18 May, while Reagan wrote a letter to Ceacescu, stating that he was recommending a year-long extension to Romania's most favoured nation status and extending the bilateral commercial agreement for three years. As a final thought, he discussed the Los Angeles Games: not only were Soviet concerns and Soviet accusations 'groundless', but the president had 'personally assured the International Olympic Committee that the US will live up to the Olympic Charter … It is our hope that … the Romanian Olympic team will participate in the games this summer.'[67] According to David Funderburk, the US ambassador to Romania, this letter was superfluous, given Romanian tensions with Moscow and its growing dependence on Western economies.[68] Ueberroth, however, took the opposite position. Not only should the president write to Ceacescu but he should also 'offer them every possible support and assistance'.[69] The same day, during a sports meeting among communist countries in Prague, Romanian minister Haralambie Alexa announced that Romanian athletes would participate in the Games. At the end of the month, a LAOOC delegation went to Bucharest and agreed on contributing to Romanian expenses. The LAOOC and the IOC would each pay $60,000 to bring the Romanian team to Los Angeles (about two-hirds of the total cost).[70]

Conclusions

At the parade of national teams during the Opening Ceremony, the Romanians, the Yugoslavs and the Chinese received ovations from 92,655 spectators, though none, according to *Sports Illustrated*, 'was so resounding as that for the immense, 573-member U.S. team, which marched in last'.[71] Statistics prove that host nations win a larger number of medals. With the Soviet and Eastern champions absent, American athletes won an incredibly large number of medals (83 gold, 61 silver, 30 bronze). The American public followed these successes with enthusiasm. The ABC TV network amplified it: non-Americans often complained about the chauvinistic bias in ABC's coverage of the Games.[72] With no little irony, had the Soviets been in Los Angeles, they would have contested, if not won, many events, limiting the American triumph.

The boycott affair and the initiatives developed by the White House are emblematic of Reagan's approach to the 1984 Los Angeles Olympics. Apparently dismissive and uninterested in the organisation of the Games, the Reagan administration constantly worked behind the scenes to ensure their success. Through a dismissive approach towards the USSR and a damage-limiting strategy, the administration isolated the Soviets and President Reagan could claim to 'have done everything [he] could to let them know the door [was] open' while promising that he 'won't make some offer that would look as if we were rewarding them for walking out'.[73]

The federal executive role in the Olympics was not limited to the boycott controversy. The Reagan administration soon identified the Games as a showcase for its new political message. The all-private nature of the LAOOC played a major role in it. Although Peter Ueberroth was cautious about the political meanings of his Games, he fully personified the neoliberalist spirit of the 1980s. He was a 'poster child' for the Reagan revolution, a symbol of the American businessman who, without government interference, was able to organise the perfect Olympic Games.[74] The motto of the Organising Committee ('we have no message; except let's have a nice Games') appeared a perfect synthesis of the Los Angeles Games: no financial support, no interference, no official message from the American government. Yet Ueberroth, the LAOOC and the Games were a shining emblem for the Reagan revolution – a neoliberal revolution yearning for limitation of the role of the state in the economy, in order to allow a free society, as American society was, to create the talents and resources needed to reaffirm American primacy.

In this Olympic apotheosis, Reagan found an example of the successes of the private sector because American athletes had 'proved the profits reaped from a free economy can be used to help our young people compete on an even footing with the state subsidized athletes of other countries'.[75] Yet there was a peculiar paradox in this Olympic vulgate: not only was the Reagan administration a co-star in staging the Games of capitalism and private initiative, but it also imagined and used the Games as a global showcase for the world on the achievements of individual freedom, free markets and the need to limit state power. This was the political message of the Los Angeles Olympic Games and its fundamental paradox: a political message which wanted to present the Los Angeles Games as government-free but, in the end, could not avoid the government meddling in it.

Notes

1 Quoted in *Los Angeles Times*, 31 July 1984.
2 Ronald Reagan Presidential Library, Simi Valley, California (hereafter RRPL), WHORM File, Alphabetical, Box Ueberroth Peter V., Folder 2, Letter, J. H. Hume to Don Regan, 4 December 1985.
3 IOC Archives, Lausanne, Collection 1984 – Boycott, Folder 24 (hereafter: CIO-call number) CIO-BOTC n.24, Clipping in IOC Archives.
4 On the Los Angeles Games as the first corporate Games see, for example, G. Whannel, 'The Five Rings and the small screen: television, sponsorship, and new media in the Olympic movement', and A. Tomlinson, 'The commercialization of the Olympics: cities, corporations, and the Olympic commodity', both in K. Young and K. B. Wamsley (eds), *Global Olympics: Historical and Sociological Studies of the Modern Games* (Bingley: Emerald Publishing, 2005). On the Los Angeles Games as the last Cold War Olympics, see P. D'Agati, *The Cold War and the 1984 Olympic Games* (Basingstoke: Palgrave Macmillan, 2013).
5 H. Edwards, 'Perspectives on Olympic sportpolitics: 1968–1984', *Black Law Journal*, Spring (1984).
6 Tomlinson, 'The commercialization of the Olympics'; B. Shaikin, *Sport and Politics: The Olympics and the Los Angeles Games* (New York: Praeger, 1988); K. Reich, *Making it Happen: Peter Ueberroth and the 1984 Olympics* (Santa Barbara, CA: Capra Press, 1986).

7 R. Edelman, 'The Russians are not coming! The Soviet withdrawal from the Games of the XXIII Olympiad', *International Journal of the History of Sport*, 32:1 (2015).

8 A. Tomlinson, 'Los Angeles 1984 and 1932: commercializing the American dream', in A. Tomlinson and C. Young (eds), *National Identities and Global Sports Events* (Albany, NY: State University of New York Press, 2006). On the 1932 Games, see also B. Keys, 'Spreading peace, democracy and Coca-Cola: sport and American cultural expansion in the 1930s', *Diplomatic History*, 28:2 (2004); M. Dyreson and M. Llewellyn, 'Los Angeles is the Olympic city: legacies of the 1932 and 1984 Olympic Games', *International Journal of the History of Sport*, 25:14 (2008).

9 W. Olins, 'Making a national brand', in J. Melissen (ed.), *The New Public Diplomacy: Soft Power in International Relations* (Basingstoke: Palgrave Macmillan, 2005), 178.

10 M. T. Harrigan to the House International Relations Subcommittee on International Organizations, 23 September 1977.

11 R. Gruneau and R. Neubauer, 'A gold medal for the market: the 1984 Los Angeles Olympics, the Reagan era, and the politics of neoliberalism', in H. Jefferson Lenskyj and S. Wagg (eds), *The Palgrave Handbook of Olympic Studies* (Basingstoke: Palgrave, 2012), 140.

12 T. Teixeira, 'The XXI Olympiad: Canada's claim or Montreal's gain? Political and social tensions surrounding the 1976 Montreal Olympics', in Jefferson Lenskyj and Wagg (eds), *The Palgrave Handbook of Olympic Studies*, 120–33. On the costs associated with the Moscow Games, see Shaikin, *Sport and Politics*, 38.

13 U. Tulli, 'Boicottare le Olimpiadi del gulag. I diritti umani e la campagna contro le Olimpiadi di Mosca', *Ricerche di Storia Politica*, 1/2013.

14 P. Ueberroth, *Made in America: His Own Story* (New York: William Morrow, 1985). On RFE/RL at the Sarajevo Games see: RRPL, Folder RFE/RL, Kenneth J. Hill collection, Box 6, 'Sarajevo Accreditation Chronology', 'Transcript of IOC Press Conference Statement', 7 February 1984, and 'Accreditation of RFE/RL', 9 February 1984; S. Mickelson, 'IOC ban on Radio Free Europe draws fire', *Los Angeles Times*, 10 February 1984; IOC Archives, D-RMOI-ETATU-021, Letter, Dante Fascell *et al.* to Samaranch, 21 March 1984. See also T. C. Rider, 'Filling the information gap: Radio Free Europe–Radio Liberty and the politics of accreditation at the 1984 Los Angeles Olympic Games', *International Journal of the History of Sport*, 32:1 (2015).

15 Associated Press Report, 'Olympic committee angry with Los Angeles, other bids welcome'.

16 LAOOC Records, UCLA; Los Angeles (hereafter LAOOC Archives), Box 61, Folder 2, KNTX newsletter, 'Tax dollars and Olympic finance', 26 January 1978, 'Protecting the taxpayer', *Los Angeles Times*, 23 February 1978; IOC Archives, doc. JO-1984S-Boyco-n.25, Lynn Morean, Letter to the IOC.

17 LAOOC Records, Box 61, Folder 2, KNTX Opinion poll, 28 November 1977.

18 LAOOC Records, Box 62, Folder 3, 'Federal participation in staging the Olympic Games'; Jimmy Carter Presidential Library (Atlanta), Staff Offices, Domestic Policy Staff – Berenson, Box 15, F. Olympics Los Angeles, Letter Tom Bradley to Jimmy Carter, September 1978; and Memorandum of a Meeting: Carter, Eizenstat, Watson, Bradley, Ferraro, Remy, Ueberroth.

19 This point is further developed in Gruneau and Neubauer, 'A gold medal for the market', 134–62.

20 Quoted in C. Lorocco, 'Rings of power: Peter Ueberroth and the 1984 Los Angeles

Olympic Games', available at www.moaf.org/publications-collections/financial-history-magazine/81/_res/id=File1/Article_81.pdf (accessed 26 May 2016).

21 S. R. Wenn, 'Peter Ueberroth's legacy: how the 1984 Los Angeles Olympics changed the trajectory of the Olympic movement', *International Journal of Sport History*, 32:1 (2015).

22 LAOOC Records, Box 1307, Folder 2, 'Montreal 1976 – International Marketing Programs'.

23 LAOOC Records, Box 1307, Folder 2, 'Montreal 1976 – International Marketing Programs'.

24 P. McMillan, 'Ueberroth's goal a profit-making Olympics', *Los Angeles Times*, 12 July 1981.

25 IOC Archives, CIO-JO-POLIT n.58, Telegram, Killanin and Berlioux to Ueberroth, 20 November 1980. See also Ueberroth, *Made in America*, 69–70.

26 C. Hill, *Olympic Politics* (Manchester: Manchester University Press, 1996).

27 Ueberroth, *Made in America*, 70.

28 R. Nader, 'The mega-corporate world of Ronald Reagan', 6 June 1984, in *Ralph Nader: A Reader* (New York: Seven Stories Press, 2000), 80.

29 R. Gruneau, 'The hamburger olympics', in A. Tomlinson and G. Whannel (eds), *Five-Ring Circus – Money, Power and Politics at the Olympic Games* (London: Pluto Press, 1984).

30 R. Reagan, Remarks at a Luncheon Meeting of the United States Olympic Committee in Los Angeles, California, 3 March1983, available at www.reagan.utexas.edu/archives/speeches/1983/30383a.htm (accessed 20 February 2015).

31 Canon Advertisement, 'Go for the gold, with Canon', *The Olympian*; IOC Archives, CIO-JO-1984S-PUB, Canon Advertisement, 'A photographic memory'.

32 See for example the advertisement published in *The Olympian*, March 1984.

33 LAOOC Records, Box 385, Folder 9, Flyer LAOOC.

34 F. Guerra, *Los Angeles Times*, 16 July 1984.

35 'L.A. Olympic aide dispatched to explain: Greeks leery of Games Torch Relay program', *Los Angeles Times*, 31 January 1984.

36 LAOOC Records, Box 64, Folder 4, Telegram from State Department to LAOOC, 'Following is text from Telegram to all Diplomatic POSTS, dated November 25, 1982'.

37 LAOOC Records, Box 64, Folder 5, Memorandum, Bill Hussey to the files, October 1982.

38 RRPL, Kenneth Hill File, Box 2, Correspondence, Unsigned Memorandum for M. Deaver, 18 September 1984.

39 RRPL, Box 1, Kenneth Hill Files, Memorandum, Charles Z. Wick to Michael Deaver, June 1984. See also J. Gygax, *Olympisme et Guerre Froide, le prix de la victoire américaine* (Paris: L'Harmattan, 2012), 407–8.

40 RRPL, Kenneth Hill File, Box 1, Folder Budget, Memorandum, Joseph R. Wright to Michael Deaver, 'U.S. Funding Associated with the L.A. Games – Additional Info', 15 September 1984.

41 LAOOC Records, Box 64, Folder 4, Memorandum from Bill Hussey to Bea Nemlaha, 'Government Relations: the USIA and the Department of State', May 1984.

42 See, for example, 'Olimpiade – Il grande spettacolo di Los Angeles rilancia il ricordo del mito hollywoodiano', *La Stampa*, 30 July 1984; 'I dollari e la perfezione', *Gazzetta dello Sport*, 21 January 1984.

43 RRPL, Kenneth Hill File, Box 2, Folder Federal Correspondence, Letter, Ronald Reagan to Samaranch, 25 October 1982.
44 LAOOC Records, Box 383, Folder 13, Telegram, State Department to LAOOC, 10 January 1983.
45 Ueberroth, *Made in America*, 153–4.
46 IOC Archives, JO-1984S-COJO n.35, Telegram, Samaranch to Ueberroth, 22 December 1982.
47 LAOOC Records, Box 64, Folder 4, Telegram, State Department to LAOOC, 'Request of S. Pavlov – President USSR Olympic Committee', 25 November 1983.
48 IOC Archives, JO-1984S-BOYCOTT et MAISON BLANCHE-24, Memorandum on discussion between the representatives of the LAOOC, IOC officials and the representatives of the National Olympic Committee of the USSR, December 1983.
49 B. J. Congelio, 'Reagan's rapprochement: a brief analysis of the Reagan administration and the 1984 Olympics', *Journal of Olympic History*, 21:3 (2013).
50 RRPL, Executive Secretariat, National Security Council Files, Box 91310, Folder NSDD 75(1), William P. Clark, Memorandum, 'NSDD 75 on U.S. Relations with the USSR', 17 January 1983, RRPL.
51 LAOOC Records, Box 65, Folder USIA, '1984 Olympics: Ban the Russians?', ABC News Nightline, 18 October 1983, transcript. For a longer perspective on Western attempts to block East Germany's participation in sports mega-events see H. Dichter, 'A game of political ice hockey: NATO restrictions on East German sport travel in the aftermath of the Berlin Wall', in H. L. Dichter and A. L. Johns (eds), *Diplomatic Games: Sport, Statecraft, and International Relations since 1945* (Lexington, KY: University of Kentucky Press, 2014), 19–52.
52 RRPL, WHORM File, ND016, casefile 174810, Memorandum from Robert B. Sims for William P. Clark, 'KAL Incident – Soviet Participation in Los Angeles Games', 19 September 1983.
53 RRPL, WHORM File, ND016, casefile 174810, Memorandum from Robert B. Sims for William P. Clark, 'KAL Incident – Soviet Participation in Los Angeles Games', 19 September 1983.
54 RRPL, Box 7, Folder Soviet Participation in Olympics, Kenneth J. Hill File, Memorandum from Ed Derwinski to the Acting Secretary, 'Soviet Participation in the 1984 Olympics', 30 September 1983.
55 RRPL, Kenneth Hill File, Box 2, Folder Correspondence, Synopsis of a Meeting on Soviet Olympic Participation, 24 January 1984.
56 IOC Archives, CIO-JO-1984s-POLIT n.58, Telegram, M. Berlioux to P. Ueberroth, 11 April 1984.
57 RRPL, Executive Secretariat, NSC Head of State File, Box 82, Folder Olympics, TASS, 8 May 1984. See, also Rider, 'Filling the information gap'.
58 Ueberroth, *Made in America*, 267–8.
59 IOC Archives, CIO-JO-1984S-BOYCO n.23, Letter, Ronald Reagan to Joseph Bloom, 14 June 1984.
60 On solidarity and tensions within the Eastern bloc relating to sport affairs, see E. Mertin, 'Steadfast friendship and brotherly help: the distinctive Soviet–East German sport relationship within the Socialist bloc', in Dichter and Johns (eds), *Diplomatic Games*, 53–84.

61 IOC Archives, CIO-JO-1984s-POLIT n.58, Telegram, M. Berlioux to William Simon (President USOC), 17 July 1981.

62 RRPL, Executive Secretariat, NSC Subject File, Box 82, Folder Olympics, 'Department of State Final Report: 1984 Summer Olympic Games'. See also Shaikin, *Sport and Politics*, 58–9.

63 RRPL, Executive Secretariat, NSC Subject File, Box 82, Folder Olympics, 'Department of State Final Report: 1984 Summer Olympic Games'.

64 RRPL, Kenneth Hill File, Box 4, Folder LAOOC, Memorandum 'Meeting – Olympics', 22 May 1984; RRPL, Kenneth Hill File, Box 1, Folder Budget, Memorandum from David Sitrin for Joe Wright, 'U.S. Olympics Status report', 14 June 1984.

65 RRPL, WHOM FO005–03, casefile 241077, USIA, Television-Worldnet, 'Video Dialogue with Peter Ueberroth, Tom Bradley and Darrell Gates', 15 June 1984; LAOOC Records, Box 65, Folder USIA, Letter, Carol C. Daniels to Rober O. Jones, 5 March 1984. See also A. A. Snyder, *Warriors of Disinformation: American Propaganda, Soviet Lies and the Winning of the Cold War* (New York: Arcade Publishing, 1995), 108–10.

66 Ueberroth, *Made in America*, 296–300.

67 RRPL, Executive Secretariat, NSC Head of State File, Box 28, Folder Romania, – Ceacescu 8203396; Letter, Reagan to Ceaucescu, 18 May 1984. See also Ueberroth, *Made in America*, 290.

68 RRPL, Executive Secretariat, NSC Head of State File, Box 28, Folder Romania, – Ceacescu 8203396, Telegram from U.S. Embassy in Bucharest to State Department, 'Proposed Presidential Letter to Ceausescu', 24 May 1984.

69 RRPL, Kenneth Hill Files, Box 4, Folder LAOOC, Letter, Ueberroth to Shultz, 24 May 1984.

70 'LAOOC, IOC helped to pay for Romanians' trip', *Los Angeles Times*, 31 July 1984. See also H. E. Wilson, 'The golden opportunity: Romania's political manipulation of the 1984 Los Angeles Olympic Games', *OLYMPIKA: The International Journal of Olympic Studies*, III (1994).

71 'Hey Russia. It's a heck of a party', *Sports Illustrated*, 6 August 1984.

72 According to journalist Frank Deford, ABC stood for 'Always Be Cheerleaders'. See F. Deford, 'Cheer, cheer, cheer for the home team', *Sports Illustrated*, 13 August 1984.

73 RRPL, WHORM CO 165 – casefile 237741, Letter Ronald Reagan to Paul Trousdale, 17 May 1984.

74 G. Troy, *Morning in America: How Ronald Reagan Invented the 1980's* (Princeton, NJ: Princeton University Press, 2005), 152.

75 R. Reagan, Remarks to United States Olympic Medal Winners in Los Angeles, 13 August 1984, available at www.presidency.ucsb.edu/ws/?pid=40252 (accessed 26 May 2016).

Post-match recovery and analysis: concluding thoughts on sport and diplomacy

Aaron Beacom and J. Simon Rofe

This concluding chapter reflects on the themes that have been identified in the book and sets out some thoughts on those that relate to the future nexus of diplomacy and sport. It begins by revisiting, in light of arguments presented in this book, the reciprocal benefits of investigating international sport and researching the reconfiguration of diplomatic practice. From there, it focuses down on the key themes developed through the book; namely conceptual issues relating to diplomacy, patterns of public diplomacy and the sports boycott as a diplomatic tool. This forms the basis for an assessment of the trajectory of sport as a dimension of the diplomatic framework. Drawing on the analysis contained in this book, what this concluding chapter captures is the increasingly entangled relationship between sport and diplomacy, where sport can itself be considered a diplomatic act, in the contexts, for example, of interest representation and mediation. In this sense the book has explored the rebalancing of their relations in a number of different spatial and temporal arenas.

Revisiting sport and diplomacy

The study of sport and diplomacy is of value in and of itself, enhancing an understanding of how this aspect of physical culture has become integral to wider political and social relations among a full range of actors in the international system. Likewise, such global phenomena which shape diplomatic practice engage with sports organisations in a variety of ways. In short, there is a relational quality to sport and diplomacy at the heart of this analysis.

The structures and institutions that have developed around sport are inherently political, reflecting, in a variety of (sometimes conflicting) ways, territorial demarcations, local and regional identities, cultural characteristics, and religious, ethnic and political allegiances. International sport can, then, provide the basis for the empirical study of the development of international relations generally and evolution of diplomatic discourses more specifically.[1]

As has been recognised for many years international sporting events can present a microcosm of international society, reflecting emerging tensions and fault lines.[2] It is unsurprising, then, that mega sport events (MSE) feature prominently throughout the book; since they have become what Iver B. Neumann identified as 'sites of diplomacy', where various rituals and exhibitions of diplomatic practice are played out. The spectacular opening ceremonies at the Olympic Games in Beijing in 2008 and London four years later speak directly to what Neumann describes as 'sublime diplomacy': the capacity of diplomacy to overwhelm and impress interlocutors that harks back to Byzantine diplomacy.[3] As such these MSE have formed the basis for public diplomacy initiatives as well as acting as a conduit for particular diplomatic practices including boycotting.

At the same time, the parameters of diplomatic activity as it relates to sport go further than such spectacular events. For example, decisions on the governance of sport, attempts to pursue development objectives through engaging with sports-based interventions, and funding of elite sport development projects as part of efforts to enhance international performances, all have implications for the representative quality of diplomatic practice that the book has demonstrated.[4]

Equally, academics from different disciplinary backgrounds are increasingly taking note of sport. As has oft been referenced in this book, Joseph Nye's conceptualisation of 'soft power' has become a touchstone for investigating influence in international affairs beyond the barrel of a gun.[5] Nye himself has used sport in explaining the power of 'attraction' in diplomacy by pointing to the allure of iconic basketball player Michael Jordan, and the opportunity taken by the People's Republic of China (PRC) to showcase China through the 2008 Olympic Games. The Chinese leadership evaluated this sufficiently successful to warrant further endeavours such as the reinvention of the Chinese Super League football tournament from 2012, and the successful bid for the 2022 Winter Olympics also to be hosted in Beijing.

It is important for those engaged in sport and diplomacy as practitioners or analysts to avoid taking an essentialist approach to sport while at the same time recognising its significance in wider international society. Though having some agency for social and political change, ultimately international sport, whether event organisation, engagement in development interventions or governance decisions, takes place within particular geopolitical contexts that determine priorities, particularly as it relates to associated diplomatic discourse. The context for the Olympic boycotts of the 1980s was the bipolarity of the Cold War that dominated the international scene at that time. Decisions on whether or not to participate in sport were linked to allegiances and concerns over resources dependent on those allegiances (the attendance of UK athletes in Moscow was in direct defiance of the government of the day and reflected a wider struggle, lost in the longer term, concerning the autonomy of sport).[6] Again from the perspective of the United Kingdom, the referendum decision to leave the European Union (EU) (23 June 2016) will inevitably have consequences on the governance of sport and the way in which it relates to regional governance: for example the transfer of players into and from the remaining EU. The Bosman Ruling was, for example, linked to the single market commitment to free movement of people, and decisions on such free movement, whether for playing, coaching or managing, will once again come under the microscope. While of little immediate consequence, the UK's referendum decision will have implications at least in terms of the presentation of the Ryder Cup, a golfing event featuring American and European teams and heavily symbolic in terms of European unity (attracting significant resourcing from the EU).[7] Sport as a physical, social and cultural activity, capable of igniting the passions of large swathes of global society while being met with supreme indifference by others, has, then, increased in its political and diplomatic significance.

Reflecting on themes developed in the book

This book's chapters have taken a broad approach to conceiving of diplomacy and its practice. In doing so it reflects long-established bastions of diplomatic thought such as Richelieu, Gucciardini, adding Harold Nicolson from the twentieth century, with the contemporary writings of Geoff Berridge, Brian Hocking, Jan Melissen and Paul Sharp, alongside the likes of Nick Cull, James Pamment, Noe Carnago and Jason Dittmer.[8] Nicolson's emphasis was on diplomacy as practice. He wrote in 1935 that he saw diplomacy as 'the practice, rather than the theory, of inter-national relations'.[9] Berridge is more specific in stating diplomacy to be an 'essentially political activity' that enables states 'to secure the objectives of their foreign policies without resort to force, propaganda or law'.[10] Dittmer takes a distinctly different account, looking at diplomacy as the output of human and nonhuman interactions, highlighting the 'contingency of human agency' with its material environment.[11] In considering this diverse heritage the book's conception of diplomacy has taken account of the activities of a wide range of actors, including stakeholders engaged in the governance of sport, as participants in the wider diplomatic process which concerns representation, communication and negotiation aimed at promoting the interests of different polities.[12]

Concepts and history of sport and diplomacy

The first section of the book focused on the conceptual debates concerning diplomacy as it relates to sport. This was addressed by highlighting the range of actors and the forms of intervention that feature in the sport diplomacy frame. Cooley's chapter served to highlight the relationship between diplomacy and the wider field of International Studies. Its consideration of the adoption of sport as part of conflict resolution and peace-building strategies highlighted the aspirational aspect of many sports-based interventions. This was reflected in attempts to engage in the governance of sport through integrative models (which in wider institutional arrangements that form part of peace-building initiatives are more generally rejected in favour of a focus on accommodative/consociational frameworks designed to reflect diversity). These are in turn predicated on assumptions around the power of sport to contribute to social cohesion and peace building. The chapter therefore contributes to the broader discussion surrounding the potential role sport has to play in addressing these issues.

This debate was given renewed prominence in early 2017 by the decision of the United Nations Secretary General to effectively transfer the mandate of the UN Office of Sport Development and Peace to the International Olympic Committee (IOC).

Cárdenas and Lang further consider the perspective on the potential of sport to contribute to peace building. In their chapter they explore how sport has been adopted as an aspect of military peace support operations (PSO). This relates to both state-based operations in the case of the armed services of the Philippines and Colombia, but also on a limited basis, in the context of United Nations Peace Keeping Operations (UNPKO). They present these initiatives as an aspect of the expanding Sport for Development and Peace (SDP) movement, and its devolution to local agencies. The multiplicity of objectives commonly associated with such sport-based interventions includes health education programmes, projects associated with gender and disability rights, and community development initiatives. In the context of peace-building interventions, the re-establishment of social relations and engagement with sport as part of psychosocial therapy to combat trauma feature prominently as objectives. The chapter identifies the challenges in realising such objectives, given the range of variables that affect outcomes. For example, sports-based interventions may be predicated on political stabilisation. In addition, the chapter recognises the potential of sport to accentuate already established divisions. In these senses, Cárdenas and Lang have contributed to the critical debate relating to the wider discourse on sport for development, and, by extension, development assistance as a tool of diplomacy.

Tomlinson's insights into the evolution of football (soccer) as a global phenomenon provide valuable context for the current struggles within the sport. The early tension between national and international institutions – in particular the Football Association and FIFA – and the roles of particular individuals as international brokers – reflect both the inherently political nature of a sport and its concomitant requirement for diplomacy as it seeks to engage actively in global events as a means of interest representation. Concerning the conceptualisation of diplomacy, of particular note is his observation that much of the writing around the subject (Beck 1999 and 2003), while not using the language of diplomacy, addresses elements of diplomatic processes relating, for example, to public diplomacy, the rise of non-governmental actors and recognition / non-recognition as a tool to influence international relations.

Dowse introduced MSE as central to debate concerning diplomatic engagement through sport. The focus on South Africa in the context of the 1995 Rugby World Cup and the 2010 Football World Cup reflected attempts by a state in rapid transition to adopt sport-appropriate mechanisms to help manage that transition. Dowse highlighted the challenges and limitations such a process faces. This includes the domestic component of securing popular support for the levels of public expenditure necessary to host (indeed, even to mount a bid to host) contemporary MSEs. In a wider sense, Dowse notes that 'MSEs used as policy tools should be treated like any other policy intervention in terms of approach and expectations. Core to this proposition is that it is unreasonable to expect any event to deliver meaningful and sustained practical policy outcomes if it is not incorporated within a multidimensional and strategic policy approach that emphasises the achievement of the policy priority over event delivery priorities or those of the event owner'. This point has been considered by a number of other commentators where to ensure effective legacy benefits, the event is planned as a 'leverage' tool, fully integrated into the wider planning process. This, it is argued, is as significant in terms of diplomacy as it is in other areas such as transport and infrastructure.

'Selling policies': sport and diplomacy as public diplomacy

The second section of the book built on the conceptual foundation and addressed the idea of sport as a dimension of public diplomacy. There is a tendency to present the historical development of diplomacy as a linear process: moving from state-centric models where the nation state provides the frame of reference with the institutions of state diplomacy representing its interests; towards what is frequently referred to as a 'new' diplomacy.[13] While this is a contested term it is frequently taken to refer to a shift away from the state and towards a multiplicity of actors engaged in representing the interests of collectives through a diverse range of activities. It is against this backdrop, and heightened by new communications technologies, that 'new' public diplomacy, engaging with other publics to shape opinions and protect interests, is presented as an emerging process.[14]

The historical perspective is developed differently in Drephal's chapter on the diplomatic dimension to Afghanistan's independence games. This sporting event began in the aftermath of the First World War and was held for the final time after the Second World War in 1947. Drephal explores the state-building qualities that sport can provide in shaping a national identity. For Afghanistan the independence games were an important annual focal point for crafting nationalism in the face of the British Empire, and so feeds into the decolonising agenda of the latter half of the twentieth century that has given rise to many sporting spectacles. Senegal's 2002 victory over reigning FIFA World Champions and former colonial power France remains a potent example of the potential sport has in this dimension; not least, as all but two of Senegal's twenty-three-man squad played their club football in France at the time.

The relationship between public diplomacy and propaganda is one that has been key to recent academic and practitioner perspectives on diplomacy and particularly public diplomacy. The linkage across previously disparate academic fields of communication studies, diplomatic studies, cultural relations and diplomatic history, while borrowing from law, politics, International Relations and sociology more broadly, provides the backdrop to the discussion of public diplomacy and propaganda.[15] The question of where public diplomacy stops and propaganda starts is implicit in Shuman's chapter on the significance of Sino-African sports delegations of the 1960s.[16] The chapter locates these efforts in opinion shaping, within the wider transition of Chinese society following the Great Leap Forward (1958–62). This was at a time when the ruling Communist Party was seeking secure stability in the domestic sphere, while simultaneously looking to enhance the Party's influence internationally. Shuman notes that the use of sport in a diplomatic context was taking root: reflected in support for

Olympic athletes, despite a lack of funding for sport in general. Nevertheless, the range of sports-based diplomatic initiatives within the African sub-continent during the 1960s demonstrated a wider commitment to project a particular ideological and cultural worldview, that would contribute towards the extension of Chinese influence at the expense of their communist relation the Soviet Union. Such relatively small-scale activities did draw significant international attention and, as Shuman indicates, demonstrates that sport diplomacy is not limited to the large-scale events associated with MSEs. At the same time these initiatives did follow the enhancement of Chinese engagement with a particular sport, namely table tennis. This engagement was articulated through its hosting of the International Table Tennis Federation World Championships in 1961. From a development perspective, Shuman's suggests that this early form of ping-pong diplomacy put China ahead of the curve, while serving to reveal an unequal relationship between the hosts and the visitors. Such an approach is noteworthy when considered in the context of more recent attempts to engage with sport as a conduit for development, and particularly twenty-first-century Chinese endeavours in Africa.

Krasnoff's chapter does however highlight the long tradition in opinion forming through international sporting contacts. A consideration of the reciprocal shaping of attitudes among young male elites resulting from the post-war basketball tours of the US by the Paris Université Club (PUC) speaks to the role of citizen diplomacy, while exhibiting echoes of so-called 'sports ambassadors' of today, including a number of other official US sport diplomacy initiatives operated by the US Bureau of Educational and Cultural Affairs.[17]

David Rowe's discussion of Australia's Asian credentials in relation to football returns to the role sport can play in shaping opinions, particularly in relation to aspects of the soft power debate. Rowe's discussion of decisions taken by sports inter-ests within Australia to move their regional football affiliation away from the Oceania Football Confederation and towards the Asian Football Confederation reflects, above all, the disjoint between aspirations for sport as a public diplomacy tool and the reality of grappling with multiple competing regional and international interests. While the move was seen as integral to a re-focusing towards Asia of wider Australian business, political and cultural interests, regional power relations quickly asserted themselves and limits to the potential of 'soccer diplomacy' to drive change were brought into sharp relief.

Boycott: no sport as diplomacy

The third section of the book is given over to the sports boycott as a particular form of diplomatic tool. In the opening chapter, Gomez places the issue of the sport boycott and sports sanctions within the wider debate concerning the efficacy of these diplo-matic tools in achieving their desired outcomes. From a historical perspective, Gomez reflects on the Cold War power-play of East and West, articulated through the boycott mechanism (later explored in Eaton's chapter). At the same time, she asks the central question: is the sporting boycott consigned to history due to the changing nature of international society, or rather, is it being reconstituted to reflect the new geopolitical context? Reference to threatened boycotting of the 2008 Beijing Olympic Games can be considered in this context. So too can the ascendency of partial boycotts in the form of non-participation or reduced participation in opening and closing ceremonies to recent Games as strategies for articulating opposition to foreign and domestic policy decisions (e.g. in the form of civil rights and the treatment of minority groups).

Vaughan's chapter on the relationship between the US and the 'two Chinas' in the context of the 1960 Winter Olympic Games underlines the trajectory of sport in international diplomacy generally, but more specifically in the context of the Cold War. Vaughan draws attention to archive material from the United States Information Agency that clearly indicates the symbolic value of sporting success by the Soviet bloc as 'a setback' for the United States that could only be countered through increased investment as part of a strategic response: placing sport firmly within the classic zero-sum Cold War lexicon. At the same time, the chapter unpicks the complexities of IOC/NOC relations in terms of international representation – and in so doing highlights the period of growing authority of the IOC as a non-governmental actor in international affairs. By focusing on tensions around representation through NOCs, around the 1960 Winter Olympic Games, Vaughan underlines the role of events in providing a point of interface between contending international allegiances, as well as international, national and local interests – and indeed state and non-state aspirations.

Eaton's analysis of the 1980 Moscow Olympics enhances our understanding of the boycott in the context of diplomacy by presenting it as a multidimensional process. Decisions to join the 1980 boycott reflected particular regional strategies rather than blanket adherence to the East–West divide. Indonesia, for example, was working to secure its place as a regional power and leading role among Islamic states. Similarly, the Egyptian decision to join the boycott of the Moscow Games reflected efforts to re-establish Egyptian influence in its own region after a period of decline. Eaton presents the decision by the PRC to join the boycott as helping to increase the speed of normalisation in relations between the PRC and the US. Here again however, a number of regional interests played a part in the PRC's decision, given the Chinese Communist Party's desire to present itself as offering a meaningful alternative to the Soviet model. Furthermore, Eaton points to the domestic dimension of boycotting. This, Eaton suggests, was particularly strong in relation to the Philippines and Ghana, where it was presented as part of a commitment by government to reduce public spending in the face of financial difficulties. What this helps to do is to underline once again the significant relationship between areas of foreign and domestic policy that sport brings together, and to characterise the conceptual underpinnings of sport and diplomacy.

Tulli's chapter on the 1984 Los Angeles Olympic Games challenges a binary 'public' versus 'private' approach to the Olympics. Despite the awarding of the Games to Los Angeles being predicated on the belief that it would mark the distancing of politics from the Olympics, following the corrosive intrusion that characterised the previous decade, Tulli questions the widely held contention that the US government was little more than a bystander at the Games. In contrast he points to the president of the LAOOC being hailed by President Ronald Reagan as the personification of entrepreneurship, drive and discipline. These characteristics underpinned Reagan's view of American values and the world – given expression in the 1984 election campaign; 'It's morning in America again'– and had a direct foreign policy counterpart in Reagan's new Cold War rhetoric. Tulli notes the role the administration took in security of the Games: albeit a role it was inevitably obliged to adopt. The administration was also inevitably drawn into the discourse over the boycott that unfolded in the lead-up to the Games. In addition, it also became engaged with what can be interpreted as a public diplomacy campaign linked to the Games. This was not inevitable Tulli argues, but rather emerged out of Reagan's conviction of the capacity to project US values through the hosting process. Reference to aggressive negotiation by LAOOC representatives, of lucrative contracts with key media organisations, is presented as a shifting of the power base away from the IOC, which was previously responsible for the negotiation of such activity, and towards the host organisation. Neumann's contemporary understanding of 'sublime diplomacy', where those conducting diplomacy endeavour to overwhelm through scale, was clearly at play here.[18] At the same time, private sector stakeholders enhanced their influence through a rapid expansion in the role and support of corporate sponsors.[19] This was an epoch-changing process in moving the Olympic Games from the state as 'old' diplomacy to including the private sector, an exemplar of 'new' diplomacy. In this regard at least, this heralded the commencement of an era that was to see the characteristics of the Olympic Games substantively change their place in international relations and embrace capitalist thinking. The 1976 Montreal Games would be seen as the apex of the Keynesian interventionist era, and the 1980 Moscow Games an anomaly – for a generation at least – in relation to the level and nature of state support they attracted.

The intertwined relationship of diplomacy and sport

In drawing this volume to a close, how then can the themes developed in the book help us to understand the evolving relationship between diplomacy and sport, provide further opportunities for research among scholars, and shape practitioners in these co-existing realms?

Soft power and mega-events

As has been shown in this book, there is particular debate over the relationship between MSEs and soft power. Such a debate is part of a wider discourse among academics and in contemporary society over the utility of soft power . Its oppositional stance to 'hard power' is a key component of this discourse. As such, soft power is perhaps most useful to consider as 'a means by which the existing hegemony is reimagined, repackaged, and reaffirmed'.[20] In other words, exercising soft power is a form of control in which increasingly its practice needs to engage with a so-called audience as a peer and co-contributor rather than as recipient. In another regard soft power is on the wane. In early 2017, Mick Mulvaney, director of the White House Office of Budget and Management, referred to the budget launched by US president Donald Trump as a 'hard-power, not a soft-power budget'.[21] The budget ought to increase federal spending on security across Defense, Homeland Security and Veterans Affairs, at the clear expense of the State Department, where cuts of over 20 per cent were proposed. The lack of appreciation for the role of diplomacy and diplomats drew a pointed response from the concept's forefather, Joseph Nye. 'It shows a profound misunderstanding', Nye told the Council on Foreign Relations. 'The question is not either/or, hard power versus soft power, but how to combine the two so that they reinforce each other, to better help you achieve your objectives. In that sense, cutting aid, public diplomacy, or other such things, which are not large, takes away attractiveness, which is a force multiplier for hard power.' Nye went on to say, 'Nobody has expressed that in simpler, more effective terms than Secretary of Defense [Jim] Mattis. He said [in 2013 Senate testimony], "If you don't fund the State Department fully, then I need to buy more ammunition ultimately."'[22]

Despite Nye's continuing appreciation of the balance and complementarity between hard and soft power, Trump's budget, its hard power focus and rhetoric are part of a wider post-2016 world of increasing nationalism where international affairs have adopted a greater realist zero-sum focus. The United Kingdom's Brexit decision, and the negotiations that will follow, equally suggest that soft power does not perhaps hold the same currency that it did in the 1990s and early 2000s. The implications for sport are not wholly clear but they do suggest a questioning of the perceived benefit of associating national identity with sport. One can point to the open and vocal opposition from millions of Brazilians who took to the streets in 2013 to protest against the government's decision to host the 2014 World Cup and 2016 Olympics. Significantly, the target for these protests evolved from outright opposition to the Brazilian government to include international tourism, which comprises a major rationale for hosting an MSE. As late in the day as June 2016 (with the Olympic Games beginning in early August), protesters held up signs at Rio Galeão-Tom Jobim International Airport written in English, 'Welcome to hell: police and firefighters don't get paid. Whoever comes to Rio de Janeiro will not be safe.'[23] The impact of such protests over a prolonged period upon the sporting spectacle are hard to assess but whatever the reality the protests altered public perception in two key regards. First, the image the Brazilian government wanted to portray, of Brazil as a rising power, one of the BRICS capable of hosting a large-scale international event was inevitably being challenged.[24] The second alteration was to palpably shift the public perception of the qualities of being a host city for the Olympic Games from Rio's immediate predecessor. While there had been some opposition to London hosting the 2012 Games, public support had been more visible, articulated for example through the extensive Games Makers volunteer programme which was characterised as the face of London and the United Kingdom. Lord Sebastian Coe highlighted their role – 'the Games-Makers stand among the heroes of London 2012' – in his closing 'Made in Britain' speech.[25] More tangibly, in terms of future MSEs in the aftermath of the first phase of protests in 2013, the host city for the 2020 Olympic Games – Tokyo – downsized its plans for 2020, with a 40 per cent reduction in its budget and there was also considerable furore over the design of British-Iraqi architect Zaha Hadid's Olympic Stadium.[26] As the perceived capacity of states to benefit diplomatically from hosting MSEs is increasingly called into question, there is pressure on International Sports Organisations to alter their bidding process. At the same time these sports organisations, mindful of the challenges they face particularly in light of reduced numbers of cities willing to bid for MSEs, are reassessing their own protocols. This includes the current IOC consideration of awarding the 2024 and 2028 Games simultaneously, revisiting the formal two-stage bidding process (originally aimed at challenging corruption) and encouraging a more open dialogue with potential bidders in an effort to allay their concerns about the process.[27]

The reduction in the number of cities/countries bidding for MSEs

There is an observable trend for fewer cities and nations to put themselves forward to host MSEs.[28] In early 2017, the Olympic Games of 2024 and FIFA World Cup of 2026 have respectively two and one bids remaining. Significantly, a number of host cities – Budapest, Rome and Hamburg – ruled themselves out of the running for the Olympic Games, and with no further creditable bids likely to emerge for the 2026 World Cup the CONCAF joint bid between Mexico, Canada and the USA is likely to be uncontested. In this light we might look back on the 1990s, culminating in the eleven bids launched for the 2004 Games, as a high point in the perceived diplomatic value of hosting MSEs. As demonstrated in table 13.1, since the bidding for the 2004 Games there has been a consistent reduction in bidding for the Olympic (and, by association, Paralympic) Games; a pattern that has continued through until the bidding round for the 2024 Games.

When this downward trend in bidding for MSEs is considered from a wider historical context, however, it should be noted that different forms of international gatherings have held prominence in different eras. A useful parallel might be drawn with the high-water mark of summitry diplomacy during the Cold War and particularly the 1970s and 1980s, which has since waned as the centrality to the world of the leaders of two nation states representing East and West coming together matters less than other forums.[29] That is not to overlook the fact that summit meetings, like sporting fixtures, still provide meaningful opportunities for discussion and serve to focus attention as venues for parley. Indeed, as one of the co-editors has written elsewhere, the annual sessions of the IOC represent 'a *summit* in Olympic terms', and 'have a mimicking quality to that of the United Nations' annual General Assembly meetings each fall'.[30] As has long been the case in diplomacy: its success reflects the evolution of the medium to cater to the need for communication and negotiation, rather than any particular form.

A further consideration in this shifting lexicon of diplomacy concerns the influence that cities as key sub-state actors exert on decisions relating to the Olympic and Paralympic Games. This influence has become as much associated with the rejection of proposals to bid for the Games (at times in defiance of national policy) as with any

Table 13.1 Bidding cities for summer Olympic Games, 2004–24

Year of Games	Applicant cities	Candidate cities	Winning city (with place and date of announcement)	Notes
2004	Istanbul Lille Rio de Janeiro St Petersburg San Juan Seville	Buenos Aires Cape Town Rome Stockholm	Athens (106th: Lausanne, 5 September 1997)	Athens was the first city to be selected under the new two-phase system of selecting candidate cities from the initial round of applicant cities
2008	Bangkok Cairo Havana Kuala Lumpur Seville	Istanbul Osaka Paris Toronto	Beijing (112th: Moscow, 13 July 2001)	Widespread concerns regarding Beijing bid on basis of human rights record. Also, concerns about air quality and impact on athletes
2012	Havana Istanbul Leipzig Rio de Janeiro	Madrid Moscow New York City Paris	London (117th: Singapore, 6 July 2005)	Accusations from Paris Delegation of violation of the IOC bidding rules by London 2012. Accusations rejected by Rogge
2016	Baku Doha Prague	Chicago Madrid Tokyo	Rio de Janeiro (121st: Copenhagen, 2 October 2009)	Doha, Baku, Madrid and Tokyo went on the register as applicant cities for the 2020 Games
2020	Baku Doha Rome*	Istanbul Madrid	Tokyo (Buenos Aires, 7 September 2013)	*Grave concerns expressed after Rome withdrew initial bid – reducing number of applications to five
2024		Hamburg* Rome** Budapest*** Los Angeles Paris	Paris (announced in Peru, 13 September 2017 – simultaneous announcement of Los Angeles to host 2028 Games)	*Withdrawal of Hamburg bid, 29 November 2015 (following referendum in city) **Withdrawal of Rome bid, 11 October 2016 ***Withdrawal of Budapest bid, 22 February 2017

Source: Updated from Beacom, *International Diplomacy and the Olympic Movement.*

other aspect of the Games cycle. In this, the capacity of civil society groups to express their opposition through a range of media, including independent referenda, while engaging with social media as a way of communicating opposition, should not be underestimated. At the same time, for cities retaining an interest in sport as part of municipal diplomacy, there are alternatives; international (as opposed to mega) sporting events that present many of the benefits without the same level of financial and other risks.[31] As an example from the UK, the Commonwealth Games of 2002, which were hosted by Manchester, were widely considered as having made a significant contribution to the rejuvenation of that city and region as it struggled with a range of socio-economic challenges linked to industrial decline.[32] Similarly, the Glasgow Commonwealth Games of 2014 were credited with contributing significantly to the strategic development of the city and region (while being linked to the ongoing debate concerning regional autonomy).[33] The non-departmental public body UK Sport's 'Gold Event Series', while linked to a wider attempt to secure a legacy from London 2012, supported (and in some contexts resourced) the relevant sports bodies together with municipal authorities, to secure a number of regional and international sporting events across the UK between 2013 and 2019.[34] It was subsequently claimed that the target of securing seventy world-class events during this period had been reached within a year of launching the initiative (the 2014 FINA Diving World Series held at London's Olympic Aquatics Centre being one of the early events in the schedule).[35]

The security agenda and the future of international sports events

A further feature of the sport and diplomacy dynamic that has been touched upon in these chapters and is ripe for further investigation is the way in which security features in the relationship. One of the enduring qualities of sport has been its accessibility to the masses. However, the participatory dimension of major sporting events, either as competitors or as spectators, has made sport a target also. The examples of the attack on the Boston marathon in April 2013 and the targeting of the France vs Germany football match at the Stade de France in the Paris attacks of November 2015 illustrate the challenges sport faces to provide a secure platform for competition. These are not new challenges to sport nor diplomacy. The 1972 Olympics were the venue for a terrorist attack that left dead eleven members of the Israeli Olympic team, a German police officer and five of the eight terrorists at the Fürstenfeldbruck airfield during a botched rescue. A longer history, with particular diplomatic resonance, can be found in the Olympic Truce, which can be traced back to the ninth century BC and has, since 1993, been revived by the United Nations General Assembly in conjunction with the Winter and Summer Olympic Games. The underpinning notion, albeit ideal rather than realised, that allows for safe passage of athletes, their families and pilgrims to the Olympic Games, has direct parallels to the immunity enjoyed by accredited diplomats in their travels. Equally, diplomatic infrastructure has consistently faced security challenges, with embassies and ambassadors the targets and victims of attacks throughout the centuries. At various points in time traditional diplomacy has sought refuge within compounds or bunkers but such actions have invariably hampered the ability to conduct diplomacy. And the infrastructure of both diplomacy and sport is no longer purely physical. While the future of e-sports is unfolding, the electronic infrastructure underpinning major sport and the conduct of diplomacy is integral in the twenty-first century and therefore vulnerable. Addressing these security challenges provides opportunities for diplomacy as well as organisational challenges and risks that increasingly go beyond the abilities of individual nations to address them. Recognising the extra-territoriality of security in sport requires multi-agency, international cooperation (particularly around the intelligence agenda). In other words, the balance for both sport and diplomacy is therefore to reconcile security with accessibility.

Leveraging a diplomatic legacy

Part of the response to the problems and limitations addressed in the book has been to consider the capacity of the Olympic and Paralympic Games to contribute to wider structural objectives, including diplomatic objectives, through what is commonly referred to as the legacy agenda. There is a fundamental difference between running an event in the hope that positive benefits will flow from it, and engaging in the conscious development of a strategy that in effect sets out to use an event as a lever to achieve wider policy objectives. Rocha identified this in relation to what he considered was the limited engagement of Brazilian politicians and diplomats in planning to leverage a positive diplomatic legacy from the Rio 2016 Olympic and Paralympic Games.[36] This was in contrast to the legacy planning that characterised the run-up to, and through, the 2012 London Games. Systematic evidence of planning for legacy was integral to the success of the bid in the face of fierce competition and at a time when it was not considered a front-runner by the majority of commentators.[37] The commitment to achieving a positive social legacy was not just a matter of using the Olympics to leverage domestic social policy objectives. It was also reflected in carefully planned efforts to project an image of the UK internationally as a caring and inclusive society, and in this respect the Paralympic Games fulfilled a particularly significant function.[38] The Olympic Legacy Park in Sheffield, some one hundred and sixty miles north of the main Olympic site, and Queen Elizabeth Park in Stratford, opened in 2017 as a centre for health and well-being, are testament as to the ways legacy can leveraged.[39]

Concern with the promotion of a positive legacy is not just an issue for the host city and government. The IOC has a direct interest in the development of its own legacy, not least as a mediator in international affairs. This has been reflected in the past through engagement with the Olympic Games as a conduit for communication between estranged states, for example North and South Korea in the context of the Sydney Games of 2000.[40] More recently in relation to the 2016 Olympic and Paralympic Games, the fielding of teams of athletes with refugee status, competing under the IOC and International Paralympic Committee (IPC) flags respectively, reflected this commitment to create a wider legacy of providing effective support in international crises.[41] The athlete development initiatives coordinated through Olympic Solidarity and, more recently, the Agitos Foundation (the international development organisations linked to the Olympic and Paralympic movements respectively) can also be considered in this context.[42] While primarily concerned with supporting athlete and infrastructure needs in resource-poor regions, such initiatives have the capacity to enhance the image of the Olympic and Paralympic movements in terms of their wider human development commitments.

At the same time, effective legacies in relation to political and social capital may emerge out of dissension towards the bidding and staging of MSEs that, when considered in a wider context, suggest the effective representation of interests hitherto mis- or underrepresented. In this context, Sengupta's reference to the rise of political activism through concerns over the treatment of the dispossessed in the preparation of the Delhi Commonwealth Games, and the subsequent creation of a new political party, is of significance.[43] In the context of successive Paralympic Games, perhaps best documented in relation to London 2012, the Paralympics have acted to varying degrees as a conduit for Disabled People's Organizations to articulate concerns and seek to inform policy makers. In this, the IPC has the capacity to engage as a global player in the diplomatic frame, representing the interests of the disability community.[44]

Technology and sport diplomacy

The capacity of technological developments to change the way in which diplomacy is carried out, namely revised approaches to communication, representation and negotiation, is a factor that has drawn extensive commentary from writers on diplomacy.[45] Social media, as one of these revised forms, has the capacity to facilitate the emergence in the diplomatic frame of civil society groups and other actors which characterise what Hocking *et al.* refer to as 'integrative diplomacy'.[46] In relation to the Paralympic Games, for example, the IPC (which as a global actor has adopted a disability advocacy role as well as its position at the apex of para-sport governance) relies increasingly on social media platforms to promote its narratives of inclusion and empowerment through the Games.[47] Social media, it would appear, enabled the Paralympic movement to engage new audiences and broaden the appeal of 'the Games and the Movement'.[48] Athlete engagement, for example, created the opportunity to provide an athlete's perspective on a range of Paralympic experiences and open up a new dimension of the Games to audiences. Developing this approach, the IPC adopted a policy of identifying athlete ambassadors, who are promoted as representing the interests and concerns of disabled athletes and, by association, the wider disabled community.[49]

Also of note was a report published by Twitter in the wake of the 2012 Games which revealed that the hashtag #Paralympics topped the table for the most trending UK sport event of 2012. It managed to beat off competition from the Olympic Games and many leading Premiership football clubs.[50] Around fifty leading athletes also took part in the Samsung Bloggers project, which saw them record and post video blogs from behind the scenes before, during and after the London 2012 Games. Over 600 video blogs were uploaded and were viewed by over 300,000 people.[51] This again can be interpreted as providing a valuable route to interest representation without depending on mainstream media formats.

Closing remarks

There are many other challenges facing sport as an aspect of global affairs; not least the re-emergence of sports events as the focus of a variety of forms of diplomatic protest. The Sochi Winter Games of 2014 in particular reflected efforts to use the medium of the Games to articulate displeasure over the actions of particular states. These Games coincided with the annexation of Crimea and hostilities in parts of Ukraine. While the Russian state had, in the lead-up to the Games, attempted to use the event as a means of promoting Russia internationally as an open and tolerant society (including legis-lating for disability rights), regional events served at least in part to derail these efforts. This was reflected through a number of diplomatic protests, particularly in response to Russian involvement in Crimea and the Ukraine. The UK and US governments decided not to send official delegations to the Games and the Ukrainian team did not participate in the parade of nations at the Opening Ceremony – beyond the presence of one athlete who carried the Ukrainian flag. This is significant in a diplomatic context since it reflects an increasing trend to engage in carefully calibrated diplomatic responses to register concerns relating to the host, while avoiding full-blown boycotts considered counterproductive on a number of fronts.[52] Protests were also reflected in advocacy group responses to controversy surrounding the change in legislation in Russia interpreted as restricting the rights of the LGBT community. The Federation of Gay Games petitioned the IPC president not to attend the Games if the Russian government did not allow the Russian Open Games – a multi-sport event for LGBT athletes due to take place just prior to the Paralympics – to go ahead. In the event, the Russian Open Games was severely disrupted due to security issues and what some commentators attributed to pressure from the Russian authorities.[53] Norway's Health Minister Bent Hoie, who is openly gay, announced he would attend the Paralympic Games with his husband in a show of solidarity to the LGBT community in Russia.[54]

Other considerations have entered the debate relating to the capacity of interna-tional sports bodies to engage in diplomacy, both in terms of interest representation and mediation. The extensively reported inherent weakness in sports governance, emerging out of lack of accountability and already referred to in this book, calls into question the aspirations of organisations such as FIFA, the IOC and the IAAF to develop their profile as international actors in a range of contexts. These concerns are accentuated when they become linked to the doping scandals that have been a feature of international sports events, in particular the 2016 Olympic Games, and the financial misconduct in football. This leads to scholarly interest in how such organisations might be reconstituted to take account of such concerns. The continued focus on developments in diplomacy as it relates to football is appropriate given the continued global prominence of the game. Tomlinson and Rowe's contributions to an expanding dialogue on 'soccer diplomacy' are significant.

Finally, we should be careful not to over-emphasise the role of sport in interna-tional diplomacy. At best it remains on the margins of international relations. This was brought into focus against the backdrop of the 2014 Winter Games in Sochi.

While the Games illustrate on a number of levels how diplomacy broadly defined can become enmeshed in the organisation and delivery, it is also a salutatory lesson in the limitations of sport to influence the trajectory of determined foreign policy interests. A stark lesson in the realpolitik diplomacy is there to address.

Overall, then, there is much here for scholars, practitioners and players to consider as the epilogue of this discussion of sport and diplomacy becomes the prologue to the next contest. The arenas of sport and diplomacy bring together manifold issues of finance, governance, gender, identity and competition that have too often been considered aside and apart from each other. The book here has sought to address those distinct realms through empirical, conceptual but overall critical analysis. That it has ended by pointing to this wide range of areas that require further attention suggests a burgeoning field of study.

Notes

1 Aaron Beacom, *International Diplomacy and the Olympic Movement: The New Mediators* (Basingstoke: Palgrave Macmillan, 2012).

2 Richard Espy, *The Politics of the Olympic Games* (Berkeley, CA: University of California Press, 1979).

3 Iver B. Neumann, *Diplomatic Sites: A Critical Enquiry* (London: Hurst, 2013), 121–46.

4 Alison Holmes and J. Simon Rofe, *Global Diplomacy: Theories, Types and Models* (Boulder, CO: Westview, 2016), 9.

5 Literature on 'soft power' is plentiful across many different fields of study and Nye's reflections on its evolution are informative in recognising this. See 'Think again: soft power', *Foreign Policy*, 23 February 2009, available at http://foreignpolicy.com/2006/02/23/think-again-soft-power/ (accessed 18 May 2017). Most relevant to the connection between soft power and public diplomacy is Nye's article 'Public diplomacy and soft power', *Annals of the American Academy of Political and Social Science – Public Diplomacy in a Changing World*, 616 (2008). Sport is a recurring theme in Nye's further writings. See 'The Olympics and Chinese soft power', *Huffington Post*, 29 September 2008. Nye's work is heavily referenced in other works, such as the eminent historian of American foreign relations, Walter Lafeber's book *Michael Jordan and the New Global Capitalism* (New York: W. W. Norton, 2002).

6 Paul Corthorn, 'The Cold War and British debates over the boycott of the 1980 Moscow Olympics', *Cold War History*, 13:1 (2012).

7 Ian Henry, *Transnational and Comparative Research in Sport: Globalisation, Governance and Sport Policy* (London: Routledge, 2007); Barrie Houlihan and Dominic Malcolm (eds), *Sport and Society* (London: Sage, 3rd edn, 2015).

8 These authors form a selection of scholars writing on diplomacy 'old' and 'new'. Francesco Gucciardini (1483–1540) and Cardinal Richelieu (1585–1642) represent some of the established thinking on diplomacy, as it was manifest in the Italian Renaissance and then in the court of the French monarch, with the latter founding the first Ministry of Foreign Affairs. See Francesco Gucciardini, *Maxims and Reflections Ricordi*, trans. Mario Domandi (Philadelphia, PA: University of Pennsylvania Press, 1972); and Armand Jean du Plessis Richelieu, Cardinal et Duc de, *The Political*

Testament of Cardinal Richelieu, trans. Henry Bertram Hill (Madison, WI: University of Wisconsin Press, 1964). Harold Nicolson's voluminous writings in the first half of the twentieth century as part of the British governing elite provide both insight and critical reflection into the then 'new' open diplomacy of the time. See Harold Nicolson, *Peacemaking 1919* (London: Faber & Faber, 1933). Of more recent vintage, now in its fifth edition, Geoff Berridge's *Diplomacy: Theory and Practice* (London: Palgrave Macmillan, 2015) is a seminal text. Berridge's contemporaries as scholars of diplomatic studies including Brian Hocking, Jan Melissen, John Young, Costas Constantinou and Paul Sharp provide further consideration across a range of publications. Two are of particular note: first, Paul Sharp's *Diplomatic Theories of International Relations* (Cambridge: Cambridge University Press, 2009); and secondly the collective piece Brian Hocking, Jan Melissen, Shaun Riordan and Paul Sharp, *Futures for Diplomacy: Integrative Diplomacy in the 21st Century* (Clingendael: Netherlands Institute of International Relations, 2012). Nick Cull's writings have evolved to focus upon public diplomacy, *Public Diplomacy: Lessons from the Past* (Los Angeles: Figueroa Press, 2007), and his contribution to the University of Southern California Annenberg School of Public Diplomacy. James Pamment's work takes a critical reading of public diplomacy in *British Public Diplomacy and Soft Power: Diplomatic Influence & Digital Disruption* (London: Palgrave Macmillan, 2016) and *New Public Diplomacy in the 21st Century: A Comparative Study of Policy and Practice* (London: Routledge, 2013). Noe Carnago's work has looked at 'para' and 'proto' diplomacy, that is, the parallel or mimicking of diplomatic practice in opposition to its traditional form by a variety of actors, including sporting institutions, and has explored this, along with Costas Constantinou and Finoa McConneel, in *Trans-Professional Diplomacy* (Leiden: Brill Research Perspectives on Diplomacy and Foreign Policy, 2016).

9 Harold Nicolson, 'Modern diplomacy and British public opinion', *International Affairs (Royal Institute of International Affairs 1931–1939)*, 145 (Sept.–Oct., 1935).

10 Berridge, *Diplomacy*, 1.

11 Jason Dittmer, *Diplomatic Material: Affect, Assemblage, and Foreign Policy* (Durham, NC: Duke University Press, 2017).

12 J. Simon Rofe has previously articulated the applicability of a global diplomacy framework and its relation to sport and diplomacy; see Rofe, 'Sport and diplomacy: a global diplomacy framework', *Diplomacy and Statecraft*, 27:2 (2016).

13 Debates on what constitutes new diplomacy are a recurring feature of literature on diplomatic studies. See Holmes and Rofe, *Global Diplomacy*, 60, 73.

14 Jan Melissen, 'The new public diplomacy: between theory and practice', in Jan Melissen (ed.), *The New Public Diplomacy: Soft Power in International Relations* (Basingstoke: Palgrave, 2005).

15 For more on the relationship between propaganda and public diplomacy, see the eponymous website of Phil Taylor at the University of Leeds, http://media.leeds.ac.uk/papers/, and Nicholas Cull, *The Cold War and the United States Information Agency: American Propaganda and Public Diplomacy, 1945–1989* (Cambridge: Cambridge University Press, 2009).

16 Holmes and Rofe, *Global Diplomacy*, 45.

17 Bureau of Educational and Cultural Affair Department of State, available at https://eca.state.gov/programs-initiatives/sports-diplomacy (accessed 17 July 2017).

18 Iver B. Neumann, *Sublime Diplomacy: Byzantine, Early Modern, Contemporary*, Clingendael, Netherlands Institute of International Relations, Discussion Papers of Diplomacy, 102, 2006, 1. See also Iver B. Neumann, 'Sublime diplomacy, Byzantine, early modern, contemporary', *Millenium*, 34:3 (2006).

19 See Noe Cornago, *Plural Diplomacies: Normative Predicaments and Functional Imperatives* (Leiden: Martinus Nijhoff, 2013).

20 Melissa Nisbett, 'Who holds the power in soft power?', *Arts & International Affairs* 3 (2016), available at https://theartsjournal.net/2016/03/13/nisbett/ (accessed 26 April 2017).

21 Michael Memoli and Noah Bierman, 'Trump's hard power budget makes sweeping cuts to EPA and State Department, boosts defence spending', *Los Angeles Times*, 16 March 2017, available at www.latimes.com/nation/la-na-pol-trump-budget-20170316-story.html (accessed 31 January 2018).

22 Joseph P. Nye, 'Hard power's essential soft side', *Council on Foreign Relations*, 29 March 2017, available at www.cfr.org/interview/hard-powers-essential-soft-side (accessed 26 April 2017).

23 Nick Butler, 'Riot police hold up signs welcoming tourists to hell as strikes threatened during Olympics and Paralympics', 29 June 2016, available at www.insidethegames.biz/articles/1039006/rio-police-hold-up-signs-welcoming-tourists-to-hell-as-strikes-threatened-during-olympics-and-paralympics (accessed 26 April 2017).

24 BRICS was a term coined by Jim O'Neil as chairman of multinational finance company and bank Goldman Sachs in 2001 comprising Brazil, Russia, India, China and South Africa. Their relationship beginning with the Bejing Olympics of 2008, in quick succession all of the other members hosted MSEs: South Africa 2010 FIFA World Cup; India 2010 Commonwealth Games; Russia Sochi 2014 Winter Olympic Games with the 2018 FIFA World Cup to followBrazil the 2014 FIFA World Cup and 2016 Olympics. The potential for a national image or brand to be shaped by an MSE is examined in Jonathan Grix and Donnal Lee, 'Soft power, sports mega-events and emerging states: the lure of the politics of attraction', *Global Society*, 27:4 (2013). The discourse on the value of MSEs to national image extends beyond the BRICS and other emerging states. See Jonathan Grix, 'Image leveraging and sports mega-events: Germany and the 2006 FIFA World Cup', *Journal of Sport and Tourism*, 17:4 (2012); and more recently, Jonathan Grix, Paul Michael Brannagan and Barrie Houlihan, 'Interrogating states' soft power strategies: a case study of sports mega-events in Brazil and the UK', *Global Society*, 29:3 (2015).

25 Lord Coe, chairman of the London Organising Committee of the Olympic and Paralympic Games, 9 September 2012.

26 Oliver Wainwright, 'Zaha Hadid's Tokyo Olympic Stadium slammed as a monumental mistake and a disgrace to future generations', *The Guardian*, 6 November 2014, available at www.theguardian.com/artanddesign/architecture-design-blog/2014/nov/06/zaha-hadids-tokyo-olympic-stadium-slammed-as-a-monumental-mistake-and-a-disgrace-to-future-generations (accessed 30 January 2018).

27 BBC News, 'IOC may award both 2024 and 2028 Olympic Games in September', 17 March 2017, available at www.bbc.co.uk/sport/olympics/39301380\ (accessed 26 April 2017).

28 The impact on certain countries and their ability to appear attractive is considered

here in relation to the 2022 FIFA World Cup in Qatar. Paul Michael Brannagan and Richard Giulianotti, 'Soft power and soft disempowerment: Qatar, global sport and football's 2022 World Cup finals', *Leisure Studies*, 34:6 (2014).

29 For further detail on the value of summitry to diplomacy, see David Dunn (ed.), *Diplomacy at the Highest Level: The Evolution of International Summitry* (Basingstoke: Palgrave, 1996); and Jan Melissen, *Summit Diplomacy Coming of Age*, Discussion Papers in Diplomacy, Netherlands Institute of International Relations (Clingendaal, 2003).

30 Holmes and Rofe, *Global Diplomacy*, 42–3.

31 Aaron Beacom 'Game on? The City and the public diplomacy of the Olympic bid', *Public Diplomacy*, Summer/Fall (2017), available at www.publicdiplomacymagazine. com (accessed 8 August 2017).

32 Andrew Cave and Alex Miller, 'A sporting gift: the renaissance of Manchester', *The Telegraph*, 4 August 2016, available at www.telegraph.co.uk/investing/business-of-sport/manchester-commonwealth-games-legacy/ (accessed 30 January 2018).

33 Social Research Unit, Scottish Government, 'An evaluation of legacy from the Glasgow 2014 Commonwealth Games: post-games report', *Scottish Government Publication*, July 2015, available at www.gov.scot/Resource/0048/00482151.pdf (accessed 30 January 2018).

34 UK Sport, 'Sports Gold Event Series to create a stage to inspire Games legacy', 14 November 2012, available at www.uksport.gov.uk/news/2012/11/14/uk-sports-gold-event-series-to-create-a-stage-to-inspire-games-legacy (accessed 26 April 2017).

35 Inside the Games, 'Gold Event Series reaches halfway target inside first year, claims UK Sport', 20 November 2013, available at www.insidethegames.biz/articles/1017205/gold-event-series-reaches-halfway-target-inside-first-year-claims-uk-sport (accessed 8 August 2017).

36 Claudio Rocha, 'Support of politicians for the 2016 Olympic Games in Rio de Janeiro', *International Journal of Sport Policy and Politics*, 35:4 (2016).

37 Ian Brittain and Aaron Beacom, 'Leveraging Paralympic legacy', *Journal of Sport and Social Issues*, 40:6 (2016).

38 House of Commons Foreign Affairs Select Committee, 'FCO and public diplomacy: the Olympic and Paralympic Games 2012' – second report of session 2010–2011. February 2011, available at www.publications.parliament.uk/pa/cm201011/cmselect/cmfaff/581/581.pdf (accessed 26 April 2017).

39 See Olympic Legacy Park, Sheffield, http://olympiclegacypark.co.uk/about (accessed 20 July 2017).

40 Aaron Beacom, *International Diplomacy and the Olympic Movement: The New Mediators* (Basingstoke: Palgrave, 2012).

41 Aaron Beacom, 'The Paralympic Movement and diplomacy: centering disability in the global frame', in Ian Brittain and Aaron Beacom (eds), *Palgrave Handbook of Paralympic Studies* (Basingstoke: Palgrave, 2018).

42 Brittain and Beacom, 'Leveraging Paralympic legacy'.

43 Mitu Sengupta, 'A window into India's development story – the 2010 Commonwealth Games', *International Journal of Sport Policy and Politics State Strategies for Leveraging Sports Mega-Events*, 9:2 (2017).

44 Aaron Beacom and Ian Brittain, 'Public diplomacy and the IPC: reconciling the roles of disability advocate and sports regulator', *Diplomacy and Statecraft*, 27:2 (2016).

45 Holmes and Rofe, *Global Diplomacy*, 47–9.
46 Brian Hocking, Jan Melissen, Shaun Riordan and Paul Sharp, 'Futures for Diplomacy: Integrative Diplomacy in the 21st Century', *Netherlands Institute of International Relations* (Clingendael: The Hague, 2011). When commenting on networks generally associated with public diplomacy, Hocking *et al.* consider the activities of new media forms in generating 'multi-directional flows' of information that have replaced the hierarchical flows of traditional diplomacy. Such information can be generated by actors who as 'producers' rather than 'consumers' of the diplomatic message, while not necessarily aiming to change policy, will often have the wider objective of influencing 'elite attitudes and policy choices'.
47 Beacom, 'The Paralympic Movement and diplomacy.
48 International Paralympic Committee, 'IPC publishes Sochi 2014 social media guidelines', 14 September 2013, available at www.paralympic.org/news/ipc-publishes-sochi-2014-social-media-guidelines (accessed 8 August 2017).
49 Aaron Beacom, Liam French and Scott Kendall, 'Impairment re-interpreted? Continuity and change in media representations of disability through the Paralympic Games', *International Journal of Sports Communication*, 9:1 (2016).
50 Brittain and Beacom, 'Leveraging Paralympic legacy'.
51 Ian Brittain, *From Stoke Mandeville to Sochi: A History of the Summer and Winter Paralympic Games* (Champaign, IL: Common Ground Publishing, 2014).
52 Beacom, 'The Paralympic Movement and diplomacy'.
53 Kathy Lally, 'Russian LGBT athletes hold Open Games despite official harassment, cancellations', *The Washington Post*, 2 March 2014, available at www.washingtonpost.com/world/russian-lgbt-athletes-hold-open-games-despite-official-harassment-cancellations/2014/03/02/b58ec98e-a213–11e3–84d4-e59b1709222c_story.html (accessed 12 October 2016).
54 Charlotte MacDonald-Gibson, 'Winter Olympics 2014: Norway's Health Minister to take his husband to Paralympics', *Independent*, 5 February 2016, available at www.independent.co.uk/sport/olympics/winter-olympics-2014-norway-s-health-minister-to-take-his-husband-to-paralympics-9110369.html (accessed 12 October 2016).

Index